THE OFFERING OF THE GENTILES

The Offering of the Gentiles

*Paul's Collection for Jerusalem in Its Chronological,
Cultural, and Cultic Contexts*

David J. Downs

WILLIAM B. EERDMANS PUBLISHING COMPANY
GRAND RAPIDS, MICHIGAN

© 2008 Mohr Siebeck Tübingen

This edition published 2016 by
Wm. B. Eerdmans Publishing Co.
2140 Oak Industrial Drive N.E., Grand Rapids, Michigan 49505

ISBN 978-0-8028-7313-2

www.eerdmans.com

to Jen

Contents

Foreword, *by Beverly Roberts Gaventa*	xi
Preface	xiii
Abbreviations	xv

Chapter 1: Introduction ... 1
  1.1 The Interpretative Context ... 3
    1.1.1 The Collection as an Eschatological Event ... 3
    1.1.2 The Collection as an Obligation ... 9
    1.1.3 The Collection as an Ecumenical Offering ... 15
    1.1.4 The Collection as Material Relief ... 19
  1.2 The Present Study ... 27

Chapter 2: The Chronology of the Collection ... 30
  2.1 Introduction ... 30
  2.2 Methodological Considerations ... 31
  2.3 Galatians 2:1–10 and the Collection from Antioch ... 33
    2.3.1 Galatians 2:1–10 ... 33
    2.3.2 Acts 11:27–30 and Assistance from Antioch ... 37
    2.3.3 Conclusion ... 39
  2.4 The Organization of the New Pauline Collection ... 40
    2.4.1 The Collection in Galatia ... 40
    2.4.2 The Collection in Corinth and Achaia ... 42
    2.4.3 The Collection in Macedonia ... 53
    2.4.4 The Collection in Asia ... 55
    2.4.5 References to the Collection in Romans ... 58
  2.5 The Book of Acts and the Delivery of the Collection ... 60
    2.5.1 Introduction ... 60
    2.5.2 Almsgiving in Acts 24:17 ... 63
    2.5.3 Conclusion ... 69
  2.6 Conclusion and Implications for the Present Study ... 70

Chapter 3: The Pauline Collection and Greco-Roman Voluntary Associations 73
3.1 Introduction: Analogies and Social Locations 73
3.2 The Pauline Churches and Greco-Roman Associations 79
3.3 Benefaction within Associations 85
    3.3.1 Types of Benefactions 89
    3.3.2 Honors for Benefactors 90
3.4 Common Funds and Monetary Collections within Associations 94
3.5 Care for the Poor within Associations 102
3.6 Translocal Economic Links among Associations 112
3.7 Conclusion 118

Chapter 4: The Collection as an Act of Worship: Paul's Cultic Rhetoric 120
4.1 Introduction 120
4.2 Methodological Considerations 121
4.3 First Corinthians 16:1–4: The Collection of Money as an Element of Worship in the Pauline Churches 127
4.4 Second Corinthians 8–9: The Collection as a Religious Offering 131
    4.4.1 8:1–6: The Example of the Macedonians 131
    4.4.2 8:7–12: Plea for Generous Giving 134
    4.4.3 8:13–15: The Aim of Equality 137
    4.4.4 8:16–24: Commendation of Delegates 138
    4.4.5 9:1–5: Boasting and Appeal 140
    4.4.6 9:6–10: Generosity That Comes from God 140
    4.4.7 9:11–15: Generosity That Glorifies God 142
    4.4.8 Conclusion 145
4.5 Romans 15:14–32: "The Offering of the Gentiles" 146
    4.5.1 Introduction 146
    4.5.2 "The Offering of the Gentiles" 147
    4.5.3 Metaphorical Mapping 156
4.6 Conclusion 157

Chapter 5: Conclusion 161

Bibliography 167
Primary Sources 167
Epigraphical and Palaeographical Sources 168
Secondary Sources 169

Index of Ancient Sources	189
1. Hebrew Bible / LXX	189
2. New Testament	190
3. Early Christian Writings	194
4. Other Greco-Roman and Jewish Writings	195
5. Inscriptions and Papyri	197
Index of Modern Authors	201
Index of Subjects	203

Foreword

In a strange twist on the contemporary mantra "spiritual but not religious" the apostle Paul might find himself labeled as "spiritual (and even religious) but not physical." Many readers of the New Testament, at least in the United States, appear to understand the apostle Paul in such terms. He is concerned with something called "salvation," meaning the eschatological redemption of the individual's spirit. As a result, he is unconcerned with, even disdainful of, the realities of the physical world in the present.

Understanding Paul this way involves considerable effort. First, the word "you" in his letters must be read as singular rather than plural. Second, Paul's comments about "flesh" must be taken to mean that the body itself is bad. To be sure, there is considerable attention (surely more than warranted by the texts) to Pauline texts concerned with human sexuality, but that attention also tends to ascribe to Paul a negative view of the human body that is itself "spiritual but not physical." Reading Paul in this way also requires ignoring his canonical context, assuming that Paul read Israel's prophets without ever noticing their comments about treatment of the poor and marginalized.

David Downs's book on the place of the collection in Paul's letters will make it exceedingly difficult to maintain this bifurcation between Paul's spiritual message and his physical concerns. Far from being tacked on as an afterthought, the collection occupies an important place in Paul's mission. In 2 Corinthians 8 and 9 Paul connects the collection with nothing less than divine generosity in the gospel itself, and in Romans 15 he links its reception to the unity of Jew and Gentile in Christ. In effect, Downs invites us to consider Paul's theology through the lens of the collection for Jerusalem.

Downs examines the collection from three interrelated angles: its place in Paul's mission, its similarity to other patterns of gift-giving in the ancient world, and its relationship to Paul's theology.

First, he examines the various references to the collection in Paul's letters and in the book of Acts in an attempt to coordinate those with the rest of what we know about Paul's mission. What is at stake here goes well beyond a particular line or two in Pauline chronology to include the contours of Paul's ministry.

Second, Downs places the collection in the wider context of ancient gift-giving by examining numerous patterns of benefaction in the voluntary associations of the Roman world. He wisely avoids attempts to identify Paul's work narrowly with a particular pattern, but he also avoids assuming that Christian benefaction was somehow unique, noting various intersections with both Jewish and "pagan" practices.

Third, the final section of the book examines the much-neglected theological significance of the collection. Here Downs unpacks the metaphors at work in Paul's discussion of the collection, metaphors that signal the deeply grace-generated character of the Pauline collection. The gift of the gospel itself gives birth to human gift-giving.

My opening suggested that this is a challenge to a particular section of North American Christianity, but that is unfair. *The Offering of the Gentiles* is a challenge to all readers of Paul to understand the holistic character of his message. While I do think that some readers of Paul attend only to the "spiritual" message, others of us are content to think of Paul as a community organizer whose talk about God is peripheral to his real concerns. Both readings are deeply flawed in their attempt to separate two issues that are integrally related. When Paul writes in 1 Corinthians 8:6 that there is "one Lord Jesus Christ, through whom are all things and through whom we exist" (NRSV), he claims that the totality of human existence belongs to God. Limiting that divine claim to the "spiritual" or to its opposite, which is parsing God out of some aspects of life as if they belonged to "us," is inimical to Paul's understanding of the gospel.

BEVERLY ROBERTS GAVENTA
Distinguished Professor of New Testament, Baylor University
Helen H. P. Manson Professor of New Testament Emerita, Princeton Theological Seminary

Preface

This book is a lightly revised version of my doctoral dissertation, which was completed at Princeton Theological Seminary in 2007. A central claim of this monograph is that the apostle Paul discourages contributors to the Jerusalem collection from receiving public acknowledgement for their act of beneficence. If I violate this Pauline strategy in these acknowledgements, it is not to follow academic convention, but to express my sincere appreciation for those whose labor and lives have contributed to the publication of this project.

First and foremost, I would like to thank my *Doktormutter*, Beverly Roberts Gaventa, for her gracious support of and interest in this project from its earliest stages. This work began, in earnest, in her seminar on the Pauline Epistles during my second semester in the Ph.D. program at Princeton Theological Seminary. From that point, and even during a year-long sabbatical, she faithfully offered numerous helpful insights and critical comments on the chapters of this monograph in their various incarnations. Her example of rigorous scholarship, constant professionalism, and enthusiastic encouragement is one that I can only hope to imitate in my own career as a scholar and teacher. Ross Wagner kindly filled in as chair *pro tem* during my first year of research and even more kindly took time away from his own sabbatical in Germany to remain involved in this project until the defense of the dissertation. Clifton Black, who also served on my committee, offered invaluable assistance and sage advice on this and many other matters during the course of my doctoral studies. While I am incredibly grateful to all the members of my dissertation committee for their input, I should hasten to add that any errors or deficiencies in the present work are, of course, no one's responsibility but my own.

I would also like to thank Judith Gundry-Volf and Jörg Frey for reading this work and granting it the honor of being published in such a distinguished series as WUNT 2. Henning Ziebritzki and his staff at Mohr Siebeck were very helpful in bringing this manuscript into print. Moreover, I would especially like to thank Susan Carlson Wood of the School of Theology Faculty Publications Services at Fuller Theological Seminary for her assistance in preparing camera-ready copy of the manuscript; the Dean of the School of Theology, Howard Loewen, for providing funds for research assistance; and J. Matthew Barnes, a doctoral student at Fuller, for his work on the indices.

Princeton Theological Seminary was a delightful place to pursue graduate study, in large part because of the collegial environment maintained by its doctoral students. I would like to thank my friends in the Biblical Studies Department, many of whom read and commented on earlier drafts of this material: Micah Kiel, Marcus Mininger, Troy Troftgruben, and Alice Yafeh. Jacob Cherian, now Vice President and Dean at Southern Asia Bible College, is especially to be thanked for sharing with me his own research on 2 Corinthians 8–9 and for his willingness to discuss economics and ethics in Paul. Gregg Gardner, a friend from the Religion Department at Princeton University, graciously read chapter three and offered many helpful comments and corrections based on his own expertise in ancient euergetism.

I am grateful for the community of All Angels' Episcopal Church in New York City, which taught me a great deal about the meaning of *koinōnia*. I would also like to thank Marianne Meye Thompson, my mentor and now colleague at Fuller Theological Seminary, who first encouraged me to think about graduate work in New Testament, and four other "mentors" from my days as a student at Fuller, who consistently remind me of how Paul's gospel can be embodied in the life of the church (and on the basketball court): Jon Crantz, Ron Eckert, Josh Smith, and Jeremy Vaccaro.

My family has done more to support this endeavor than they will ever know. My parents, John and Donna Downs, and my brother Jared have always been a source of much laughter and love. Thanks also to my in-laws, Beth Truax and Bill Alzos, who welcomed me into their lives even before I had my driver's license. It has been a pleasure to have shared a church and a city with my dear friend and sister-in-law, Lauren Alzos.

Finally, I dedicate this study to my wife, Jen. Her love, companionship, and sense of humor have made this project possible. Moreover, her deep commitment to the task of caring for the poor and marginalized in her own vocation as a physician has challenged me to remember that an academic study of a gift for the "poor among the saints" is incomplete without a concomitant quest for justice and service in one's own context. She has enriched this study and my life in too many ways to count.

DAVID J. DOWNS
May 2008
Fuller Theological Seminary
Pasadena, California

Abbreviations

In addition to the items listed below, abbreviations for collections of epigraphical inscriptions follow those provided in G. H. R. Horsley and John A. L. Lee, "A Preliminary Checklist of Abbreviations of Greek Epigraphic Volumes," *Epigraphica* 56 (1994): 129–69. For epigraphical texts published after 1994, I have used the abbreviations found in the online database of Greek inscriptions maintained by the Packard Humanities Institute (http://epigraphy.packhum.org/inscriptions).

AB	Anchor Bible
ABR	*Australian Biblical Review*
AGSU	Arbeiten zur Geschichte des Spätjudentums und Urchristentums
AJPh	*American Journal of Philology*
AncSoc	*Ancient Society*
ANF	The Ante-Nicene Fathers
ANRW	*Aufstieg und Niedergang der römischen Welt: Geschichte und Kultur Roms im Spiegel der neueren Forschung.* Edited by H. Temporini and W. Haase. Berlin: W. de Gruyter, 1972– .
ANTC	Abingdon New Testament Commentaries
ATDan	Acta theologica danica
AThR	*Anglican Theological Review*
BCH	*Bulletin de correspondance hellénique*
BDAG	Bauer, Walter, Frederick William Danker, W. F. Arndt, and F. W. Gingrich, eds. *A Greek-English Lexicon of the New Testament and Other Early Christian Literature.* 3d ed. Chicago and London: University of Chicago Press, 2000.
BDF	Blass, F., A. Debrunner, and R. W. Funk, *A Greek Grammar of the New Testament and Other Early Christian Literature.* Chicago: University of Chicago Press, 1961.
BECNT	Baker Exegetical Commentary on the New Testament
BETL	Bibliotheca ephemeridum theologicarum lovaniensium
Bib	*Biblica*
BibInt	*Biblical Interpretation*
BNTC	Black's New Testament Commentaries
BTB	*Biblical Theology Bulletin*
BWSG	Beiträge zur Wirtschafts und Sozialgeschichte

BZNW	Beihefte zur Zeitschrift für die neutestamentliche Wissenschaft
CBQ	*Catholic Biblical Quarterly*
CBQMS	Catholic Biblical Quarterly – Monograph Series
CGTSC	Cambridge Greek Testament for Schools and Colleges
CIG	*Corpus inscriptionum graecarum*
CIJ	*Corpus inscriptionum judaicarum*
CIL	*Corpus inscriptionum latinarum*
CJZC	*Corpus jüdischer Zeugnisse aus der Cyrenaika.* Edited by Gert Lüderitz and Joyce M. Reynolds. Wiesbaden: Reichert, 1983.
CurTM	*Currents in Theology and Mission*
EKKNT	Evangelisch-katholischer Kommentar zum Neuen Testament
ExpTim	*Expository Times*
HNT	Handbuch zum Neuen Testament
HNTC	Harper's NT Commentaries
HTKNT	Herders theologischer Kommentar zum Neuen Testament
HTR	*Harvard Theological Review*
HTS	Harvard Theological Studies
HUT	Hermeneutische Untersuchungen zur Theologie
ICC	International Critical Commentary
IG	*Inscriptiones graecae*
IGSK	Inschriften griechischer Städte aus Kleinasien
IJO	*Inscriptiones judaicae orientis*
ILS	*Inscriptiones latinae selectae*
Int	*Interpretation*
JAC	*Jahrbuch für Antike und Christentum*
JBL	*Journal of Biblical Literature*
JECS	*Journal of Early Christian Studies*
JETS	*Journal of the Evangelical Theological Society*
JHMAS	*Journal of the History of Medicine and Allied Sciences*
JJS	*Journal of Jewish Studies*
JNES	*Journal of Near Eastern Studies*
JR	*Journal of Religion*
JRS	*Journal of Roman Studies*
JSJ	*Journal for the Study of Judaism in the Persian, Hellenistic, and Roman Periods*
JSNT	*Journal for the Study of the New Testament*
JSNTSup	Journal for the Study of the New Testament – Supplement Series
JSOTSup	Journal for the Study of the Old Testament – Supplement Series
JSP	*Journal for the Study of the Pseudepigrapha*
JTS	*Journal of Theological Studies*
KEK	Kritisch-exegetischer Kommentar über das Neue Testament (Meyer-Kommentar)
KNT	Kommentar zum Neuen Testament
LCL	Loeb Classical Library

LHBOTS	Library of Hebrew Bible/Old Testament Studies
LPS	Library of Pauline Studies
LSAM	*Lois sacrées de l'Asie Mineure*
LSCG	*Lois sacrées des cités grecques*
LSJ	Liddell, Henry G., Robert Scott, and Henry S. Jones, eds. *A Greek-English Lexicon.* 9th ed. Oxford: Clarendon, 1996.
MAMA	*Monumenta Asiae Minoris Antiqua*
NAC	New American Commentary
NEchtB	Neue Echter Bibel
Neot	*Neotestamentica*
NewDocs	*New Documents Illustrating Early Christianity*
NICNT	New International Commentary on the New Testament
NIGTC	New International Greek Testament Commentary
NovT	*Novum Testamentum*
NovTSup	Novum Testamentum, Supplements
NSBT	New Studies in Biblical Theology
NTOA	Novum Testamentum et Orbis Antiquus
NTS	*New Testament Studies*
OCD	*The Oxford Classical Dictionary.* Edited by Simon Hornblower and Antony Spawforth. 3d rev. ed. Oxford: Oxford University Press, 2000.
PSB	*Princeton Seminary Bulletin*
ResQ	*Restoration Quarterly*
RevExp	*Review and Expositor*
RHPR	*Revue d'histoire et de philosophie religieuses*
RSPT	*Revue des sciences philosophiques et théologiques*
SBEC	Studies in the Bible and Early Christianity
StBL	Studies in Biblical Literature
SBLDS	Society of Biblical Literature Dissertation Series
SBLRBS	Society of Biblical Literature Resources for Biblical Study
SBLSymS	Society of Biblical Literature Symposium Series
SBT	Studies in Biblical Theology
SD	Studies and Documents
SE	*Supplementum Ephesium*, herausgegeben von Michael Alpers und Helmut Halfmann (Universität Hamburg) in Zusammenarbeit mit John Mansfield (Cornell University) und Christoph Schäfer (Universität Regensburg), gefördert von der Deutschen Forschungsgemeinschaft. Hamburg, 1995.
SEG	Supplementum epigraphicum graecum
SIG[3]	*Sylloge inscriptionum graecarum*
SNTA	*Studiorum Novi Testamenti Auxilia*
SNTSMS	Society for New Testament Studies Monograph Series
SP	Sacra pagina
SSEJC	Studies in Early Judaism and Christianity
STAC	Studien und Texte zu Antike und Christentum

STDJ	Studies on the Texts of the Desert of Judah
SVTQ	*St. Vladimir's Theological Quarterly*
TANZ	Texte und Arbeiten zum neutestamentlichen Zeitalter
TDNT	*Theological Dictionary of the New Testament.* Edited by G. Kittel and G. Friedrich. Translated by G. W. Bromiley. 10 vols. Grand Rapids: Eerdmans, 1964–1976.
TLNT	*Theological Lexicon of the New Testament.* C. Spicq. Translated and edited by J. D. Ernest. 3 vols. Peabody, Mass.: Hendrickson, 1994.
THKNT	Theologischer Handkommentar zum Neuen Testament
TPINTC	TPI New Testament Commentaries
TSAJ	Texte und Studien zum antiken Judentum
WBC	Word Biblical Commentary
WTJ	*Westminster Theological Journal*
WUNT	Wissenschaftliche Untersuchungen zum Neuen Testament
ZNW	*Zeitschrift für die neutestamentliche Wissenschaft und die Kunde der älteren Kirche*

Chapter 1

Introduction

Whether reflected in Paul's statements about support obtained from some of his churches (1 Cor 9:3–12; 2 Cor 11:8; Phil 4:10–20), in his vigorous refusal to request or receive compensation for his work from others (1 Thess 2:9–12; 1 Cor 9:8–18; 2 Cor 2:17; 11:7–11), or in his willingness to incur personal debts for the sake of a "beloved brother" (Phlm 18–19), the Pauline epistles are rich with information about the economic life of the earliest Christian communities. Perhaps not coincidentally, all of the undisputed epistles of Paul refer to financial transactions on behalf of the Pauline mission – while those letters deemed pseudepigraphical typically refrain from mentioning the funding of missionary work.[1] Clearly, pecuniary matters play an important role in Paul's letters to his churches. Pauline theology, therefore, cannot be dissociated from the seemingly mundane world of coins and credit.

One economic endeavor of signal importance for the apostle Paul was the relief fund that he organized among the largely Gentile churches of his mission in Macedonia, Achaia, and Galatia for the Jewish-Christian community in Jerusalem, a project commonly called "the collection for the saints" (ἡ λογεία εἰς τοὺς ἁγίους, 1 Cor 16:1).[2] It would be difficult to overstate the significance of this collection for Paul's mission as apostle to the Gentiles. That the organization and implementation of the relief fund demanded a considerable amount of Paul's time and energy over the course of a number of years is revealed in his comments about the project in 1 Cor 16:1–4; 2 Cor 8:1–9:15; and Rom 15:14–32. So portentous was the collection for Paul that he reports in Rom 15:30–31 his willingness to risk both his life and the possible rejection of his efforts by the Jerusalem church in order to deliver the funds personally to Jerusalem.

Given its importance for Paul's mission and theology, this subject has not received the scholarly attention it merits. Until recently, the only two monographs

---

[1] This point is made by Mark Kiley in *Colossians as Pseudepigraphy* (Sheffield: JSOT Press, 1986), 46–47.

[2] Unless otherwise indicated, all translations in this work are my own. Throughout this monograph, I shall use the term "Jewish-Christian" to refer to the believing community in Jerusalem. Although I understand that the term "Christian" is technically anachronistic when applied to Paul's period, scholarly convention still recognizes the usefulness of this designation. Similarly, usage of the term "pagan" to refer to individuals and/or groups that were neither Jewish nor Christian carries no negative connotations.

on the Jerusalem collection were Keith Nickle's dissertation *The Collection: A Study in Paul's Strategy* and the *Habilitationschrift* by Dieter Georgi, *Die Geschichte der Kollekte des Paulus für Jerusalem*, written independently of one another in the 1960s.[3] While this lacuna has been partially addressed by the publication of three more monographs on the collection in the last seven years, the Jerusalem collection is still a relatively under-explored area of New Testament research.[4] In particular, focus on the historical and socio-cultural context of the collection has tended to obscure the theological dynamics of the relief fund.[5] While hoping to contribute to both the historical and socio-cultural understanding of the collection, this book seeks also to explore the properly theological aspects of the relief fund for Jerusalem. Indeed, a central claim of the work that follows is that careful attention to the chronological and socio-cultural contexts of the Pauline collection for Jerusalem offers the promise of a much richer understanding of the place of the relief fund in Paul's theology. Therefore, the next three chapters of this monograph – which focus, respectively, on the chronology, the socio-cultural context, and the theology of the collection – aim to build off one another in such a way as to present a coherent picture of Paul's efforts to raise money on behalf of the "poor among the saints" in the Jerusalem church. First, however, it is necessary to locate this project in the context of previous research on the Pauline collection for Jerusalem.

---

[3] Keith Nickle, *The Collection: A Study in Paul's Strategy* (SBT 48; Naperville, Ill.: Allenson, 1966); Dieter Georgi, *Remembering the Poor: The History of Paul's Collection for Jerusalem* (Nashville: Abingdon, 1992); trans. of *Die Geschichte der Kollekte des Paulus für Jerusalem* (Theologische Forschung 38; Hamburg: H. Reich, 1965).

[4] The most recent contributions include Burkhard Beckheuer, *Paulus und Jerusalem: Kollekte und Mission im theologischen Denken des Heidenapostels* (Europäische Hochschulschriften 23; Frankfurt am Main: Peter Lang, 1997); Stephan Joubert, *Paul as Benefactor: Reciprocity, Strategy and Theological Reflection in Paul's Collection* (WUNT 2:124; Tübingen: Mohr Siebeck, 2000); and Byung-Mo Kim, *Die paulinische Kollekte* (TANZ 38; Tübingen: Francke, 2002). See also Hans Dieter Betz's commentary *2 Corinthians 8 and 9: A Commentary on Two Administrative Letters of the Apostle Paul* (Hermeneia; Philadelphia: Fortress, 1985); Verlyn D. Verbrugge, *Paul's Style of Church Leadership Illustrated by His Instructions to the Corinthians on the Collection* (San Francisco: Mellen Research University Press, 1992); Kieran J. O'Mahony, *Pauline Persuasion: A Sounding in 2 Corinthians 8–9* (JSNTSup 199; Sheffield: Sheffield Academic Press, 2000); and the section on the Jerusalem collection in James R. Harrison's *Paul's Language of Grace in Its Graeco-Roman Context* (WUNT 2:172; Tübingen: Mohr Siebeck, 2003), 294–324; Jacob Cherian, "Toward a Commonwealth of Grace: A Plutocritical Reading of Grace and Equality in Second Corinthians 8:1–15" (Ph.D. diss., Princeton Theological Seminary, 2007).

[5] For this point, see Beverly Roberts Gaventa, "The Economy of Grace: Reflections on 2 Corinthians 8 and 9," in *Grace upon Grace: Essays in Honor of Thomas A. Langford* (ed. Robert K. Johnston, L. Gregory Jones, and Jonathan R. Wilson; Nashville: Abingdon, 1999), 51–62, esp. 53.

1.1 The Interpretative Context

In the history of scholarly study of the Jerusalem collection, four main interpretations of the offering have arisen.[6] As we shall see, these interpretations are not necessarily mutually exclusive. A brief overview and analysis of the literature will provide a context for the present project by illuminating some promising avenues of investigation while at the same time exposing some interpretative dead-ends.

1.1.1 The Collection as an Eschatological Event

Since the publication of Johannes Munck's influential book *Paulus und die Heilsgeschichte* in 1954 (ET 1959) many interpreters, including Nickle and Georgi, have followed Munck's lead in reading the Pauline collection in light of Old Testament and early Jewish traditions concerning an eschatological pilgrimage of the nations to Jerusalem. The importance of this scriptural tradition for New Testament studies can probably be traced back to Joachim Jeremias's delivery of the Franz Delitzsch lectures in 1953.[7] Here Jeremias argues that Jesus' views with respect to the Gentiles were shaped by a biblical tradition that the Göttingen professor called *"the eschatological pilgrimage of the Gentiles to the Mountain of God."*[8] For Jeremias, who in his sketch of this tradition endeavors to eschew "all the questions and conclusions of modern historical and literary criticism of the Old Testament," the eschatological pilgrimage of the Gentiles to Zion was marked by five distinctive features: (1) the epiphany of God to the nations (Isa 2:2; 11:10; 40:5; 60:3; 62:10; Zech 2:13); (2) the call of God to all the peoples of the world (Ps 96:3, 10; Isa 50:1; 55:5; 66:19–24); (3) the response to that call, which results in a journey of the Gentiles (Isa 2:3; 60:5–14; 66:18–20; Jer 3:17; Mic 7:12, 17; Hag 2:7; Zech 8:21–23; 14:16); (4) worship at the world-sanctuary (Pss 22:28; 72:9–11; 96:8; Isa 19:24–25; 45:14, 23; 49:23; 56:7; 66:18; Jer 16:19; Zeph 3:9); and (5) the Messianic banquet on the world-mountain (Isa 25:6–8).[9]

---

[6] See Scot McKnight, "Collection for the Saints," in *Dictionary of Paul and His Letters* (ed. Gerald F. Hawthorne and Ralph P. Martin; Downers Grove, Ill.: InterVarsity Press, 1993), 143–47.

[7] Joachim Jeremias, *Jesus' Promise to the Nations: The Franz Delitzsch Lectures for 1953* (trans. S. H. Hooke; London: SCM, 1958). The first German edition of Munck's *Paulus und die Heilsgeschichte* (Acta Jutlandica; Aarsskrift for Aarhus Universitet, Theologisk Serie 6; København: Universitetsforlaget I Aarhus, 1954) was published in 1954, but in it Munck draws on an earlier essay in which Jeremias had discussed "the eschatological pilgrimage of the nations to God's holy mountain"; see Joachim Jeremias, "The Gentile World in the Thought of Jesus," *SNTA* 3 (1952): 18–28.

[8] Jeremias, *Jesus' Promise*, 57 (italics original).

[9] Given the diverse pool of scriptural sources from which this collection of texts is gathered, one can justifiably ask whether the so-called eschatological pilgrimage tradition should even be considered a well-defined "tradition" within the Old Testament and early Jewish literature, especially considering Jeremias's admittedly uncritical methodology. The motif is, at the very least, concentrated in a select number of texts (Third Isaiah, Zechariah), and the picture that Jeremias

Building on the work of Jeremias, Munck claims in his treatment of the Pauline collection that, along with a large contingent of representatives from his Gentile churches (Acts 20:4; 1 Cor 16:3–4; 2 Cor 8:16–24), Paul undertook a final, perilous journey to Jerusalem as part of a prophetic missionary strategy intended "to provoke the Jews to jealousy, so that a certain number of them accept the Gospel and are saved; and the fullness of the Gentiles will bring with it the salvation of all Israel."[10] Citing Isa 2:2–4, Mic 4:1–2, and Isa 60:5, Munck asserts that the large group of Gentile delegates that accompanied Paul to Jerusalem – here Munck is dependent upon Acts – symbolized the fulfillment of the Old Testament prophecies that forecast the Gentiles flocking with gifts to Zion in the last days. This group also represented the "full number of the Gentiles" (τὸ πλήρωμα τῶν ἐθνῶν) about which Paul speaks in Rom 11:25.[11] Munck, therefore, sees a close affinity between Paul's collection for Jerusalem and the apostle's statements about the Gentile mission in Rom 11: "It is his intention to save the Jews by making them jealous of the Gentiles, who are accepting the Gospel in great numbers; and now he is going up to the stronghold of Israel, to the disobedient, as he calls them, with a representative company of believing Gentiles."[12] Munck, then, appears to have been the first scholar to connect the collection with certain Jewish prophetic traditions that envision Gentiles bringing gifts to Jerusalem in the last days, although he does not attempt to explain how or where these scriptural traditions are reflected in Paul's explicit discussions of the Jerusalem collection.

Munck's position was followed and expanded in two monographs on the history and theological significance of the collection, one by Dieter Georgi, the other by Keith Nickle. Like Munck, Georgi argues for an eschatological interpretation of the collection. Although Georgi highlights some differences between the pilgrimage tradition and Paul's strategy, on the one hand, and posits a

---

paints does not represent the diversity of Jewish views on the Gentiles (see E. P. Sanders, *Jesus and Judaism* [Minneapolis: Fortress, 1985], 213–18). For a more recent discussion of this tradition, see Terence L. Donaldson, "Proselytes or 'Righteous Gentiles'? The Status of Gentiles in Eschatological Pilgrimage Patters of Thought," *JSP* 7 (1990): 3–27.

[10] Johannes Munck, *Paul and the Salvation of Mankind* (Atlanta: John Knox, 1959), 301.

[11] For a thorough critique of the relationship between Israel's "jealousy" and Israel's salvation in Munck's interpretation of Rom 11 (though regrettably without reference to Munck's discussion of the Pauline collection), see Murray Baker, "Paul and the Salvation of Israel: Paul's Ministry, the Motif of Jealousy, and Israel's Yes," *CBQ* 67 (2005): 469–84.

[12] Munck, *Paul*, 303. As Leander Keck ("The Poor among the Saints in the New Testament," *ZNW* 56 [1965]: 126–27) observes, "Munck takes the oblique reference to the offering in Acts 24:17 (though he never says so!), which says that the money was 'for my nation,' and couples this with Romans 9–11 in order to argue that the offering and the large delegation that brought it were designed 'to save the Jews by making them jealous of the Gentiles.' This desperate device fails on all counts, for not only is there no hint of Paul's trip or of the fund in Rom. 9–11, but the entire construction stems from a steadfast refusal to believe what Paul himself says in Rom. 15:30f."

development of Paul's conception of the project over the years of its organization, on the other, he also suggests a "provocative" purpose – fully in line with Jewish prophetic traditions – behind the delivery of the collection to Jerusalem by "a major delegation of non-circumcised Gentiles."[13] This was, according to Georgi, a "symbolic act" that "simply had to revive in Jewish eyes the old concept of the eschatological pilgrimage of the peoples."[14] Nickle, in his chapter on "The Theological Significance of the Collection," helpfully proposes an interrelation of three purposes behind the collection: "(1) the realization of Christian charity, (2) the expression of Christian unity, (3) the anticipation of Christian eschatology."[15] In the last of these three sections, however, Nickle follows Munck in arguing that the collection was related to Paul's reversal of the common Jewish view of the *ordo salutis*. With a statement that reveals the influence of both Jeremias and Munck on his work, Nickle concludes his discussion of the eschatological significance of the collection with a salient summary of the prevailing paradigm:

> The delegates from the contributing Gentile churches, who accompanied Paul to deliver the collection to Jerusalem, were the first-fruits of an expectation long associated in Judaism with the coming eschatological judgement of the world [he cites Munck in a footnote]. This was the expectation that all the nations would stream to Zion to worship the true God, the God of Israel [he cites Jeremias].... From his understanding of the role that the Gentiles were to fulfil in the scheme of redemption, Paul made an audacious alteration in the prevalent Jewish conception of the eschatological role of Jerusalem. The Gentile Christians, represented by the delegates from the churches, were to stream to Jerusalem, but not as the seekers and petitioners of Israel. They were coming as the true Israel of God, those already chosen by his grace to participate though faith in Christ in salvation. Further, they were coming to fulfil the function in the 'Heilsgeschichte' assigned by the prophets to Israel. That is, they were coming to proclaim the salvation of God instead of to receive the salvation through the mediation of Israel.[16]

The theological vision of this paragraph – in particular its last sentence – is difficult to reconcile with the picture of the collection painted in Rom 15:14–32, where the Gentile churches of Paul's mission are depicted as inheritors of spiritual blessings through the Jewish saints in Jerusalem. That Paul understood his band of Gentile Christians as the "true Israel of God" hardly seems likely given his wrestling with God's faithfulness to Israel – in spite of Israel's rejection of the gospel – in Rom 9–11.[17] In order for Paul's final journey to Jerusalem to

---

[13] Georgi, *Remembering the Poor*, 119.

[14] Ibid., 118, 119.

[15] Nickle, *The Collection*, 100.

[16] Ibid., 138–39.

[17] On the meaning of the phrase ἐπὶ τὸν Ἰσραὴλ τοῦ θεοῦ in Gal 6:16 and the difference between this locution in Galatians and Paul's view of Israel in Romans, see J. Louis Martyn, *Galatians: A New Translation with Introduction and Commentary* (AB 33A; New York: Doubleday, 1997), 574–77.

represent a fulfillment of pilgrimage texts, however, it was necessary for the apostle to have envisioned an "audacious alteration" of the Jewish eschatological pilgrimage tradition, an important facet of which (at least according to Jeremias) is that the journey of the Gentiles to Zion *follows* the restoration of Israel.

A good deal of the more recent literature on the collection has followed the lead of Munck, Georgi, and Nickle in viewing the monetary gift from Paul's churches to the saints in Jerusalem in light of the eschatological pilgrimage of the nations to Zion.[18] Perhaps the most thorough outworking of this position is Burkhard Beckheuer's 1997 Göttingen dissertation *Paulus und Jerusalem*.[19] Beckheuer, who views the collection from beginning to end in terms of the eschatological vision of Third Isaiah, places particular emphasis on Rom 9–11 and Rom 15:14–21 as passages infused with reference to the Isaianic pilgrimage of the nations. Since the so-called eschatological pilgrimage tradition represents one of the more positive strands of Jewish universalism in the Old Testament, this reading does present an attractive potential background for Paul's mission to the Gentiles. Moreover, to the extent that certain passages (Isa 56:6–8; 60:1–14) actually portray the Gentiles bearing gifts as they stream into Zion to worship God in the holy sanctuary, the pilgrimage tradition would seem to correspond, at least on a broad level, with Paul's efforts to transport a monetary contribution to Jerusalem, especially when it is assumed that a large contingent of delegates from the Gentile churches accompanied Paul to Jerusalem (cf. Acts 20:4).

There are at least three significant problems with the eschatological interpretation of the collection for Jerusalem, however. The first and most daunting is the absence of any pilgrimage texts in connection with Paul's statements about the collection in 1 Corinthians, 2 Corinthians, and Romans.[20] In an endeavor to dispel the view that the universality of Paul's gospel had its origins in the eschatological pilgrimage tradition, Terence Donaldson, for example, has pointed

---

[18] See Ben Witherington III, *Conflict and Community in Corinth: A Socio-Rhetorical Commentary on 1 and 2 Corinthians* (Grand Rapids: Eerdmans, 1995), 423. Scholars who interpret the collection as a fulfillment of the pilgrimage tradition include Roger D. Aus, "Paul's Travel Plans to Spain and the 'Full Number of the Gentiles of Rom. XI 25," *NovT* 21 (1979): 232–62; E. P. Sanders, *Paul, the Law, and the Jewish People* (Minneapolis: Fortress, 1983), 171; Victor P. Furnish, *II Corinthians: Translated with Introduction, Notes, and Commentary* (AB 32A; Garden City: Doubleday, 1984), 412; James D. G. Dunn, *Romans* (2 vols.; WBC 38; Dallas: Word, 1988), 2:874; F. F. Bruce, "The Romans Debate – Continued," in *The Romans Debate: Revised and Expanded Edition* (ed. Karl P. Donfried; Peabody, Mass.: Hendrickson, 1991), 175–94; Thomas R. Schreiner, *Romans* (BECNT; Grand Rapids: Baker, 1998), 776–77; and Sze-kar Wan, "Collection for the Saints as Anticolonial Act: Implications of Paul's Ethnic Reconstruction," in *Paul and Politics: Ekklesia, Israel, Imperium, Interpretation; Essays in Honor of Krister Stendahl* (ed. Richard H. Horsley; Harrisburg, Pa.: Trinity, 2000), 191–215.

[19] Beckheuer pays scant attention to the socio-economic aspects of the collection.

[20] For a more thorough assessment of the potential allusion to Isaiah 66 in Rom 15:16, see pp. 224–29.

to the "virtual absence of eschatological pilgrimage texts" in Paul's letters.[21] This claim is perhaps not as decisive with respect to Romans as it is for the other epistles, since there may be several places in Romans where Paul does in fact draw on texts connected to the pilgrimage tradition. One thinks, for instance, of the citation of Isa 11:10 in Rom 15:12, which Donaldson himself acknowledges as a potential "counterexample" to his claim that Paul does not cite from the pilgrimage tradition,[22] or, perhaps more allusively, of the use of the verb εἰσέρχομαι in Rom 11:25, which some have seen as an echo of the pilgrimage tradition.[23] But whatever one makes of these potential allusions to the pilgrimage tradition in Romans – and it can be argued that these examples do not reflect the so-called pilgrimage tradition – they only throw into sharper relief the absence of any reference to pilgrimage texts in Paul's explicit comments about the collection in Rom 15:25–32. Those who would find Paul evoking the pilgrimage tradition in Rom 11:25 or 15:12 are hard pressed to explain why, when Paul in Rom 15:25–32 writes about his impending trip to Jerusalem to deliver the collection to the Jewish-Christian community, he does not frame his journey in terms of the eschatological pilgrimage of the nations.

A second problem with the attempt to relate the collection to the eschatological pilgrimage tradition concerns the nature of the entourage that traveled with Paul to Jerusalem in order to administer the offering of the Gentiles. We know from 1 Cor 16:3–4 and 2 Cor 8:16–24 (cf. 2 Cor 9:3) that some churches participating in the Pauline collection apparently selected delegates to assist Paul in his fundraising efforts and to convey the offering to Jerusalem, although according to Paul the primary motivation for this practice seems to have been the avoidance of impropriety (2 Cor 8:20). These representatives would have included at least Titus (2 Cor 8:16), "the brother whose praise in the gospel has gone through all the churches" (2 Cor 8:18–19), and another unnamed brother (2 Cor 8:22). By conflating Acts 20:4, 1 Cor 16:3–4, and 2 Cor 8:16–9:4, Munck calculates a party of "at least ten men," which he labels, without supporting evidence, an "uncommonly large number of travelling-companions."[24] The problems with using Acts as a source for the historical reconstruction of Paul's activity are well known and will be addressed in greater detail in the following chapter. Acts is especially problematic on this particular point because the author of

---

[21] Terence L. Donaldson, *Paul and the Gentiles: Remapping the Apostle's Convictional World* (Minneapolis: Fortress, 1997), 194.

[22] Ibid., 194.

[23] E.g., Aus, "Paul's Travel Plans," 249–52.

[24] Munck, *Paul*, 303. The use of evidence from Acts 20 here is methodologically problematic, as will be shown in the following chapter. Nickle (*The Collection*, 68–69), who also employs Acts as a source for information about the collection and its delivery, produces a list of delegates that includes the eight individuals named in Acts 20:4 (including the author), the Corinthian delegates, and additional representatives picked up along the way from Troas, Philippi, Tyre, Ptolemais, Caesarea, and perhaps Cyprus and Ephesus – a crowded contingent indeed!

that work nowhere mentions the collection for the saints. The identification of the individuals in Acts 20:4 with the delegation responsible for delivering the Pauline collection to Jerusalem is, therefore, tenuous at best. While it is reasonable to assume that some delegates from Paul's Gentile churches accompanied the relief fund to Jerusalem, we simply do not know how large this envoy may have been.

More revealing, in Paul's own description of the anticipated delivery of the collection in Rom 15:14–32, he essentially places the onus of the delivery squarely on his own shoulders, making no mention of traveling companions. He does not request prayers for representatives from his Gentile churches, but only asks that the Romans join him in praying for his own rescue from unbelievers in Judea and that *his* ministry (ἡ διακονία μου) might be acceptable to the saints in Jerusalem (15:31). It would seem that, if the presence of a large coterie of Gentile companions was essential for Paul's vision of the collection's theological significance, he would have commented on the role of this party in the delivery of the gift to Jerusalem in Rom 15:25–32. That he does not do so places the eschatological pilgrimage reading of the collection in doubt.

Additionally, the claim that Paul's trip to Jerusalem with an assembly of Gentiles would have been interpreted by the Jews of that city as a symbolic act reminiscent of eschatological prophetic traditions seems implausible. In the biblical passages where reference is made to the wealth of the nations flowing into Jerusalem in the last days, the destination of the Gentile gifts and offerings is almost always the temple of the Lord (Isa 56:6–8; Isa 60:1–14; cf. Isa 2:1–4; 66:18–20). Yet there is no evidence in Paul's letters that the collection was intended for the Jerusalem temple.[25] On the contrary, Paul indicates in Rom 15:25 that the collection was especially designated for the "poor among the saints" of the Jerusalem church (Rom 15:25; cf. 1 Cor 16:1; 2 Cor 8:4; 9:1). Even if the collection had been delivered to the temple, it would not necessarily have been controversial, since Gentile offerings to the Jerusalem temple were by no means uncommon during the first century (cf. Josephus, *J.W.*, 2.408–411; *Ant.* 11.329–30; 16.14; Philo, *Legat.* 23). If unbelieving Jews in Jerusalem had taken any notice of the monetary gift that Paul and his Gentile companions were delivering to the Jewish-Christian community in that city, it is hardly likely that they would have been provoked to jealousy by the supposedly inflammatory nature of the gesture. Paul, at least, does not draw attention to the provocative *heilsgeschichtlich* message

---

[25] If Acts 21:17–26 represents an attempt by Luke to describe a sort of compromise reached by Paul and the Jerusalem leaders that led to the acceptance of the collection after Paul had financed the Nazarite vows of four members of the Jerusalem church (Acts 21:23–24), this might bring the collection into some relationship with the temple within Luke's narrative. For this proposal, see Joubert, *Paul as Benefactor*, 204–15. It can only be said that the scene in Acts 21 does not mention the collection and does not fit with what Paul says about the project (not to mention the law and the temple) in his extant letters. On the Jerusalem collection and the end of Acts, see ibid., pp. 91–107.

of the collection in Rom 15:25–32. In fact, Paul's request for prayer in Rom 15:31 appears to draw a distinction between what might happen to him ("that I might be rescued from the unbelievers in Judea") and what might happen to his monetary offering ("that my service to Jerusalem might be acceptable to the saints").[26]

For these reasons, I conclude that the eschatological pilgrimage tradition (so-called) did not inform Paul's organization of a relief fund for the Jerusalem church. Despite some surface similarities between the collection for the saints in Jerusalem and Old Testament passages regarding the wealth of the nations streaming into Zion in the last days, a close examination of Paul's travel plans in Rom 15:14–32 reveals no mention of the pilgrimage tradition in the one place within the Pauline correspondence in which the apostle reflects on the actual delivery of the collection to Jerusalem. Paul does not cite pilgrimage texts; he does not mention the importance of his entourage; and he does not imply that the delivery of the collection to Jerusalem was intended to be an act of eschatological provocation.[27]

1.1.2 The Collection as an Obligation

A second interpretation of the Jerusalem collection advocated by a number of scholars holds that the request that Paul and Barnabas "remember the poor" in Gal 2:10 is an indication that the collection was an obligation placed upon Paul by the authorities of the Jerusalem church. This view was first advanced in an influential essay on Paul's conception of the church by Karl Holl in 1921, in which Holl suggested that the Jerusalem community possessed "a certain right of taxation over the entire church" ("ein gewisses Besteuerungsrecht über die ganze Kirche").[28] From the point of view of the foundational community in Jerusalem,

---

[26] The parallels that Georgi (*Remembering the Poor*, 119) adduces between Rom 15:31 and Rom 9–11 are unconvincing except for the use of ἀπειθέω in 15:31 and 11:30–31: (1) It hardly does justice to Rom 9–11 to classify that section as "one of Paul's two programmatic statements on his missionary strategy and activity"; and (2) Rom 15:7–13 is a summary of themes developed throughout the whole epistle, rather than, as Georgi asserts, a recapitulation "of thoughts previously dealt with in a more general way in chapters 9–11."

[27] Though he doubts whether an eschatological motivation lies behind Paul's collection for Jerusalem, David Horrell ("Paul's Collection: Resources for a Materialist Theology," *Epworth Review* 22 [1995]: 76) also rejects this eschatological interpretation because of its (negative) implications for present-day theology: "The eschatological, salvation-historical motivation is certainly rooted in a particular conception of what God is doing to work for the salvation of all creation (Rom. 11:25–32; 8:18–25), though it is probably the hardest for us to use as a contemporary theological resource, and the most alien to our way of thinking, not least because it implies that the consummation of all things was imminent around the time when Paul delivered the collection."

[28] Karl Holl, "Der Kirchenbegriff des Paulus in seinem Verhältnis zu dem der Urgemeinde," Sitzungsbericht der Berliner Akademie (1921): 920–47; repr. in *Gesammelte Aufsätze zur Kirchengeschichte, II* (Tübingen: J. C. B. Mohr, 1928), 44–67.

the collection represented an obligation due to "the poor" in Jerusalem. According to Holl, both the terms οἱ πτωχοί and οἱ ἅγιοι functioned as technical designations for the *Urgemeinde* in Jerusalem. The Jerusalem community's identity as the center of the early Christian movement, reflected in official titles that ascribed to it righteous poverty and holiness, meant that both the Antioch church and the Gentile congregations of Paul's mission were under a legal obligation to provide financial support to the mother-church. Paul, therefore, uses legal terminology to describe the collection.[29] While Holl himself did not suggest an analogy between the Pauline collection and the Jewish temple-tax, a connection between these two forms of giving has been asserted by scholars both before and after Holl.[30]

Two articles published by Leander Keck in the mid-1960s, however, seriously challenge Holl's claim that the term οἱ πτωχοί in Gal 2:10 (cf. Rom 15:26) functions as a technical designation for the Jerusalem church as a whole rather than as a reference to a group of destitute believers within that community (see below).[31] More substantially, Holl's interpretation rests on the inaccurate assumption that Gal 2:10 refers to the origins of the Pauline collection for Jerusalem instead of to a request directed specifically to the delegation from Antioch, of which Paul and Barnabas were members. Furthermore, while there are some surface parallels between the monetary gift raised among the congregations of Paul's mission for the poor among the saints in Jerusalem, on the one hand, and the Jewish temple tax, on the other, the differences are more substantial than the similarities: whereas the half-shekel tax was used to subsidize the daily sacrifices in the Jerusalem temple, the only connection between the Gentile offering and the temple cultus is found in Paul's metaphorical language for the collection (see chapter four); the temple tax was compulsory and paid annually, whereas the Pauline collection was voluntary and seems to have been a one-time donation; and the amount of the temple tax was uniform and set by legislation, whereas Paul encourages contributors to the relief fund freely to give according to their

---

[29] Ibid., 60: "Paulus bezeichnet die Abgabe bald mit erbaulichen Ausdrücken als κοινωνία und διακονία (Röm. 15,25f. 31), χάρις (2. Kor. 8,4.6.7.19), εὐλογία (2. Kor. 9,5), bald mit mehr rechtlich Klingenden als ἁδρότης (2. Kor. 8,20), λειτουργία (2. Kor. 9,12; *vgl.* Phil 2,25.30), λογία (1. Kor. 16,1)."

[30] Holl notes the suggestions of Pfleider and Holtzmann (see "Der Kirchenbegriff," 58 n. 1). The most extensive comparison between Paul's collection for Jerusalem and the Jewish temple tax is presented in Nickle, *The Collection*, 74–93; cf. Wan, "Collection for the Saints," 201–3; James Chacko, "Collection in the Early Church," *Evangelical Review of Theology* 24 (2000): 178; Murray J. Harris, *The Second Epistle to the Corinthians* (NIGTC; Grand Rapids: Eerdmans: 2005), 94–96. On the payment of the temple tax as an identity marker in Second Temple Judaism, see Mikael Tellbe, "The Temple Tax as a Pre-70 CE Identity Marker," in *The Formation of the Early Church* (ed. Jostein Ådna; WUNT 183; Tübingen: Mohr Siebeck, 2005), 19–44.

[31] Keck, "The Poor among the Saints in the New Testament," 100–29; idem, "The Poor among the Saints in Jewish Christianity and Qumran," *ZNW* 57 (1966): 54–78.

means (1 Cor 16:2; 2 Cor 8:3).³² Additionally, the notion that the collection was a legal obligation placed upon Paul by the authorities of the Jerusalem church is difficult to reconcile with what the apostle actually says about the offering in his extant correspondence. Although Paul does indicate in Rom 15:26–27 that the Gentile contributors are "debtors" (ὀφειλέται) of the poor among the saints – a term that suggests some sense of duty behind the offering – this note of obligation needs to be balanced by Paul's rather consistent emphasis on the voluntary nature of the gift elsewhere in his letters (2 Cor 8:3, 8, 10, 17; 9:5, 7; Rom 15:26: εὐδόκησαν).³³

Klaus Berger takes a slightly different approach to the issue of obligation, arguing that the collection for Jerusalem reflects the tradition of redemptive almsgiving in Judaism, an institution through which God-fearing Gentiles were able to demonstrate their solidarity with God's people.³⁴ Reading the reference to alms (ἐλεημοσύνη) in Acts 24:17 as an allusion to the Jerusalem collection, Berger contends that the uncircumcised Gentiles of Paul's mission were required to display their faith in the one true God through their act of charity on behalf of the poor in the Jerusalem church, thus allowing them to be included in the covenant community. Yet Berger is unable to cite any evidence that Gentiles who donated alms to Jerusalem were regarded as full members of God's covenant people, and there is "no apparent precedent for regarding almsgiving as a complete substitute for circumcision."³⁵ Moreover, given Paul's refusal to accept such distinctively Jewish identity markers as circumcision, dietary laws, and Sabbath observance as necessary preconditions for Gentile inclusion into the community of God's holy people, it is difficult to imagine that the apostle to the Gentiles would have recognized another ethnic identity marker – such as payment of the temple tax or alms for the poor – as a legitimate means of Gentile

---

³² See the discussion in Nickle, *The Collection*, 90–93; cf. M. E. Thrall, *A Critical and Exegetical Commentary on the Second Epistle to the Corinthians* (2 vols.; ICC; London: T & T Clark, 1994, 2000), 512.

³³ So Harrison, *Paul's Language of Grace*, 309. As Verbrugge (*Paul's Style of Church Leadership*, 315) points out, "According to [Paul's] perspective, the Gentiles owe this money to the poor in Jerusalem, not because the authorities in Jerusalem say so but because Paul as the leader of his churches says so."

³⁴ Klaus Berger, "Almosen für Israel," *NTS* 23 (1977): 180–204. Berger's thesis concerning the Jerusalem collection is endorsed by Bengt Holmberg (*Paul and Power: The Structure of Authority in the Primitive Church as Reflected in the Pauline Epistles* [Philadelphia: Fortress, 1978], 39–43) and Jost Eckert ("Die Kollekte des Paulus für Jerusalem," in *Kontinuität und Einheit: Für Franz Mussner* [ed. Paul-Gerhard Müller and Werner Stenger; Freiburg: Herder, 1981], 65–80). Byung-Mo Kim's dissertation *Die Paulinische Kollekte* presents a thorough reading of 2 Cor 8–9 in light of "das Almosenmodell der Kollekte." A more theologically focused study of the tradition of redemptive almsgiving in both early Judaism and nascent Christianity can be found in Roman Garrison, *Redemptive Almsgiving in Early Christianity* (JSNTSup 77; Sheffield: Sheffield Academic Press, 1993).

³⁵ Nicholas Taylor, *Paul, Antioch and Jerusalem: A Study in Relationships and Authority in Earliest Christianity* (JSNTSup 66; Sheffield: Sheffield Academic Press, 1992), 119.

acceptance.³⁶ While it is, of course, quite possible that the leadership of the Jerusalem church maintained a different conception of the offering than did Paul,³⁷ we have access only to *Paul's* statements about the relief fund, and nowhere in his extant comments about the collection does Paul speak of the contribution as an act of almsgiving. The term ἐλεημοσύνη is, in fact, entirely absent from the Pauline corpus. Finally, as we shall see in the following chapter, the attempt to read Acts 24:17 as a reference to the Pauline collection for the saints is unconvincing, for it fails to account for the distinctive role that the activity of almsgiving plays in the larger narrative of Acts.

More recently, Stephan Joubert has claimed that the Pauline collection for Jerusalem should be interpreted in light of the framework of reciprocal relationships of benefit exchange in ancient Mediterranean societies.³⁸ According to Joubert, "The bestowal of gifts initiated the establishment of long-term relationship that involved mutual obligations and clear status differentials between the transactors."³⁹ With respect to the Pauline collection, Joubert interprets the Jerusalem church's recognition of Paul's "Law-free gospel" (Gal 2:1–10) as a benefaction offered to the apostle.⁴⁰ Paul and Barnabas, therefore, were obligated to reciprocate this benefaction by fulfilling the charge of the Jerusalem leaders "to remember the poor" (Gal 2:10). When the church in Antioch failed to meet its obligation in this matter, Paul initiated the organization of a monetary collection among the Gentile-Christian communities of his own mission, which "were included as *beneficiaries* in the reciprocal relationship between [Paul] and the Jerusalem church."⁴¹ Paul, according to Joubert, adopted a variety of rhetorical strategies and theological appeals in order to encourage his Gentile churches to support this reciprocal exchange, particularly emphasizing "the religious nature

---

³⁶ So also James D. G. Dunn, *The Partings of the Ways between Christianity and Judaism and Their Significance for the Character of Christianity* (London: SCM, 1991), 84–85.

³⁷ A point argued by Holmberg, *Paul and Power*, 39.

³⁸ Joubert, *Paul as Benefactor*, passim. See also idem, "Coming to Terms with a Neglected Aspect of Ancient Mediterranean Reciprocity: Seneca's View on Benefit Exchange in *De beneficiis* as the Framework for a Model of Social Exchange," in *Social Scientific Models for Interpreting the Bible: Essays by the Context Group in Honor of Bruce J. Malina* (ed. John J. Pilch; Biblical Interpretation Series 53; Leiden: Brill, 2001), 47–63; idem, "Religious Reciprocity in 2 Corinthians 9:6–15: Generosity and Gratitude as Legitimate Responses to the *Charis Tou Theou*," *Neot* 33 (1999): 79–90. G. W. Peterman (*Paul's Gift from Philippi* [SNTSMS 92; Cambridge: Cambridge University Press, 1997], 175–83) also addresses the Jerusalem collection primarily in terms of the theme of social obligation. For another representative of the obligation interpretation of the collection, see Holmberg, *Paul and Power*, 35–43.

³⁹ Joubert, *Paul as Benefactor*, 6.

⁴⁰ One might object that this is most certainly not how Paul understands the matter of his commissioning as apostle to the Gentiles. In Galatians 1–2, Paul is emphatically insistent that his law-free gospel and apostolic calling come from no other source than the "apocalypse of Jesus Christ" (Gal 1:12; cf. 1:1, 6–11, 15–17; 2:2, 6).

⁴¹ Ibid., 6.

of the project, which involved his communities in a reciprocal relationship not only with Jerusalem, but also with God."[42] Yet the contingent arguments in support of the collection remain, for Joubert, subordinate to Paul's attempt "to secure his future role as benefactor of Jerusalem."[43] That is, "[in] order to ensure the completion of the collection, Paul offered various contextual (re)interpretations of the nature, function and advantages of this project for all parties involved by constantly relating it to the basic framework of benefit exchange."[44] Paul's fears that Jerusalem would ultimately reject his gift, and thus terminate the reciprocal relationship that had obtained between Pauline Christianity and the believing community in Jerusalem, led the apostle to present "a new ideological angle to the collection at a late stage in this project (Rom 15,25ff), over against his previous theological reflection that focussed on securing the successful completion of the project (cf. 1 Cor 16,1–4; 2 Cor 8–9; Gal 2,10).... He did this by shifting the emphasis away from the generally accepted views on reciprocity ('gifts must be rewarded with counter gifts'), to giving according to the principles of selfless service, and fulfilling of one's responsibilities, irrespective of the response on the side of the recipients. Paul thus turned the collection into an 'eleventh hour success' from his own communities' point of view."[45] Once Paul arrived in Jerusalem with the gift in hand, he and James "devised an emergency solution to ensure the eventual acceptance of the collection by the Jerusalem church"[46]; this solution involved Paul acting as the benefactor to the Jerusalem church by paying for the Nazirite vows of some of its members (Acts 21:17–26).

Joubert's work on the Jerusalem collection is both promising and problematic. Positively, Joubert's emphasis on the religious nature of Paul's language in 2 Cor 8–9 is an important contribution to the study of the relief fund, for it underscores the specifically religious dimensions of Paul's rhetoric.[47] In chapter four of this monograph, I shall attempt to contextualize the cultic language used with reference to the collection in 1 Cor 16:1–4; 2 Cor 8:1–9:15; and Rom 15:14–32 by arguing that Paul metaphorically frames the collection as an act of cultic worship. Unlike Joubert, however, I do not view Paul's comments about the collection in Rom 15 as representing "a new ideological angle of incidence on the collection," since I argue that the collection is consistently presented as an act of cultic worship throughout Paul's various comments about the fund. An additional strength of Joubert's study is that, like the work of G. W. Peterman on Phil 4:10–20, Joubert is able to show how Paul involves the contributors to the

---

[42] Ibid.
[43] Ibid., 7.
[44] Ibid.
[45] Ibid.
[46] Ibid.
[47] See also Richard S. Ascough, "The Completion of a Religious Duty: The Background of 2 Cor 8.1–15," *NTS* 42 (1996): 584–99.

relief fund in a three-way relationship that involves themselves, the poor among the saints in Jerusalem, and God.[48]

Yet Joubert's interpretation of the collection as an obligation placed upon Paul by the Jerusalem authorities is unconvincing for several reasons. If, as the next chapter on the chronology of the collection attempts to demonstrate, the request of the leaders of the Jerusalem church in Gal 2:10 *does not refer* to the collection that Paul later organized among the Gentile churches of his mission (1 Cor 16:1–4; 2 Cor 8:1–9:15; Rom 15:14–32), then Joubert's entire thesis is called into question. Indeed, Joubert does not adequately explain why Paul should have feared the specter of Jerusalem's rejection of his fundraising efforts, if the collection was nothing more than the fulfillment of the request reported in Gal 2:10. Additionally, Joubert's claim that Paul's comments about the collection in Rom 15:25–32 represent "a new ideological angle of incidence on the collection" not only fails to appreciate the continuity of Paul's language about the collection throughout his epistles, it also is unable to explain why Paul should have needed a new perspective on the collection – one that accounted for the possibility of Jerusalem's rejection. Joubert's explanation that, once the collection was actually raised, Paul finally shifted "his attention to the expected impact and symbolic value of the collection on present and future relations between himself, Jerusalem and his communities" makes Paul a remarkably short-sighted figure and still does not indicate why the church in Jerusalem would refuse a gift that it had requested. Moreover, Joubert's reliance on Acts in order to reconstruct the final chapter of the collection's history is methodologically problematic, which I shall demonstrate in the following chapter.

Finally, although his work does not fit easily into this category, James Harrison's suggestive comparison of Paul's language about the collection with the terminology of benefaction from Greek honorific inscriptions has built on the work of Joubert. As part of his larger attempt to locate Paul's use of the concept of χάρις in the context of the Hellenistic reciprocity system, Harrison argues that Paul never merely accepts but also critiques and transforms the values of Greco-Roman patronage. With respect to Paul's appeals on behalf of the collection in 2 Cor 8–9, Harrison writes, "the emphasis of Paul on voluntariness and divine grace as the dynamic of human generosity was probably designed to extricate the Corinthians from the burdensome demands of the Graeco-Roman reciprocity system. At the very least, it challenged the Corinthians to understand the obligation of reciprocity differently to the prevailing ethos of their culture. The language of abundance associated with grace also liberated them from the tyranny of commensurability that characterised the reciprocity system."[49] Paul's language of grace, according to Harrison, offers to the contributors to the fund

---

[48] Peterman, *Paul's Gift from Philippi*, 157–61; see also Bart B. Bruehler, "Proverbs, Persuasion and People: A Three-Dimensional Investigation of 2 Cor 9.6–15," *NTS* 48 (2002): 209–24.

[49] Harrison, *Paul's Language of Grace*, 323.

for Jerusalem a new, countercultural model of obligation and reciprocity within the Christian community, shaped by Paul's theological and cruciform convictions.

1.1.3 The Collection as an Ecumenical Offering

Some scholars, noting the frequency with which the word κοινωνία and its cognates occur in connection with the collection (2 Cor 8:4, 23; 9:3, 13; Rom 15:26; cf. Gal 2:9), have emphasized the ecumenical aim of the relief fund, contending that the contribution was primarily a voluntary expression of Christian unity. Perhaps the most famous proponent of this position is Oscar Cullmann.[50] On what he calls the "real significance" of the collection for the poor in Jerusalem, Cullmann writes, "It is much more than a humanitarian collection. It is an ecumenical affair and assumes for Paul definite theological character."[51] The ecumenical interpretation of the collection is developed in greater detail by Josef Hainz in his monograph *Koinonia: "Kirche" als Gemeinschaft bei Paulus*.[52] In contrast to earlier scholars whom he believes guilty of underestimating the role of the collection in unifying Jews and Gentiles, Hainz concludes:

> Damit dürfte deutlich geworden sein, daß die Kollekte von Anfang an für Paulus nicht nur den wirtschaftlichen Aspekt materieller Hilfeleistung hatten, sondern Ausdruck dieser Haltung dankbaren Gedenkens und Zeichen des Gemeinschaftswillens sein sollte.... Die κοινωνία, welche die christlichen Gemeinden miteinander verbindet, ist demnach eine durch Gott gestiftete, an dessen Gnadenhandeln sie alle gemeinsam teilhaben.[53]

With that it becomes clear that from the beginning the collection for Paul entailed not only the economic aspect of material help, but also that this stance should be an expres-

---

[50] Oscar Cullmann, "The Early Church and the Ecumenical Problem," *AThR* 40 (1958): 181–89, 294–301. As the result of his study of the Jerusalem collection, Cullmann calls for a collection to be taken up in modern times by Protestants and Catholics in order to symbolize the unity of these two branches of the Christian church. See also Maurice Goguel, "La collecte en faveur des Saints," *RHPR* 5 (1925): 301–18; Nickle, *The Collection*, 111–29; Thrall, *2 Corinthians*, 514–15.

[51] Cullmann, "The Early Church," 296.

[52] Josef Hainz, *Koinonia: "Kirche" als Gemeinschaft bei Paulus* (Biblische Untersuchung 16; Regensburg: Pustet, 1982), 122–161, esp. 151–61. See also idem, "Gemeinschaft (κοινωνία) zwischen Paulus und Jerusalem (Gal 2,9f.): Zum paulinischen Verständnis von der Einheit der Kirche," in *Kontinuität und Einheit: Für Franz Mussner* (ed. Paul-Gerhard Müller and Werner Stenger; Freiburg: Herder, 1981), 30–42.

[53] Hainz, *Koinonia*, 161. Earlier Hainz writes, "Die Kollekte wäre demnach zu verstehen als eine Konkretion bzw. als Ausdruck und Beweis zwischen Jerusalem und den heidenchristlichen Kirchen bestehenden 'Gemeinschaft'" (152). Other scholars who highlight the unifying and ecumenical significance of the collection include: Nickle, *The Collection*, 111–29; Richard R. Melick, "The Collection for the Saints: 2 Corinthians 8–9," *Criswell Theological Review* 4 (1989): 102–3; C. H. Talbert, "Money Management in Early Mediterranean Christianity: 2 Corinthians 8–9," *RevExp* 86 (1989): 360; G. W. Peterman, "Romans 15.26: Make a Contribution or Establish Fellowship?" *NTS* 40 (1994): 461; Joubert, *Paul as Benefactor*, 207–8; Thrall, *2 Corinthians*, 515; Harrison, *Paul's Language of Grace*, 307–8.

sion of thanks and a sign of willing partnership. The κοινωνία, which links the Christian communities with one another, is therefore one established by God, at whose gracious action they jointly share.

This interpretation of the collection has much to commend it. Even if, as I shall argue in the following chapter, Paul's effort to collect money for the saints in Jerusalem was not the direct result of the Jerusalem conference reported in Gal 2:1–10 – one outcome of which is the extension of κοινωνία by the pillar apostles to Paul and Barnabas (Gal 2:9) – the relief fund organized among the largely Gentile churches of the Pauline mission clearly served an ecumenical purpose. According to Paul, the collection is a tangible expression of the mutual relationship shared by Jews and Gentiles through the gracious manifestation of the gospel of Jesus Christ. That Paul designates the contributors to this relief fund τὰ ἔθνη in Rom 15:27 indicates that the apostle conceived of the offering as a gift that would demonstrate the unity of Gentile and Jewish believers, even though he nowhere explicitly calls the recipients of the aid οἱ Ἰουδαῖοι, preferring instead terms like οἱ ἅγιοι (1 Cor 16:1; 2 Cor 8:4; 9:1, 12; Rom 15:25, 31), οἱ πτωχοὶ τῶν ἁγίων τῶν ἐν Ἰερουσαλήμ (Rom 15:26), ἄλλοι (2 Cor 8:13), and Ἰερουσαλήμ (1 Cor 16:3; Rom 15:31).[54] As Paul writes in Rom 15:26, "For Macedonia and Achaia were pleased to make a certain partnership-forming contribution (κοινωνίαν τινὰ ποιήσασθαι) for the poor among the saints in Jerusalem."

There is some debate about whether the abstract noun κοινωνία, when it is used in connection with the collection in 2 Cor 8:4; 9:13; and Rom 15:26 (cf. Gal 2:9), reflects the social relationship between Jews and Gentiles established by the collection or instead refers to the concrete, material sign of that relationship in the form of a monetary contribution. Thus some translations of the construction κοινωνίαν τινὰ ποιήσασθαι in Rom 15:26 emphasize the former ("to establish fellowship," Peterman; "to establish a rather close relation w. the poor," BDAG; "ein gewisses Gemeinschaftswerk zu betreiben," Hainz) while others emphasize the latter ("to share their resources," NRSV; "to make a certain communicativeness," Nickle; "to make a contribution," NIV, Cranfield, Dunn). It is not necessary to view κοινωνία in Rom 15:26 as designating only one of these two semantic options, however, and the slightly clumsy translation "to make a certain

---

[54] Paul's identification of the contributors from his churches as τὰ ἔθνη in Rom 15:27 (cf. Rom 15:16) might also give us pause before accepting Sze-kar Wan's claim that the collection was intended to broaden *Jewish* boundaries for inclusion. Wan writes, "the collection lay at the heart of Paul's concern with redefining Jewish group boundaries to include gentile converts. In so doing, he constructed an all-embracing sociopolitical order that stood in contradistinction to and in criticism of colonial powers" ("Collection as Anticolonial," 192). The Gentiles contributed to the saints in Jerusalem as *Gentiles*, however, not as Jews. In spite of the unity of these groups accomplished though the gospel, Paul's distinction between these two ethnic categories is nevertheless consistently maintained, for example, throughout the epistle to the Romans (cf. 1:16; 11:13; 15:7–9).

partnership-forming contribution" is intended to highlight both the material and the social aspects of κοινωνία in Paul's theological vision.⁵⁵ For Paul, κοινωνία is formed when κοινωνία is materially demonstrated; that is, the collection itself is a tangible manifestation of financial assistance at the same time that it symbolizes the bond of fellowship, established on account of the gospel, between the Gentiles of the Pauline churches and the saints in Jerusalem.⁵⁶

The ecumenical interpretation of the collection identifies a crucial, though not the only, reason for the organization of a relief fund for Jerusalem among the largely Gentile communities of Paul's mission. Doubtless the collection represented a challenge to the opponents of Paul's missionary enterprise in Jerusalem (cf. Gal 2:4, 12), for the acceptance of this benefaction for the poor within the Jerusalem church would solidify the spiritual unity of Jewish and Gentile believers (Rom 15:27). On the other hand, as Paul is well aware, the rejection of this offering would pose a serious threat to the singularity of the one body of

---

⁵⁵ See Furnish, *II Corinthians*, 401. In an attempt to argue that Rom 15:26 means "establish fellowship" rather than "make a contribution," G. W. Peterman ("Romans 15.26," 459) cites two parallel texts in which the relatively rare construction κοινωνίαν ποιήσασθαι appears to mean "establish fellowship" (Polybius, *Histories*, 5.35.1; Plato, *Rep.* 371b5–6). This construction also appears in Demosthenes, however, and this text clearly suggests that κοινωνία can also refer to material assistance. In one of his four speeches against Philip II of Macedonia, the fourth-century Athenian orator Demosthenes assails the inability of the independent Greek states to join together in opposition to Philip's tyranny. Demosthenes writes: "And yet while we Greeks see and hear all this, we do not send ambassadors to one another and express our vexation with these things. We are in such a poor state, we are so entrenched in our several cities, that to this very day we can do nothing for our common interests or needs, nor can we band together, nor can we establish a fellowship of aid or friendship (οὐδὲ κοινωνίαν βοηθείας καὶ φιλίας οὐδεμίαν ποιήσασθαι), but we overlook the growing power of this man" (Demosthenes, *3 Philip*. 28.1–6). That the noun κοινωνία is qualified by both βοήθεια ("help, aid," perhaps also "force of auxiliaries," LSJ, 320) and φιλία indicates that Demosthenes desired more than mere fellowship among the Greek states; had they manifested κοινωνία through financial sharing and military assistance, the tyrant might have been resisted. Moreover, among the examples of the construction φιλίαν ποιήσασθαι cited by Peterman as having "the abstract meaning 'friendship,'" several indicate that φιλία is, in fact, demonstrated through military or financial assistance (Josephus, *Ant.* 7.107; 12.414–419; 13.259–264; 14.10). To cite but one example, when Alexander makes a "league of friendship" with the Arabians, Gazites, and Ashkelonites in *Ant.* 14.10, he does so by means of "many and large presents, that made them his fast friends." This is not merely "abstract" friendship, as if such a thing ever existed in the ancient world. On the economic aspects of friendship in antiquity, see Richard Saller, "Patronage and Friendship in Early Imperial Rome: Drawing the Distinction," in *Patronage in Ancient Society* (ed. Andrew Wallace-Hadrill; London and New York: Routledge, 1989), 49–61. I would like to thank Prof. Peterman for providing me with a copy of his unpublished paper "Romans 15.26 Eleven Years Later: Make a Contribution or Establish Fellowship?" (paper presented at the annual meeting of the Society of Biblical Literature, Philadelphia, Pa., November 19, 2005) and for corresponding with me on this issue.

⁵⁶ Horrell's assertion ("Paul's Collection," 76) that Paul's "own statements hardly formulate this [ecumenical understanding of the collection] explicitly" fails to account for Paul's use of the κοινων- terminology in Rom 15:26, 27; 2 Cor 8:4; 9:13 (cf. Rom 12:13).

Christ (Rom 12:4–5; 1 Cor 12:27). Recognizing the very real possibility that the saints in Jerusalem might rebuff his efforts on their behalf (Rom 15:31), Paul nevertheless persists in the attempt to demonstrate through the collection the κοινωνία of Jews and Gentiles. In some sense, the collection may even have functioned as a test of whether Paul's Judaizing opponents in Judea would acknowledge the validity and the equality of Gentile Christianity, or whether they would actively seek to terminate fellowship with Paul's mission.[57]

It is necessary to make one additional point. While the monetary collection for Jerusalem undoubtedly exemplified the solidarity of Jewish and Gentile believers, it has not often been observed that the collection also served to strengthen ties between the separate *Gentile* churches of the Pauline mission spread across the cities of the Eastern Mediterranean.[58] Certainly Paul's letters and the messengers who delivered them testify to the existence of a vast web of Christian communities linked not only by shared faith but also by a network of translocal exchange and communication.[59] Embedded in Paul's epistles are numerous passages that highlight regional connections within Pauline Christianity, including greetings from members of one community to members of another (Rom 16:3–16, 21–23; 1 Cor 16:19–20; Phil 4:21–22; Phlm 23; cf. Col 4:10–17), letters of recommendation (Rom 16:1; 1 Cor 16:10–12; cf. Col 4:7–10), references to travel delegates (1 Cor 1:11; 2 Cor 7:2–16; 8:16–24; 9:3–5; Phil 2:25–30; 1 Thess 3:6), and requests for hospitality (Rom 15:24; Phlm 22; cf. Col 4:19). At the same time, since many of these references center on the activity of Paul and his closest associates, it is possible to overestimate the extent to which Paul's churches established relationships with Christian communities in other cities. In fact, as Richard Ascough has pointed out, Paul's fundraising problems in Corinth might have been due to the fact that Corinthians "remained unconvinced that they had a social and religious obligation to an otherwise unknown group. What confuses the Corinthians is not the fact that they have to donate, but that the monies are going to Jerusalem rather than the common fund of the local congregation."[60] As we shall see in chapter three, which looks at instances of translocal

---

[57] So Jürgen Becker, *Paul: Apostle to the Gentiles* (trans. O. C. Dean; Louisville: Westminster John Knox, 1993), 260.

[58] But see now Harrison, *Paul's Language of Grace*, 298 n. 33; cf. Harris, *Second Epistle*, 100. Abraham Malherbe ("The Corinthian Contribution," *ResQ* 3 [1959]: 225 n. 18) makes the point that, while the primary purpose of the collection may have been to unite Gentiles and Jews, focus on a common concern may also have prevented the fragmentation of the Corinthian house churches.

[59] See Wayne A. Meeks, *The First Urban Christians: The Social World of the Apostle Paul* (New Haven and London: Yale University Press, 1983), 107–10; see also Michael B. Thompson, "The Holy Internet: Communication between Churches in the First Christian Generation," in *The Gospels for All Christians: Rethinking the Gospel Audiences* (ed. Richard Bauckahm; Grand Rapids: Eerdmans, 1998), 49–70.

[60] Richard S. Ascough, *Paul's Macedonian Associations: The Social Context of Philippians and 1 Thessalonians* (WUNT 2:161; Tübingen: Mohr Siebeck, 2003), 104.

giving among Greco-Roman voluntary associations, Paul's effort to gather funds from communities in a number of geographical regions for the Jewish-Christian community in Jerusalem may not represent a unique form of gift-giving in antiquity, but it at least offered a relatively uncommon type of benefaction, especially for pagan converts familiar with traditions of civic euergetism and local patronage. The Jerusalem collection, then, would have presented the members of Paul's churches with the opportunity to combine their donations with monies raised in other localities. As 2 Cor 8:1–6 and 9:2–5 reveal, Paul was not above using the positive example of one congregation to stir up support for the collection in another. Perhaps even more than promoting any sense of competition among the Pauline churches in terms of their financial support of the saints in Jerusalem, however, this rhetorical strategy reminded the members of these congregations that they were partners in the gospel with one another, no less than with the poor among the saints in Jerusalem.

1.1.4 The Collection as Material Relief

Finally, a number of interpreters have stressed the caritative aspects of the collection. Proponents of this materialist reading often claim that other scholars have minimized or ignored the economic dimensions of the collection and that the chief objective of the project was the material relief of the saints in Jerusalem and the equal distribution of goods.[61]

The issue of the economic significance of the collection has sometimes been clouded by the theory, originally advanced by Karl Holl, that the term "the poor" (οἱ πτωχοί), by which designation the recipients of financial assistance for Jerusalem are identified in Gal 2:10 and Rom 15:26, is a technical title ("ein feststehender, geläufiger Name") for the Jerusalem church as a whole, derived from the Hebrew אביונים, and thus not a socio-economic categorization of a destitute segment of that community.[62] Holl argues that the Jerusalem church adopted this title from the Jewish tradition, reflected in a number of Old Testament and early Jewish texts, of concern for the poor as a group with special status before God.[63] Holl's thesis is supported by Georgi, who agrees that "the absolute use of this appellation in Galatians 2:10 and the fact that it does not need any explanation show that it must have been a title commonly bestowed upon [the Jerusalem] congregation."[64] Georgi also adds an eschatological dimension to this self-designation, since it is "the poor," according to Georgi, who are specifically associated with the restoration of Zion in the last days (Isa 14:30–32; Zeph 3:9–12). This reading of οἱ πτωχοί in Gal 2:10 also received some support with the

---

[61] See Nickle, *The Collection*, 100–11; Horrell, "Paul's Collection," 74–83.
[62] Holl, "Der Kirchenbegriff," 60.
[63] For a discussion of the significant texts, see E. Bammel, "πτωχός, πτωχεία, πτωχεύω," *TDNT* 6:888–902.
[64] Georgi, *Remembering the Poor*, 34.

discovery of the Dead Sea Scrolls, for in several instances the Qumran sect appears to supplement more common community self-designations like יחד, ברית, and עדה with the use of titles אביונים or ענוים (1QpHab XII, 2–3; 1QM XIII, 12–14; 4Q171 II, 9–10; III, 10).[65]

There are a number of problems with this interpretation of οἱ πτωχοί with reference to the recipients of the Pauline collection, however. Aside from the difficulties of associating the request in Gal 2:10 "to remember the poor" with the Pauline collection as such – an issue that will be addressed in the following chapter on the chronology of the collection – Leander Keck has shown that, while this self-designation is not impossible, there is no evidence in the New Testament or other early Christian literature to suggest that the Aramaic-speaking church in Jerusalem referred to itself as "the poor."[66] One would at least expect to find traces of this appellation in the book of Acts, for example, not only because a large portion of that narrative is devoted to the history of the early community in Jerusalem, but also because the author of that work displays no small level of interest in issues of wealth and poverty.[67] Holl's theory is based solely on his reading of Gal 2:10 and Rom 15:26, yet these passages do not support his conclusions. In Gal 2:10, while Paul is essentially reporting the request of the leaders of the Jerusalem church, his use of the noun πτωχός does not signal the honorable piety of "the poor" in Jerusalem, for not only would such a subtle evocation of the Jewish tradition of honorific poverty be fairly unintelligible to his Gentile readers in Galatia, but drawing upon this tradition would also undercut the somewhat negative portrayal of Jerusalem elsewhere in the letter to the Galatians.[68] Πτωχός in this context means the economically disadvantaged, as is the case in Rom 15:26. As even Georgi concedes, the phrase εἰς τοὺς πτωχοὺς τῶν ἁγίων τῶν ἐν Ἰερουσαλήμ in Rom 15:26 should be understood in a partitive sense, that is, as a reference to the materially poor *among* the saints in Jerusalem.[69]

If the collection for Jerusalem was, in fact, designated for a destitute segment of the Jerusalem church, then charity must also been seen as a major motivating factor in Paul's concern to contribute to the needs of the poor among the saints. After reviewing the eschatological and ecumenical interpretations of the collec-

---

[65] See the discussion in Keck, "The Poor among the Saints in Jewish Christianity," 68–77.

[66] Keck, "The Poor among the Saints in the New Testament," 100–29; idem, "The Poor among the Saints in Jewish Christianity," 54–78.

[67] Keck, "The Poor among the Saints in the New Testament," 103–12.

[68] See J. Louis Martyn, "A Tale of Two Churches," in *Theological Issues in the Letters of Paul* (Nashville: Abingdon, 1997), 25–36. I cannot agree with Keck's argument that Paul did not need to explain to the Galatians the identity of "the poor" because he had already begun raising funds in Galatia for the Jerusalem collection, however. This does not fit with the overall chronology of a fundraising project initiated *after* the writing of Galatians (see the following chapter).

[69] Georgi, *Remembering the Poor*, 175–76 n. 51. So also Dunn, *Romans*, 875; Thrall, *2 Corinthians*, 506–9.

tion, David Horrell suggests that the reason "which emerges most clearly as Paul's fundamental motivation for the collection is the desire to relieve the poverty of the poor among the saints in Jerusalem."[70] According to Horrell, Paul's deeply theological understanding of God's grace manifested itself in the material task of raising money for the poor among the saints in Jerusalem. "For Paul," Horrell writes of 2 Cor 8:13–14, "the divine objective of equality is to be realised through the generous actions of Christian people, inspired as they are by the grace of God." The collection is, then, both an outstanding example of and the foundational resource for what Horrell labels "materialist theology," by which term he means "a theology which engages with social, economic, and political realities, a theology which insists that the gospel has to do with the whole of life, including the material conditions and socio-economic relationships in which people are enmeshed."[71]

If Horrell presents a coherent reading of the Pauline collection based on a careful examination of the role of the fundraising project in Paul's mission and its significance for modern readers, the same is not true of the work of Petros Vassiliadis, another proponent of the materialist reading of the collection, who has published two articles and one book on the subject.[72] In his critique of previous work on the collection, Vassiliadis consistently emphasizes the neglect of "the *social* aspects of that project."[73] Vassiliadis claims, "According to [Paul's] argument in 2 Cor 8–9, the ultimate purpose of the collection project was to realize the social ideal of *the equal distribution and permanent sharing of material wealth*."[74]

Yet Vassiliadis's work on the social aspects of the collection is marred at a number of points by confusing and, at times, inaccurate assertions. First, Vassiliadis consistently speaks of the aim of the collection as "sharing the surplus with *the needy of the society at large*."[75] There is no indication in Paul's letters, however, that the collection was intended for any group other than the Jewish-Christian community in Jerusalem. The apostle consistently designates the recipients of the relief fund οἱ ἅγιοι (1 Cor 16:1; 2 Cor 8:4; 9:1, 12; Rom 15:25, 26, 31). Even when Paul uses the metonym Ἰερουσαλήμ in 1 Cor 16:3 and Rom 15:31,

---

[70] Horrell, "Paul's Collection," 76.

[71] Ibid., 79.

[72] Petros Vassiliadis, "Equality and Justice in Classical Antiquity and in Paul: The Social Implications of the Pauline Collection," *SVTQ* 36 (1992): 51–59; idem, "The Collection Revisited," *Deltion Biblikon Meleton* 11 (1992): 42–48; idem, *ΧΑΡΙΣ–ΚΟΙΝΩΝΙΑ–ΔΙΑΚΟΝΙΑ: Ο κοινωνικός χαρακτήρας του παύλειου προγράμματος της λογείας* (Εισαγωγή και ερμηνευτικό υπόμνημα στο Β Κορ 8–9) (Bibliotheca Biblica 2; Thessaloniki: Pournaras, 1985).

[73] Vassiliadis, "The Collection Revisited," 42.

[74] Vassiliadis, "Equality and Justice," 57 (italics original).

[75] Ibid. (italics added); cf. "The Collection Revisited," 43, 44. Vassiliadis ("The Collection Revisited, 44) includes a clause that appears to clarify that with the phrase "society at large" he means the non-Christian poor, for he writes that the collection illustrated "the social ideal of equal distribution and permanent sharing of material means *in the Christian community and the society at large*" (italics added).

context clearly indicates that he is speaking of the poor among the believing community in that city rather than the poor in general. To imply that the gift was offered to "the needy of the society at large" misses the ecclesiocentric focus of the relief fund in Paul's mission and theology. Second, Vassiliadis opines that, while the Pauline collection may have been modeled after the Jewish temple tax, nevertheless "it was St. Paul himself who made this project a unique phenomenon in world history, both religious and social."[76] The dangers of characterizing any element of early Christianity as "unique" are well known, however, and are no less pertinent in the description of the Pauline collection, an activity for which analogous forms of benefaction are readily available, as even Vassiliadis's own comparison with the temple tax implies.[77] Finally, Vassiliadis claims that Paul envisioned economic equality within the church as a permanent goal. The aim of the collection, according to Vassiliadis, "was to realize the social ideal of *the equal distribution and permanent sharing of material wealth*."[78]

This last point, which is not developed in great detail in Vassiliadis's articles, raises the question whether the Pauline collection for Jerusalem was a one-time act of charity or part of a continued effort on behalf of the Gentile churches of Paul's mission to provide financial assistance to the impoverished believers among the Jerusalem congregation. This issue is also central to the discussion of the collection in Justin Meggitt's recent monograph *Paul, Poverty and Survival*.[79] Meggitt's assessment of the collection for Jerusalem is part of his larger polemic against the so-called New Consensus concerning the socio-economic status of the members of Paul's churches. This consensus, according to Meggitt, incorrectly views the earliest Pauline communities as "incorporating individuals from a cross section of first-century society, including some from the higher strata (who would be, amongst other things, economically affluent)."[80] Meggitt contends, on the other hand, that *all* members of the Pauline circles were "poor," by which term he means, adopting a definition from Peter Garnsey and Greg Woolf, the ninety-nine percent of the population that lived "at or near subsis-

---

[76] Vassiliadis, "Equality and Justice," 56. Vassiliadis even goes so far as to suggest that the account of the Antiochean collection in Acts 11:27–30 "was modeled after the Pauline project rather than the other way around" (56–57). On historical grounds alone this theory is impossible; by all accounts, Paul had split with the church in Antioch long before the organization of the relief fund mentioned in 1 Corinthians, 2 Corinthians, and Romans.

[77] On the tendency of an earlier generation of Christian scholars to describe Christianity as "unique," see Jonathan Z. Smith, *Drudgery Divine: On the Comparison of Early Christianities and the Religions of Late Antiquity* (Jordan Lectures in Comparative Religion 14; Chicago: University of Chicago Press, 1990), esp. 36–46.

[78] Vassiliadis, "Equality and Justice," 57 (italics original).

[79] Justin J. Meggitt, *Paul, Poverty and Survival* (Studies of the New Testament and Its World; Edinburgh: T & T Clark, 1998), esp. 155–78.

[80] Ibid., 99–100. Meggitt attributes this consensus to scholars like Gerd Theissen (*The Social Setting of Pauline Christianity: Essays on Corinth* [ed. and trans. John Schütz; Philadelphia: Fortress, 1982] and Wayne Meeks (*The First Urban Christians*).

tence level, whose prime concern it is to obtain the minimum food, shelter, and clothing necessary to sustain life, whose lives are dominated by the struggle for physical survival."[81] The vast majority of inhabitants of the Roman Empire, the *plebs urbana*, was characterized by widespread poverty, destitution, and subsistence existence, a fate escaped only by the very small number of urban elites who comprised less than one percent of the population.

Meggitt lists a number of survival strategies adopted by members of Paul's churches for dealing with their subsistence existence. These strategies include self-sufficiency (αὐτάρκεια; Phil 4:11; cf. 2 Cor 9:8), the giving and receiving of alms (Gal 6:9), hospitality (Phlm 22; Rom 12:13), and, finally, what Meggitt calls "mutualism." The first three practices were, according to Meggitt, relatively uncommon in the Pauline churches, but the fourth, mutualism, was prominent. Meggitt defines mutualism as "the implicit or explicit belief that *individual and collective well-being is attainable above all by mutual interdependence.*"[82]

Two factors lead Meggitt to identify the collection for Jerusalem as the chief example of the practice of mutualism among the early Christian communities. The first is his belief that the collection was aimed principally at the promotion of *"material well being"* and *"the relief of the economically poor in the Jerusalem church,"* although eschatological, ecumenical, and other concerns doubtless played a role in the organization of the fund.[83] Second, Meggitt views the collection as truly mutual in character because of his conviction that *all* members of *all* churches were expected to contribute and that the relief fund was not a one-time act of charity. Instead, *"the material assistance given was understood as something that would, in time, be returned, when the situation was reversed."*[84] Rejecting the typical strategy of reading 2 Cor 8:14 ("At the present time your abundance is for their need, so that their abundance may be for your need, so that there may be equality") in light of the material-spiritual exchange described in Rom 15:27, Meggitt contends that Paul's statement to the Corinthians envisions a situation in which the Jerusalem church will repay the Corinthians with financial assistance in the future, when there is a material shortage in Corinth. Since the "problem facing the Jerusalem church was almost certainly brought about by a localized food shortage, it is quite feasible that Paul would have had such economic reciprocation in mind."[85] Thus, "By meeting the needs of the Jerusalem congregation, the communities were contributing to their own, long-term, economic stability."[86]

---

[81] Meggitt, *Paul, Poverty and Survival*, 5; citing Peter Garnsey and Greg Woolf, "Patronage of the Rural Poor in the Roman World," in *Patronage in Ancient Society* (ed. Andrew Wallace-Hadrill; Routledge: London, 1990), 153.

[82] Meggitt, *Paul, Poverty and Survival*, 158 (italics original).

[83] Ibid., 159 (italics original).

[84] Ibid. (italics original).

[85] Ibid., 160–61.

[86] Ibid., 161.

Meggitt's provocative thesis concerning the economic status of Paul and the members of his churches and the material significance of the collection for Jerusalem represents a bold challenge to a developing consensus among New Testament scholars, and his work has garnered significant attention.[87] Yet there are several problems with Meggitt's work on the Jerusalem collection. First, Meggitt's dichotomous reading of the socio-economic world of Greco-Roman society – with a wealthy elite comprising one percent (or less) of the population and an undifferentiated mass of the destitute and poor comprising ninety-nine percent (or more) of the population – is entirely too simplistic to be convincing, and hardly accounts for the diversity in terms of wealth and status, not only among the members of Paul's churches in particular, but also in the ancient world in general.[88] Even if there are difficulties in using the category of "social status" in the economic analysis of the Pauline churches, as Meggitt shows, what is needed is more – not less – precision in the discussion of wealth and benefaction within early Christianity. Steven J. Friesen, for example, has recently attempted to move beyond the binary categories of "rich/poor" by developing and then applying to Pauline Christianity a poverty scale with seven categories ranging from "below subsistence level" to "imperial elites."[89] Friesen's approach is far more fruitful for the attempt to understand the social and economic location(s) of the members of Paul's churches than Meggitt's undifferentiated analysis.

Second, Meggitt's claim that the collection "was not a one-off act of charity" is based upon his assumption that "the problem facing the Jerusalem church was almost certainly brought about by a localised food shortage."[90] It is no doubt true that the Pauline collection was organized to render material assistance to impoverished believers in Jerusalem (2 Cor 8:14). Given the ubiquity of food

---

[87] Between 2001–2003, the *Journal for the Study of the New Testament* published three lengthy reviews of Meggitt's monograph as well as a response by Meggitt to two of the reviews. See Dale B. Martin, "Review Essay: Justin J. Meggitt, *Paul, Poverty and Survival*," *JSNT* 24 (2001): 51–64; Gerd Theissen, "The Social Structure of Pauline Communities: Some Critical Remarks on J. J. Meggitt, *Paul, Poverty and Survival*," *JSNT* 24 (2001): 65–84; Justin J. Meggitt, "Response to Martin and Theissen," *JSNT* 24 (2001): 85–94; Gerd Theissen, "Social Conflicts in the Corinthian Community: Further Remarks on J. J. Meggitt, *Paul, Poverty and Survival*," *JSNT* 25 (2003): 371–91.

[88] For a strong critique of this point, see Martin, "Review Essay," 54–56. As Martin points out, greater than one percent of the population in Greco-Roman antiquity owned slaves, which should surely indicate that those members of the non-elite who owned slaves were relatively better off than those who did not. Yet Meggitt claims that "the inclusion of a slave in a person's household can therefore indicate little about the householder's socio-economic status" (*Paul, Poverty and Survival*, 131).

[89] Steven J. Friesen, "Poverty in Pauline Studies: Beyond the So-called New Consensus," *JSNT* 26 (2004): 323–61. See also the responses by John Barclay, "Poverty in Pauline Studies: A Response to Steven Friesen," *JSNT* 26 (2004): 363–66; and Peter Oakes, "Constructing Poverty Scales for Graeco-Roman Society: A Response to Steven Friesen's 'Poverty in Pauline Studies,'" *JSNT* 26 (2004): 367–71.

[90] Meggitt, *Paul, Poverty and Survival*, 159, 160–61.

shortages in antiquity, poverty among the saints in Jerusalem certainly could have been caused by a localized limitation in the available food supply, although other reasons have also been suggested, such as a reduction in capital and land resources caused by the Jerusalem church's experiment in communal living (cf. Acts 2:42–47; 4:32–37).[91] At the same time, we should not overstate the severity of the financial crisis facing the Jerusalem church, for the very fact that Paul seems to have taken a number of years to coordinate the delivery of a relief fund among the churches of his mission suggests that the situation in Jerusalem may not have been as dire as Meggitt suspects. Paul's instructions about the delivery of the relief fund lack the urgency that one would expect, if the gift were intended to stave off the imminent threat of starvation among a segment of the Jewish-Christian community in Jerusalem. There is reason to believe, in fact, that the Pauline collection for Jerusalem was a one-time caritative project. In his discussion of his plans to deliver the fund in Rom 15:25–32, Paul does not indicate that he plans to continue his fundraising efforts after this journey to Jerusalem, nor does he encourage the church in Rome to begin gathering a follow-up offering for Jerusalem.

Finally, and perhaps most significantly, Meggitt's identification of the collection as an example of the survival strategy known as "mutualism" is problematic. While Meggitt is right to warn against the danger of reading the material/spiritual dichotomy of Rom 15:27 (τὰ πνευματικὰ vs. τὰ σαρκικὰ) into 2 Cor 8:14, there are hints even in 2 Cor 8:1–9:15 that Paul's readers in Corinth are to imagine an exchange of material support for spiritual blessings from the Jerusalem church. At the conclusion of his appeal for the Corinthians to contribute to the fund, for example, Paul writes, "Through the testing of this ministry you glorify God by your obedience to the confession of the gospel of Christ and by the abundance of your partnership-forming contribution for them and for all, while they, too, with prayer on your behalf, are longing for you because of the surpassing benefaction of God among you" (2 Cor 9:13–14). While the material/spiritual exchange is not as explicit here as it is in Rom 15:27, Paul does seem to intimate that the return that the Corinthians will receive for their generous benefaction is not material assistance in the future but "prayer on your behalf." Meggitt's argument rests, in part, on his assumption that *all* members of the Corinthian churches were, like the believers in Jerusalem, "poor"; if some of the Corinthians

---

[91] The classic study of food shortages in antiquity remains Peter Garnsey, *Famine and Food Supply in the Graeco-Roman World: Responses to Risk and Crisis* (Cambridge: Cambridge University Press, 1988); see now also several of the essays in Margaret Atkins and Robin Osborne, eds., *Poverty in the Roman World* (Cambridge: Cambridge University Press, 2006). For evidence of famine in Palestine, see Bruce W. Winter, "Acts and Food Shortages," in *The Book of Acts in Its Graeco-Roman Setting* (ed. David W. J. Gill and Conrad Gempf; vol. 2 of *The Book of Acts in Its First Century Setting*, ed. Bruce W. Winter; Grand Rapids: Eerdmans, 1994), 59–78. Those who have tied the poverty within the Jerusalem church to the communal practices described in Acts 2 include Holl, "Der Kirchenbegriff," 35; Nickle, *The Collection*, 102; Harris, *Second Epistle*, 88.

were relatively well-off (a possibility that Meggitt rejects on questionable historical grounds), their wealth, and with it their ability to live beyond subsistence means, would call into question Meggitt's proposal that "the apostle foresaw a time when the [economic] situation would be reversed."[92] Moreover, it is striking that in his discussion of the Pauline collection, Meggitt produces no ancient parallels to the early Christian practice of mutualism. As Dale Martin rightly objects in his review of Meggitt's book:

One would have thought that, if Christian mutualism "emerged to meet a very real need,"

> then it would have emerged among groups besides Paul's churches. Weren't the rest of the 99 per cent as much in need of a "survival strategy" as Pauline Christians? Meggitt, though, is in the uncomfortable position of positing a new, distinctive, indeed *unique* invention on the part of the Pauline Christians – a social economic strategy found nowhere else in the ancient world (see pp. 173, 175, 179). Historians are rightly skeptical of absolute uniqueness in historical accounts.[93]

Meggitt's work, then, raises the question of the relationship between the Pauline collection for the poor among the saints in Jerusalem and other means of dealing with economic scarcity in the Greco-Roman world. As we shall see, Meggitt appears to understate the role that care for the poor played in Greco-Roman society, particularly among pagan and Jewish voluntary associations.[94] Also worthy of mention in this context is Verlyn Verbrugge's monograph on the Jerusalem collection. In a section in which he considers three fundraising models in Greco-Roman antiquity that might have influenced Paul's appeal in 2 Cor 8–9 – involuntary liturgies (λειτουργίαι), clubs and associations, and the Greek system of ἐπίδοσις ("subscriptions") – Verbrugge concludes that "the notion of ἐπίδοσις does serve as a true parallel to Paul's notion of raising money for the poor in Jerusalem," although he does also recognize significant differences.[95] An ἐπίδοσις was an occasional, public appeal for civic assistance, often used to finance the construction of sanctuaries or municipal buildings, military expenses in times of war, or, occasionally, grain or oil in times of food shortage.[96] While there are indeed some similarities between Paul's fundraising efforts on behalf of the poor in the Jerusalem church and the Greek system of ἐπίδοσις, recent scholarship that has explored analogies between the Pauline churches and Greco-Roman voluntary associations has cleared the way for a reexamination of the phenomenon of benefaction within pagan and Jewish associations.

---

[92] Meggitt, *Paul, Poverty and Survival*, 161.
[93] Martin, "Review Essay," 63.
[94] See esp. the discussion of Greco-Roman *collegia* in Meggitt, *Paul, Poverty and Survival*, 170–72.
[95] Verbrugge, *Paul's Style of Church Leadership*, 157.
[96] See Léopold Migeotte's major study *Les souscriptions publiques dans les cités grecques* (Geneva: Droz, 1992), which was unavailable when Verbrugge published his dissertation.

1.2 The Present Study

This overview of previous research on the Pauline collection for Jerusalem suggests that, while major lines of interpretation have already been drawn, there remains significant room for a fresh study of the history of the "offering of the Gentiles" (Rom 15:16) and its attendant place in Paul's mission and theology. There are three aspects of the Jerusalem collection in particular that merit more careful examination: (1) the chronology of the collection, an issue of no small importance in the attempt to determine the significance of the relief fund for Paul's mission; (2) the relationship between the Jerusalem collection and other forms of benefaction in the ancient world; and (3) the religious rhetoric used by Paul in his discussions of the collection and the importance of the collection for Pauline theology.

Chapter two, "The Chronology of the Collection," attempts to locate the collection in Pauline chronology with more methodological rigor than is sometimes afforded this difficult topic.[97] It is no exaggeration to say that every noteworthy monograph devoted to the Jerusalem collection works with the assumption that the project originated in the request of the Jerusalem leadership that Paul and Barnabas, as delegates of the Antioch church, "remember the poor," an appeal which is reported by Paul in Gal 2:10. In recent years, however, some scholars have begun to question this assumption, positing instead that there is no evidence in Gal 2:10 that Paul was actively engaged in organizing the collection when he wrote to the churches in Galatia and, moreover, that the collection that Paul eventually organized was *not* the result of a previously established pact with Jerusalem.[98] If the request of the Jerusalem church in Gal 2:10 is seen as a reference to a relief fund that Paul had earlier organized as a representative of Antioch (cf. Acts 11:27–30), then the collection mentioned in the Corinthian correspondence and in Romans can be viewed as a project of Paul's own initiative, which may also explain the apostle's trepidation vis-à-vis the gift's acceptance in Jerusalem (Rom 15:31).[99] This, of course, raises substantial questions for those who would claim that the collection was an obligation placed upon Paul and his congregations by the authoritative church in Jerusalem.

If this represents a problem with how scholars have interpreted the origins of the Pauline collection for Jerusalem, there are also difficulties with most reconstructions of the fate of the relief fund, the vast majority of which rely heavily –

---

[97] For an earlier but unsuccessful attempt to do this, see Charles H. Buck, "The Collection for the Saints," *HTR* 43 (1950): 1–30.

[98] See A. J. M. Wedderburn, "Paul's Collection: Chronology and History," *NTS* 48 (2002): 95–110; Martyn, *Galatians*, 225; François Vouga, *An die Galater* (HNT 10; Tübingen: Mohr Siebeck, 1998), 3–5.

[99] To the best of my knowledge, the only monograph devoted to the collection from Antioch is Valentin Weber's *Die antiochenische Kollekte, die übersehene Hauptorientierung für die Paulusforschung: Grundlegende Radikalkur zur Geschichte des Urchristentums* (Würzburg: Echterhaus, 1917).

and for the most part uncritically – on information from the book of Acts. In chapter two, I shall argue that, because it cannot be shown that the author of Acts possessed knowledge of the Pauline collection for Jerusalem, the narrative of Acts cannot be used as a reliable source of information concerning the eventual outcome of the offering. In short, there is room for a reevaluation of the chronology of the collection using the rather simple, but too often neglected, methodological principle articulated by John Knox more than fifty years ago: "We may, with proper caution, use Acts to supplement the autobiographical data of the letters, but never to correct them."[100]

Chapter three, "The Pauline Collection and Greco-Roman Voluntary Associations," aims to explore the socio-cultural context of the collection for the saints by focusing on the phenomenon of benefaction within ancient pagan and Jewish voluntary associations. There have been a number of proposed analogies to and backgrounds of the Jerusalem collection in the ancient world, including the eschatological offering of the Gentiles (Munck, Georgi, Nickle), the Jewish temple tax (Holl, Wan), the Jewish tradition of redemptive almsgiving (Berger, Kim), the general exchange of benefits and obligations in the Mediterranean world (Joubert, Harrison), and the Greek tradition of ἐπίδοσις (Verbrugge). Building on the work of recent scholarship that has suggested Greco-Roman voluntary associations as a helpful comparative model for understanding the organization and activity of the Pauline churches, chapter three examines benefaction, monetary collections, and the sharing of resources within ancient associations. The attempt to frame the social context of the Pauline collection for Jerusalem must carefully tread a fine line between two extreme positions. On the one hand, there is the temptation to force Paul's fundraising efforts on behalf of the Jerusalem church to conform to some already existing model. On the other hand, recognizing that Paul's activity and financial practices are firmly rooted in a particular historical context, one must also avoid the temptation to set up the Jerusalem collection as a unique, unparalleled event in world history. Jonathan Z. Smith's book *Drudgery Divine*, a treatise on the comparison of nascent Christianity with the religions of late antiquity, offers a helpful methodological perspective on the task of negotiating the Scylla of sameness and the Charybdis of uniqueness with respect to the socio-cultural context of the Jerusalem collection.

Chapter four, "The Collection as an Act of Worship: Paul's Cultic Rhetoric," offers a detailed exegetical examination of those passages in which Paul explicitly discusses the collection for the saints (1 Cor 16:1–4; 2 Cor 8:1–9:15; and Rom 15:14–32), focusing particularly on Paul's use of cultic metaphors to frame the collection as a religious offering consecrated to God. Using the theoretical perspective on "conceptual metaphors" developed by George Lakoff and Mark Johnson, I shall argue that Paul metaphorically frames his readers' responsive

---

[100] John Knox, *Chapters in a Life of Paul* (rev. ed.; ed. Douglas R. A. Hare; Macon, Ga.: Mercer University Press, 1987), 19.

participation in the collection as an act of cultic worship, and in so doing he underscores the point that benefaction within the community of believers results in praise to God, the one from whom all benefactions ultimately come. This rhetorical strategy not only minimizes the competition for honor among the members of Paul's churches, it also suggests that even the very human action of raising money for those in material need originates in ἡ χάρις τοῦ θεοῦ and will eventuate in χάρις τῷ θεῷ (2 Cor 9:14–15). Thus, careful attention to the chronological and socio-cultural contexts of the Pauline collection for Jerusalem offers the promise of a much richer understanding of the place of the relief fund in Paul's theology.

Chapter 2

The Chronology of the Collection

2.1 Introduction

The attempt to construct an accurate chronological framework for Paul's life and letters is one of the perennially problematic issues in New Testament studies. This conundrum threatens to capture even the savviest Pauline interpreters in a morass of guesses, inferences, and speculations. Nevertheless, the quest for the history of the Pauline mission continues unabated, in large part because of the vital importance that a reliable chronology of Paul's activity and correspondence holds, both for the history of earliest Christianity and for the endeavor to locate possible developments or changes in Paul's theology.[1]

Any study of Paul's collection for Jerusalem must risk venturing into this difficult area of research because understanding of the Pauline collection is influenced to a significant degree by understanding of Pauline chronology, and vice versa. On the one hand, one's view of the details regarding the origin, organization, and outcome of the relief fund will shape one's conception of the theological significance of that project for Paul's mission as apostle to the Gentiles. On the other, as A. J. M. Wedderburn has observed, "The presence or absence of references to Paul's collection can be a valuable aid in determining the relative chronology of the various Pauline letters."[2] The timeline of Paul's efforts on behalf of the monetary contribution for Jerusalem, therefore, holds valuable clues for the development of the Pauline mission and for the significance of the relief fund for Paul's theology.

This chapter aims to provide an overview of the chronology of the collection organized among the largely Gentile churches of Paul's mission and delivered to the saints in Jerusalem. After a brief discussion of method, I shall first evaluate

---

[1] See A. J. M. Wedderburn, "Paul's Collection: Chronology and History," *NTS* 48 (2002): 95–110.

[2] Wedderburn, "Paul's Collection," 95; see also J. Louis Martyn, *Galatians: A New Translation with Introduction and Commentary* (AB 33A; New York: Doubleday, 1997), 223. This point was made earlier by Paul S. Minear in his essay, "The Jerusalem Fund and Pauline Chronology," *AThR* 25 (1943): 389–96, esp. 390. See now Gregory Tatum, *New Chapters in the Life of Paul: The Relative Chronology of His Career* (CBQMS 41; Washington, D.C.: The Catholic Biblical Association of America, 2006), 94–122.

the theory that the Pauline collection originated in the request of the Jerusalem leadership, reported in Galatians, that Paul and his associates "remember the poor" (Gal 2:10). Next, I shall attempt to construct a narrative detailing the involvement in the Jerusalem collection among the Pauline churches in the regions of Galatia, Achaia, Macedonia, and Asia. Finally, I shall turn to the book of Acts, endeavoring critically to discern what information, if any, regarding the Jerusalem collection's outcome can be culled from that narrative. Some of this chronological work has, of course, been undertaken before, but each interpreter must wrestle with this difficult issue on his or her own, building on the work of previous scholarship, while simultaneously avoiding needless argumentation for well-established conclusions. Moreover, problematic chronological assumptions in several recent studies of the collection, particularly with regard to the issue of method, demand that greater attention be paid to the history of the relief fund.

2.2 Methodological Considerations

Chronological studies of Paul's life and letters must proceed on the basis of a simple, yet too often ignored, methodological principle, first articulated by John Knox nearly seventy years ago and now aptly summarized by J. Louis Martyn: "Our first and decisive attempt to discern the chronology of Paul's work is to be made on the basis of the letters alone. As a second and separable step, we may turn to Acts. Even in that second step, however, one accepts from Acts only points of confirmation and supportive elucidation."[3] It is necessary to restate this principle because scholars writing on the chronology of the Pauline mission, including the history of Paul's organization of a monetary contribution for Jerusalem, regularly confuse and conflate the primary source of historical information

---

[3] Martyn, *Galatians*, 17. The classic statement of this position is found in two seminal articles by John Knox in the 1930s: "'Fourteen Years Later': A Note on the Pauline Chronology," *JR* 16 (1936): 341–49; and "The Pauline Chronology," *JBL* 58 (1939): 15–29. There is an extensive bibliography devoted to the study of Pauline chronology; see especially Rainer Riesner, *Paul's Early Period: Chronology, Mission Strategy, Theology* (trans. Doug Stott; Grand Rapids: Eerdmans, 1998); A. Suhl, "Paulinische Chronologie im Streit der Meinungen," *ANRW* 26.2:939–1188; Gerd Lüdemann, *Paul, Apostle to the Gentiles: Studies in Chronology* (trans. F. Stanley Jones; Philadelphia: Fortress, 1984); Niels Hyldahl, *Die paulinische Chronologie* (ATDan 19; Leiden: Brill, 1986); John Knox, *Chapters in a Life of Paul* (rev. ed.; ed. Douglas R. A. Hare; Macon, Ga.: Mercer University Press, 1987), 1–73; Robert Jewett, *A Chronology of Paul's Life* (Philadelphia: Fortress, 1979); the essays by Jewett, Lüdemann, and Knox in *Colloquy on New Testament Studies: A Time for Reappraisal and Fresh Approaches* (ed. Bruce Corley; Macon, Ga.: Mercer University Press, 1983); Karl Paul Donfried, "Chronology: The Apostolic and Pauline Period," in *Paul, Thessalonica, and Early Christianity* (Grand Rapids: Eerdmans, 2002), 99–117; and Tatum, *New Chapters*, passim. The earlier period of Paul's missionary activity is addressed in meticulous detail in Ruth Schäfer's *Paulus bis zum Apostelkonzil: Ein Beitrag zur Einleitung in den Galaterbrief, zur Geschichte der Jesusbewegung und zur Pauluschronologie* (WUNT 2:179; Tübingen: Mohr Siebeck, 2004).

(the letters of Paul) with a secondary one (the book of Acts).[4] As we shall see, especially with regard to Paul's involvement with a collection from the church in Antioch, the narrative of Acts may at times proffer valuable historical information concerning Paul's life and work, but this data should only be used with caution to supplement information already obtained from the letters.[5] At the same time, since this is a chapter on the limited subject of the "Chronology of the Collection" and not a general study of the "Chronology of Paul's Life," I shall refrain from addressing questions regarding the overall usefulness of the portrait of the Pauline mission in Acts. The story of Paul's second missionary journey in Acts 15:36–19:41, for example, is often mined by those who wish to obtain from it data for a chronological account of Paul's activity in the cities of Philippi, Thessalonica, Beroea, Athens, Corinth, and Ephesus. That is not how information from Acts will be used here, however, where I shall focus primarily on material from Paul's letters, considering only evidence from Acts that bears directly (or is alleged to bear directly) on our understanding of Paul's collection for Jerusalem.

A second, related methodological principle active in the present study is that this chapter will attempt only to discern a relative chronology for the Pauline collection, leaving aside the issue of an absolute dating of Paul's mission.[6] Apart from the brief mention of Paul's dramatic escape from Damascus during the

---

[4] To call Acts a secondary source is, of course, already to render a judgment on the very difficult question of the sources of Acts, for if the author of the so-called "we" passages (16:10–17; 20:5–15; 21:1–18; 27:1–28:16) was a traveling companion of Paul, then at least those sections of the narrative might justifiably be labeled primary sources. There is not space here to discuss in detail my understanding of the "we" passages in Acts. I do not think that these sections necessarily reflect the eyewitness testimony of a historical observer, however – either that of the author of Acts or one of his sources. I find stylistic and literary explanations of the "we" passages far more convincing, such as the theory that the use of first-person discourse testifies to Paul's obedience to divine missionary instructions. See, e.g., William Sanger Campbell, *The 'We' Passages in the Acts of the Apostles: The Narrator as Narrative Character* (StBL 14; Atlanta: Society of Biblical Literature, 2007). For other recent assessments of the "we" passages, see Susan Marie Praeder, "The Problem of First Person Narration in Acts," *NovT* 29 (1987): 193–218; A. J. M. Wedderburn, "The 'We'-Passages in Acts: On the Horns of a Dilemma," *ZNW* 93 (2002): 78–98; Samuel Byrskog, "History or Story in Acts – A Middle Way? The 'We' Passages, Historical Intertexture, and Oral History," in *Contextualizing Acts: Lukan Narrative and Greco-Roman Discourse* (ed. Todd Penner and Caroline Vander Stichele; SBLSymS 20; Atlanta: Society of Biblical Literature, 2003), 257–83.

[5] Cf. Knox, *Chapters in a Life*, 19: "The distinction between primary and secondary sources in [the case of Paul and Acts] is of such importance that we can justly say that a fact only suggested in the letters has a status which even the most unequivocal statement of Acts, if not otherwise supported, cannot confer. We may, with proper caution, use Acts to supplement the autobiographical data of the letters, but never to correct them."

[6] For a tentative chronology of Paul's activity, see David J. Downs, "Chronology of the New Testament," in *The New Interpreter's Dictionary of the Bible* (ed. Katharine Doob Sakenfeld; Nashville: Abingdon, 2006), 1:633–36.

reign of the Nabataean king Aretas (2 Cor 11:32–33), the Pauline epistles provide no other absolute dates from which the apostle's activity may be connected to events in world history.[7] The quest for an absolute Pauline chronology inevitably involves evidence from Acts, even if a relative chronology is first constructed from the epistles.[8] While data from Acts will be evaluated as it is relevant to our understanding of the chronology of the collection, in order to limit the scope of the present study, this chapter will focus only on the events associated with the organization and delivery of the collection in their *relative* chronological order. This sequence can and will be constructed from the epistles alone.

2.3 Galatians 2:1–10 and the Collection from Antioch

2.3.1 Galatians 2:1–10

"Remember the poor." This, according to Paul's recollection in Gal 2:10, represents the content of a request made by the leaders of the Jerusalem church on the occasion of Paul, Barnabas, and Titus's visit to Jerusalem. It is frequently maintained that Paul's collection for the poor among the believing community in Jerusalem had its origins in this appeal. For example, in his study of the collection in light of conventions of benefit exchange in the Greco-Roman world, Stephan Joubert makes the agreement between Paul and the pillar apostles described in Gal 2:1–10 the starting point of his analysis of the Pauline collection. For Joubert, the compact reached during the Jerusalem conference and recounted in Gal 2:1–10 initiated a relationship of reciprocal exchange in which Paul was indebted to the leaders of the Jerusalem church because of their validation of his mission to the Gentiles. According to Joubert, then, Paul's endeavor to raise a monetary contribution designed to meet the needs of the poor believers in Jerusalem represents the apostle's attempt to fulfill his obligations to the Jerusalem leadership by returning proper (material) benefits to those who had authorized his law-free gospel during the Jerusalem conference.[9]

---

[7] Even this incident is difficult to date with precision, although in a recent article arguing that this episode occurred between 36–37 C.E., Douglas A. Campbell has suggested that this datum "could constitute the chronological anchor that Pauline biographers so desperately need; one to which an entire biographical framework for his life could eventually be connected" ("An Anchor for Pauline Chronology: Paul's Flight from 'the Ethnarch of King Aretas' (2 Corinthians 11:32–33)," *JBL* 121 [2002]: 279–302).

[8] This is the method rigorously adopted by Lüdemann in *Paul, Apostle to the Gentiles*.

[9] Stephan Joubert, *Paul as Benefactor: Reciprocity, Strategy and Theological Reflection in Paul's Collection* (WUNT 2:124; Tübingen: Mohr Siebeck, 2000), esp. 73–115. Others who connect the request in Gal 2:10 with the beginnings of Paul's collection efforts include Keith Nickle, *The Collection: A Study in Paul's Strategy* (SBT 48; Naperville, Ill.: Allenson, 1966), 40–73; Byung-Mo Kim, *Die paulinische Kollekte* (TANZ 38; Tübingen: Francke, 2002), 137–80; Victor P. Furnish, *II*

A number of interpreters have questioned the assumption that Gal 2:10 refers to the beginnings of the Pauline collection as such, however. Instead, these scholars contend that there is no evidence in Galatians that Paul was actively engaged in organizing the collection when he wrote that letter and, moreover, that the collection that Paul eventually organized was *not* the immediate result of the pact with Jerusalem related in Gal 2:1–10.[10] It may be more accurate, then, to speak, as Martyn does, of Paul's "collections," recognizing that Paul was involved in the delivery of a relief fund from the church of Antioch – an activity reflected in Gal 2:10 – long before he organized a collection among the Gentile churches of his own mission.[11] Several relevant pieces of information make this a more acceptable hypothesis.

First, when Paul writes in Gal 2:9–10 that James, Cephas, and John – "those who were acknowledged pillars" (οἱ δοκοῦντες στῦλοι εἶναι) – extended to him and to Barnabas the right hand of fellowship, along with the singular request that Paul and his companions "remember the poor" (μόνον τῶν πτωχῶν ἵνα μνημονεύωμεν), Paul does not in that context highlight the significance of this agreement for his readers in Galatia – a striking omission if Paul were engaged in gathering a collection at the time Galatians was written.[12] Indeed, in spite of Hurtado's ingenious but ultimately unconvincing attempt to read Gal 6:6–10 as an exhortation for the Galatians to contribute to the collection, nowhere in all of Galatians does one find mention of the offering for Jerusalem, if one does not count Gal 2:10 as such.[13]

Corinthians: Translated with Introduction, Notes, and Commentary (AB 32A; Garden City: Doubleday, 1984), 410–11; Lüdemann, *Paul, Apostle to the Gentiles*, 83–87; Jürgen Becker, *Paul: Apostle to the Gentiles* (trans. O. C. Dean; Louisville: Westminster John Knox, 1993), 22–26; and Ralph P. Martin, *2 Corinthians* (WBC 40; Waco, Tex.: Word, 1986), 251.

[10] The basic chronological outline of this alternative view was provided by Dieter Georgi, although Georgi still maintains that Paul's collection represented a "new start" to a project that had been abandoned, rather than a different collection altogether. See Dieter Georgi, *Remembering the Poor: The History of Paul's Collection for Jerusalem* (Nashville: Abingdon, 1992), 43–67. See also Nicholas Taylor, *Paul, Antioch and Jerusalem: A Study in Relationships and Authority in Earliest Christianity* (JSNTSup 66; Sheffield: Sheffield Academic Press, 1992), 197–204; Martyn, *Galatians*, 222–28; M. E. Thrall, *A Critical and Exegetical Commentary on the Second Epistle to the Corinthians* (2 vols.; ICC; London: T & T Clark, 1994, 2000), 504–6. In a recent essay, Bruce W. Longenecker has advanced the provocative thesis that the reference to "the poor" in Gal 2:10 should not be taken as a reference to the Jerusalem poor at all: "Instead, their stipulation was that Paul should ensure that Gentile Christians should care for the poor and needy within their own local contexts" (Bruce W. Longenecker, "Good News to the Poor: Jesus, Paul, and Jerusalem," in *Jesus and Paul Reconnected: Fresh Pathways into an Old Debate* [ed. Todd D. Still; Grand Rapids: Eerdmans, 2007], 58).

[11] Martyn, *Galatians*, 222–28. On this issue, see also the brief but illuminating comments in Thrall, *2 Corinthians*, 503–20.

[12] Georgi, *Remembering the Poor*, 45; Wedderburn, "Paul's Collection," 96–97.

[13] Larry W. Hurtado, "The Jerusalem Collection and the Book of Galatians," *JSNT* 5 (1979): 46–62. Not only does Hurtado's interpretation strain the rather obvious meaning of the text, but

Second, the connection with Antioch in Gal 2 is important. On the one hand, although Paul asserts in Gal 2:2 that he went up to Jerusalem "because of a revelation" (κατὰ ἀποκάλυψιν), he nevertheless serves, along with Barnabas and Titus, as a representative of the Antioch community (cf. 1:21; 2:11–13). The request of the Jerusalem leadership, phrased in the first-person plural verb μνημονεύωμεν (2:10), should be understood as a petition directed to the believers in Antioch and mediated through the agency of their delegates. On the other hand, there is no evidence that Antioch actually participated in the Pauline collection mentioned in the Corinthian correspondence and Romans. This detail is not at all surprising, if the events narrated in Gal 2:11–14 imply a break between Paul and Antioch and, later, Paul's founding of an independent missionary venture.[14] From Paul's perspective, the agreement regarding the Gentile mission reached earlier during the Jerusalem conference and reported in Gal 2:1–10 may have been voided by the controversy in Antioch surrounding the objection of "certain people from James" (Gal 2:12) to table fellowship between Jews and Gentiles. If so, and if Paul split with Antioch after this controversy, these developments explain the cessation of Paul's fundraising efforts for Jerusalem as a representative of Antioch.[15] In fact, if Paul was being charged by his opponents in Galatia with abandoning his promise to remember the poor in Jerusalem because of his divorce from Antioch, this clarifies his emphatic insistence that remembrance of the poor in Jerusalem was exactly a pledge that he had already fulfilled at some point prior to the dissolution of his relationship with the Antiochene community: "this is the very thing that I *was* eager to do" (ὃ καὶ ἐσπούδασα αὐτὸ τοῦτο ποιῆσαι).[16]

Third, as Wedderburn points out, "nowhere in all his explicit mentions of the collection (if one does not count Gal 2:10 as such) does Paul connect the project with the carrying out of an agreement reached between himself and the Jerusalem church; nothing suggests that in the raising of the collection he saw himself as carrying out his side of that particular bargain."[17] Indeed, it is very difficult to

---

it also requires that ὁ κατηχούμενος in 6:6b be seen as a reference to Jerusalem, hardly a designation one would expect given Paul's consistently negative stance toward the Jerusalem church elsewhere in the letter (so Martyn, *Galatians*, 551–52). Also, while there are obvious parallels between the sowing and reaping metaphor found in Gal 6:7–9 and 2 Cor 9:6, this metaphor is employed elsewhere in Paul's letters without reference to the collection for Jerusalem (cf. 1 Cor 9:7, 11; 15:36–44; Rom 1:13). See also Michael Winger, "Act One: Paul Arrives in Galatia," *NTS* 48 (2002): 552–53.

[14] Georgi, *Remembering the Poor*, 43–48; Taylor, *Paul, Antioch and Jerusalem*, 145–81.

[15] So also A. J. M. Wedderburn, *The Reasons for Romans* (Studies of the New Testament and Its World; Edinburgh: T & T Clark, 1988), 38–41.

[16] Martyn, *Galatians*, 225. Georgi writes: "that particular wording refers to Paul's eagerness to help fulfill the second point of the agreement of Jerusalem as a past effort, long behind him, when he wrote the epistle to the Galatians (from Ephesus or some place nearby)" (*Remembering the Poor*, 45).

[17] Wedderburn, "Paul's Collection," 99. This point highlights a crucial weakness in Stephan

explain Paul's trepidation about the possibility of Jerusalem's rejection of his efforts in Rom 15:30–31 if, in fact, he is doing nothing more than fulfilling an accord previously established with the Jerusalem leadership.

Fourth, separating the stipulation in Gal 2:10 from the collection later organized among Paul's churches helps to make sense of the problematic aorist verb ἐσπούδασα used by Paul to summarize his response to the leaders of the Jerusalem church. This verse has often been viewed as a *crux interpretum*, not only because the first-person singular awkwardly follows the first-person plural subjunctive μνημονεύωμεν, but also because the Jerusalem church's request for a continual remembrance is followed by an indication that Paul has already fulfilled this petition: "They asked only one thing, that we continue to remember the poor, which was the very thing I was eager to do" (Gal 2:10). Knox accurately and succinctly distinguishes three ways in which this response can be understood: (1) as an indication of "a regular, more or less constant effort on Paul's part to raise and send money to Jerusalem, which he is now asked to continue and which he expresses himself as eager to do"; (2) "as a reference to some special collection for Jerusalem that antedates the offering being raised in the period of the Corinthian letters"; and (3) as an allusion to the Pauline collection mentioned in 1–2 Corinthians and Romans.[18] Knox and many commentators settle for the third of these options.[19] However, in light of the considerations identified above, it is much more probable that Paul intends with the aorist ἐσπούδασα to refer to a collection already completed, either at the time of the Jerusalem conference or shortly thereafter (but before the writing of Galatians).[20] This also explains the present subjunctive verb μνημονεύωμεν, which should be rendered "that we continue to remember," denoting a regular, ongoing activity of the Antioch community that may have started already on the occasion of this visit to Jerusalem.[21] This reading of Gal 2:10, therefore, suggests that Paul was involved

---

Joubert's argument that the collection among the Gentiles originated in the context of reciprocal benefit exchange between Paul and the Jerusalem leadership (see *Paul as Benefactor*, esp. 73–115).

[18] Knox, *Chapters in a Life*, 37–38. All three options refer to the actual organization of relief funds. Paul could, of course, simply be indicating that he already possessed the *intent* to help the poor in Jerusalem before the pillar apostles asked him and Barnabas to do so. Yet had Paul only intended to fulfill this request and not actually carried it out, doubtless his opponents in Galatia would have seized on the apostle's capriciousness.

[19] See Kim, *Die paulinische Kollekte*, 148; Furnish, *II Corinthians*, 410.

[20] D. R. Hall ("St. Paul and Famine Relief: A Study in Galatians 2:10," *ExpTim* 82 [1971]: 310) points out that the aorist form of σπουδάζω in Gal 2:10 may have the sense of an English pluperfect: "I had made an effort to do this very thing prior to my visit." See also Richard N. Longenecker, *Galatians* (WBC 41; Word: Dallas, 1990), 60–61; F. F. Bruce, *The Epistle to the Galatians: A Commentary on the Greek Text* (NIGTC; Grand Rapids: Eerdmans, 1982), 126; C. F. D. Moule, *An Idiom Book of New Testament Greek* (2d ed.; Cambridge: Cambridge University Press, 1959), 16.

[21] So Martyn, *Galatians*, 206–7; Longenecker, *Galatians*, 60. As Martyn points out, "Two misreadings are to be avoided: (1) Luedemann has seen in the present subjunctive verb *mnêmoneuômen*

in the organization of a minimum of two relief funds to Jerusalem: at least one from Antioch and one from the communities of his own mission many years later. On the basis of statements in Paul's letters alone, then, it is possible to conclude that the apostle played an active role in the organization and delivery of more than one relief fund to the poor among the saints in Jerusalem. It is at this point that evidence from Acts may enter the discussion, for in that narrative there is a brief vignette detailing Paul's involvement with a monetary contribution from Antioch to Jerusalem (Acts 11:27–30).

2.3.2 Acts 11:27–30 and Assistance from Antioch

According to the story in Acts 11:27–30, the Christians in Antioch learned from the Spirit-inspired prediction of Agabus, who had come to their city with other prophets from Jerusalem, that there would be "a severe famine over all the world" (ἐφ' ὅλην τὴν οἰκουμένην, 11:28). The author of Acts locates this food shortage temporally during the reign of Tiberius Claudius (41–54 C.E.). In response, the disciples in Antioch decided, "each according to one's ability, to send aid (διακονία) to the brothers and sisters who live in Judea" (11:29). After reporting that this relief is sent to the elders (presumably of the Jerusalem church) by Barnabas and Saul, the vignette ends without further comment.[22] In Acts, this

---

– and even in the aorist verb *espoudasa poiēsai*! – evidence that 'the collection is still fully in progress' as Paul writes to the Galatians (*Chronology*, 80). In fact, the tense of *mnēmoneuōmen* gives no indication as to the state of affairs with the collection at the time at which Paul is writing the latter … (b) The motif of regularity has been taken to point to an annual subvention analogous to the Jewish temple tax" (*Galatians*, 206).

[22] The matter is actually slightly more complicated since, as is well known, the earliest and best manuscripts of Acts 12:25 include the phrase εἰς Ἰερουσαλὴμ after the statement "Paul and Barnabas returned" (ℵ, B, 81). Apparently uncomfortable with this difficult reading, which is hard to reconcile with the implication of the narrative that Paul and Barnabas have never left Jerusalem, some witnesses substitute the prepositional phrase εἰς Ἀντιοχειαν (E, 104, 323, 945, 1175, 1739) or change the preposition from εἰς to ἐξ (P74, A, 33, 945, 1739) or ἀπό (D, E, Ψ, 36, 323, 453). See J. Dupont, "La misson de Paul 'à Jérusalem' (Actes xii, 25)," *NovT* 1 (1956): 275–303; Bruce M. Metzger, *A Textual Commentary on the Greek New Testament* (2d ed.; New York: United Bible Societies, 1994), 350–52. If the more difficult and better attested reading is accepted, it may be possible to take εἰς Ἰερουσαλὴμ with the following participle πληρώσαντες: "they returned, having completed their ministry to Jerusalem" (so Joseph Fitzmyer, *The Acts of the Apostles: A New Translation with Introduction and Commentary* [AB 31; New York: Doubleday, 1998], 493). Buck suggests, rather implausibly, that this verse "must mean that Paul and Barnabas, having delivered the relief from Antioch, left Jerusalem to complete the collection and returned to Jerusalem with the proceeds of this further effort" (Charles H. Buck, "The Collection for the Saints," *HTR* 43 (1950): 16). This assertion becomes the basis for Buck's unlikely claim that the collection described in Paul's letters followed very shortly after the first delivery of the relief fund in Acts 11:27–30, which leads Buck to a "drastic revision of the accepted chronology of Paul's life and writing" in which 1 Corinthians, Galatians, Romans, 2 Corinthians 1–9, and 2 Corinthians 10–13 are all dated before 48 C.E. (16). On the transitional function of this pericope in the

trip represents the second of five (post-conversion) visits of Paul to Jerusalem (the others being 9:26–27; 15:1–29; 18:22; and 21:15–23:30).

This episode is difficult to harmonize with what is known about events in ancient history broadly and with the chronology of the Pauline mission more narrowly. Regional famines are attested throughout the period of Claudius's rule, particularly in the eastern part of the empire (Pliny, *Nat.* 5.58; 18.1168; Suetonius, *Claud.* 18–19; IG 2712). Josephus chronicles a severe famine in Judea circa 46–48 C.E., during which Helena, Queen of Adiabene, while on a trip to Jerusalem to worship God in the temple, observed many people dying for want of food and "sent some of her attendants to Alexandria to buy grain for large sums and others to Cyprus to bring back a cargo of dried figs."[23] Yet there is no extant evidence of a "worldwide" famine during this period, which may indicate that Luke's language at this point is characteristically hyperbolic.[24]

In spite of some differences between Acts 11:27–30 and Gal 2:1–10, there are reasons to believe that both accounts refer to the same visit to Jerusalem.[25] First, and most obviously, both Barnabas and Paul (or Σαῦλος, as he is designated in Acts 11:30) function as representatives of Antioch in Acts 11:27–30 and Gal 2:1–10. Second, if the present tense of the request ἵνα μνημονεύωμεν in Gal 2:10 is stressed ("that we continue to remember the poor"), this may indicate that Paul and his associates delivered assistance to Jerusalem on the occasion of the visit reported in Gal 2:1–10. Third, Paul insists, rather emphatically, in Gal 1–2 that the occasion of his meeting with the apostles described in Gal 2:1–10 was his second – and only his second – visit to Jerusalem (post-conversion), occurring fourteen years after his first journey there. Given Paul's forceful avowal of his truthfulness in Gal 1:20 ("And the things that I am writing to you – behold, as God is my witness, I am not lying!"), his autobiographical outline should be considered accurate, or else his opponents would have seized upon his deceit for their own advantage.[26] However we evaluate the five post-conversion

---

overall structure of the narrative of Acts, see Bruce W. Longenecker, "Lukan Aversion to Humps and Hollows: The Case of Acts 11.27–12.25," *NTS* 50 (2004): 185–204.

[23] Josephus, *Ant.* 20.51–53 (Feldman, LCL); cf. *Ant.* 3.320–22.

[24] See also Acts 19:27 (cf. Luke 2:1), where the phrase ὅλη ἡ Ἀσία καὶ ἡ οἰκουμένη is used in a similarly exaggerated fashion. For a helpful summary of the evidence of famines during the reign of Claudius, see Bruce W. Winter, "Acts and Food Shortages," in *The Book of Acts in Its Graeco-Roman Setting* (ed. David W. J. Gill and Conrad Gempf; vol. 2 of *The Book of Acts in Its First Century Setting*, ed. Bruce W. Winter; Grand Rapids: Eerdmans, 1993), 59–78.

[25] For a detailed defense of this position, see Longenecker, *Galatians*, lxxx–lxxxiii. This view is also related to arguments for rejecting the identification of Gal 2:1–10 with Acts 15:1–30 (see Longenecker, *Galatians*, lxxvii–lxxx; Nickle, *The Collection*, 51–59; Moisés Silva, *Interpreting Galatians: Explorations in Exegetical Method* [2d ed.; Grand Rapids: Baker Academic, 2001], 129–39). I agree that Gal 2:1–10 cannot be squared with Acts 15:1–30 but will not enter into that debate in the present chapter.

[26] On this point, I tend to place more confidence in Paul's account as a source of accurate autobiographical data than does Jack T. Sanders, "Paul's 'Autobiographical' Statements in Gala-

visits of Paul to Jerusalem recounted in the narrative of Acts, the journey reported in 11:27–30 is the second visit, a fact that has led many scholars to conclude that this is the same visit as that recorded in Gal 2:1–10.[27] Fourth, the lack of reference to the apostolic decree in Galatians would mean that that decision (if it was rendered as Luke describes it) took place sometime after the conference visit reported in Gal 2:1–10. This argument has in its favor the likelihood that the events of Gal 2:11–14 took place after the events in Gal 2:1–10. If the apostolic decree had been issued at the time of this controversy in Antioch, it is hard to explain why Paul would not have referred to it in his argument with Peter. Finally, although this point must remain somewhat speculative, it is at least possible that with the statement "I went up [to Jerusalem] *because of a revelation* (κατὰ ἀποκάλυψιν)" Paul is referring to the prophecy of Agabus recorded in Acts 11:28. Clearly Paul's rhetoric in Gal 1:11–12 demands the view that he received the gospel through an ἀποκάλυψις of Jesus Christ, and not, as Paul says, "from a human" (Gal 1:11). The use of the word ἀποκάλυψις in Gal 2:2, however, does not eliminate the possibility that Paul's "revelation" concerning the necessity of a visit to Jerusalem was mediated to him through a human agent (cf. 1 Cor 14:6, 26), though he does not directly attribute this revelation to the prophecy of Agabus. Of course, given the circumstances in which the letter to the Galatians was written, such an omission would be entirely understandable.[28]

2.3.3 Conclusion

Acts 11:27–30, therefore, appears to provide an independent witness that connects Paul and Barnabas, as representatives of the congregation in Antioch, with the delivery of material assistance (διακονία) to the believing community in Jerusalem. That the narrative in Acts 11:27–30 corresponds broadly, though not in every detail, to the account in Gal 2:1–10 should be taken as evidence collaborating the theory that Paul was involved in the organization and delivery of a relief fund to "the poor" in Jerusalem during his association with the church in Antioch. After his split with Antioch, however, Paul later organized a monetary collection among the churches of his own mission. This is the project to which reference is made in 1 Cor 16:1–4; 2 Cor 8:1–9:15; and Rom 15:14–32.

---

tians 1–2," *JBL* 85 (1966): 335–43. While it is certainly true that Paul's aim in Gal 1–2 is not merely to provide a chronicle of his activity (see Beverly R. Gaventa, "Galatians 1 and 2: Autobiography as Paradigm," *NovT* 28 [1986]: 309–26), I believe that the basic credibility of Paul's description of his activity can be assumed because, were it false, his opponents in Galatia would have exploited the apostle's pretense.

[27] Longenecker, *Galatians*, lxxx–lxxxiii; Bruce, *Galatians*, 126; Joe Morgado, "Paul in Jerusalem: A Comparison of His Visits in Acts and Galatians," *JETS* 37 (1994): 55–68; cf. the discussion in Jewett, *Chronology*, 69–75.

[28] On the potential link between Gal 2:2 and Acts 11:27–30, see Longenecker, *Galatians*, 47. Bruce (*Galatians*, 108) disputes this connection.

2.4 The Organization of the New Pauline Collection

2.4.1 The Collection in Galatia

Probably sometime after the completion of the letter to the Galatians, but before writing 1 Corinthians, Paul conceived the idea of gathering a collection for the saints in Jerusalem from the largely Gentile churches of his mission. The origins of and the reasons for this new project are now almost entirely obscured – lost along with the letters in which Paul must surely have addressed these important issues – and it is wise to exercise caution in speculating on these matters. It is possible, however, to sketch at least a very bare outline of the beginning of this fresh effort on behalf of the Jerusalem church's poor. We start with the story of the Galatians' participation in the project, though the earliest evidence for their involvement comes from Paul's correspondence with the Corinthians.

Initially, Paul would have communicated his plan for a collection, perhaps in the form of a letter, to the church in Corinth. Although this communication – whether written or oral – is no longer extant, it may have been contained in the lost missive mentioned in 1 Cor 5:9.[29] We can only surmise that Paul broached the idea of the collection with the Corinthians in this earlier correspondence because of the fact that, in turn, the Corinthians appear to have asked Paul about the project in their written response to him, a communiqué alluded to in 1 Cor 7:1. Five times in 1 Corinthians Paul uses the formulaic construction περὶ δέ ostensibly to respond to specific questions asked of him by the Corinthian congregation in this letter (7:1, 25; 8:1; 12:1; 16:1, 12; cf. 8:4).[30] In 1 Cor 16:1, Paul

---

[29] On the issue of whether this exchange was written or oral, see Lüdemann, *Paul, Apostle to the Gentiles*, 81–83. Lüdemann lists the following possibilities for the means by which the collection plan was introduced to the Corinthians: (1) "the Corinthians received news from the Galatians that a collection was being taken up in the Pauline congregations in Galatia"; (2) Paul initiated the collection during a stay in Corinth; (3) "Paul had Timothy, Titus, or other assistants convey instructions for the collection to Corinth"; and (4) "Paul wrote about the collection that should be begun also in Corinth in the 'previous letter' (1 Cor 5:9)" (82). Lüdemann wisely rules out the first option, preferring instead option four. Given the likelihood that the Corinthians asked Paul about the collection in their previous letter to him, combined with the duration of time between Paul's founding visit and the writing of 1 Corinthians, Lüdemann's conclusion is entirely reasonable: it is most likely the Paul presented the idea of the collection to the Corinthians in the letter mentioned in 1 Cor 5:9.

[30] In an article in which she presents a thorough comparison of the περὶ δέ construction in 1 Corinthians and Hellenistic literature, Margaret M. Mitchell cautions against assuming that περὶ δέ in every instance in 1 Corinthians refers to a topic contained in the Corinthians' letter mentioned in 7:1; see her, "Concerning ΠΕΡΙ ΔΕ in 1 Corinthians," *NovT* 31 (1989): 229–56. Mitchell concedes, however, "What we can say definitely is that each of the topics Paul introduces with the formula περὶ δέ (virgins, idol meat, spiritual people/things, the collection and Apollos) is readily known to both the Corinthians and Paul *from some element of their shared experience*" (256; emphasis original). While recognizing the important methodological contribution of Mitchell's essay, I would still maintain that the use of the phrase περὶ δέ in 1 Cor 16:1 implies

writes, "Now concerning the collection for the saints: just as I directed the churches in Galatia, you yourselves should also do likewise" (Περὶ δὲ τῆς λογείας τῆς εἰς τοὺς ἁγίους ὥσπερ διέταξα ταῖς ἐκκλησίαις τῆς Γαλατίας, οὕτως καὶ ὑμεῖς ποιήσατε). This statement implies (1) that before Paul wrote 1 Corinthians the Corinthian church was aware of the collection project and possessed enough knowledge of it to inquire of Paul about specific procedures for gathering the fund, and (2) that Paul had, in some form, already communicated these same fundraising procedures – and thus the plan for the collection – to the Galatians.

It is unfortunately impossible to determine with more specificity when, exactly, Paul broached the subject of the collection, along with the method for its procurement, with the Galatians. Did he do so before writing Galatians in some exchange that was not preserved, and then refrain from mentioning this earlier project in the heat of his polemical epistle to the churches in Galatia? Did he do so when he learned that the canonical letter to the Galatians had led to at least a partial victory over those who opposed his teaching in those congregations?[31] Or, did he do so, as Martyn speculates, "soon after sending the angry letter, perhaps thinking that the idea of a collection for Jerusalem could itself increase the likelihood of his letter's being heard as he wished it to be heard?"[32] It is theoretically possible that Paul could have sent a letter to the Galatians concerning his plan for the collection only a day or two after he had written his forceful epistle, in hopes that it would assuage tensions over his rather negative characterization of Jerusalem in that letter, but certainty in this matter is prevented by our lack of evidence.[33] Paul's statements in 1 Cor 16:1–2 indicate nothing about the response of the Galatians to his instructions, although the very fact that Paul is confident enough to "direct" (διατάσσω) the Galatians in this matter may indicate his belief (or hope?) that his earlier letter met with some degree of success.[34]

---

that Paul is responding to a specific question asked by the Corinthians, since in this context he provides specific instructions concerning the method of fundraising. The phrase ὥσπερ διέταξα ταῖς ἐκκλησίαις τῆς Γαλατίας, οὕτως καὶ ὑμεῖς ποιήσατε in 1 Cor 16:1 is a natural response to a question such as Τί οὖν ποιήσωμεν περὶ τῆς λογείας.

[31] So Georgi, *Remembering the Poor*, 49.

[32] Martyn, *Galatians*, 226 n. 79.

[33] On the characterization of Jerusalem in Galatians, see J. Louis Martyn, "A Tale of Two Churches," in *Theological Issues in the Letters of Paul* (Nashville: Abingdon, 1997), 25–36. Admittedly, it remains a curiosity why the canonical letter to the Galatians was preserved but the epistle in which Paul asked the Galatians to begin collecting money for Jerusalem was not.

[34] On the use of διατάσσω as a command, see 1 Cor 7:17; 9:14; 11:34. See also David Horrell, "'The Lord Commanded ... But I Have Not Used': Exegetical and Hermeneutical Reflections on 1 Cor 9:14–15," *NTS* 43 (1997): 587–603. Joubert (*Paul as Benefactor*, 157) assumes that the mere fact of Paul's command was enough to ensure the completion of the project among the churches in Galatia. The problems that Paul encountered in Corinth alone, however – to say nothing of the lack of evidence indicating that the Galatians ultimately contributed to the

Whether Paul's confidence in the Galatians' commitment to the collection was finally well-founded is impossible to say with any certainty, but Paul's comments about the collection in his later epistles make it probable that the Galatians ultimately failed to support the Pauline collection for Jerusalem. Nowhere in his discussions of the collection after 1 Cor 16:1–4 does Paul mention the fundraising activity of the Galatians, and this absence alone is more than a little revealing. While arguments from silence are always problematic, it is highly suggestive that, in his attempt to persuade the Corinthians to renew their commitment to the project (see below), Paul praises the commendable behavior of the churches of *Macedonia* in 2 Cor 8:1–6. That the apostle does not mention the enthusiasm or compliance of the Galatians could be brushed aside as mere coincidence, if the Corinthians were not already familiar with Paul's effort to raise a contribution in Galatia. If the Galatians had demonstrated the same "wealth of generosity" (2 Cor 8:2) as the Macedonians, why would Paul not cite their exemplary behavior, since they had already served in 1 Cor 16:1–4 as something of a model for the Corinthians to imitate? Also, if the Galatians had already assembled the collection and sent it on to Jerusalem, as Becker and Joubert suggest, then Paul could easily have cited the enthusiasm of the Galatians as a spur to motivate renewed vigor for the project among the Corinthians.[35] Moreover, in his final comments about the collection for the saints in Rom 15:25–32, Paul declares to his readers in Rome that "*Macedonia* and *Achaia* were pleased to make a certain partnership-forming contribution" (Rom 15:26). Again, Paul's failure to mention the Galatians in Rom 15 would be surprising if they had, in fact, actively contributed to the fund. On the other hand, if the Galatians had dropped out of the project altogether sometime after the writing of 1 Corinthians and disassociated themselves from the Pauline mission, not an unlikely possibility considering the conflict that occasioned Paul's polemical letter to them, such an omission is entirely comprehensible. It seems most likely, then, that the Galatians did not participate in the offering of the Gentiles.

2.4.2 The Collection in Corinth and Achaia

As we have seen, the beginning of Paul's attempt to organize a collection for Jerusalem in the region of Galatia occurred at roughly the same period of time as his efforts to introduce the collection to the province of Achaia and, in particular, to the believing community founded by Paul and his associates in its capital city, Corinth. The story of the Corinthian involvement in the relief fund can be sketched more fully than the sparse and inconclusive narrative that can be pieced together for the Galatians. The extra information available for Paul's fundraising

---

fund (see below) – are enough to question the assumption that Paul's instructions would have been obeyed without hesitation in Galatia.

[35] Becker, *Paul*, 24–25; Joubert, *Paul as Benefactor*, 157. For this point, see also Wedderburn, "Paul's Collection," 103.

2.4 The Organization of the New Pauline Collection

efforts in the province of Achaia is due, of course, to the lengthy and valuable correspondence between Paul and the Corinthians preserved in the pages of the New Testament. The history of this exchange is muddled, however, by the fact that the canonical book of 2 Corinthians preserves at least two and possibly as many as four different letters from Paul to Corinth (1:1–6:13, 7:2–8:24; 9:1–15; 10:1–13:14; 6:14–7:1). The canonical letter of 2 Corinthians also contains an allusion to another important epistle sent from Paul to Corinth that we no longer possess (2 Cor 2:4).[36] Drawing on evidence from the Pauline epistles alone, the major events in this unfolding drama can be outlined briefly as follows.

A New Collection in Corinth

Paul, Silvanus, and Timothy founded a church in the Roman colony of Corinth (2 Cor 1:19; cf. 1 Cor 2:1–5). Sometime after departing this city for further missionary work, Paul transmitted a letter (Letter A) to the believers in Corinth. This letter has not been preserved, but we know of its existence because Paul himself mentions in 1 Cor 5:9 instructions he had written to the Corinthians regarding the avoidance of associating with immoral individuals: "I wrote to you in my letter not to keep company with sexually immoral persons" ("Ἔγραψα ὑμῖν ἐν τῇ ἐπιστολῇ μὴ συναναμίγνυσθαι πόρνοις). It is possible that Paul broached the subject of the collection for Jerusalem with the Corinthians at this point in their communication with one another, because in the next known event in this exchange – a letter sent from Corinth to Paul (1 Cor 7:1) – the congregation in Corinth is not only aware of but also curious about how to organize the relief fund (cf. 1 Cor 16:1). While we cannot eliminate the possibility that Paul introduced the idea of a collection for Jerusalem earlier in his history with the Corinthians, perhaps as early as his founding visit, the fact that Paul in 1 Cor 16:1–4 appears to respond to specific questions among the Corinthians raised by Letter A suggests that the notion of a collection was introduced via this epistle.

Questions about Organization

In response to Letter A, Paul in turn received both an epistle (1 Cor 7:1) and a delegation from the Corinthian church (1 Cor 1:11; 16:7–8); some of the substance of the written communication can be reconstructed from Paul's allusions to this missive in his responses in 1 Corinthians to specific questions posed by the Corinthians (7:1, 25; 8:1; 12:1; 16:1, 12; cf. 8:4). Paul's reply to this situation is represented in 1 Corinthians (Letter B), a document that is considered by the majority of scholars to be a literary unity in its canonical form.[37] One of the is-

---

[36] Attempts to identify the "letter of tears" mentioned in 2 Cor 2:1–4 with 2 Cor 10–13 are unconvincing; see Thrall, *2 Corinthians*, 13–20. This section benefits from the work of the many scholars who have already addressed the complicated history of the Corinthian correspondence. See the extensive discussion in Thrall, *2 Corinthians*, 13–20.

[37] For overview of the major partition theories and a defense of the unity of the epistle, see

sues addressed in Letter B, of course, is the collection for the saints (1 Cor 16:1–4). At this point in the project's history in Corinth, Paul appears confidently to assume that sufficient progress in the raising of funds will permit the gift to be ready for delivery to Jerusalem, by those with letters of recommendation and possibly by Paul himself, at the time of Paul's next visit to Corinth (1 Cor 16:3–4), a journey scheduled in the not too distant future.[38] According to the travel plans articulated in 1 Cor 16:5–9, Paul asserts that he intends to visit Corinth after passing through Macedonia, perhaps even staying with the Corinthians through the winter before journeying to Jerusalem. In the meantime, however, he will remain in Ephesus, the city from which 1 Corinthians was written, until Pentecost (ἕως τῆς πεντηκοστῆς; 1 Cor 16:8).

Change of Travel Plans and Conflict

Although in 1 Cor 16:5–7 Paul avows that he intends to visit Corinth after passing through Macedonia, a change in plans ensued before the writing of 2 Cor 1–9: Paul reports in 2 Cor 1:15 that he desired instead to visit Corinth on his way to Macedonia. We have from Paul only the cryptic statement in 2 Cor 1:15–16 to explain this alteration in his itinerary: "I wanted to come first to you (i.e., the Corinthians) in order that you might have a double benefit (ἵνα δευτέραν χάριν σχῆτε), desiring to pass through you on to Macedonia, and again from Macedonia to come to you, and to be sent on by you to Judea." It appears that Paul met with harsh criticism in Corinth because of his vacillating schedule, for he clearly feels the need in 2 Cor 1:17–22 to provide a theological defense of his course of action.

There is good reason to believe that Paul's desire for the Corinthians to have a "double benefit" was in some way related to the issue of money. While the phrase δευτέραν χάριν is frequently interpreted as some form of (spiritual) blessing actively bestowed by Paul upon the Corinthians – such as the blessing of his presence – Gordon Fee has shown that χάρις in this context is instead "active from the perspective of the Corinthians," representing something that

---

Anthony C. Thiselton, *The First Epistle to the Corinthians: A Commentary on the Greek Text* (NIGTC; Grand Rapids: Eerdmans, 2000), 36–41; see also Raymond F. Collins, *First Corinthians* (SP 7; Collegeville, Minn.: Liturgical, 1999), 10–14; Margaret M. Mitchell, *Paul and the Rhetoric of Reconciliation: An Exegetical Investigation of the Language and Composition of 1 Corinthians* (Louisville: Westminster John Knox, 1991). The discovery of P[46] was a boon to proponents of the unity of the epistle. An intriguing but complex mediating position is developed by Martinus C. de Boer, "The Composition of 1 Corinthians," *NTS* 40 (1994): 229–45.

[38] Verbrugge's claim that 1 Cor 16:1–2 represents the genre of a "commanding letter" is mistaken for a number of reasons: he is unable to prove that such a clearly defined genre existed in Greco-Roman literature; his thesis does not account for the place of 1 Cor 16:1–2 in a much larger document; and he fails to explain the relationship between vv. 1–2 and vv. 3–4. Verlyn D. Verbrugge, *Paul's Style of Church Leadership Illustrated by His Instructions to the Corinthians on the Collection* (San Francisco: Mellen Research University Press, 1992), 25–69.

the Corinthians themselves will demonstrate twice as they render material benefits to Paul through their financial support of his mission.[39] Later in the same letter χάρις has a material meaning where it clearly denotes the collection itself (2 Cor 8:4, 6, 7; 19; cf. 1 Cor 16:3). In 2 Cor 1:15, then, Paul speaks of his desire that the Corinthians enjoy two opportunities for displaying χάρις toward him, namely, in terms of an additional occasion to subsidize his travels.[40] Paul's refusal to accept financial assistance from the Corinthians during his period of residency in Corinth had already been a contentious issue between the church and its apostle (cf. 1 Cor 9:3–18). This dispute seems to have arisen from Paul's unwillingness, reflected in a rather consistent fiscal policy, to request or receive money from a church in a city in which he was actively working to establish a mission.[41] Having completed his residency in Corinth, however, Paul was able, in good conscience, to accept, and even to call for, financial support from the Corinthians, an opportunity that he had denied them in the past.

Upon arriving in Corinth from Ephesus, Paul experienced some distressing crisis within the community.[42] This conflict was significant enough for Paul to label this visit "painful" and to withdraw from the situation to Asia (2 Cor 2:1–4, 12). It is at this point that Paul, instead of confronting the Corinthians again in

---

[39] Gordon Fee, "ΧΑΡΙΣ in II Corinthians I.15: Apostolic Parousia and Paul-Corinth Chronology," *NTS* 24 (1977): 533–38.

[40] James R. Harrison (*Paul's Language of Grace in Its Graeco-Roman Context* [WUNT 2:172; Tübingen: Mohr Siebeck, 2003], 294) clearly misunderstands Fee when he states, "If, as G. Fee argues, χάρις in 2 Cor 1:15 also refers to the 'kindness' of the Jerusalem collection, there exist (at most) five Pauline references to grace as a description of human beneficence (1 Cor 16:3; 2 Cor 1:15; 8:6, 7, 19)." In a footnote Harrison affirms, "the twofold mention of Macedonia (2 Cor 1:16a, 16b; cf. 8:1; 9:2, 4) probably seals the case for the referent being the Jerusalem collection" (294 n. 17). Fee does not, however, claim that χάρις in 2 Cor 1:15 refers to the Jerusalem collection. Instead, he views the "benefit" (χάρις) of the Corinthians in terms of their "service toward others (in this case Paul and his companion)" (ΧΑΡΙΣ, 536). Indeed, later Fee explicitly declares, "The first part of this double visit was surely not to pick up the collection, but perhaps to pick up some of the brothers to accompany him (cf. I Cor. xvi. 3–4). In any case, it was an added opportunity for the church to do something they had not yet had a hand in – ministering to *Paul's needs*" (538, emphasis added).

[41] On these issues in Corinth, see Peter Marshall, *Enmity in Corinth: Social Conventions in Paul's Relations with the Corinthians* (WUNT 23; Tübingen: J. C. B. Mohr, 1987); and John K. Chow, *Patronage and Power: A Study of Social Networks in Corinth* (JSNTSup 75; Sheffield: Sheffield Academic Press, 1992). See also Stephen E. Fowl, "Know Your Context: Giving and Receiving Money in Philippians," *Int* 56 (2002): 45–58.

[42] This assumes that Paul's second visit to Corinth (cf. 2 Cor 12:14; 13:1–2; in these passages, Paul speaks of plans to visit Corinth a third time) occurred during the interval between the sending of 1 Corinthians and the writing of 2 Corinthians 1–8. For a discussion of this issue and a defense of this position, see Thrall, *2 Corinthians*, 49–56; Murray J. Harris, *The Second Epistle to the Corinthians* (NIGTC; Grand Rapids: Eerdmans: 2005), 194–95. With C. K. Barrett (*The Second Epistle to the Corinthians* [HNTC; New York: Harper & Row, 1973], 7), I see the second visit – that is, the implementation of the first part of the travel plan in 2 Cor 1:15–16 – as the cause of, rather than a response to, the conflict in Corinth.

person, penned his so-called "letter of tears" (Letter C), an epistle in which he addressed the conflict he experienced during his second visit to Corinth (2 Cor 2:3–4; 7:8–12). Because this "letter of tears" has not survived, it is, again, difficult to say what precipitated this dispute in Corinth; the reasons for the controversy can only be pieced together from Paul's statements in 2 Cor 2:1–11 and 7:5–16. Traditionally, "the offender" (ὁ ἀδικηθείς) of 2 Cor 2:5–11 and 7:12 has been regarded as the sexually immoral man identified in 1 Cor 5:1–5.[43] But Paul himself seems to have been the victim of the offender's behavior, or else his disclaimers in 2 Cor 2:5, 10 make little sense, and this is hardly likely to have been the case if the offender identified in 2 Cor 2:5–11 is the same incestuous man of 1 Corinthians. While there are undoubtedly some linguistic and thematic similarities between these three passages,[44] differences in Paul's attitudes towards the offenders in 1 and 2 Corinthians (cf. the severity of the penalties proposed in each situation), among other factors, suggest that, in fact, 2 Cor 2:5–11 and 1 Cor 5:1–5 deal with two distinct conflicts.

Margaret Thrall has advanced the following explanation of the cause of the conflict during Paul's second visit to Corinth, which, if convincing, bears on our understanding of the history of Paul's collection efforts in Corinth:

> After Paul arrived in Corinth on his second visit, one of the church members handed over to him for temporary safekeeping the money he had saved to contribute to the collection. This money was then stolen, in circumstances which suggested that some other member of the congregation was responsible. But this man denied the charge. It was Paul's word against his, and the church was uncertain whom to believe. Because the apostle's view of the matter was not immediately accepted, he began to suspect that other members of the congregation, perhaps a fair number of them, might have had something to do with the theft. Since he was unable to persuade them to take action against the man he suspected, he returned to Ephesus. He then wrote a letter which caused a revulsion of feeling amongst the Corinthians and moved them to further investigation, which resulted in the offender's confession and punishment.[45]

Thrall's hypothesis is both creative and attractive, but the following scenario is equally plausible, and perhaps provides a simpler sequence of events:[46] Having

---

[43] For a careful discussion of the similarities and differences between these passages, see Furnish, *II Corinthians*, 164–68. Furnish concludes that the cause of the offense in 2 Cor 2:5–11 was slander against Paul, and not the behavior of the immoral man of 1 Cor 5:1–5. Problematic also, as Furnish shows, are attempts to identify the "letter of tears" with 2 Cor 10–13.

[44] Cf. ὁ τοιοῦτος in 2 Cor 2:6 and 1 Cor 5:5; and the reference to Σατανᾶς in 1 Cor 5:5 and 2 Cor 2:11.

[45] Thrall, *2 Corinthians*, 68. See also Margaret Thrall's earlier essay, "The Offender and the Offence: A Problem of Detection in 2 Corinthians," in *Scripture: Meaning and Method; Essays Presented to Anthony Tyrrell Hanson for His Seventieth Birthday* (ed. Barry P. Thompson; Hull: Hull University Press, 1987), 65–77.

[46] Thrall's overly complex solution also raises several questions: Why would a member of the Corinthian church entrust the funds he had saved for the collection to Paul when the apostle

altered his travel plans (for reasons unknown), Paul arrived in Corinth expecting, and perhaps even asking for, monetary assistance for his upcoming journey to Macedonia; this is the first part of the itinerary detailed in 2 Cor 1:15–16. Combined with his earlier refusal to accept financial support from the Corinthians, this expectation caused a serious misunderstanding, and one member of the congregation in particular insulted Paul and accused him of corruption. Puzzled by Paul's apparent change in policy, the majority of the congregation refused to come to the apostle's defense. From their perspective, Paul's inconsistent fiscal policy would have been the source of no small amount of frustration: formerly Paul had protested vigorously against receiving funds from the congregation; now, after a surprise visit, he expected the Corinthians to subsidize his travels, first to Macedonia and then to Jerusalem. Perhaps some in the congregation, led by ὁ ἀδικήσας, felt that Paul was even demanding personal support from the funds that they had collected and saved specifically for the poor in Jerusalem. Following a painful confrontation in which his integrity was slandered by one member of the community, and unable to find support among the other members of the church, Paul retreated from Corinth to Troas. After his departure, Paul decided against the option of returning to Corinth, figuring that another visit would be too painful ("I made up my mind not to come again to you in sorrow," 2 Cor 2:1) and instead wrote to the Corinthians "out of much distress and anguish of heart and with many tears" (2 Cor 2:4).

2 Corinthians 1–9

After departing from Asia, Paul arrived in Macedonia, where he learned of successful efforts to raise a collection in that region (2 Cor 2:13; 7:5; 8:1–6). In Macedonia, he also obtained from Titus, whom he had missed during his stay in Troas (2 Cor 2:13), a report that his severe letter (Letter C) had grieved the Corinthians and led to their repentance (2 Cor 7:6–12). In response, Paul composed 2 Cor 1–9 (Letter D). In the address of 2 Cor 1:1, Paul refers to the existence of believers in Achaia outside the city limits of Corinth by distinguishing between ἡ ἐκκλησία τοῦ θεοῦ τῇ οὔσῃ ἐν Κορίνθῳ and οἱ ἅγιοι πᾶσιν τοῖς οὖσιν ἐν ὅλῃ τῇ Ἀχαΐᾳ. Although 1 Thess 3:1 indicates that Paul spent time in Athens, technically a city in Achaia, the apostle's assertion in 1 Cor 16:15 that the members of the household of Stephanas in Corinth were the first believers he had

---

was only planning to stop over in Corinth on his way to Macedonia? Was it really safer to deliver the money to Paul than to keep it at home in a safe-box (*arca*)? That said, it is hardly likely that Paul would have encouraged the Corinthians to deposit the funds in a pagan temple, despite the fact that temples were used (much as modern banks) to provide security for cash. See Thomas Wiedemann, "The Patron as Banker," in *'Bread and Circuses': Euergetism and Municipal Patronage in Roman Italy* (ed. Kathryn Lomas and Tim Cornell; London and New York: Routledge, 2003), 12–27. On Plutarch's identification of Corinth as a major financial center in his day in *Moralia* 831, see Jean Andreau, *Banking and Business in the Roman World* (trans. Janet Lloyd; Cambridge: Cambridge University Press, 1999), 58.

baptized in Achaia implies that Paul understood the term Ἀχαΐα in a more restricted sense than as a reference to all of Greece. That is, if 2 Cor 1–9 was a circular letter sent both to Corinth and to believers in the region of "Achaia," the circle must not have been too large.

In spite of the joy with which the apostle received news of the Corinthian church's reconciliation to him, Paul also felt the need cautiously to exhort the Corinthians to resume their efforts on behalf of the collection for the saints, which he does in 2 Cor 8:1–9:15. In order to accomplish this, along with this written encouragement he also sent Titus back to Corinth, "so that as he had previously started, so he should also complete this benefaction among you as well" (ἵνα καθὼς προενήρξατο οὕτως καὶ ἐπιτελέσῃ εἰς ὑμᾶς καὶ τὴν χάριν ταύτην) (2 Cor 8:6). As Thrall observes, the verb προενάρχομαι seems to imply "a time more remote in the past than that to which chap. 7 refers," which may mean that Titus was involved in organizing the collection in Corinth as early as the period of Letter A.[47] Paul encourages the Corinthians to display the same zeal for the project that they had demonstrated "last year" (ἀπὸ πέρυσι; 2 Cor 8:10; 9:2), perhaps a reference to the enthusiastic questions reflected in 1 Cor 16:1–4.[48]

Along with his associate Titus, Paul also dispatched to Corinth two unnamed brothers – called "messengers of the churches" (ἀπόστολοι ἐκκλησιῶν) in 2 Cor 8:23 – the purpose of whose presence in this delegation seems to have been not only to work for the collection but also to ensure the financial integrity of the relief fund (2 Cor 8:20; 9:3), a necessary precaution if Paul had earlier received severe criticism in Corinth that impugned his own motives in raising these funds. The first anonymous brother is said to have been "appointed by the churches (χειροτονηθεὶς ὑπὸ τῶν ἐκκλησιῶν) to be our fellow-traveler while this benefaction is being administered by us, for the glory of the Lord himself and to show willingness [to help]" (2 Cor 8:19).[49] Knowledge of the churches that were responsible for the selection of these men for this service is unattainable, though acquaintance with the identity of these congregations would add crucial information to our understanding of the history of the collection. It is implausible that they were representatives from Jerusalem, as some have suggested.[50] The best option is that Paul is referring to the churches of Macedonia, since that is Paul's location when he writes the present letter, though Paul's residency in

---

[47] Thrall, *2 Corinthians*, 528.
[48] So Thrall, *2 Corinthians*, 537.
[49] Cf. Martin, *2 Corinthians*, 275–76.
[50] *Pace* Nickle, *The Collection*, 18–22. Had Jerusalem been responsible for these delegates, not only would Paul likely have mentioned it, but it would also be hard to explain Paul's worry about the possibility of Jerusalem's rejection of the collection in Rom 15:30–32. Moreover, elsewhere in his letters when Paul refers to the Judean churches, he is clear on the matter (so Furnish, *II Corinthians*, 434). Equally improbable is Antioch (as Nicholas Taylor suggests [*Paul, Antioch and Jerusalem*, 202]), since Paul had apparently split with that congregation long before writing 2 Cor 1–9.

Ephesus prior to his trip to Macedonia requires that the Asian churches cannot be ruled out.[51] Although Paul seems reasonably hopeful that this embassy will have met with success in Corinth (2 Cor 9:5), the apostle holds out the warning that he – to say nothing of his readers themselves – will be shamed if he comes to Achaia with a coterie of Macedonians and finds that the contribution is not ready (2 Cor 9:4). At this point, Paul transmitted what is now 2 Corinthians 1–9 (Letter D) to Corinth.

There exists, of course, a significant debate about the literary unity of 2 Corinthians, and the decision to regard 2 Cor 1:1–9:15 as a unified composition is by no means an easy one, for strong arguments can be brought forward in favor of the theory that 2 Cor 1:1–8:24 and 2 Cor 9:1–15 were originally distinct letters. At the same time, the choice to view 2 Cor 1–9 as a literary unity does not significantly affect the chronology of the Jerusalem collection, for even if chapter 9 is viewed as a separate epistle, it was probably written shortly after 8:1–24 – not more than a few months, if that long.[52] In spite of the reasonable case that can be made for the theory that 2 Cor 9:1–15 represents a distinct literary composition, there are enough factors to tip the balance in favor of the literary unity of 2 Cor 1–9 that I am inclined, with some hesitation, to regard 2 Cor 1:1–9:15 (with the possible exception of 6:14–7:1) as a unified composition.[53]

---

[51] Harris (*Second Epistle*, 603) also argues that the appointing churches were Macedonian.

[52] The prepositional phrase ἀπὸ πέρυσι in 9:2 would then refer to the same time period as that designated by the identical phrase in 8:10, namely, the enthusiasm displayed by the Corinthians in their questions about how to go about raising money for Jerusalem (1 Cor 16:1–4). Rudolf Bultmann (*The Second Letter to the Corinthians* [trans. Roy A. Harrisville; Minneapolis: Augsburg, 1985], 256) regards chapter 9 as earlier than chapter 8, arguing that the report that Paul had given the Macedonians of Achaia's προθυμία (9:1) had provoked the Macedonian zeal reflected in 8:2–5. However, Furnish, following Hans Windisch and Dieter Georgi, lists three reasons that chapter 8 should be seen as the earlier of the two letters, if the two are viewed as distinct: "'(1) chap. 9 presumes the collection is near completion, while chap. 8 urges that it be completed; (2) chap. 9 presumes that the brothers introduced in chap. 8 are already known; and (3) chap. 9 alludes to an impending visit of Paul (v. 4), while chap. 8 does not" (*II Corinthians*, 431).

[53] I shall not enter into the detailed debate here. Careful and balanced discussions of this issue, which come to differing conclusions, are found in Furnish, *II Corinthians*, 429–33; and Thrall, *2 Corinthians*, 36–47. See also Margaret M. Mitchell, "Paul's Letters to Corinth: The Interpretative Intertwining of Literary and Historical Reconstruction," in *Urban Religion in Roman Corinth: Interdisciplinary Approaches* (ed. Daniel N. Schowalter and Steven J. Friesen; HTS 53; Cambridge: Harvard University Press, 2005), 307–38. Proponents of the unity of these chapters include Harris, *Second Epistle*, 24–29; Furnish, *II Corinthians*; Kieran J. O'Mahony, *Pauline Persuasion: A Sounding in 2 Corinthians 8–9* (JSNTSup 199; Sheffield: Sheffield Academic Press, 2000); Ben Witherington III, *Conflict and Community in Corinth: A Socio-Rhetorical Commentary on 1 and 2 Corinthians* (Grand Rapids: Eerdmans, 1995); Frank J. Matera, *II Corinthians: A Commentary* (The New Testament Library; Louisville: Westminster John Knox, 2003), 23; Frances Young and David F. Ford, *Meaning and Truth in 2 Corinthians* (Grand Rapids: Eerdmans, 1988), 27–59; Jan Lambrecht, *Second Corinthians* (SP 8; Collegeville, Minn.: Liturgical, 1999), 148–51; and Kim, *Die paulinische Kollekte*, 123–36. Advocates of separation include: Hans Dieter Betz, *2 Corinthians 8 and 9: A Commentary*

2 Corinthians 10–13

Paul had reason to worry. Having learned of a rapidly deteriorating situation in Corinth, triggered by the influx of those whom he labels "super-apostles" (2 Cor 11:5; 12:11), Paul sent off a biting, polemical letter, now preserved as 2 Corinthians 10–13 (Letter E). While the identity and message of the opponents whose presence in Corinth occasioned this missive letter is highly debated, it is possible that, among their many criticisms of Paul, they had pounced on memories of the earlier conflict associated with Paul's alleged abuse of the Corinthian finances.[54] Twice in 2 Cor 10–13 Paul defends his actions in Corinth with respect to monetary matters. First, in 2 Cor 11:7–12 Paul explains once again (cf. 1 Cor 9:3–18) why he had preached the gospel in Corinth without charge and without accepting financial support from the Corinthians. He declares:

> Did I commit a sin by humbling myself so that you might be lifted up, because I preached the gospel of God to you without payment? Instead, I "robbed" other churches by accepting support from them in order to minister to you. And when I was present with you and was in need, I did not burden anyone, for the brothers who came from Macedonia supplied my needs. In all ways I kept myself from being a burden to you, and I will continue to do so. As surely as the truth of Christ is in me, this boast of mine will not be silenced in the districts of Achaia. How so? Is it because I do not love you? God knows that I do! And what I do I will continue to do, in order that I may deny an opportunity to those who are seeking an opportunity to be recognized as our equals in what they boast about.

Paul's refusal to accept support from the Corinthians during his ministry in Corinth may have been regarded by the so-called "super-apostles" as a "sin" (ἁμαρτία; 2 Cor 11:7), for this policy appears to contradict material in the Jesus tradition that allows for, and even requires, material support for missionaries. In the commissioning of the seventy in Luke 10:1–16, for example, Jesus instructs

---

on *Two Administrative Letters of the Apostle Paul* (Hermeneia; Philadelphia: Fortress, 1985); Georgi, *Remembering the Poor*, 75–79; Thrall, *2 Corinthians*; Martin, *2 Corinthians*; Burkhard Beckheuer, *Paulus und Jerusalem: Kollekte und Mission im theologischen Denken des Heidenapostels* (Europäische Hochschulschriften 23; Frankfurt am Main: Peter Lang, 1997), 151–52; and Mitchell, "Paul's Letters to Corinth."

Rhetorical approaches to 2 Cor 8–9 do not shed much light on this problem, since different rhetorical studies of these chapters produce opposing results. So, for example, Hans Dieter Betz's important rhetorical analysis of this passage suggests two distinct letters (*2 Corinthians 8 and 9*, 38–41, 87–90), while Kieran J. O'Mahony's proposed rhetorical structure of these same chapters suggests a literary unity (*Pauline Persuasion*, 164–81). This may simply highlight some of the problems with employing the categories of classical rhetoric to analyze the Pauline epistles, however.

[54] For a treatment of Paul's opponents in 2 Corinthians, see Jerry L. Sumney, *Identifying Paul's Opponents: The Question of Method in 2 Corinthians* (JSNTSup 40; Sheffield: JSOT Press, 1990); cf. Harris, *Second Epistle*, 67–87. For an earlier, and somewhat problematic approach, see Dieter Georgi, *The Opponents of Paul in Second Corinthians* (Philadelphia: Fortress, 1986).

2.4 The Organization of the New Pauline Collection

the disciples, "Remain in the same house, eating and drinking whatever is provided by them, for the worker is worthy of his wage" (Luke 10:7; cf. the parallel in Matt 10:10; cf. also 1 Cor 9:14–15; Matt 10:1–15; Mark 6:7–11; Luke 9:1–5). Gerd Theissen has noted that in 2 Cor 10–13 "whenever [Paul] speaks of the superlative apostles (2 Cor. 11:15; 12:11) he goes on to speak about his renunciation of his right to support, and does so in such a way as to defend himself against the charge of ἁμαρτία or ἀδικία." The norm that Paul was charged with violating because of his self-sufficiency in Corinth, according to Theissen, is the standard of "charismatic poverty" reflected in the Gospel tradition. That is:

> Paul's renunciation of the "privilege" of support might be seen in a quite different way: the charge could be leveled at him that he has deliberately evaded the requirements of charismatic poverty, and that his work as a craftsman displays a lack of trust in the grace of God, who will also supply the material needs of his missionaries. Seen this way Paul is dependent on his work; he is not free and is no real apostle ([1 Cor] 9:1), for he has offended against the norm of the primitive Christian ideal of itinerant charismatics set down by Jesus himself.[55]

Paul's second defense of his fiscal policy in Corinth in 2 Cor 10–13 comes in 2 Cor 12:13–18. With more than a tinge of sarcasm, he writes:

> How were you worse off than the other churches, except that I myself did not burden you? Forgive me this wrong! Look, I am ready to come to you this third time, and I will not be a burden, for I seek not your possessions but you. For children ought not to save up for their parents, but parents for their children. I will most gladly spend and be spent on your behalf. If I love you more, will I be loved less? Let us assume that I did not burden you. Yet, "since I am crafty, I took you in with deceit"? Did I take advantage of you through any of those whom I sent to you? I urged Titus to go, and I sent the brother with him. Titus did not take advantage of you, did he? Did we not conduct ourselves with the same spirit? Did we not take the same steps?

If in 2 Cor 11:7–12 the sensitive issue is Paul's enjoinment of Corinthian assistance, the hostile rhetoric in 12:13–18 reflects an underlying accusation of financial malfeasance by Paul and his associates. While there is no specific mention of the collection in 2 Cor 10–13, the reference to Titus's visit in 12:17–18 implies, as Furnish states, that "the Corinthians have become so suspicious of Paul's motives that they are refusing to fulfill their commitment to the collection." Furnish goes on to suggest:

> Thus one immediate, practical result of the activity of rival apostles in Corinth was probably the failure of Titus' second mission, which was to ensure that the collection would be completed by the time of Paul's arrival, en route to Jerusalem. If so, the sense of urgency and frustration which permeates the whole Letter E [i.e., 2 Cor 10–13] may

---

[55] Gerd Theissen, *The Social Setting of Pauline Christianity: Essays on Corinth* (ed. and trans. John Schütz; Philadelphia: Fortress, 1982), 43; cf. Horrell, "'The Lord Commanded ... But I Have Not Used...'": 587–603.

be due to more than the deterioration of his relationship with the Corinthians. It may be due, as well, to Paul's fear of what this could mean for his collection project as a whole, and thus for his planned trip to Jerusalem and meeting with the apostles there.[56]

Unfortunately, these matters are not addressed directly in 2 Cor 10–13, probably because Paul intended to tackle them on the occasion of his upcoming visit to Corinth. The warning of 13:1–3, however, does seem to imply a connection between the reason for the conflict during Paul's second visit (the slander against Paul) and the accusations against which he is prepared to defend himself on the occasion of his third visit: "This is the third time I am coming to you. 'Every matter is established on the evidence of two or three witnesses.' As I said during my second visit and now say while absent: I will not spare again those who sinned previously and all the rest, since you seek proof that Christ is speaking in me."

It is likely, then, that Paul's opponents had learned of his history of financial inconsistency with the Corinthians – the issue that had provoked the first spark of conflict during Paul's second visit – and used it to their advantage. They not only pointed out that Paul had disobeyed the Lord's commandment by refusing financial support during his stay in Corinth, but they also assailed Paul's trustworthiness with respect to the collection. Perhaps they also publicly recalled the issue of the "double benefit" that had so troubled some members of the Corinthian congregation during Paul's second visit by noting the discrepancy between Paul's refusal of money during his stay in Corinth and his demand for travel assistance on his return. In the eyes of his opponents, Paul's questionable financial tactics were factors in the invalidation of his apostolic authority. We might imagine the following charge from the mouth of one of Paul's opponents:

> How can you Corinthians entrust your money to a fickle man like Paul? He boasts about proclaiming the good news free of charge, yet he disobeys the command of Jesus that the worker should receive his wages. Moreover, despite the insult you suffered though his denial of your opportunity to support his mission in Corinth, he even granted this same privilege to the churches in Macedonia. Then he showed up on your doorstep during his second visit asking you to support his travels, when he had refused your gracious benefactions while he was living among you. Now, after all this, he has sent representatives from Macedonia to collect money from you! And for his own personal profit! He lives according to the flesh (2 Cor 10:2) and his inconsistency is manifested in the difference between the strong words you receive from him in letters and his weak actions when he is in Corinth (2 Cor 10:10).

Thus, these opponents were able to rekindle the flames of opposition in Corinth that Paul thought he had extinguished with his "letter of tears."

---

[56] Furnish, *II Corinthians*, 45–46.

The Conclusion of the Collection Effort in Corinth

Finally, after sending Letter E (2 Cor 10–13), a letter that anticipates an impending visit by the apostle to Corinth (2 Cor 12:14; 13:1–2), Paul returned to Corinth and, by all accounts, achieved something of a restoration with the Corinthians once again. If, as many commentators conclude, Rom 16:1–27 was part of the original letter to Rome, evidence from these verses, such as the commendation of Phoebe from Cenchreae (Rom 16:1–2) and the greetings of Gaius (Rom 16:23; cf. 1 Cor 1:14), suggests that Romans was penned in Corinth.[57] In that letter Paul asserts that he is presently departing to Jerusalem in order to deliver a contribution from "Macedonia and Achaia" (Rom 15:25–26). Does this mean that the Corinthians ultimately gave to the relief fund? Or does Paul's reference to the province of Achaia subtly hide the fact that the community in Corinth eventually abandoned the project while other churches throughout the region contributed? Although the evidence is far from certain, the reference to Achaia's delight in contributing in Rom 15:26, combined with the fact that Romans appears to have been written from Corinth, strongly supports the conclusion that the Corinthians did not finally leave Paul in the lurch and did, in the end, participate in the fund.[58]

2.4.3 The Collection in Macedonia

The little that can be known about the history of Paul's collection efforts in Macedonia can be gleaned, interestingly, not from Paul's letters to the churches in that region (1 Thessalonians and Philippians) – exchanges in which the Jerusalem collection is not mentioned – but rather from allusions to the organization of the collection in Macedonia in both 2 Corinthians and Romans. It is, unfortunately, impossible to know precisely when Paul introduced the notion of a relief

---

[57] I regard the debate over the literary integrity of Romans 1–16 as settled in favor of the view that Rom 16 was originally a part of the epistle; see Harry Gamble Jr., *The Textual History of the Letter to the Romans: A Study in Textual and Literary Criticism* (SD 42; Grand Rapids: Eerdmans, 1977); and Peter Lampe, *From Paul to Valentinus: Christians at Rome in the First Two Centuries* (trans. Michael Steinhauser; Minneapolis: Fortress, 2003), 153–83. If Erastus ὁ οἰκονόμος τῆς πόλεως in Rom 16:23 is the same Erastus who is identified as the holder of the civic office of *aedile* in an inscription from Corinth, this would count as further support that Rom 16:1–27 was penned in Corinth. For the inscription see J. H. Kent, *Inscriptions 1926–1950: Corinth viii. Part Three* (Princeton: American School of Classical Studies at Athens, 1966), 99. For detailed arguments for and against, respectively, the identification of these two figures, see Bruce Winter, "An Early Christian Benefactor and Prominent Citizen," in *Seek the Welfare of the City: Christians as Benefactors and Citizens* (Grand Rapids: Eerdmans, 1994), 179–97; and Justin J. Meggitt, *Paul, Poverty and Survival* (Studies of the New Testament and Its World; Edinburgh: T & T Clark, 1998), 135–41.

[58] So also Becker, *Paul*, 27; Harris, *Second Epistle*, 93. Harris also points out "that Clement, writing in about A.D. 96, would [not have] complimented the Corinthians for 'giving more gladly than receiving' (ἥδιον διδόντες ἢ λαμβάνοντες [*1 Clement* 2:1, alluding to the saying of Jesus cited in Acts 20:35]), if in fact the church had earlier failed to contribute to Paul's collection in spite of his urgent appeals" (93).

fund for Jerusalem to the communities associated with his mission in Macedonia, in the cities of Thessalonica and Philippi. By the time that 2 Cor 8:1–9:15 was written, the Macedonians had proven themselves to be wholehearted supporters of the fund. In 2 Cor 8:1–6, Paul writes of the enthusiasm with which the Macedonians had approached the collection:

> We make known to you, brothers and sisters, the benefaction of God that has been given to the churches of Macedonia; for during a great ordeal of affliction the abundance of their joy and their deep poverty have abounded in the wealth of their sincere concern. For in accordance with their means, I testify, and beyond their means, they gave of their own volition, petitioning us earnestly for the benefit of partnership in the ministry for the saints, and not simply as we expected, but they gave themselves first to the Lord and to us through the will of God, so that we urged Titus that, as he had previously started, so he should also complete this benefaction among you as well.

In 2 Cor 9:2–4, written from Macedonia, Paul reports that he has also boasted to the Macedonians about the eagerness of Achaia and alludes to the possibility that some Macedonians, along with their contribution to the fund, may accompany him to Corinth before taking the collection to Jerusalem. Later, as we have seen, Paul looks back in Rom 15:26–27 upon the fact that Μακεδονία has fulfilled its obligation to Jerusalem by sharing with them in "material things" (ἐν τοῖς σαρκικοῖς). In all these statements, it appears that the collection effort in Macedonia sailed on smooth waters compared to the stormy seas present in the "renegade congregations" in Galatia and Corinth.[59]

Preferring the general term "Macedonians" in all three passages listed above, Paul does not specify which churches in that region contributed to the collection, but given the affirmation bestowed upon the Philippians for their generous financial support of Paul's ministry in Phil 4:10–20 (cf. 1:3–5), it is highly likely that they participated joyfully in the project. About the Thessalonians (or the Beroeans, if one counts the evidence from Acts 17) nothing specific can be said, but the Philippians must not have been the only church in Macedonia that supported the fund.

That the collection is mentioned neither in 1 Thessalonians nor in Philippians is understandable if these letters are dated, respectively, to the period before and the period after Paul's involvement with the collection for Jerusalem. As Martyn notes, "Once Paul had conceived the plan for his collection, it occupied a place in his thinking so large as to make it unlikely that he would subsequently write a letter to any of his churches without mentioning it."[60] With regard to 1 Thessalonians, Wedderburn points out that the silence regarding the collection in the Thessalonian correspondence "only becomes problematic if one places the apostolic council of Gal 2.1–10 before the missionary journey of Acts

---

[59] Lüdemann, *Paul, Apostle to the Gentiles*, 96.
[60] Martyn, *Galatians*, 228 n. 83.

16–18 *and* interprets Gal 2.10 as meaning that Paul was from that point of time on actively promoting his collection project in fulfillment of that part of the agreement."[61] While this chapter has not considered the evidence from Acts 16–18, the argument that Gal 2:10 does not refer to the foundation of the Pauline collection sufficiently explains why this fund is not mentioned in 1 Thessalonians, in spite of the fact that economic concerns do play a role in this epistle (1 Thess 2:9–10).[62]

With regard to Philippians, Paul does, of course, refer to the pecuniary assistance of the community in Philippi in 4:10–20, but this particular gift is rendered to him alone and not to the church in Jerusalem (4:15–18).[63] The absence of references to the Jerusalem collection in Philippians, combined with the reasonable assumption that the Philippians were active participants in the collection, then, suggests that this letter was written either before or after the organization of the Pauline collection.[64] Martyn places Philippians in the period before the beginning of the collection.[65] However, given the likelihood that Philippians was written late in Paul's life (1:20–21), and quite possibly during a period of imprisonment in Rome (cf. 1:13; 4:22), it is more reasonable to conclude that this epistle was written after the completion and delivery of the collection to Jerusalem.[66]

2.4.4 The Collection in Asia

Since 1 Cor 16:1–20 clearly indicates that the collection for Jerusalem was being organized during the period of Paul's residency in Ephesus, it is natural to wonder why Ephesus is nowhere mentioned in the Pauline letters as a participant in that project.[67] On the basis of Acts 20:4, which lists Tychius and Trophimus as

---

[61] Wedderburn, "Paul's Collection," 102.

[62] Like many scholars, I count 2 Thessalonians among the Pauline pseudepigrapha. For a balanced discussion of the recent debate, which defends the authenticity of 2 Thessalonians, see Abraham Malherbe, *The Letters to the Thessalonians: A New Translation with Introduction and Commentary* (AB 32B; New York: Doubleday, 2000), 349–375.

[63] The literary integrity of Philippians is often doubted. If the canonical book of Philippians were a compilation of various letters (e.g., 4:10–20; 1:1–3:1; 3:2–4:3), this would complicate the question of why the collection is not mentioned in any of these exchanges. On the other hand, the absence of references to the Jerusalem collection in Philippians could presumably be interpreted as an indication of the letter's integrity, since, given the importance of the project for Paul's mission, there is a greater chance that the apostle would have mentioned it at least once in three different letters to Philippi. This point is immaterial, however, because I side with those who view Philippians in its present form as a literary unity. For a recent defense of this position, see Paul A. Holloway, *Consolation in Philippians: Philosophical Sources and Rhetorical Strategy* (SNTSMS 112; Cambridge: Cambridge University Press, 2001), esp. 7–33.

[64] So Wedderburn, "Paul's Collection," 102.

[65] Martyn, *Galatians*, 228.

[66] Wedderburn, "Paul's Collection," 102.

[67] It is possible that the Asian churches, including Ephesus, are those who have elected the nameless delegates in 2 Cor 8:16–24, but this identification is uncertain.

"Asians" who accompany Paul on his final journey to Jerusalem in that narrative, Georgi assumes that Ephesus did contribute to the fund. This evidence from Acts is tenuous, however, and cannot be used to answer the question satisfactorily (on Acts, see below). On the other hand, citing the hardships described in 1 Cor 15:32 and 2 Cor 1:8, Lüdemann suspects that "Asia (Ephesus) did not organize a collection because the apostle could not (any longer?) gain a foothold there."[68]

John Knox, who possesses a high estimation of the importance of Ephesus for Paul's mission, demurs from Lüdemann's skepticism. Knox posits that Paul maintained a close relationship with the church in Ephesus that lasted over eight years and included a substantial amount of time spent by Paul in that city.[69] In response to Lüdemann's doubts regarding Ephesian participation in the collection, Knox writes:

> Yet, can there be any question but that the Asian churches, particularly the church at Ephesus, were involved [in the collection]? To be sure, Luedemann thinks there is such a question and, consistent with his opinion about the Galatians, holds that the Ephesians, too, "did not organize a collection because the apostle could not (any longer?) gain a foothold there." He cited 1 Cor. 15:32 and 2 Cor 1:8 in this connection. I must differ from him at this point. There would be no disagreement between us, I feel sure, as to the fact that Paul worked (himself and through his aides) for a considerable period in Ephesus and in other parts of Asia (witness Colossae, Laodicea and Hierapolis; no doubt there were other cities) and that his relations with these churches were warm and close, even in the very period when the collection effort was being made (1 Cor. 16:19).... In considering the fact of Paul's silence about the collection in Asia, it may be well to reflect that we should know little about Paul's effort in Macedonia and Achaia if it were not for the Corinthian letters. But there *is* no letter to the Ephesians! And may not this fact itself point to his having his base or headquarters there?[70]

Knox is correct that we would, indeed, know little about Paul's effort in Macedonia if it were not for the Corinthian letters. But there is no letter to the Macedonians that mentions the collection, either. We are only aware of Paul's fundraising activity in Macedonia because Paul speaks of it in the Corinthian correspondence. That Paul does not also refer to Ephesian involvement in the contribution in these same letters only complicates the matter. Given the evidence that a Pauline community continued to exist in Ephesus well into the second century (cf. 1 Tim 1:2–4; cf. 2 Tim 1:18; 4:12; Ign. *Eph.*), it is true that Paul's mission to and contacts with that city may not have ended altogether with his

---

[68] Lüdemann, *Paul, Apostle to the Gentiles*, 86; cf. the chapter entitled "Paul in Ephesus," in Rick Strelan, *Paul, Artemis, and the Jews in Ephesus* (BZNW 80; Berlin: Walter de Gruyter, 1996), 126–65.

[69] Knox, *Chapters in a Life*, 63.

[70] Ibid., 63–64.

2.4 The Organization of the New Pauline Collection

departure to Corinth.[71] However, local troubles for Paul in Ephesus may have prevented the active involvement necessary to organize a collection in that city. On balance, then, Lüdemann's suspicion seems like the better option, for if the Ephesians had supported the relief fund, why would Paul not mention their gift anywhere in his letters?[72]

Knox may also overestimate Paul's success among and influence within the Ephesian church. In challenging the received scholarly tradition that Paul had much greater success among Gentiles in Ephesus than among Jews, Rick Strelan concludes his careful study of the evidence concerning the Pauline ministry in Ephesus from both Paul's letters and Acts with the following observation:

The second aim [of this study] has been to show that Paul's work in Ephesus was

> marked by a struggle which at times was life-threatening and that he himself claimed little success for his efforts there. Paul never holds up the Ephesians as a model to be emulated by Christians elsewhere – whatever he does say about Ephesus is nearly always negative. What success Paul does have is not from among gentiles in the city, but from among Jews, so that it is possible to speak of Pauline Jewish Christianity in Ephesus. That is the evidence of both Paul himself and Luke. The conclusion that Paul worked with, at the very least, equal success among Jews as among gentiles in Ephesus, and that Christians in Pauline communities there may have been predominantly of Jewish background raises the question whether other centers traditionally known as Pauline and gentile also ought to be re-examined.[73]

Writing independently of Strelan, Matthias Günther reaches similar conclusions concerning the struggle, and the eventual dissolution, of the Pauline mission in Ephesus.[74] While this is certainly a larger debate than can be entered here, Strelan's work not only supports Lüdemann's theory that Paul's collection efforts in Ephesus were impeded by local persecution, but also supplies another intriguing explanation of why Ephesus is not mentioned as a participant in the

---

[71] See Paul Trebilco, *The Early Christians in Ephesus from Paul to Ignatius* (WUNT 2:166; Tübingen: Mohr Siebeck, 2004).

[72] If Ephesians were an authentic Pauline epistle, 2:11–4:16 would be a natural location for a treatment of the ecumenical significance of the collection, along the lines of what Paul says in Rom 15:25–27. That Ephesians contains no such discussion is perhaps indicative that the significance or memory of the collection had faded by the late first century, even within Pauline circles. Manuscripts of Eph 1:15 do contain some version of the clause καὶ τὴν ἀγάπην τὴν εἰς πάντας τοὺς ἁγίους (ℵ², D², Ψ), but this appears to be a derivation from Col 1:4 and is not a reference to the Jerusalem collection.

[73] Strelan, *Paul, Artemis and the Jews in Ephesus*, 295. See also the review essay by Eckhard Schnabel, "Die ersten Christen in Ephesus: Neuerscheinungen zur frühchristlichen Missionsgeschichte," *NovT* 41 (1999): 349–82.

[74] Matthias Günther, *Die Frühgeschichte des Christentums in Ephesus* (Arbeiten zur Religion und Geschichte des Urchristentums 1; Frankfurt: Lang, 1995). The conclusions of both Günther and Strelan are disputed by Trebilco, who tends to rely more heavily on evidence from Acts.

gift for Jerusalem. If the Ephesian church was predominately Jewish, as Strelan maintains, would that community have been exempt from contributing to what Paul calls in Rom 15:16 the "offering of the Gentiles"? This question cannot be answered with surety, but considering all the available evidence, it does appear (contra Knox) that the churches in Asia did not partake in the collection for the saints.

2.4.5 References to the Collection in Romans

The importance of Paul's discussion of the Jerusalem collection in Rom 15:25–32 has already been noted. In this passage the apostle reflects on the collection on the eve of its delivery and outlines his plans to travel from Corinth to Rome, and then to Spain, by way of Jerusalem:

> But now I am going to Jerusalem to minister to the saints. For Macedonia and Achaia were pleased to make a certain partnership-forming contribution for the poor among the saints in Jerusalem. For they were pleased to do this and, indeed, they are their debtors. For if in spiritual blessings the Gentiles have received a contribution from them, the Gentiles ought also to be of service to them in material blessings. Therefore, when I have discharged this task and sealed to them this fruit, I will go through you to Spain; and I know that when I come to you, I will come in the fullness of the blessing of Christ. But I urge you, brothers and sisters, by our Lord Jesus Christ and by the love of the Spirit, to contend with me in prayers to God on my behalf, that I may be rescued from the disobedient in Judea and that my ministry to Jerusalem may be acceptable to the saints, so that in joy, by God's will, I may come to you and be refreshed by you.

Of significance here, aside from the itinerary and the identification of "Macedonia and Achaia" as contributors to the fund, is Paul's genuine concern for his own personal safety and for the successful reception of the collection by the believers in Jerusalem. Paul asks the Romans to pray not only that he will be rescued from "those Jews who regard him as a renegade and a serious threat to the ancestral religion," but also that his "ministry to Jerusalem" (ἡ διακονία μου ἡ εἰς Ἰερουσαλὴμ), by which he means the collection (cf. 15:25), will be deemed acceptable by the saints in Jerusalem.[75] Against Cranfield, who rationalizes Paul's anxiety with his own experiential, modern-day explanation that charitable gifts are not always heartily received, Paul's fear reflects the very real threat that the Jewish Christians in Jerusalem would reject this monetary gift from the Gentile congregations.[76] Given the staunch opposition to Paul's law-free gospel in Judea,

---

[75] Brendan Byrne, *Romans* (SP 6; Collegeville: Minn.: Liturgical, 1996), 442; cf. Kim, *Die paulinische Kollekte*, 179.

[76] C. E. B. Cranfield (*A Critical and Exegetical Commentary on the Epistle to the Romans* [2 vols.; ICC; Edinburgh: T & T Clark, 1979], 2:778) writes, "Some tension there undoubtedly was; but any one who has had any considerable experience not just in organizing a church's collection of money for charitable purposes but also in the actual passing on of it to those in need will know full well that its being εὐπρόσδεκτος is no foregone conclusion, and will be more likely to recognize in these words evidence of Paul's spiritual and human sensitivity and freedom from self-

the likelihood that Paul's new attempt to bring money to Jerusalem would rekindle memories of his abandonment of the collection efforts in Antioch, and the possibility of an increasingly nationalistic aversion to Gentile benefactions (cf. Josephus, *J.W.* 2.409–10),[77] Paul was understandably nervous. Moreover, his uncertainty with regard to Jerusalem's response to the contribution supports the claim that the collection raised among the Gentile communities of the Pauline mission was *not* a project that resulted from an agreement reached between Paul and the leadership of the Jerusalem church. Instead, Paul, of his own initiative, conceived the idea of gathering monetary assistance for the saints in Jerusalem from his Gentile churches, and in Rom 15:30–31 he reckons with the genuine possibility that this manifestation of grace will not be considered εὐπρόσδεκτος by its recipients.

There are two other possible allusions to the collection in Romans that merit brief consideration. First, some scholars have suggested that Rom 1:13 also pertains to the Jerusalem collection, which would mean that the collection was not a one-time gift but rather part of a continued effort by Paul to enlist the churches of his mission and believers in congregations not founded by him in a campaign to provide financial support to believers in Jerusalem.[78] This reading would provide some support for those who maintain that the collection was an obligation, or even a tax, imposed upon the Pauline mission by the authorities in Jerusalem. In Rom 15:28, Paul asserts with reference to the collection that, "after having sealed this fruit [τὸν καρπὸν τοῦτον]," he plans to come via Rome to Spain. In Rom 1:13 he writes, "I want you to know, brothers and sisters, that I have often intended to come to you (but thus far have been prevented), in order that I may have some fruit [τινὰ καρπὸν] among you just as (I had) among the rest of the Gentiles." It is argued that the καρπός of Rom 1:13, both that which Paul expects in Rome and that which he has already obtained from other Gentiles, is related to the "fruit" that he is presently delivering to Jerusalem, namely, the collection. An allusion to the collection in Rom 1:13 is not demanded by the use of καρπός elsewhere in Romans (cf. 6:21–22), but this is not an altogether common word in Paul's letters (cf. 1 Cor 9:7; Gal 5:22; Phil 1:11, 22; 4:17).

However, καρπός in Rom 1:13 should not be interpreted as a reference to the collection. It would be rather crass, and equally unwise, for Paul at the beginning

---

centered complacency than to draw from them any confident conclusions about the tension between the Jerusalem church and Paul."

[77] So Sze-kar Wan, "Collection for the Saints as Anticolonial Act: Implications of Paul's Ethnic Reconstruction," in *Paul and Politics: Ekklesia, Israel, Imperium, Interpretation; Essays in Honor of Krister Stendahl* (ed. Richard H. Horsley; Harrisburg, Pa.: Trinity, 2000), 202.

[78] Nickle, *The Collection*, 69–70; M. A. Krüger, "*Tina Karpon*, 'Some Fruit,' in Rom. 1:13," *WTJ* 49 (1987): 167–73; James Chacko, "Collection in the Early Church," *Evangelical Review of Theology* 24 (2000): 179; Mark Nanos, *The Mystery of Romans: The Jewish Context of Paul's Letter* (Minneapolis: Fortress, 1996), 206–7.

of his letter to tell the Romans that the reason for his long-anticipated visit to Rome is to reap a monetary harvest among them. Additionally, the absence of a reference to Jerusalem suggests that καρπός in Rom 1:13 is used, as it is also in Phil 1:22, to refer to "fruitful labor" of his missionary endeavors. As Moo puts it, "'Harvest' refers to the product of his apostolic labors (cf. Phil 1:22), including here probably both an increase in the number of Christians through evangelization 'among' the Romans and a strengthening of the faith of the Roman Christians themselves (cf. v. 11b)."[79]

Second, it will be argued in much more detail in chapter four that the phrase "the offering of the Gentiles" (ἡ προσφορὰ τῶν ἐθνῶν) in Rom 15:16 should be interpreted not as an appositional or objective genitive, as it is taken by almost all commentators, but rather as a subjective genitive that refers to an offering made by the Gentiles themselves, namely, the collection. This alternative reading does not affect our understanding of the chronology of the collection, though it does have deep significance for our view of Paul's theological understanding of the relief fund.

2.5 The Book of Acts and the Delivery of the Collection

2.5.1 Introduction

In spite of the fact that Paul may have written letters (such as Philippians and Philemon) after the journey anticipated in Rom 15 from Corinth through Jerusalem to Rome (and then to Spain?), his last remaining comments about the collection are found in Rom 15:25–32.[80] We have, then, no firsthand testimony about the actual delivery of the relief fund to Jerusalem. For this reason, scholars searching for evidence concerning the outcome of the collection have often turned to the book of Acts, the final chapters of which provide a fairly detailed narrative of Paul's ultimate journey to Jerusalem, his arrest, and his eventual im-

---

[79] Douglas J. Moo, *The Epistle to the Romans* (NICNT; Grand Rapids: Eerdmans, 1996), 61. Even if καρπός in Rom 1:13 is taken monetarily, a stronger case could be made that it refers to financial support of Paul's missionary expenses. This may be how the word is used in Phil 1:11 (πεπληρωμένοι καρπὸν δικαιοσύνης τὸν διὰ Ἰησοῦ Χριστοῦ εἰς δόξαν καὶ ἔπαινον θεοῦ). The "harvest" of Rom 1:13, then, would designate the sort of assistance mentioned more directly by Paul in Rom 15:24 when he speaks of his desire "to be sent on" (προπεμφθῆναι) by believers in Rome to Spain. Contextually, however, this reading is far less compelling than the view that by καρπός Paul looks forward to a fruitful missionary experience in Rome.

[80] This section is adapted from my article "Paul's Collection and the Book of Acts Revisited," *NTS* 52 (2006): 50–70. For a different perspective on the collection in Acts, see Friedrich Wilhelm Horn, "Die Kollektenthematik in der Apostelgeschichte," in *Die Apostelgeschichte und die hellenistische Geschichtsschreibung: Festschrift für Eckhard Plümacher zu seinem 65. Geburtstag* (ed. Cilliers Breytenbach and Jens Schröter; AGSU 57; Leiden: Brill, 2004), 135–56.

prisonment in Rome (21:1–28:30). Two of the latest studies of Paul's collection, for example, both rely heavily on material from Acts in their reconstructions of the collection's chronology.[81] Stephan Joubert's recent monograph on the collection, *Paul as Benefactor*, is a case in point. Recognizing that Acts "is silent about the actual delivery of the collection," Joubert nonetheless assumes that "Luke did in fact possess some basic knowledge about the collection project."[82] He supports this claim with a reference to Acts 24:17. Joubert goes on to assert that the author of Acts had more than a modicum of reliable historical information about the collection, including "the basic reason for the collection; the main parties involved; (some of) the theological meanings attached to this project; the delivery journey to Jerusalem; and Paul's meeting with the Jerusalem leadership."[83]

The assumption on which this assertion is based, namely, that Luke had reliable information about the Pauline collection, is invalid. Unfortunately, the author of Acts makes no mention of Paul's collection for Jerusalem anywhere in his narrative. For this reason, material from the book of Acts cannot be used, as it often is, to write the final chapter of the historical reconstruction of the Pauline collection. Theories about the collection – its history or its theological significance for Paul's ministry – based on the book of Acts are bound to remain nothing more than unverifiable speculations. In order to justify this skepticism concerning the efficacy of turning to Acts for details about the Pauline collection, it is necessary to comment briefly on the two passages in Acts to which appeal is most often made by those who claim (or assume) that the narrative of Acts offers historical information about the offering of the Gentiles.

The book of Acts does, of course, briefly mention two instances in which Paul is associated with the bringing of money to Jerusalem, and both of these references have sometimes been connected with the Pauline collection. First, as we have seen, in Acts 11:27–30, reacting to the prophecy of severe famine by the Jerusalem prophet Agabus, the church in Antioch dispatches Barnabas and Saul on a mission to bring "aid to the brothers and sisters living in Jerusalem" (11:29). Some have suggested that this incident is a misplaced or transposed account of Paul's final visit to Jerusalem to deliver the relief fund raised among his Gentile communities.[84] This chapter has earlier argued that, while Act 11:27–30 may indeed preserve an authentic tradition of Paul and Barnabas representing the church in Antioch by delivering a relief fund to Jerusalem, this tradition can

---

[81] Joubert, *Paul as Benefactor*, 210–15; Kim, *Die paulinische Kollekte*, 137–80.
[82] Joubert, *Paul as Benefactor*, 212.
[83] Ibid., 212.
[84] Paul J. Achtemeier, *The Quest for Unity in the New Testament Church: A Study in Paul and Acts* (Philadelphia: Fortress, 1987), 46; Taylor, *Paul, Antioch, and Jerusalem*, 52, 214–17; Gerhard Schneider, *Die Apostelgeschichte, II. Teil: Kommentar zu Kap. 9,1–28,31* (HTKNT 5:2; Freiburg: Herder, 1982), 113; Martin Dibelius, "The Acts of the Apostles as an Historical Source," in *Studies in the Acts of the Apostles* (ed. Heinrich Greeven; trans. Mary Ling; London: SCM, 1956), 106–7; Buck, "Collection for the Saints," 1–30. Cf. Lüdemann, *Paul, Apostle to the Gentiles*, 149–52.

more plausibly be connected with the request of the leaders of the Jerusalem church in Gal 2:10 that Paul and Barnabas "continue to remember the poor," however, and not with the fundraising project that Paul undertook among the congregations of his own mission many years later.

The second reference in Acts to Paul bringing money to Jerusalem comes in Paul's defense before the Roman governor Felix at Caesarea, an oration in which the apostle declares, "Now after many years I came to give alms to my nation and sacrifices" (24:17). The vast majority of interpreters takes the reference to "almsgiving" (ἐλεημοσύνη) in this context as an allusion to Paul's collection for Jerusalem.[85] Joseph Fitzmyer's comment is typical: "At length, Luke allows Paul to mention the collection that he had taken up in the Gentile Christian churches founded by him in Galatia, Macedonia, and Achaia."[86] This interpretation, however, makes little sense of the narrative of Acts, which until this statement in 24:17 has given the reader no indication that Paul has been involved in raising a contribution among his Gentile churches to be distributed during his final journey to Jerusalem. Fitzmyer himself appears to be conscious of this tension: "Readers of Acts may, indeed, not be aware of the importance of that collection in Paul's sight, because Luke has not emphasized it to the same extent as did Paul himself. How could he have known about its importance, not being with Paul when he wrote those important letters?"[87]

---

[85] Scholars who view Acts 24:17 as an allusion to the Pauline collection include Horn, "Die Kollektenthematik," 152–56; Joubert, *Paul as Benefactor*, 92, 210–215; Fitzmyer, *Acts of the Apostles*, 736; C. K. Barrett, *A Critical and Exegetical Commentary on the Acts of the Apostles, XV–XXVIII* (ICC; Edinburgh: T & T Clark, 1998), 1107–8; Ben Witherington, *The Acts of the Apostles: A Socio-Rhetorical Commentary* (Grand Rapids: Eerdmans, 1998), 712; Paul W. Walaskay, *Acts* (Westminster Bible Companion; Louisville: Westminster John Knox, 1998), 216; Justin Taylor, *Les Actes Des Deux Apôtres, VI: Commentaire Historique (Act. 18,23–28,31)* (Paris: Librairie Lecoffre, 1996), 107–9, 170–71; J. D. G. Dunn, *The Acts of the Apostles* (Narrative Commentaries; Valley Forge, Pa.: Trinity, 1996), 313–14; Brian Rapske, *The Book of Acts and Paul in Roman Custody* (vol. 3 of *The Book of Acts in Its First Century Setting*, ed. Bruce W. Winter; Grand Rapids: Eerdmans, 1994), 163; F. F. Bruce, *The Acts of the Apostles: The Greek Text with Introduction and Commentary* (3d ed.; Grand Rapids: Eerdmans, 1990), 481; Hans Conzelmann, *Acts of the Apostles* (Hermeneia; trans. James Limburg, A. Thomas Kraabel, and Donald H. Juel; Philadelphia: Fortress, 1987), 199; Rudolf Pesch, *Die Apostelgeschichte (Apg 13–28)* (EKKNT 2:5; Zürich: Neukirchener, 1986), 258; Schneider, *Apostelgeschichte*, 348–49; I. Howard Marshall, *The Acts of the Apostles: An Introduction and Commentary* (Grand Rapids: Eerdmans, 1980), 378–79; Klaus Berger, "Almosen für Israel," *NTS* 23 (1977): 180–204; Johannes Munck, *The Acts of the Apostles: Introduction, Translation, and Notes* (AB 31; Garden City, N.Y.: Doubleday, 1967), 230; Nickle, *The Collection*, 70, 148–50; Paton J. Gloag, *A Critical and Exegetical Commentary on the Acts of the Apostles* (Edinburgh: T & T Clark, 1870), 340.

[86] Fitzmyer, *Acts of the Apostles*, 736.

[87] Ibid., 736. Cf. the statement by Conzelmann: "Finally the collection is mentioned, but only in passing and ad hoc, in order to refute the charge of στάσις, 'insurrection,' and to demonstrate the solidarity of Paul with his people. *The reader of Acts can scarcely understand the allusion here*; it is clear that Luke knows more than he says" (*Acts of the Apostles*, 199; emphasis added).

2.5.2 Almsgiving in Acts 24:17

Scholars more attuned to the narrative contours of Acts have occasionally challenged the consensus view that Acts 24:17 is an allusion to the collection. For example, both Robert Tannehill and Beverly Gaventa have suggested that 24:17 refers more directly to the activity of worship, which has been the subject of Paul's speech since 24:11.[88] The prevailing sentiment, however, is that Acts 24:17 provides at least a hint of Luke's knowledge of the collection, information which, for a variety of proposed reasons, he has ostensibly suppressed in his narrative. In fact, the scholarly consensus has hardly changed since Clayton R. Bowen asked over eighty years ago, "[Does] Acts 24:17 refer to the collection at all?" With a few notable exceptions, Bowen's answer could appropriately describe the situation today: "No commentator has, to the present writer's knowledge, hitherto doubted it."[89] A careful analysis of Paul's speech before Felix, along with an examination of the role that almsgiving plays in the larger narrative of Acts, will show that Acts 24:17, far from being a reference to the collection, identifies Paul before his accusers as a faithful Jew whose individual piety is demonstrated by almsgiving and worship.

The Journey to Jerusalem

The difficulty begins in Acts 19:21, which sounds the first note of necessity with reference to Paul's final trip to Jerusalem: "After these things had been fulfilled, Paul resolved in the Spirit to go through Macedonia and Achaia, and then to go on to Jerusalem. He said, 'After I have gone there, I must also see Rome.'" Although the phrase ἔθετο ὁ Παῦλος ἐν τῷ πνεύματι can be translated either "Paul resolved in the Spirit" or "Paul set in his own spirit," it is more likely that this verse evokes the theme of guidance by the Holy Spirit. Such a reading makes

---

[88] Robert C. Tannehill, *The Narrative Unity of Luke-Acts: A Literary Interpretation* (2 vols.; Minneapolis: Fortress, 1986–1990), 2:300; Beverly Roberts Gaventa, *The Acts of the Apostles* (ANTC; Nashville: Abingdon, 2003), 328. John B. Polhill (*Acts* [NAC 26; Nashville: Broadman, 1992], 484 n. 117) appears to follow Tannehill in questioning whether 24:17 is, in fact, a reference to the collection. Earlier in his commentary, however, Polhill maintains, with an appeal to 24:17, that Luke was clearly informed of the collection yet deliberately deemphasized its importance: "[Luke] was certainly aware that Paul took a collection to Jerusalem, for it is mentioned explicitly in Paul's later speech before Felix (24:17)" (417).

[89] Clayton R. Bowen, "Paul's Collection and the Book of Acts," *JBL* 42 (1923): 49–58, esp. 53. Bowen's insightful essay has unfortunately never received the attention it deserves, either by commentators on Acts or by authors dealing with the Pauline collection for Jerusalem. For example, among the important monographs on the collection, Bowen's article is not listed in the bibliographies of Georgi (*Remembering the Poor*), Nickle (*The Collection*), Beckheuer (*Paulus und Jerusalem*); Joubert (*Paul as Benefactor*), or Kim (*Die paulinische Kollekte*). Somewhat surprisingly, the article is listed in Fitzmyer's bibliography (*Acts of the Apostles*, 737), but Fitzmyer does not interact with Bowen's thesis in his commentary. The present section is, of course, fundamentally indebted to the questions posed and the answers offered by Bowen, although the main features of my own argument were developed before I located Bowen's work.

sense of the divine purpose that often compels and controls the missionary work in Acts (cf. 13:1–2, 4; 16:6–10), and which is more directly signaled in the declaration that Paul "must" (δεῖ) see Rome.[90] As Gaventa writes, "Journeying to Rome reflects neither Paul's personal desire for travel nor his own discernment of what the witness requires but the divine will, conveyed to him by means of the Holy Spirit."[91]

Apart from the assertion of divine necessity, Luke initially provides no other reason for Paul's final visit to Jerusalem. This is problematic for interpreters of Acts because, as readers of Paul's letters, they know very well the reason for this journey to Jerusalem: Paul intended to deliver the collection raised among his largely Gentile churches. As Paul himself announces to believers in Rome in his last remaining comments about the collection: "But now I am going to Jerusalem to minister to the saints. For Macedonia and Achaia were pleased to make a certain partnership-forming contribution for the poor among the saints in Jerusalem" (Rom 15:25–26; cf. 1 Cor 16:3).[92] Yet the narrative of Acts provides little indication of the reason that Paul is obliged to travel to Jerusalem. The trace of a motivation emerges in 20:16, where it is stated that Paul "was eager to be in Jerusalem, if possible, on the day of Pentecost." This verse, however, only raises the question: *Why* must Paul reach Jerusalem by Pentecost?[93]

---

[90] *Pace* Charles H. Cosgrove, "The Divine ΔΕΙ in Luke-Acts," *NovT* 26 (1984): 168–90, esp. 178. Cosgrove's perceptive article helpfully draws attention to the parallel between 19:21 and 20:22, the latter of which speaks of Paul "being bound in the Spirit." However, Cosgrove states of 20:22, "Here the 'spirit' is clearly distinguished from the Holy Spirit in that the following verse speaks explicitly of τὸ πνεῦμα τὸ ἅγιον" (178 n. 26). The close connection between vv. 22 and 23 actually mitigates Cosgrove's argument, for τὸ πνεῦμα in v. 22 should interpreted in light of its usage in the following verse (so also Fitzmyer, *Acts of the Apostles*, 677).

[91] Gaventa, *Acts*, 268.

[92] On the debate over this rendering of the construction κοινωνίαν τινὰ ποιήσασθαι, see G. W. Peterman, "Romans 15.26: Make a Contribution or Establish Fellowship?" *NTS* 40 (1994): 457–63.

[93] It could be objected that the list of names in Acts 20:4 constitutes evidence that Luke was indeed aware that a large party of delegates (seven named individuals plus at least one included in the "we" of 20.5) from the churches of Macedonia and Greece traveled with Paul to Jerusalem in order to deliver the collection (cf. 1 Cor 16:3–4; 2 Cor 8:19; 9:4). This view has significant proponents (recently, Dietrich-Alex Koch, "Kollektenbericht, 'Wir'-Bericht und Itinerar: Neue [?] Überlegungen zu einem alten Problem," *NTS* 45 [1999]: 367–90). A. J. M. Wedderburn, for example, calls this "one of those pieces of detailed information that Acts contains, and that many are disposed to regard as traditional, particularly if their content does not seem to serve an obvious purpose in the story that the author of Acts wishes to tell" ("Paul's Collection," 103–4). Wedderburn then suggests that this verse, along with 24:17, indicates that Luke was aware of Paul's collection but suppressed mention of it in his account because the gift was rejected by Jerusalem (104 n. 27).

There are two problems inherent in Wedderburn's assertion, however. First, it is incorrect to claim that this verse "does not seem to serve an obvious purpose in the story that the author of Acts wishes to tell." Rather, this list symbolizes the growth and success of Paul's ministry in the

The problem is intensified as the narrative continues. Paul's farewell speech to the Ephesian elders portrays Jerusalem as a destination that the apostle, literally bound by God's will, cannot avoid: "And now, as a captive to the Spirit, I am going to Jerusalem, not knowing what will happen to me there, except that the Holy Spirit warns me in every city that imprisonment and persecutions are waiting for me" (20:22–23). That this speech forebodes Paul's eventual death is suggested not only by the reference to imprisonment and persecutions, but also by the note of reservation evident in Paul's view of his own future (20:24), by the pronouncement that none of the believers in Ephesus will ever see Paul's face again (20:25), and by the pathos of the final scene (20:36–38).[94] Similar episodes appear in the following chapter: in Tyre, the disciples plead with Paul not to continue on to Jerusalem (21:4); in Caesarea, the prophet Agabus returns to predict Paul's arrest and the people urge Paul not to go up to Jerusalem (21:10–14). A sense of finality is achieved in 21:14 when the narrator remarks, "Since he would not be persuaded, we remained silent except to say, 'The Lord's will be done' (τοῦ κυρίου τὸ θέλημα γινέσθω)." This declaration underscores the extent to which the narration of Paul's final journey to Jerusalem depicts that expedition as motivated by nothing other than the will of God. In Luke's account, it is divine necessity, and not the collection, that compels Paul on his fateful trip to Jerusalem.

The Defense before Felix

Interestingly, Paul's speech before the Roman governor Felix in Acts 24 provides a slightly different motivation for the trip to Jerusalem, although one not necessarily at odds with the allusion to Pentecost in 20:16. Paul's defense is intended to reply to the charges leveled against him by the orator Tertullus, who

---

larger regions of Macedonia, Greece, and Asia, as well as in particular localities like Beroea, Thessalonica, Derbe (so Tannehill, *Narrative Unity*, 2:246; Gaventa, *Acts*, 277–78). The entourage may also draw attention to yet another of the many parallels between Jesus and Paul, both of whom embark on ill-fated journeys to Jerusalem accompanied by a coterie of followers (so F. Scott Spencer, *Acts* [Sheffield: Sheffield Academic Press, 1997], 278). Second, the list in Acts 20:4 does not include representatives from churches that are known to have participated in Paul's collection, specifically Corinth and Philippi (so Gerd Lüdemann, *Early Christianity according to the Traditions in Acts: A Commentary* [trans. John Bowden; Minneapolis: Fortress, 1989], 225; Becker, *Paul*, 26; cf. 1 Cor 16:1–4; 2 Cor 8:1; Rom 15:26). It is doubtful, therefore, that this list should be seen as an indication of Luke's knowledge of the collection's delivery, particularly since only Trophimus is named in the account of Paul's stay in Jerusalem (21:29). (Aristarchus strangely reappears on the ship bound to Rome in 27:2.) As Becker (*Paul*, 26) states, "If we consider further that in the list in Acts 20:4 even Philippi and Corinth, for example, are completely missing, and Gaius of Derbe does not fit the Pauline information at all, we must regard with skepticism the list from Acts and not harmonize it with the Pauline data but rather regard the latter alone as reliable."

[94] *Pace* Witherington, *Acts of the Apostles*, 618–20, who argues that Luke does not portend Paul's death.

had accused Paul before the Roman official of being an agitator and troublemaker, a ringleader of the sect of the Nazarenes, and one who had attempted to profane the temple (24:5–6). In response, after beginning with a brief *captatio benevolentiae* that acknowledges the "many years" that Felix has served as a judge for the nation,[95] Paul states, "As you are able to perceive, it is not more than twelve days since I went up to worship in Jerusalem [ἀνέβην προσκυνήσων εἰς Ἰερουσαλήμ]" (24:11).[96]

Since this assertion stands in tension with the reason given for Paul's pilgrimage to Jerusalem in the epistles, commentators often struggle to read Acts on its own terms at this point. For example, C. K. Barrett writes of v. 11, "This cannot be said to be a complete statement of Paul's purpose in coming to Jerusalem; he came as the bearer of a gift from the Gentile world (cf. v. 17), and probably with a view to some form of consultation with the leaders of the Jerusalem church."[97] Although most scholars would readily acknowledge the perils of reading information from the book of Acts into the Pauline epistles, in this case the reverse danger of reading information from Paul's letters into the narrative of Acts seems to be entirely ignored. We only know from the Corinthian correspondence and from Romans that Paul was engaged in organizing a monetary collection that would eventually take him to Jerusalem. To say that Luke has provided an incomplete statement of Paul's purpose in coming to Jerusalem is to force Acts into a Pauline mold and to fail to treat Acts as a narrative with distinctive theological interests in its own right.

Nevertheless, Barrett is surely correct to draw attention to the parallel between vv. 11 and 17, for that latter verse introduces the concluding section of Paul's carefully constructed discourse (vv. 17–21) in a way that picks up themes developed in vv. 11–13. The syntactical similarities between vv. 11 and 17 make this clear: in each sentence a first-person aorist verb of motion (ἀνέβην, παρεγενόμην) is combined with a future participle (προσκυνήσων, ποιήσων) indicating purpose.[98] Both of these units focus on the innocence of Paul's actions in Jerusalem, whereas vv. 14–16 detail Paul's relationship with "the Way." In all three of these sections, however, the activity of worship is prominent: this speech affirms that Paul "went up to Jerusalem to worship" (24:11); that Paul "worships the God of our ancestors" (24:14); and that Paul came to the temple

---

[95] See Bruce W. Winter, "The Importance of the *Captatio Benevolentiae* in the Speeches of Tertullus and Paul in Acts 24:1–21," *JTS* 42 (1991): 505–31.

[96] Here the future participle προσκυνήσων indicates purpose (cf. v. 17; Fitzmyer, *Acts of the Apostles*, 735).

[97] Barrett, *Acts of the Apostles, XV–XXVII*, 1102. Cf. Fitzmyer's comment: "No mention is made of the purpose of Paul's visit to Jerusalem, about which he himself writes (Rom 15:25–32), bringing the collected aid for the poor (cf. 1 Cor 16:1–4; 2 Cor 8:1–9:15). Paul will mention it in v. 17" (*Acts of the Apostles*, 735).

[98] Bowen, "Paul's Collection," 55.

to participate in acts of corporate worship, namely, almsgiving, sacrifices, and purification rites (24:17–18).

The speech before Felix, then, like Paul's first two defense speeches in Acts (22:1–21; 23:1–10), is specifically structured to highlight Paul as a faithful Jew. The central section of the speech accomplishes this aim by drawing attention to Paul's fidelity to the Jewish scriptures ("believing in all that is according to the law and written in the prophets," v. 14) and his hope in the Jewish doctrine of the resurrection (v. 15). Moreover, throughout the address there is an emphasis on Paul's piety, which is achieved through the depiction of his actions in Jerusalem as nothing more than peaceful worship offered by a devout Jew (vv. 12–13). It is in this context that the reference to almsgiving in v. 17 should be interpreted. Paul has come to Jerusalem in order to worship (24:11), and he has declared himself to be a worshipper of "the God of our ancestors" (24:14). Thus, his statement in v. 17 is a reiteration of this motif of worship: "Now after some years I came to give alms to my nation and sacrifices." Almsgiving, which cannot be separated from the parallel act of offering sacrifices, is an activity of worship and a demonstration of religious devotion. The most direct antecedent for the feminine relative pronoun αἷς at the beginning of v. 18 is προσφοράς, which identifies Paul's offerings as temple offerings.[99] However, because both of the feminine plural nouns ἐλεημοσύνας and προσφοράς in v. 17 are subordinated to the same future participle (ποιήσων), the construction ἐν αἷς in v. 18 should be taken as a reference to *both* almsgiving and offerings. Verse 18 could thus be paraphrased, "While I was in the temple offering alms and sacrifices, they found me completing the rite of purification, without a crowd or disturbance." This reading would locate Paul's act of almsgiving in the vicinity of the temple (cf. Acts 3:1–10) and would suggest that the recipients of this gift were not, according to Luke's narrative, members of the Christian community in Jerusalem.[100] Luke says nothing of these alms being designated for "the poor among the saints," and, more decisively, the prepositional phrase εἰς τὸ ἔθνος μου demands a wider object for this gift, namely, the Jewish nation as a whole, perhaps through the agency of its temple.[101] Therefore, far from being an allusion to the

---

[99] Tannehill, *Narrative Unity*, 2:300.

[100] *Pace* Stanley E. Porter, who avows that "Paul came to Jerusalem with a charitable gift for the Christians there (v. 17; the only mention of the gift in Acts)" ("Paul's Apologetic Speeches in Acts," in *Paul in Acts* [LPS; Peabody, Mass.: Hendrickson, 2001], 156); cf. Bruce, *Acts of the Apostles*, 480.

[101] Again, Fitzmyer's view of the phrase εἰς τὸ ἔθνος μου shows an inability to accept the narrative of Acts on its own terms. He writes, "This phrase must mean what Paul himself calls 'my brothers, my kinsmen by descent' (Rom 9:3). *In reality, however, the alms were meant for converted Jews, as one learns in Rom 15:26* ('God's dedicated people there'), but his reference also to 'unbelievers in Judea' (Rom 15:31) would not mean that he would exclude 'people of my race' from sharing in that help being brought" (*Acts of the Apostles*, 736; emphasis added). That this explana-

offering of the Gentiles, the reference to Paul's almsgiving and sacrifices in 24:17 is intended to underscore Paul's piety expressed in worship. Two other pieces of evidence from the narrative of Acts support this claim.

First, the language of almsgiving (ἐλεημοσύνη) is used seven times in three stories in the narrative of Acts, not including the reference in chapter 24 (Acts 3:2, 3, 10; 9:36; 10:2, 4, 31). Significantly, in each episode almsgiving is either connected to the activity of worship at the temple (3:1–10) or it is used to establish the piety of certain individuals (9:36–43; 10:1–33). Acts 3:1–10, for instance, reports that a lame man would customarily be placed at the gate of the Jerusalem temple where he would "ask for alms [ἐλεημοσύνην] from those entering into the temple" (3:2). Although Peter and John, when they pass by on their way into the temple, do not give this man alms upon his request (3:3), the narrative does imply a certain connection between almsgiving and temple worship similar to that found in 24:17. Next, in Acts 9:36–43 the act of almsgiving highlights the faithfulness of the female disciple Tabitha and her importance for the community of believers in Joppa. Finally, the bracketing of the Cornelius episode (10:1–33) with references to his almsgiving (10:2, 4, 31) establishes his devotion to and even favorable status before God ("Cornelius, your prayer has been heard and your alms [αἱ ἐλεημοσύναι σου] have been remembered before God!"). This triptych of stories suggests a particular nuance to the word ἐλεημοσύνη in Acts, namely, that the giving of alms is associated either with worship at the temple or acts of individual piety. This corresponds to and illuminates the depiction of Paul as a faithful Jew in the defense speech before Felix in Acts 24:10–21.

Second, closely related to Paul's avowal before Felix that he had come to Jerusalem "to give alms to my nation and sacrifices" (24:17) is the episode recounted in 21:17–26, shortly after Paul's arrival in Jerusalem. There, in response to the request of James and the elders in Jerusalem, and as a way of defending himself against accusations of disregard for the law, Paul joins in a rite of purification with four men "who are under a vow" (εὐχὴν ἔχοντες ἐφ' ἑαυτῶν) and funds the shaving of their heads. Whatever the exact nature of this vow,[102] the language of purification in 21:24, 26 undoubtedly corresponds to Paul's declaration before Felix in 24:18 that he was accosted while he was "engaged in completing the rites of purification in the temple." Not only do these three verses represent the only instances of the verb ἁγνίζω in the book of Acts, but the only occurrences of the noun προσφορά are limited to the narrative of Paul's religious activity in the temple in chapter 21 and his defense before Felix in chapter 24 (21:26; 24:17). According to the narrative of Acts, then, one plausible answer to

---

tion directly contradicts the interpretation of the gift offered in Acts 24 is symptomatic of a consistent (mis)reading of Pauline evidence *into* the narrative of Acts.

[102] Stanley Porter nicely lays out the options in "Acts 21:17–26 and Paul, the Man for All Seasons, or the Man Betrayed by his Friends," in *Paul in Acts* (LPS; Peabody, Mass.: Hendrickson, 2001), 172–86, esp. 180–81.

2.5 The Book of Acts and the Delivery of the Collection 69

the question of what exactly Paul did with the alms mentioned in 24:17, is that this money was in part used to finance the purification rites in the temple. Again, the connection to worship and piety could not be stronger.[103] This fits, also, with the note in 20:16 that Paul wanted to be in Jerusalem by the day of Pentecost and makes sense of Paul's journey to Jerusalem in the book of Acts. As Bowen recognized long ago:

> [Paul's monetary gift] was brought as a religious offering, so accepted and so presented, in the temple, in religious rites. Acts thus offers a perfectly clear and consistent picture throughout, from 20:16 to 24:17. To be sure, it is not a historic picture. Paul's letters show us that this whole construction is in error; it is none the less a perfectly coherent and possible picture....[104]

2.5.3 Conclusion

From the claim that Paul's relief fund for Jerusalem is not mentioned in Acts follows the corollary that information from the book of Acts cannot be used to complete the story of the Pauline collection left unfinished in Rom 15:25–32. The absence of any direct references or even allusions to the collection in Acts will not stop readers of Acts, who are almost always also readers of Paul's letters, from asking *why* Luke does not refer to the Pauline collection, even indirectly. Luke's silence regarding the collection does not necessarily imply his ignorance of it, although it may. Did Luke have any knowledge of the collection at all, or was this vital aspect of Paul's mission simply neglected in his sources? Without the benefit of Paul's letters, modern historians would have no knowledge of Paul's collection. If, as most think, it were true that Luke did not have access to the epistles, then he would have been entirely dependent upon his sources for information about the collection.[105] If Luke did possess some basic information about the collection, why did he refrain from mentioning it? Did he fail to understand its significance?[106] Did he know that it was illegal, a violation of Roman law concerning the transportation of money?[107] Was he aware of its rejection by the Jerusalem leadership?[108] Since Luke's failure to mention the collection prevents us from determining if he was even aware of it, these questions are essentially unanswerable, and scholars would be wise to exercise a certain degree of

---

[103] Gaventa, *Acts*, 300: "The stipulation that Paul would pay the expenses for the shaving of the heads would itself be generous indication of his piety."

[104] Bowen, "Paul's Collection," 56.

[105] Fitzmyer (*Acts of the Apostles*, 88), for example, brushes aside the question of Luke's knowledge of the epistles with but one sentence: "Lastly, I have made no mention of Paul's letters as a source of Acts, because I do not think that Luke read any of them."

[106] Ibid., 736.

[107] Nickle, *Collection*, 149–50; see also Wan, "Collection for the Saints," 191–215.

[108] Achtemeier, *Quest for Unity*, 46.

critical restraint when speculating on the reasons for the collection's absence in the narrative of Acts.

Caution should also be employed by those researching the history and theological significance of the Pauline collection itself. The obvious differences between the authentic Pauline epistles and the narrative of Acts regarding the collection have not prevented scholars from appealing to Acts in order to speculate on the final outcome of the Jerusalem collection. Stephan Joubert's use of Acts was mentioned above. With a similar appropriation of material from Acts, Byung-Mo Kim closes his section on "Die Geschichte der Kollekte" by summarizing the journey to Jerusalem described in Acts 20:4–21:17 and then by paraphrasing the account of Paul's meeting with the Jerusalem leaders and the narrative of his arrest in the temple in 21:18–36. Kim then concludes, "Die Kollekte wurde zwar dennoch von Jakobus und den sich um ihn scharenden Judenchristen angenommen, aber wohl nur inoffiziell."[109]

This section has argued, however, that such readings as Kim's stem from the improper mixing of primary and secondary sources. Events known only from the Pauline letters cannot uncritically be introduced into the narrative of Acts, and vice versa. Since it cannot be demonstrated that Luke possessed knowledge of Paul's relief fund for Jerusalem, the narrative of Acts cannot serve as a source for the chronological framework of the collection. Our knowledge of the history of the collection ends with Paul's statements in Romans 15. This is undoubtedly disappointing for interpreters who desire to know the outcome of this important economic endeavor, which demanded so much of Paul's time and attention, but historians must occasionally admit the limitations of their sources. The story of the collection for Jerusalem concludes with an open ending.

2.6 Conclusion and Implications for the Present Study

It is now possible to draw these observations together and place the events associated with the organization of a collection for Jerusalem among the Pauline churches into a relative chronological order according to the sequence arrived at above:

Before the Pauline collection:
  Paul and Barnabas travel to Jerusalem with assistance from Antioch; Jerusalem conference (Gal 2:1–10; Acts 11:27–30)
  Paul's split with Antioch and the end of his fundraising on behalf of Antioch
  1 Thessalonians
  Galatians

---

[109] Kim, *Die paulinische Kollekte*, 180; so also Nickle, *The Collection*, 70: "[It] may be confidently conjectured that the collection was well received."

The Pauline collection:
  Pauline collection and method for procurement introduced to Galatia
  Corinthians A (cf. 1 Cor 5:9); Pauline collection introduced to Corinth
  Letter and delegation from Corinth to Paul (cf. 1 Cor 1:11; 7:1)
  Corinthians B (1 Corinthians); method for collection's procurement introduced to Corinth (1 Cor 16:1–4)
  [Galatian churches abandon the collection][110]
  Paul's travel plans change; second visit to Corinth; conflict over finances (cf. 2 Cor 1:15–2:11)
  Corinthians C (Letter of Tears) sent to Corinth from Asia (2 Cor 2:1–4)
  Paul travels to Macedonia (to introduce the collection?) (2 Cor 2:13; 7:5)
  Titus brings news of Corinth's repentance to Paul (2 Cor 7:5–16)
  Corinthians D (2 Cor 1–9); Titus sent back to Corinth with the brothers
  Titus's mission fails in Corinth
  News reaches Paul of troubles involving the "super-apostles" and criticism of the collection in Corinth (cf. 2 Cor 11:7–12; 12:13–18)
  Corinthians E (2 Cor 10–13) from Macedonia
  Funds gathered in Macedonia; Paul returns to Corinth
  Collection completed in Corinth; Paul writes Romans
  Journey to Jerusalem in order to deliver the collection (Rom 15:25–32)

After the Collection:
  Philippians and Philemon[111]

What significance does this sequence of events hold for Paul's theological conception of the collection and for its meaning for the Gentile mission? At least three relevant observations can be made based on this chronological outline. First, it is immediately apparent how much time and energy Paul must have spent in the organization and delivery of the relief fund. Not only would the travels on behalf of the collection by both Paul and his delegates have demanded a considerable amount of resources, but Paul's personal zeal for the project, in spite of harsh opposition from a number of his churches, also testifies to the apostle's abiding dedication to the completion of the fund. The collection mattered greatly to Paul, both personally and theologically. To retrace the long and arduous history of the collection effort in Corinth, for example, is to be reminded that the seemingly mundane task of fundraising was for Paul a deeply

---

[110] The relative location of this development is uncertain, but I would favor a short period of time between the writing of Galatians (which does not mention the collection), the introduction of the collection to Galatia, and the failure of the collection in that region. This brief sequence is all the more likely because Paul does not mention trouble with the Galatian contribution in the Corinthian correspondence.

[111] This sequence draws on the chronological outlines of Thrall, *2 Corinthians*, 74–75, and Harris, *Second Epistle*, 101–5.

theological endeavor, one which demanded his total commitment and perseverance though intense struggle. Though the modern economic dictum tells us that "time is money," Paul's work on behalf of the collection for the saints instead reveals that, for the apostle, both time and money were worthwhile investments in a higher economy, the economy of God.[112]

Second, this chronological scenario poses a serious challenge to several earlier interpretations of the collection. Having its origins not in the agreement between Jerusalem and Antioch reflected in Gal 2:1–10, but rather in Paul's own initiative, the Pauline collection for the saints was not an obligation placed upon Paul by the authorities of the Jerusalem church. Thus, Holl's thesis that the collection was a tariff, analogous to the Jerusalem temple tax, and Stephan Joubert's attempt to analyze the collection through the framework of reciprocal relationships of benefit exchange in ancient Mediterranean societies are both called into question by the simple observation that Paul's activity on behalf of the collection was not spurred by a specific request from Jerusalem. The collection for the saints is very much an endeavor initiated and organized by the apostle Paul.

Third, this historical overview, which has covered Paul's activity in the regions of Galatia, Achaia, Asia, and Macedonia, highlights the truly translocal nature of Pauline Christianity. While the goal of the collection was first and foremost assistance for the poor among the believing community in Jerusalem, the process of organizing the fund also strengthened or created inter-city and interregional links among the various Pauline churches. The ecumenical purpose of the collection – a theme rightly stressed by a number of scholars – not only effected unity between Jews and Gentiles, but also unity among the many Gentile churches of Paul's mission. This point will become more pertinent in the next chapter, when we turn to consider analogies to the collection among the financial practices of Greco-Roman voluntary associations.

---

[112] The last phrase in this sentence comes from the provocative chapter entitled "The Economy of God: Exploring a Metaphor," in Young and Ford, *Meaning and Truth*, 166–185.

Chapter 3

The Pauline Collection and Greco-Roman Voluntary Associations

3.1 Introduction: Analogies and Social Locations

As the opening chapter demonstrated, scholars interested in the social context of the Pauline collection have proposed a number of analogies to and backgrounds for the relief fund for Jerusalem. Candidates include the temple tax paid by Jews throughout the Mediterranean world (Nickle, Wan), the Jewish custom of redemptive almsgiving (Berger, Kim), the eschatological offering of the Gentiles in the Old Testament and Second Temple Jewish literature (Munck, Beckheuer), the Greek tradition of ἐπίδοσις (Verbrugge), and the general exchange of benefits and obligations in the Mediterranean world (Joubert, Harrison). Some of these suggestions have proved more promising than others. The Jewish temple tax, for example, does bear certain similarities to Paul's collection for Jerusalem, at least in terms of the overall organizational strategies (cf. Philo, *Spec. Laws*, 1.76–78) and the general direction of the fund (that is, to Jerusalem). At the same time, there is no indication that the Pauline contribution was directed to the temple or its authorities. Other options, such as redemptive almsgiving and the eschatological pilgrimage, have, upon closer examination, proved less attractive.

If the chronological findings of the previous chapter are accurate, then Paul's collection for Jerusalem seems to have been modeled after, but not identical to, his involvement in the administration of a contribution for the church in Jerusalem during his association with the Christian community in Antioch (Acts 11:27–30). That is, when Paul conceived of and introduced the idea of a collection for Jerusalem to the congregations of his mission in Galatia and Achaia, the most obvious antecedent for the organization and delivery of the fund would have been the earlier collection from Antioch. This observation is of no small importance, for any attempt to discuss analogies to or the social context of the Pauline collection must account for the relationship between these two relief funds, in spite of the different actors and motivations involved in each offering. This is significant for at least two reasons. First, while the sources of historical information for this earlier relief fund are sparse – consisting only of Paul's allusive mention of the fund in Gal 2:10 and the brief vignette of Agabus's visit to Antioch in Acts 11:27–30 – there is no indication in the extant evidence that the

Antioch collection was modeled after traditions of the eschatological pilgrimage or redemptive almsgiving. Instead, a concern to meet the material needs of the poor in Jerusalem in the face of an imminent economic crisis seems to have been the primary motivation (Acts 11:28; Gal 2:10). Second, to judge from Luke's account, the gift was offered in response to the threat of a famine and resulted from the collective activity of the individual members of the church in Antioch (Acts 11:29: καθὼς εὐπορεῖτό τις ὥρισαν ἕκαστος αὐτῶν). Also, the organization of this collection – or at least the introduction of the notion of a gift from Antioch to Jerusalem – seems to have taken place in the context of a Christian worship assembly, a point that will become important in the following chapter. The Pauline collection for Jerusalem, then, was no unique event in world history, but was modeled on at least one earlier instance of collective assistance within the nascent Christian community.

The aim of the present chapter is to probe the socio-cultural context of the Pauline collection for Jerusalem by focusing on an additional, and heretofore underexplored, social framework for the relief fund, namely, the phenomenon of benefaction within pagan and Jewish voluntary associations.[1] Joubert's work on benefaction and obligation within ancient Mediterranean societies and Harrison's short chapter on the collection in light of Greek honorific inscriptions have pointed the way forward in the attempt to discern the socio-historical context of the collection.[2] Building on the work of recent scholarship that has suggested Greco-Roman voluntary associations as a helpful comparative model for understanding the organization of the Pauline churches, this chapter will look at benefaction, monetary collections, and the sharing of resources within ancient

---

[1] The two most recent works that attempt to situate Paul's collection for Jerusalem in the context of Greco-Roman benefaction traditions do not discuss voluntary associations (Stephan Joubert, *Paul as Benefactor: Reciprocity, Strategy and Theological Reflection in Paul's Collection* [WUNT 2:124; Tübingen: Mohr Siebeck, 2000]; James R. Harrison, *Paul's Language of Grace in Its Graeco-Roman Context* [WUNT 2:172; Tübingen: Mohr Siebeck, 2003]). Conversely, Thomas Schmeller's comparison of the Pauline communities and Greco-Roman associations, with its almost exclusive focus on 1 Corinthians, does not address the Jerusalem collection (*Hierarchie und Egalität: Eine sozialgeschichtliche Untersuchung paulinischer Gemeinden und griechisch-römischer Vereine* [Stuttgarter Bibelstudien 162; Stuttgart: Katholisches Bibelwerk, 1995]). Some brief but very helpful observations may be found in Richard S. Ascough, *Paul's Macedonian Associations: The Social Context of Philippians and 1 Thessalonians* (WUNT 2:161; Tübingen: Mohr Siebeck, 2003), 149–51. Verlyn D. Verbrugge (*Paul's Style of Church Leadership Illustrated by His Instructions to the Corinthians on the Collection* [San Francisco: Mellen Research University Press, 1992], 150–57) considers the relationship between fundraising within Greco-Roman clubs and associations, on the one hand, and the Pauline churches, on the other, but concludes that there is not "any parallel to what Paul does in 2 Corinthians 8 and 9, namely, to appeal to a large group of people for the voluntary donations [*sic*] of funds." For a fresh comparison of the communal practices of the Jerusalem community as reported in the early chapters of Acts with Greco-Roman voluntary associations, see Markus Öhler, "Die Jerusalemer Urgemeinde im Spiegel des antiken Vereinswesens," *NTS* 51 (2005): 393–415.

[2] Joubert, *Paul as Benefactor*, passim; Harrison, *Paul's Language of Grace*, 294–332.

associations. What can literary and epigraphical evidence teach us about the monetary practices of associations in antiquity, and what light do these practices shed on the socio-cultural context of the collection for Jerusalem that was organized among the churches of Paul's mission? Did pagan or Jewish associations care for the poor? Did associations establish financial links with and offer monetary support to related groups in other cities? In short, do the pecuniary practices of ancient associations offer analogous forms of giving to the Pauline collection for Jerusalem?

To speak of "analogous forms of giving" is not to suggest a genealogical relationship between the collection for the saints in Jerusalem and any one form or instance of benefaction within pagan or Jewish associations.[3] New Testament scholarship is characterized by a long and unhelpful history of seeking to identify beliefs and practices which the earliest Christian groups must have "borrowed" from any number of religious or cultural groups in antiquity, whether it be the Essenes, the mystery cults, the philosophical schools, or some other organization. Conversely, other New Testament scholars have worked to pinpoint that which is "unique" about early Christianity, oftentimes equating "unique" with "pure" and "uncorrupted," and therefore "superior." Instead, following the method for the comparative study of religions in antiquity developed by Jonathan Z. Smith, this chapter will focus on *analogies* to the Pauline collection.[4] That is, rather than concentrating on direct genealogical antecedents for the collections with which Paul was involved from the church of Antioch and the churches of his own mission, this chapter will examine comparative forms of giving within Greco-Roman associations, highlighting both similarities to and differences from the Pauline collection for Jerusalem. As Richard Ascough, in a different context, sums up his adoption of Smith's method:

> In an analogical investigation the comparative process is not undertaken to find direct relationships. One is not looking for the "earlier" exemplar, nor is one trying to determine the direction of borrowing. Rather, one type of association is compared to another in order to highlight both similarities *and* differences. Indeed, what is inherently interesting in the comparative process is not so much the similarities among various groups, although these are important, but the differences. It is precisely in finding difference that one is invited into "negotiation, classification and comparison." It is only in defin-

---

[3] See the statement by F. Cumont (*Les religions orientales dans le paganisme romain* [Paris: Leroux, 1929], ix): "Un mot n'est pas une démonstration, et il ne faut pas se hâter de conclure d'une analogie à une influence." Cited in S. C. Barton and G. H. R. Horsley, "A Hellenistic Cult Group and the New Testament Churches," *JAC* 24 (1981): 7.

[4] Jonathan Z. Smith, *Drudgery Divine: On the Comparison of Early Christianities and the Religions of Late Antiquity* (Jordan Lectures in Comparative Religion 14; Chicago: University of Chicago Press, 1990). Although Keith F. Nickle's earlier study of the collection devotes a chapter to "Analogies to Paul's Collection in Contemporary Judaism," it is clear that Nickle is really interested in Paul's "borrowing" of Jewish traditions (see *The Collection: A Study in Paul's Strategy* [SBT 48; Naperville, Ill.: Allenson, 1966], 99).

ing peculiarities that one is able to note what was distinctive about early Christian groups.[5]

After an initial summary of recent scholarship comparing the Pauline churches with Greco-Roman associations, this chapter will focus on a cluster of four interrelated issues that may shed light on the analogical relationship between the monetary practices of associations and clubs in antiquity, on the one hand, and the Pauline collection for Jerusalem, on the other. We shall consider (1) benefaction within associations; (2) common funds and monetary collections within associations; (3) care for the poor within associations; and (4) translocal economic links among associations. Much of the available evidence for these practices comes from epigraphical sources, and is therefore both geographically and temporally diverse. I shall try to focus on evidence for associations in the Greek East, for the most part omitting information from the Roman *collegia* in the West. Some data from Greek associations in the Roman West will be considered, however. Given the tendency of inscriptions to follow rather formalized patterns of language, combined with nature of the comparative task, which focuses on analogical rather than chronological relationships, I have included evidence from a fairly broad temporal range, considering epigraphical sources from a few centuries before and a few centuries after the life of Paul.[6] Finally, since much recent research on associations in antiquity has incorporated evidence from Jewish synagogues – drawing on comments from Josephus and Philo, inscriptional evidence, and comparisons between the Essenes and Greco-Roman associations – where appropriate this chapter will make use of information from Jewish as well as pagan groups.[7] Indeed, it is now considered axiomatic that, while these institu-

---

[5] Ascough, *Paul's Macedonian Associations*, 2. Quotation from Smith, *Drudgery Divine*, 42. See also Jonathan Z. Smith, *To Take Place: Toward Theory in Ritual* (Chicago: University of Chicago Press, 1987), 13–14. There Smith writes, "It is axiomatic that comparison is never a matter of identity. Comparison requires the acceptance of difference as the grounds of its being interesting, and a methodological manipulation of that difference to achieve some stated cognitive end. The questions of comparison are questions of judgment with respect to difference: What differences are to be maintained in the interests of comparative inquiry? What differences can be defensibly relaxed and relativized in light of the intellectual tasks at hand?"

[6] On the formulaic nature of epigraphical language, particularly in honorific inscriptions, see Bradley H. McLean, *An Introduction to Greek Epigraphy of the Hellenistic and Roman Periods from Alexander the Great down to the Reign of Constantine* (323 B.C.–A.D. 337), 181–214, 228–45; and Friedemann Quass, "Bemerkungen zur 'Honoratiorenherrschaft' in den griechischen Städten der hellenistischen Zeit," *Gymnasium* 99 (1992): 422–34.

[7] For comparisons of the Essenes and collegia, see Moshe Weinfeld, *The Organizational Pattern and the Penal Code of the Qumran Sect: A Comparison with Guilds and Religious Associations of the Hellenistic-Roman Period* (NTOA 2; Göttingen: Vandenhoeck & Ruprecht, 1986); Matthias Klinghardt, "The Manual of Discipline in Light of Statutes of Hellenistic Associations," in *Methods of Investigation of the Dead Sea Scrolls and the Khirbet Qumran Site: Present Realities and Future Prospects* (ed. Michael O. Wise, Norman Golb, John J. Collins, and Dennis G. Pardee; Annals of the New York Academy of Sciences 722; New York: New York Academy of Sciences, 1994), 251–70; Sandra

tions were never identical, pagan associations, Jewish synagogues, and Christian churches were nevertheless formed in response to and conducted their activities in the midst of similar economic, social, and political conditions, and are therefore worthy of comparative inquiry.[8] To the outside observer, associations, synagogues, and churches may have been nearly indistinguishable. Sharp distinctions between these groups, either in terms of internal organization or legal classification, are, then, no longer justifiable.[9]

A brief word of caution on the use of inscriptional evidence is in order. While inscriptions do shed important light on the beliefs and practices of ancient associations, these public monuments represent a very different medium of information than Paul's letters. The "epigraphic habit in the Roman Empire," as Ramsay MacMullen memorably dubbed the common ancient convention of inscribing and advertising certain facts on stone, served an important public func-

---

Walker-Ramisch, "Graeco-Roman Voluntary Associations and the Damascus Document: A Sociological Analysis," in *Voluntary Associations in the Ancient World* (ed. John S. Kloppenborg and Stephen G. Wilson; London and New York: Routledge, 1996), 128–45; and Albert Baumgarten, "Graeco-Roman Voluntary Associations and Ancient Jewish Sects," in *Jews in a Graeco-Roman World* (ed. Martin Goodman; Oxford: Clarendon, 1998), 93–111.

[8] The fact that evidence from three different types of communities will be considered actually serves to assist the comparative task. As Smith points out, comparison necessarily implies three rather than two objects of observation. Thus, the statement "*x* resembles *y*" is "logically incomplete," for what is really intended is "*x* resembles *y* more than *z* with respect to ..." (*Drudgery Divine*, 51). Smith goes on to say, "the statement of comparison is never dyadic, but always triadic; there is always an implicit 'more than,' and there is always a 'with respect to'" (*Drudgery Divine*, 51).

[9] See Peter Richardson, "Early Synagogues as Collegia in the Diaspora and Palestine," in *Voluntary Associations in the Graeco-Roman World* (ed. John S. Kloppenborg and Stephen G. Wilson; London and New York: Routledge, 1996), 90–109; and Philip A. Harland, *Associations, Synagogues, and Congregations: Claiming a Place in Ancient Mediterranean Society* (Minneapolis: Fortress, 2003), passim. Vincent Gabrielsen ("The Rhodian Associations and Economic Activity," in *Hellenistic Economies* [ed. Zofia H. Archibald, John Davies, Vincent Gabrielsen, and G. J. Oliver; London and New York: Routledge, 2001], 218) writes: "[Historically] specific associations (here, those of Rhodes) [are] components of an overarching but temporally multi-layered structure which covered an infinitely larger spatial and chronological horizon, and which, according to a fourth-century BC thinking, owed its existence to the deep-seated mental habit of pooling and articulating human action through *koinoniai* (Arist. *Pol.* 1253a30–31): hence the semantic as well as historical spaciousness of the word *koinon*. Supra- or pre-*polis* organizations are as much part of that larger structure as are the '*polis*'-version of a political community and its constituent parts (public or private), 'such as (those of) *phrateres* or *orgeones* or business partnerships' (Arist. *Eth. Eud.* 1241b25–27). Religious or cultic orientation and conviviality are putatively among the earliest and definitely least transient layers of that structure, bringing into some degree of contact such (synchronically and/or diachronically) discrete groups as the *gene*, *orgeones*, the various *thiasoi*, the 'hell-fire clubs' at Athens, the *philosophiai* (notably the Epicurean and Stoic schools), the plethora of Roman *collegia*, the Therapeutai near Alexandria and their (altogether different in character) namesakes on Delos, the worshippers of Mithras and the Khirbet Qumran covenanters – to mention only some."

tion in antiquity, and inscriptional evidence is a boon for social historians.[10] Yet "inscriptions do not tell the whole story, and it is the things that were taken for granted and were not worth recording that we most want to know."[11] As Philip Harland points out, "We have personal letters pertaining to early Christian groups (reflecting personal interactions), but rarely have we any literary or epistolary evidence for the internal life of associations."[12] Moreover, since inscriptions broadcast only what groups wanted to make public, there is a high likelihood that the epigraphic production of Greco-Roman voluntary associations accentuated the official and competitive aspects of corporate activity, while minimizing the more informal elements of group life.[13] The rhetoric of inscriptions, therefore, may conceal as much as it reveals. In addition, while inscriptions and papyri may give us "the clearest 'window' into 'popular culture',"[14] the prohibitive cost of engraving a text on stone means that the voices of the poorest members of society, including the impoverished within associations, are not likely to be preserved in the epigraphic record.[15]

---

[10] Ramsay MacMullen, "The Epigraphic Habit in the Roman Empire," *AJPh* 103 (1982): 233–46.

[11] Russell Meiggs, *Roman Ostia* (2d ed.; Oxford: Clarendon, 1973), 313. Occasionally inscriptions allow us a peek behind the curtains, so to speak, to glimpse something of the reality behind the stone. Guy M. Rogers's article "Demosthenes of Oenoanda and Models of Euergetism," *JRS* 81 (1991): 91–100 offers a fascinating look at the tensions and conflicts between one civic benefactor, C. Iulius Demosthenes, and city councilors in Oenoanda as they carefully negotiated the establishment of a festival sponsored by Demosthenes.

[12] Philip A. Harland, "Familial Dimensions of Group Identity: 'Brothers' ('Αδελφοί) in Associations of the Greek East," *JBL* 124 (2005): 495.

[13] Gabrielsen, "The Rhodian Associations and Economic Activity," 219.

[14] Justin J. Meggitt, *Paul, Poverty and Survival* (Studies of the New Testament and Its World; Edinburgh: T & T Clark, 1998), 30.

[15] See the helpful comments in Onno M. Van Nijf, *The Civic World of Professional Associations in the Roman East* (Dutch Monographs on Ancient History and Archaeology 17; Amsterdam: J. C. Gieben, 1997), 23–28. Evidence from the earliest Christian communities is, of course, noticeably absent from the epigraphic record. While this absence may be no more than an accident of history, MacMullen's attempt to provide a psychological explanation for the decrease in epigraphical output in the Roman empire after about the middle of the second century C.E. may shed some light on the seeming avoidance of inscriptions among the early Christians. MacMullen ("Epigraphic Habit," 246) writes, "Apparently the rise and fall of the epigraphic habit was controlled by what we can only call the sense of audience. In the exercise of the habit, people (I can only suppose) counted on their world still continuing in existence for a long time to come, so as to make nearly permanent memorials worthwhile; and they still felt themselves members of a special civilization, proud (or obliged) to behave as such. Later, in not bothering any more to record on stone their names or any other claim to attention, perhaps they expressed their doubts about the permanence or importance of that world. Perhaps. At least I cannot see in the evidence anything less than the sign of some very broad psychological shift." Might the eschatological expectations of the earliest Christians also be counted as one factor in their apparent aversion to the epigraphic habit?

3.2 The Pauline Churches and Greco-Roman Associations

Voluntary associations may be defined as "associations of persons more or less permanently organized for the pursuit of a common end, and so distinguishable both from the state and its component elements on the one hand, and on the other from temporary unions for ephemeral purposes."[16] Although Greek associations and clubs are attested as early as classical Athens, during the Imperial period numerous ethnic, professional, cultic, and artistic associations flourished in the urban centers of the Greco-Roman world.[17] Known by a variety of names – including κοινόν, θίασος, ἔρανος, and *collegium* – and serving assorted purposes, these diverse groups provided alternative and sometimes competing forms of social organization to both kinship and the *polis*.[18] While it was once popular in the study of associations to classify these groups according to their primary purpose – either occupational, cultic, or burial – recent scholarship has emphasized the need for greater taxonomic flexibility, especially given the fact that associations chartered specifically for burial purposes do not seem to have existed before the time of Hadrian.[19] John Kloppenborg has suggested that "a better taxonomy of collegia would be based on the profile of their membership, especially since the actual functions of various collegia overlapped to a substantial degree."[20] Thus, members of associations might be united by household connections, ethnic identity, occupational ties, or common cultic devotion.[21] In reality, however, it is often difficult to draw clear distinctions, particularly with respect to religion, since every association in the Hellenistic and Roman periods sponsored cultic as well as social activities.[22]

---

[16] Marcus Niebuhr Tod and Simon Hornblower, "Clubs, Greek," *OCD*, 351. See also S. G. Wilson, "Voluntary Associations: An Overview," in *Voluntary Associations in the Graeco-Roman World* (ed. John S. Kloppenborg and Stephen G. Wilson; London and New York: Routledge, 1996), 1–15; Walker-Ramisch, "Graeco-Roman Voluntary Associations and the Damascus Document," 131.

[17] On associations in classical Athens, see Nicholas F. Jones, *The Associations of Classical Athens: The Response to Democracy* (New York and Oxford: Oxford University Press, 1999).

[18] On the relationship between associations and the *polis*, see Paul Foucart, *Les associations religieuses chez les Grecs: Thiases, éranes, orgéons* (Paris: Klincksieck, 1873), 50–53; Gabrielsen, "The Rhodian Associations and Economic Activity," 215–44; Wayne A. Meeks, *The First Urban Christians: The Social World of the Apostle Paul* (New Haven and London: Yale University Press, 1983), 31. For a more complete list and discussion of names for associations, see Franz Poland, *Geschichte des griechischen Vereinswesens* (Leipzig: Teubner, 1909), 5–172.

[19] John S. Kloppenborg, "Collegia and *Thiasoi*: Issues in Function, Taxonomy and Membership," in *Voluntary Associations in the Graeco-Roman World* (ed. John S. Kloppenborg and Stephen G. Wilson; London and New York: Routledge, 1996), 20–22; and Frank M. Ausbüttel, *Untersuchungen zu den Vereinen im Westen des römischen Reiches* (Frankfurter Althistorische Studien 11; Kallmünz: Michael Lassleben, 1982), 22–29.

[20] Kloppenborg, "Collegia and *Thiasoi*," 23.

[21] See Harland, *Associations, Synagogues, and Congregations*, 28–53.

[22] Cf. the statement by Franz Poland (*Geschichte des griechischen Vereinswesens*, 5): "In gewissem

There is a long history of comparing the earliest Christian churches to Greco-Roman associations. Indeed, some of the first opponents and observers of nascent Christianity made explicit connections between churches and *collegia*. Pliny's letters reveal that, in the early years of the second century C.E., Christians in Bithynia-Pontus had ceased meeting after an edict, authorized by Trajan, banned political clubs (*Ep. Tra.* 10.96.7), a revelation which suggests that both the Christians and their persecutors ranked Christian assemblies with pagan associations (*quod ipsum facere desisse post edictum meum, quo secundum mandata tua hetaerias esse vetueram*). Lucian of Samosata (born ca. 120 C.E.) calls the charismatic yet duplicitous figure Peregrinus, during his spell as a Christian, a "prophet, cult-leader, head of the synagogue, and everything, all by himself" (προφήτης καὶ θιασάρχης καὶ ξυναγωγεὺς καὶ πάντα μόνος αὐτὸς ὤν; *Peregr.* 11). Lucian also characterizes Jesus as the initiator of a mystery cult (τελετής; *Peregr.* 11), employing a term that is used in inscriptions to refer to officials of associations (cf. SEG 46:745). Later, Tertullian (ca. 160–ca. 240) includes the Christian community among the associations when he asks, "Should not this school have been classed among tolerated associations (*licitas factions sectam istam deputari oportebat*), when it commits no such actions as are commonly feared from unlawful associations?" (*Apol.* 38.1).

Following the spate of epigraphical publications focused on Greco-Roman clubs and guilds in the nineteenth and early twentieth centuries,[23] a number of modern scholars began to draw attention to connections between churches and associations. Edwin Hatch, for example, in the 1880 Bampton Lectures at Oxford University, highlighted several parallels between these groups:

> [To] the eye of the outside observer [the Christian communities] were in the same category as the associations which already existed. They had the same names for their meetings, and some of the same names for their officers. The basis of association, in the one case as the other, was the profession of a common religion. The members, in the one case as in the other, contributed to or received from a common fund, and in many cases, if not universally, shared in a common meal. Admission was open, in the one case

---

Sinne ist jeder Verein ein Kultverein, weil die religiösen Vorstellungen, vor allem die religiösen Feste fast überall von grosser Bedeutung sind." This same idea is expressed also in the pioneering work of Edwin Hatch (*The Organization of the Early Christian Churches: Eight Lectures Delivered Before the University of Oxford in the Year 1880* [Bampton Lectures; London: Rivingtons, 1881], 27–28): "Almost all associations seem to have had a religious element: they were under the protection of a tutelary divinity, in the same way as at the present day similar associations on the continent of Europe invoke the name of a patron saint."

[23] E.g., Theodore Mommsen, *De collegiis et sodaliciis romanorum* (Kiliae: Libraria Schwersiana, 1843); Foucart, *Les associations religieuses*; Willy Liebenam, *Zur Geschichte und Organisation des römischen Vereinswesens: Drei Untersuchungen* (Leipzig: Teubner, 1890); J. P. Waltzing, *Étude historique sur les corporations professionnelles chez les Romains depuis les origines jusqu'à la chute de l'empire d'Occident* (4 vols.; Louvain: Peeters, 1895–1900).

as in the other, not only to free-born citizens, but to women and strangers, to freedmen and slaves.[24]

These observations were part of Hatch's larger attempt to explain the origin of the offices of bishop, elder, and deacon in the early church as positions of financial management, similar in many ways to the ἐπιμελητής of a Greco-Roman association (cf. CIG 119, 120; IG II² 1261, 1324). Hatch's basic thesis was not broadly accepted, however, and the widespread rejection of Hatch's work may have been due in part to the desire among contemporaries of Hatch to insulate early Christianity from the tainting of pagan influence.[25] Yet several other researchers in Hatch's day, including Ernest Renan and Georg Heinrici, found fruitful comparisons for the early church among cultic associations.[26]

In more recent times, a number of New Testament scholars have continued the exploration of Greco-Roman voluntary associations as a possible social analogy to the Pauline churches.[27] Some have drawn attention to the numerous similarities between the groups, particularly in terms of organizational structures, open membership (including membership for women), the socio-economic status of members, cultic and ritual practices, linguistic terminology, and financial activities. Others, like Wayne Meeks in his influential book *The First Urban Christians*, have found the comparison interesting but ultimately wanting.[28] Meeks points to a number of similarities between these two groups – including size, membership by choice rather than birth, cultic activities and common meals, burial provisions, dependence (to some extent) on the benefaction of patrons, and democratic organization.

In the end, however, Meeks concludes that several significant differences indicate that "the Christian groups did not consciously model themselves on the associations."[29] Meeks points to four variations that militate against the conclu-

---

[24] Hatch, *Organization of the Early Christian Churches*, 30–31.

[25] See Smith, *Drudgery Divine*, 58–62.

[26] See the helpful article by John S. Kloppenborg, "Edwin Hatch, Churches, and *Collegia*," in *Origins and Method: Towards a New Understanding of Judaism and Christianity; Essays in Honour of John C. Hurd* (ed. Bradley H. McLean; JSNTSup 86; Sheffield: JSOT Press, 1993), 212–38; see also Ascough, *Paul's Macedonian Associations*, 3–10; and Dietrich-Alex Koch and Dirk Schinkel, "Die Frage nach den Vereinen in der Geistes- und Theologiegeschichte des 19. und 20. Jahrhunderts," in *Vereine, Synagogen und Gemeinden im kaiserzeitlichen Kleinasien* (ed. Andreas Gutsfeld and Dietrich-Alex Koch; STAC 25; Tübingen: Mohr Siebeck, 2006), 129–48.

[27] A summary of modern scholarship may be found in Richard S. Ascough, *What Are They Saying About the Formation of the Pauline Churches?* (New York and Mahwah, N.J.: Paulist, 1998), 71–94.

[28] Meeks, *First Urban Christians*, 77–80.

[29] Ibid., 79. In the comparative task elucidated by Jonathan Z. Smith, where the focus is on similarities and differences, one is not so much interested in the question of what the earliest churches may have "consciously modeled" their community on, even if we possessed adequate evidence to determine such an intentional emulation. Another interesting methodological approach is Loveday Alexander's "ancient reader-response criticism," which she applies to the relationship between Paul's churches and ancient schools. Alexander's interest lies in what a curious

sion that nascent Christian congregations were analogous to pagan associations. First, "Christian groups were exclusive and totalistic in a way that no club nor even any pagan cultic association was."[30] For the Pauline churches, according to Meeks, "the sect was intended to become virtually the primary group for its members, supplanting all other loyalties."[31] Second, Christian communities were "much more inclusive in terms of social stratification and other social categories than were the voluntary associations."[32] Third, Meeks highlights "the almost complete absence of common terminology for the groups themselves or for their leaders."[33] Fourth, the associations did not experience the same "extralocal linkages of the Christian movement": "Each association, even those that served the internationally popular deities, was a self-contained local phenomenon."[34] According to Meeks, therefore, among the several models of community to which the earliest Pauline groups might profitably be compared – including the household, the voluntary association, the synagogue, or the philosophic or rhetorical school – the household "remains the basic context within which most if not all the local Pauline groups established themselves," and the synagogue stands as "the nearest and most natural model."[35]

Upon closer examination of the primary evidence, however, Meeks's four objections need to be nuanced, if not altogether eliminated. First, recent scholarship has challenged Meeks's sectarian approach to group identity and its attendant claim that both synagogues and churches were "exclusive and totalistic in a way that no club nor even any pagan cultic association was."[36] On the one hand, there is evidence that points to the involvement of Jews and Christians with both civic and associational bodies, suggesting that membership in a synagogue or a church did not demand that one cut off other social ties.[37] On the other hand,

---

Greek or Roman observer might have thought of the Pauline communities had she or he stumbled across one of their meetings. See Loveday Alexander, "Paul and the Hellenistic Schools: The Evidence of Galen," in *Paul in His Hellenistic Context* (ed. Troels Engberg-Pedersen; Minneapolis: Fortress, 1995), 60–83; idem, *"IPSE DIXIT*: Citation of Authority in Paul and in the Jewish and Hellenistic Schools," in *Paul Beyond the Judaism/Hellenism Divide* (ed. Troels Engberg-Pedersen; Louisville: Westminster John Knox, 2001), 103–27.

[30] Meeks, *First Urban Christians*, 78.

[31] Ibid., 78.

[32] Ibid., 79.

[33] Ibid.

[34] Ibid., 80. For other scholars who make this particular point, see Wayne O. McCready, "*Ekklēsia* and Voluntary Associations," in *Voluntary Associations in the Graeco-Roman World* (ed. John S. Kloppenborg and Stephen G. Wilson; London and New York: Routledge, 1996), 63–64; and Barton and Horsley, "Hellenistic Cult Group," 28.

[35] Meeks, *First Urban Christians*, 84, 80.

[36] Ibid., 30. For a refutation of this view, see Harland, *Associations, Synagogues, and Congregations*, 182–95.

[37] Harland, *Associations, Synagogues, and Congregations*, 183–212. One thinks, for example, of the donations to the city of Smyrna from a group of Jews during the reign of Hadrian (IJO 2:40), or

associations did occasionally make exclusive claims on their members (PLond 2710; PLond 2193).[38] It is, of course, true that individuals could often maintain membership in numerous, and in some instances even dozens of, pagan associations (cf. IG II[2] 1325, 1326, 1327).[39] An inscription from Hellenistic Rhodes (IG XII/1 155), for example, shows that in the second century B.C.E. one Dionysodoros from Alexandria was a member of no less than four Rhodian associations, serving as chief-eranistes of the Haliadai and Haliastai association for some twenty-three years, while concurrently holding the same position in the Paniastai *koinon*.[40] At the same time, associations did compete with one another for members and benefactions, and there is some evidence for claims of religious exclusivity among some pagan voluntary associations.[41]

Second, it does not appear that the Christian groups were in every instance more inclusive than pagan associations, or that the membership of pagan associations was necessarily more "socially homogeneous." While the Pauline house churches in Corinth do seem to have been composed of a wide cross-section of society – including slaves, freedmen, wealthy individuals, and perhaps even members of the local elite – some of Paul's churches may have been more demographically homogeneous. Richard Ascough, for example, has recently argued that, given the abundant references to manual labor in the Thessalonian correspondence (cf. 1 Thess 2:9; 4:11), the church in Thessalonica was similar to a professional voluntary association, its members workers in the same guild (and perhaps also predominantly male, an exception among the Pauline churches).[42] At the same time, while the social composition of the Pauline churches may not

---

of Erastus's coterminous involvement with the Corinthian church and his service as ὁ οἰκονόμος τῆς πόλεως of Corinth (Rom 16:23; cf. the first-century inscription identifying an Erastus as *aedile* in Corinth in J. H. Kent, *Inscriptions 1926–1950: Corinth viii. Part Three* [Princeton: The American School of Classical Studies at Athens, 1966], 99; Bruce W. Winter, *Seek the Welfare of the City: Christians as Benefactors and Citizens* [Grand Rapids: Eerdmans, 1994], 179–97).

[38] See C. H. Roberts, T. C. Skeat, and A. D. Nock, "The Guild of Zeus Hypsistos," HTR 29 (1936): 39–88.

[39] On membership in multiple associations, see Meiggs, *Roman Ostia*, 321–23; Ascough, *Paul's Macedonian Associations*, 87–91; Philip A. Harland, "Spheres of Contention, Claims of Preeminence: Rivalries among Associations in Sardis and Smyrna," in *Religious Rivalries and the Struggle for Success in Sardis and Smyrna* (ed. Richard S. Ascough; SSEJC 14; Waterloo, Ontario: Wilfrid Laurier University Press, 2005), 53–63, esp. 59–61.

[40] Vincent Gabrielsen, "The Rhodian Associations Honouring Dionysodoros from Alexandria," *Classica et Mediaevalia* 45 (1994): 137–60.

[41] Harland, *Associations, Synagogues, and Congregations*, 183; Ascough, *Paul's Macedonian Associations*, 88–91; cf. ISardH 4; PLond 2193. The evidence for competition and exclusivity among pagan associations is discussed in Harland, "Spheres of Contention," 53–63.

[42] Ascough, *Paul's Macedonian Associations*, 162–90. There is no need to assume a uniform model of church in the letters of Paul. The diverse geographical and socioeconomic locations of the Pauline mission will have led to different organizational and demographic patterns in different churches. See Kloppenborg, "Edwin Hatch," 232; and David J. Downs, "'Early Catholicism' and Apocalypticism in the Pastoral Epistles," CBQ 67 (2005): 647.

have been as consistently diverse as is often assumed, many pagan associations were more socially and economically inclusive than Meeks admits. For instance, an inscription from a first-century association of fishermen and fishmongers in Ephesus records the donations made by about one hundred members of the group for the construction of a customs house for fishers (NewDocs 5:5). The contributions, which are listed roughly in order of value from greatest to least, range from the funds for the construction of four columns, to fifty denarii, to five denarii at the end of the list. If the value of these donations is any indication of the economic status of the individual members of the group, we should expect that this association was characterized by some degree of socio-economic diversity. More explicitly, the regulations of a first-century B.C.E. cultic association in Philadelphia are emphatically inclusive: three times the formula "men and women, free people and slaves" (ἄνδρες καὶ γυναῖκες ἐλεύθεροι καὶ οἰκέται) is repeated in the description of those to whom access to the *oikos* is permitted (SIG³ 985 = LSAM 20, *lines* 5–6, 15–16, 53–54).[43]

Third, the issue of terminological overlap needs to be revisited. A diverse array of designations was used to refer to pagan associations and their leaders in the Greco-Roman world, and these do often overlap with technical terms used within Pauline and Jewish communities.[44] For example, although the most common titles for pagan associations include κοινόν, θίασος, ἔρανος, and συναγωγή, there are several instances in which an association is referred to as an ἐκκλησία (IDelos 1519 = Foucart 43; LBW 1381, 1382; OGI 488). Moreover, while the Pauline communities were characterized by a variety of leadership titles and structures, several leadership designations that do occur in the Pauline corpus (ἐπίσκοπος, διάκονος, and προστάτις) are also found in the context of pagan associations.[45] Aside from similarities in the terms used for groups and leaders, Greek associations and Jewish synagogues, like the Pauline churches, occasionally employed the rhetoric of fictive kinship and other expressions of familial

---

[43] A text, translation, and commentary are provided in Barton and Horsley, "Hellenistic Cult Group," 7–41. Recently, Stanley K. Stowers ("A Cult from Philadelphia: Oikos Religion or Cultic Association," in *Early Christianity in Its Context: Essays in Honor of Everett Ferguson* [ed. Abraham J. Malherbe, Frederick W. Norris, and James W. Thompson; NovTSup 90; Leiden and Boston: Brill, 1998], 287–301) has argued that SIG³ 985 represents the regulations of a household cult rather than a cultic voluntary association. His reading of this inscription is open to debate, however, and his admission that "friends and relatives of the household living outside may also have played a part" in the cultic activities highlights the difficulty of drawing sharp distinctions between voluntary and household associations. On the issue of inclusivity among pagan associations, see also Bradley H. McLean, "The Agrippinilla Inscription: Religious Associations and Early Church Formation," in *Origins and Method: Towards a New Understanding of Judaism and Christianity; Essays in Honour of John C. Hurd* (ed. Bradley H. McLean; JSNTSup 86; Sheffield: JSOT Press, 1993), 239–70.

[44] Kloppenborg, "Edwin Hatch," 231–34.

[45] For a discussion of these technical titles see Kloppenborg, "Edwin Hatch," 231–34; Ascough, *Paul's Macedonian Associations*, 79–83.

identity to symbolize the nature of the community formed within these groups (cf. IKilikiaBM 2:201).[46]

Finally, it is not necessarily the case that pagan voluntary associations lacked "extralocal linkages." An important article by Richard Ascough has demonstrated that Meeks overstates the extralocal nature of many early Christian groups, on the one hand, and neglects evidence that points to translocal links among pagan associations, on the other.[47] Several of these translocal connections will be addressed below.

This reconsideration of the primary evidence in light of the four points of difference between the Pauline churches and Greco-Roman clubs and guilds highlighted by Meeks suggests that pagan and Jewish voluntary associations can, in fact, serve as a helpful analogical model for the social formation of the congregations of Paul's mission. It is to the comparison of the financial practices of these different groups that we now turn.

3.3 Benefaction within Associations

In his treatise on the giving and receiving of benefits, the Roman philosopher and politician Lucius Annaeus Seneca calls the practice of bestowing benefactions "the chief bond of human society" (*Ben.* 1.4.2; *maxime humanam societatem alligat*).[48] Modern study of gift-giving in antiquity has confirmed the acuity of Seneca's observation. Social institutions such as patronage and benefaction were deeply integral aspects of the distribution of goods and services in the Greco-Roman world. Urban centers throughout the Mediterranean region were crowded with architectural commemorations – in the form of tombs, honorific inscriptions, monuments, and statues – that memorialized and praised wealthy patrons and benefactors who had rendered assistance to cities and other private organizations, including voluntary associations.

Historians and sociologists typically draw upon two models to understand gift-giving practices in the cities of the late-Hellenistic and Roman eras: *patronage* and *benefaction*. In the Roman West, much attention has been paid to the subject of patronage (*patrocinium*). Richard Saller, in his pioneering monograph *Personal*

---

[46] Harland, "Familial Dimensions of Group Identity"; idem, "Familial Dimensions of Group Identity (II): 'Mothers' and 'Fathers' in Associations and Synagogues of the Greek World," *JSJ* 38 (2007): 57–79; cf. Öhler, "Die Jerusalemer Urgemeinde," 399–401.

[47] Richard S. Ascough, "Translocal Relationships among Voluntary Associations and Early Christianity," *JECS* 5 (1997): 223–41.

[48] For a study of Seneca's views of gift-giving, see Stephan Joubert, "Coming to Terms with a Neglected Aspect of Ancient Mediterranean Reciprocity: Seneca's Views on Benefit-Exchange in *De beneficiis* as the Framework for a Model of Social Exchange," in *Social Scientific Models for Interpreting the Bible: Essays by the Context Group in Honor of Bruce J. Malina* (ed. John J. Pilch; Biblical Interpretation 53; Leiden: Brill, 2001), 47–63.

Patronage under the Early Empire, provides the standard sociological definition of Roman patronage:[49]

> First, it involves the *reciprocal* exchange of goods and services. Secondly, to distinguish it from commercial transaction in the marketplace, the relationship must be a personal one of some duration. Thirdly, it must be asymmetrical, in the sense that the two parties are of unequal status and offer different kinds of goods and services in the exchange – a quality which sets patronage off from friendship between equals.[50]

Patronal relationships pervaded ancient society, even, one may argue, where the terminology of patronage was not expressly employed or where it was, as in the case of classical Athens, consciously avoided.[51] Studies of patronage in antiquity tend to focus on the relationships of individual patrons to individual clients,[52]

---

[49] I call Saller's definition "sociological" in the sense that he avoids the more legal/institutional approach to patronage, which asserts that patronal relationships existed only when the corresponding terminology of patronage – *patrocinium, patronatus, cliens* – is present. The legal/institutional approach, therefore, would deny that patronage existed in the Greek world. A sociological model of patronage is presented in S. N. Eisenstadt and Louis Roniger, "Patron-Client Relations as a Model of Structuring Social Exchange," *Comparative Studies in Society and History* 22 (1980): 42–77. For a recent defense of the legal/institutional understanding of patronage, see Claude Eilers, *Roman Patrons of Greek Cities* (Oxford Classical Monographs; Oxford: Oxford University Press, 2002); cf. G. E. M. De Ste. Croix, "Suffragium: From Vote to Patronage," *British Journal of Sociology* 5 (1954): 33–48.

[50] Richard Saller, *Personal Patronage under the Early Empire* (Cambridge: Cambridge University Press, 1982), 1. To Saller's definition should be added the qualification that patronage represents a *voluntary relationship*, which sets it apart from slavery, for example. So Peter Garnsey and Greg Woolf, "Patronage of the Rural Poor in the Roman World," in *Patronage in Ancient Society* (ed. Andrew Wallace-Hadrill; London and New York: Routledge, 1989), 154.

[51] See Paul Millett, "Patronage and Its Avoidance in Classical Athens," in *Patronage in Ancient Society* (ed. Andrew Wallace-Hadrill; London and New York: Routledge, 1989), 15–47; and John Rich, "Patronage and Interstate Relations in the Roman Republic," in *Patronage in Ancient Society* (ed. Andrew Wallace-Hadrill; London and New York: Routledge, 1989), 117–35. One problem with the legal/institutional approach to patronage is that it runs the risk of ignoring obviously patronal relationships simply because the explicit language of patronage is not present. As Rich shows, the Romans rarely, if ever, referred to their "client states" as *clientela*, choosing instead more polite designations like *amicus* ("friend") and *socius* ("ally"). This does not mean that Rome was not a patron of those territories it conquered, however. The absence of the terminology does not indicate the absence of the relationship. One thinks in this context of Paul Veyne's twinkle-eyed critique of the historian Premerstein: "The great historian has been the victim of a philological convention, that of seeking to interpret the realities of an epoch solely through the concepts and symbols of that epoch. Consequently one is not allowed to assert that the sky over Rome was blue and that the Romans had two arms and two legs, if chance has it that these facts are not mentioned in any of the ancient writings which have survived" (*Bread and Circuses: Historical Sociology and Political Pluralism* [trans. Brian Pearce; London and New York: Penguin, 1990], 346; trans. of *Le Pain et le cirque* [Paris: Éditions du Seuil, 1976]).

[52] See, e.g., the illustrative statement by Holland Hendrix ("Benefactor/Patron Networks in the Urban Environment: Evidence from Thessalonica," *Semeia* 56 [1991]: 40): "Generally speaking, the use of the term 'benefactor' (*euergetes*) and other associated terms such as 'good will'

perhaps because of the assumption that "promoting vertical ties of solidarity above horizontal ones led to a conflict with other forms of solidarity between social equals, such as private associations."[53] Yet Garnsey and Woolf suggest that patronage was, in fact, able to "coexist" with other forms of social exchange, such as "charity and euergetism (philanthropy or public benefaction), and support provided by other members of the poor man's family, village or town."[54] Moreover, there is ample evidence for the existence of patronal relationships – using the language of *patrocinium* and *patronus* (or the Greek transliteration πάτρων) – between members of the Roman elite, on the one hand, and civic bodies and municipalities, on the other, evidence which indicates that both Romans and Greeks were able to conceptualize patronage as a system of exchange between individuals and communities.[55] Finally, along with serving as patrons of cities, wealthy men and women also patronized numerous *collegia*, both in Italy and in the Greek East, as a number of recent studies have shown.[56]

The second model used to understand gift-giving practices in the cities of the Greco-Roman world is that of benefaction, or "euergetism."[57] Greek society was also characterized by the importance of networks of benefaction and gift exchange. Citizens of the *polis*, as well as wealthy foreigners, were able to accumulate significant public honor and praise by disseminating benefactions, or *euergesiai*, which might have come in the form of the construction of civic buildings or temples, the funding of religious festivals or banquets, or the subsidizing of grain prices during times of food shortage. Here the civic nature of benefaction is paramount, as is seen in Philippe Gauthier's definition of euergetism:

(*eunoia*), 'commitment to the good' (*philagathia*), and 'manifest excellence' (*arete*) reflects *corporate activity*. A durable corporate group with fixed structural properties grants corporate honors and amenities to one who has benefited the group. Patron-client terminology generally reflects *a more individualized phenomenon* in which one party is bound to another through specific transactions or the assumption of particular obligations" (emphasis added). That Hendrix goes on to cite and discuss epigraphical evidence that challenges this statement is an indication that his pragmatic distinction between "benefaction" as a corporate activity and "patronage" as an individual relationship is ultimately unhelpful.

[53] Van Nijf, *Civic World of Professional Associations*, 77.

[54] Garnsey and Woolf, "Patronage of the Rural Poor," 154.

[55] See the valuable discussion in Eilers, *Roman Patrons of Greek Cities*, which provides an appendix with 164 inscriptions recording Roman patronage of Greek cities through the Imperial period. In this context, one thinks also of the example of municipal patronage found in the Roman alimentary schemes of the late first century C.E. designed to feed children in Italy; see Greg Woolf, "Food, Poverty and Patronage: The Significance of the Roman Alimentary Schemes in Early Imperial Italy," *Papers of the British School at Rome* 58 (1990): 197–228.

[56] Van Nijf, *Civic World of Professional Associations*, 77–79; Guido Clemente, "Il patronato nei collegia dell'impero Romano," *Studi classici e orientali* 21 (1972): 142–229; Koenraad Verboven, "The Associative Order: Status and Ethos among Roman Businessmen in Late Republic and Early Empire," *Athenaeum* 95 (2007): 861–93.

[57] The neologism "euergetism" was popularized, but not invented, by Paul Veyne in his classic book *Bread and Circuses*, 10.

"l'action, l'influence et le prestige des notables, citoyens et étrangers, au sein des cités."[58] Paul Veyne, in fact, contends that *euergesiai* were, by definition, collective benefactions to the *polis* as a whole: "By collective benefits or services we mean those satisfactions which, owing to their external nature, are, like the radio or national defence, at the disposal of all users, without being in principle objects of competition between them."[59]

The exclusive focus of Gauthier and Veyne – authors of the two most influential monographs on the subject – on the civic context of euergetism is potentially misleading, however. It is no doubt true that, while both authors trace the historical emergence of this socio-political system to different factors, euergetism played a crucial role in the development of the political structures and activities of the post-classical *polis*.[60] Yet there is abundant evidence to suggest that "euergetism" in Greek cities was by no means limited to the official *boulē* or *dēmos*. Private groups and associations within cities also competed for and received benefactions from wealthy notables, and these private groups reciprocated gifts with honorific inscriptions that employed the same language and rewards as those erected by municipal officials. In fact, Onno van Nijf has concluded, "the ancient sources appear to offer no support for any conceptual distinction between generosity towards cities and generosity towards smaller groups such as civic subdivisions and collegia...."[61] Voluntary associations, therefore, competed with other groups, including official civic bodies, for access to the gifts and benefactions of wealthy donors.

Recent scholarship has emphasized the importance of understanding social institutions like benefaction and patronage as components of a larger system of social exchange.[62] For the purposes of this study, I shall assume that Roman patronage and Greek benefaction were slightly different but essentially overlapping

---

[58] Philippe Gauthier, *Les cités grecques et leur bienfaiteurs (IVe-Ier avant J.-C.): Contribution à l'histoire des institutions* (Suppléments du bulletin de correspondance hellénique 12; Athènes: École Française D'Athènes, 1985), 1; cf. Veyne's brief definition: "Euergetism means private liberality for public benefit" (*Bread and Circuses*, 10). Veyne goes on to write, "Euergetism would be incomprehensible outside the city of antiquity.... As a town, the city was the principle setting for voluntary euergetism. As a city, it was the primary cause of political euergetism" (34–35).

[59] Veyne, *Bread and Circuses*, 12.

[60] According to Veyne, euergetism cannot exist as such in a democratic society. It was not until the "regime of the notables," which is for Veyne the normal outcome of a direct democracy such as existed in classical Athens, that the conditions for euergetism were ripe. Gauthier, on the other hand, is skeptical of Veyne's neat historical categories. The establishment of the Hellenistic monarchies was an important political development, but its impact on the political institutions of the independent cities should not be overestimated. Essentially, Gauthier finds in the second century B.C.E. what Veyne claimed to have existed as early as the fourth century.

[61] Van Nijf, *Civic World of Professional Associations*, 81.

[62] See Stephen Charles Mott, "The Power of Giving and Receiving: Reciprocity in Hellenistic Benevolence," in *Current Issues in Biblical and Patristic Interpretation: Studies in Honor of Merrill C. Tenney Presented by His Former Students* (Grand Rapids: Eerdmans, 1975), 60–72.

forms of what Ekkehard and Wolfgang Stegemann have called "general reciprocity."[63] This asymmetrical form of social exchange takes place between two parties of unequal status; unlike "balanced reciprocity," in which gifts of equal value are exchanged among parties of equal social status, benefactions that fall into the category of "general reciprocity" are reciprocated, not in kind, but rather with "homage and loyalty or political support or information."[64] Given that both "patrons" and "benefactors" could support both individuals and groups, including Greco-Roman voluntary associations – not to mention the overlap of Greek and Roman culture during the Imperial period – it is very difficult, if not impossible, to draw sharp distinctions between these two social institutions.[65] The point to be made here, and demonstrated in the following section, is that pagan and Jewish voluntary associations participated in this system of generalized reciprocity. Voluntary associations received support from benefactors and, in turn, honored those who patronized their societies. We shall look first at the types of assistance – both material and nonmaterial – that these associations received from benefactors; then we shall examine the honorific practices through which associations symbolized their gratitude to and their relationships with wealthy patrons.

3.3.1 Types of Benefactions

Voluntary associations typically drew upon two sources of income to fund their activities: membership dues (which we shall look at in more detail below) and substantial benefactions from wealthy individuals or families. Inscriptions speak of benefactors "establishing" the association (IG X/2 58: καταστήσαντι τὸν οἶκον) or of noteworthy individuals serving as προστάτης (IG X/2 192, 220; SEG 47:954; SEG 24:1233) or εὐεργέτης (IDelos 1791; IMakedD 1104; SIRIS 123) to the group. Other inscriptions record the specific contributions of money by affluent members (CIL III 703; CIL III 704; CIL III 707; IKnidos 1:23; IG XII/1 937). In Thessalonica in the first century C.E., for example, Julius set up a dedicatory inscription to Zeus commemorating his donation of a vineyard to an

---

[63] Ekkehard W. Stegemann and Wolfgang Stegemann, *The Jesus Movement: A Social History of Its First Century* (trans. O. C. Dean Jr.; Minneapolis: Fortress, 1999), 34–38.

[64] Ibid., 36; see also Zeba A. Crook, *Reconceptualising Conversion: Patronage, Loyalty, and Conversion in the Religions of the Ancient Mediterranean World* (BZNW 130; Berlin: Walter de Gruyter, 2004), 56–59; cf. Zeba A. Crook, "Reflections on Culture and Social-Scientific Models," *JBL* 124 (2005): 515–20.

[65] Recently, Stephan Joubert has argued that benefaction ("euergetism") and patronage represented two distinct forms of social exchange, which should not be confused or collapsed into one category (see Joubert, *Paul as Benefactor*, 17–72; idem, "One Form of Social Exchange or Two? 'Euergetism,' Patronage, and Testament Studies," *BTB* 31 [2001]: 17–25). Joubert's analysis of the data is problematic, however, and his attempt to distinguish neatly between these two exchange relationships is unconvincing. For a trenchant critique of Jobuert's work, see now Crook, *Reconceptualising Conversion*, 59–66.

association of *mystai*, the proceeds of which were to be used to fund banquets for the group and to maintain a shrine in which the inscription was placed (IG X/2 259). The donation of vineyards, other parcels of land, and money could also occur after death; these benefactions would then be recorded on gravestones, often with regulations for the proper use of the land or money by the association (cf. IG X/2 260; IMakedD 920). Benefactors and patrons were frequently members of the associations to which they contributed donations, but that was not always the case. There are numerous examples of nonmembers patronizing associations, sometimes with financial distributions, sometimes with food (e.g., IHistria 57).[66] The assistance provided by elite members of society to voluntary associations was not always material, however. A powerful patron might also be counted on to serve as a legal advocate for an association (cf. *Digest* 3.4.1.1), brokering benefits from civic or imperial authorities in the form of tax breaks, construction projects, or conflict mediation (cf. IDelos 1520).[67]

3.3.2 Honors for Benefactors

Since these distributions took place within a system of generalized reciprocity, the support given to voluntary associations was not offered without the expectation of a return, for patrons anticipated, and were offered, public honor for their benefactions from those whom they had assisted. In the language of French sociologist Pierre Bourdieu, benefactors exchanged economic capital for symbolic capital.[68] In return for the assistance that they received, associations, like cities, would reciprocate with appropriate honors, such as the awarding of honorific inscriptions, privileged seats at festivals, and crowns. To cite but one example, when an honorific inscription was erected for Dionysodoros the Alexandrian at Rhodes in the mid-second century B.C.E (IG XII/1 155), commemorating his support and leadership of several Rhodian associations, the monument provides an extensive inventory of the honors he received from at least four different *koina*: the title "Benefactor" (εὐεργέτας); numerous crowns of gold, laurel, and poplar (στεφανωθεὶς ὑπὸ τοῦ κοινοῦ, cf. *lines* 46–49; 76–80); immunity from duties (ἀτελείαι πάντων); and the proclamation of his honors forever (εἰς τὸν ἀεὶ χρόνον) at the burial grounds of the Paniastai association and by the Haliadi and Haliastai *koinon*.[69] As has often been noted, these public honors also increased the likelihood of further benefactions from the same patron, and at the same time they enhanced the possibility that other benefactors might attempt to

---

[66] Poland, *Geschichte des griechischen Vereinswesens*, 270–73. Meiggs (*Roman Ostia*, 316–20) discusses examples of guilds in Ostia electing as patrons individuals who were not members of the society.

[67] Van Nijf, *Civic World of Professional Associations*, 95–100.

[68] Pierre Bourdieu, "Ökonomisches Kapital, kulturelles Kapital, soziales Kapital," in *Soziale Ungleichheiten* (ed. Reinhard Kreckel; Göttingen: Otto Schartz, 1983), 183–98.

[69] See Gabrielsen, "The Rhodian Associations Honouring Dionysodoros from Alexandria," 137–60.

outshine their rivals among the civic elite in a competition for acclaim.[70] That Dionysodoros probably commissioned and paid for this inscription during his own lifetime, inscribing onto one stele all the awards he had received from the associations in his network of social exchange, only highlights the extent to which the accumulation and advertisement of public honor was highly valued in the Mediterranean world.

Indeed, the importance for benefactors of receiving glory, honor, praise, and thanksgiving in the euergetic context of Greco-Roman antiquity can scarcely be overstated. In a society in which the love of honor (φιλοτιμία) – that is, "the value of a person in his or her own eyes … *plus* that person's value in the eyes of his or her social group"[71] – was a highly prized cultural virtue, the public (and, in the case of inscriptions, permanent) advertisement of one's magnanimity and virtue was something to which members of the civic elite unabashedly aspired.[72] As Dio Chrysostom opines in a speech intended to dissuade citizens of Rhodes from dishonoring benefactors with their practice of recycling monuments by merely inscribing the names of newly honored patrons on old statues, "many in times past have even give up their lives in order that they might get a statue and have their name announced by the herald or receive some other honor and leave a succeeding generation a fair name and remembrance of themselves" (*Rhod.* 31.16 [Cohoon and Crosby, LCL]).[73] For benefactors of clubs and guilds, many of whom might not have had access to the realm of civic power, patronizing these private societies would have offered opportunities for prestige unavailable to them in the official civic structures, allowing them to "to play the role of esteemed civil service officials, of members of councils and planning committees."[74] Benefactors doubtless dispensed *euergesiai* for many reasons, including, we might imagine, a genuine love and concern for the cities or associations that received their gifts. Moreover, "fear of what might happen if conspicuous donations were not made" was also a motivating factor, as the occasional appearance of a riotous crowd on the steps of a parsimonious grain hoarder makes clear.[75] But it is the ability to accumulate public honor that best accounts for the systematic distribution of benefactions by members of the wealthy elite to cities and associations in the ancient world. As Onno Van Nijf nicely sums up:

---

[70] On "agonistic" giving, see Joubert, *Paul as Benefactor*, 49, 54–56.

[71] Bruce Malina, *The New Testament World: Insights from Cultural Anthropology* (3d ed.; Atlanta: John Knox, 2001), 30.

[72] See Harrison, *Paul's Language of Grace*, 26–63; David A. deSilva, *Honor, Patronage, Kinship and Purity: Unlocking New Testament Culture* (Downers Grove, Ill.: InterVarsity Press, 2000), 23–42; Malina, *The New Testament World*, 27–57; Robert Jewett, "Paul, Shame, and Honor," in *Paul in the Greco-Roman World: A Handbook* (ed. J. Paul Sampley; Harrisburg, Pa.: Trinity, 2003), 551–74.

[73] For an instructive account of the ideology of benefaction in Dio's writings, see C. P. Jones, *The Roman World of Dio Chrysostom* (Cambridge: Harvard University Press, 1978), 104–14.

[74] F. W. Danker, "On Stones and Benefactors," *CurTM* 8 (1981): 352.

[75] Harland, *Associations, Synagogues, and Congregations*, 99–100.

Public generosity was usually repaid by the award of public honor, which came in the form of an honorific monument, with accompanying inscription, in a public location in the city. Tedious and repetitive though these monuments and their inscriptions may seem to us, they were of considerable social and political importance to their honorands…. Honorific inscriptions were the counter-gifts in the exchange relationships between collegia and their patrons and benefactors. Patrons valued them highly because they were a form of symbolic capital: a source of prestige, on which their position of social and political prominence relied. Collegia capitalized on this and used the honorific monuments to establish a place for themselves alongside the recognized official institutions of the city, a process which we may describe as 'status association.' By assisting the *demos* and the *boule* in their honorific practices and by emulating their honorific language, they showed that they subscribed to an underlying world view, and to the political order of a provincial town in a huge empire. In this way collegia were able to present themselves as loyal and dependable institutions, as 'integral elements' of the ancient city.[76]

Of course, some individuals and communities might express reservations about, or elect not to endorse, this "underlying world view" of the Roman Empire in which the accrual of public honor and praise was so highly coveted. There appears to have existed among some Jews in antiquity an unwillingness to embrace, and occasionally even an explicit critique of, the emphasis on the accumulation of honor in the system of civic euergetism. The writings of both Josephus and Philo, for example, contain condemnations of the ideology of pagan benefaction.[77] In *Against Apion*, Josephus declares, with reference to the practice of honoring benefactors, that the reward for those who live according to the law of Moses is not "is not silver or gold; nor is it a crown of olive branches or of parsley," but rather the confidence that comes from obeying God and the hope of a better life (*Ag. Ap.* 2.217; cf. 2.74; 2.205). Similarly, Philo begins his treatise *On the Decalogue* with the question of why God gave the law "not in cities but in the deep desert." The answer lies in the inherent immorality of cities, an evil seen most unmistakably, according to Philo, in human lust for pride (τῦφος): whence comes "the most treacherous of all things, namely pride, and is implanted, which some people esteem and worship, magnifying vain opinions, with golden crowns and purple robes" (*Decal.* 1.4). Although the highest honor ought to be ascribed by mortals to "divine concerns," in cities rightly placed honors are usurped by human pride (τύφῳ γὰρ καὶ τὰ θεῖα ἐξωλιγώρηται, καίτοι νομιζόμενα τῆς ἀνωτάτω τυγχάνειν τιμῆς; *Decal.* 1.6; cf. *Cher.* 117; *Det.* 33–34). In *On the Cherubim*, Philo provides an even more explicit critique of what he perceives to be the contractual nature of pagan benefaction, arguing that all gifts and possessions originate from and belong to God:

---

[76] Van Nijf, *Civic World of Professional Associations*, 117, 127–28.

[77] For a very helpful study of the ways in which Jews interacted with the model of euergetism, see Gregg Gardner, "Jewish Leadership and Hellenistic Civic Benefaction in the Second Century B.C.E.," *JBL* 126 (2007): 327–43.

Look round you and you shall find that those who are said to bestow benefits sell rather than give, and those who seem to us to receive them in truth buy. The givers are seeking praise or honor [ἔπαινον ἢ τιμὴν] as their exchange and look for the repayment of the benefit, and thus, under the specious name of gift, they in real truth carry out a sale; for the seller's way is to take something for what he offers. The receivers of the gift, too, study to make some return, and do so as opportunity offers, and thus they act as buyers. For buyers know well that receiving and paying go hand in hand. But God is no salesman, hawking his goods in the market, but a free giver of all things, pouring forth eternal fountains of free bounties, and seeking no return. For He has no needs Himself and no created being is able to repay His gift. (*Cher.* 122–123 [Colson and Whitaker, LCL)

This is not to suggest that all Jews consistently refrained from bestowing honors upon the benefactors of their communities.[78] Jewish synagogues, which to the outside observer may have been indistinguishable from pagan associations, also participated in networks of benefaction and exchange. Two honorific inscriptions from Delos, for example, tentatively dated by their editor on palaeographical grounds to between 150–50 B.C.E. and between 250–175 B.C.E., recognize the benefactions of two separate individuals to an association of Samaritans on that island (SEG 32:809–810).[79] The first inscription documents the awarding of a golden crown to one Sarapion for an unknown benefaction to the association (εὐεργεσίας ἕνεκεν τῆς εἰς ἑαυτούς); the second bestows the same honor upon Menippos and his descendents, ostensibly for some construction project, though the bottom of the text is mutilated. Both inscriptions begin with the phrase "the Israelites of Delos who contribute to sacred ['and holy,' SEG 32:810] Mount Gerizim," indicating that the association sent monies to the temple of the Samaritans (cf. IJO 1: Mac1). Diaspora Jews not only occasionally honored benefactors with the same language and the same rewards as their pagan neighbors, they also sometimes used donations to demonstrate their loyalty to the cities in which they lived, as seems to have been the case with the group of Judeans in Smyrna who donated funds to the *polis* (IJO 3:40).[80]

Tessa Rajak's careful of study inscriptions in the Jewish Diaspora, however, has shown that, with some exceptions, Jews tended to avoid awarding lavish honors to human benefactors. Rajak identifies several strategies employed by Jews in order to diminish the influence of donors within the community: (1) by avoiding the language of honor altogether, or (2) "by asserting the act of giving

---

[78] Nor do I mean to imply that patrons did not sometimes play important roles in Pauline churches. Paul explicitly identifies Phoebe, deacon of the church of Cenchreae, as a patron (προστάτις), both to him and to many others (Rom 16:1–3). Schmeller's contention that the term προστάτις in Rom 16:2 does not indicate that Phoebe is a patron like patrons of Greco-Roman associations but rather "ist deshalb doch eher mit 'Beistand' weiderzugeben" is thoroughly unpersuasive (*Hierarchie und Egalität*, 58–59). For a more balanced perspective, see Caroline F. Whelan, "*Amica Pauli*: The Role of Phoebe in the Early Church," *JSNT* 49 (1993): 67–85.

[79] P. Bruneau, "Les Israélites de Délos et la juiverie délienne," *BCH* 106 (1982): 465–504; see also NewDocs 8:12.

[80] Harland, *Associations, Synagogues, and Congregations*, 202–10.

as a communal and equalizing activity, not a field for display," or (3) by describing a benefaction as the gift of God rather than as coming from an individual's personal assets.[81] This leads Rajak to conclude:

> The different strategies I have pointed to will not have been employed with equal enthusiasm in all communities at all times. Local patterns can be dimly discerned. Yet it is not fanciful to detect also a certain consistency of principle, limits beyond which Jewish communities could not allow themselves to go in adopting local modes of giving and honouring, limits which allow us to suggest that somewhere in this area lay one of the defining marks which were seen by Diaspora Jews as distinguishing them form their neighbors. If this suggestion is right, then they will have been striking an extremely delicate balance, doing things the Greek way up to a point, but stopping short where it mattered to them. It is the setting of that sticking point which constitutes the art of Diaspora living, and perhaps the art of being an ethnic or religious minority of any kind.[82]

Reluctance to endorse the ideology of benefaction among some Jews may have served as one point of distinction between pagan associations and Jewish synagogues. In the following chapter, I hope to demonstrate that Paul, with his insistence that the collection originates in ἡ χάρις τοῦ θεοῦ and will eventuate in χάρις τῷ θεῷ, attempts to minimize the honor and thanksgiving that contributors to the relief fund might have anticipated for their donations, maintaining a position very close to Rajak's third strategy, namely, that human benefaction is ultimately a gift from God.[83]

3.4 Common Funds and Monetary Collections within Associations

That members of the Pauline churches would have contributed monies to a collective fund is by no means unusual. While it may be the case that the purpose of the Pauline collection – namely, to support the poor among the saints in Jerusa-

---

[81] Tessa Rajak, "Benefactors in the Greco-Jewish Diaspora," in *Geschichte-Tradition-Reflexion: Festschrift für Martin Hengel zum 70. Geburtstag*, vol. 1 (ed. Hubert Cancik, Hermann Lichtenberger, and Peter Schäfer; Tübingen: J.C.B. Mohr, 1996), 312, 316–17. Marianne Palmer Bonz reaches a similar conclusion in her study of Jewish synagogue inscriptions in antiquity, "Differing Approaches to Religious Benefaction: The Late Third-Century Acquisition of the Sardis Synagogue," *HTR* 86 (1993): 139–54. Bonz ends her essay with a discussion of Philo's claim that, as she puts it, "[J]ewish people of every financial circumstance were happy and eager to give this tithe [for the temple] because they believed that in honoring God (the only true benefactor) they would receive every benefaction worth having" (151–52; cf. Philo, *Spec.* 1.76–78).

[82] Rajak, "Benefactors," 318.

[83] Although Rajak does not cite any specific inscriptions, she speaks of the "Sardis formula, where a contribution, instead of being described as coming from the individual's own resources in the customary fashion, is instead specified as the gift of God, or, more often, of the divine *pronoia*" ("Benefactors," 317). The inscriptions from the Sardis synagogue have recently been published; see now John H. Kroll, "The Greek Inscriptions of the Sardis Synagogue," *HTR* 94 (2001): 5–127; Frank Moore Cross, "The Hebrew Inscriptions from Sardis," *HTR* 95 (2002): 3–19.

lem – was somewhat distinctive, a claim that will be assessed in more detail below, the practice of pooling resources into a common fund is attested in numerous Greco-Roman voluntary associations. Both donations from wealthy benefactors and contributions from less affluent members of the association were frequently collected into a common chest, from which purse the social and religious activities of the association were funded.[84] Indeed, the second-century jurist Gaius indicates that the ability to share property and money in common became a special right of Roman *collegia*:

> Partnerships, collegia, and bodies of this sort may not be formed by everybody at will; for this right is restricted by statutes, senatus consulta, and imperial constitutiones. In a few cases only are bodies of this sort permitted. For example, partners in tax farming, gold mines, silver mines, and saltworks are allowed to form corporations. Likewise, there are certain collegia at Rome whose corporate status has been established by senatus consulta and imperial constitutiones, for example, those of the bakers and certain others and of the shipowners, who are found in the provinces too. Those permitted to form a corporate body [*corpus*] consisting of a collegium or partnership [*societatis*] or specifically one or the other of these have the right on the pattern of the state to have common property [*res communes*], a common treasury [*arcam communem*], and an attorney or syndic through whom, as in a state, what should be transacted and done in common is transacted and done.[85]

Even as early as the eighth century B.C.E., Hesiod's poem *Works and Days* celebrates meals "shared in common" (ἐκ κοινοῦ), with the implication that participants donated to a common fund in order to finance the banquet.[86] By the time of the classical period, and continuing into the Imperial era, voluntary associations had adopted institutionalized practices of communal monetary collections. Some associations collected fees from members at initiation, while others required members to pay regular dues (usually during monthly meetings) to the association's common chest, or κοινόν, which was maintained by a specially appointed treasurer (ταμίας).[87] Funds from this treasury were typically used to pur-

---

[84] See the discussion in J. Albert Harrill, *The Manumission of Slaves in Early Christianity* (HUT 32; Tübingen: J. C. B. Mohr, 1995), 129–57.

[85] *Digest* 3.4.1.1 (trans. from Alan Watson, ed., *The Digest of Justinian* [2 vols.; Philadelphia: University of Pennsylvania Press, 1998]).

[86] Hesiod, *Op.* 723. An honorific inscription for Boidas, a gymnasiarch in Thebes (third to second century B.C.E.), uses similar language in describing the rewards that will be given Boidas and his progeny, which are to be paid "from the common expenses" (ἀναλώματα δοθῆναι ἐκ κοινοῦ; SEG 8:694).

[87] See Ascough, *Paul's Macedonian Associations*, 63 n. 82 for a list of texts. The famous Lanuvium inscription (ILS II/2, 7212) requires members to pay both an entry fee, consisting of 100 sesterii and an amphora of wine, and monthly dues of 5 asses. For a commentary on this text, see Eva Ebel, *Die Attraktivität früher christlicher Gemeinden: Die Gemeinde von Korinth im Spiegel griechisch-römischer Vereine* (WUNT 2:178; Tübingen: Mohr Siebeck, 2004), 12–72; cf. Meiggs, *Roman Ostia*, 334; A. R. Hands, *Charities and Social Aid in Greece and Rome* (Aspects of Greek and Roman Life; Ithaca, N.Y.: Cornell University Press, 1968), 187–88. For an example of a subscription list of the

chase or pay rent on group-owned property, to subsidize banquets, to finance the maintenance of cultic practices, or to endow honors for wealthy benefactors who had supported the association.[88] For example, an inscription from the Bacchic society at Athens (178 C.E.) stipulates that each new member shall pay an entrance fee of fifty denarii and a libation, except for the sons of members, who receive a discounted rate of twenty-five denarii (SIG³ 1109; cf. IG II² 1368). During the monthly meetings, the members of this Bacchic association are also responsible for "the designated monthly contribution for the wine" (καταβάλλων μηνιαίαν τὴν ὁρισθεῖσαν εἰς τὸν οἶνον φοράν, *lines* 47–48). Failure to pay the entrance fee is cause for exclusion from the banquet (*lines* 104–108), a regulation which suggests that these dues were used to finance the community meal, as well as the religious sacrifices offered during meetings. Members of Jewish associations, likewise, contributed to a common fund that was used to pay for group activities. Josephus declares that, when Gaius banned cultic societies (θίασοι), the emperor nevertheless still permitted Jews "to bring in contributions for common dinners and sacred rites" (χρήματα εἰς σύνδειπνα καὶ τὰ ἱερὰ εἰσφέρειν, *Ant.* 14.214–216). A papyrus from Apollinopolis Magna (Egypt) also preserves a fragmentary register of offerings for the common feasts of a Jewish association, celebrated on the 15th and 16th of an unknown month (CPJ 139).

Contributions to the common chest of Greco-Roman voluntary associations were also used to fund the burial expenses of deceased members. We find evidence for this practice even among associations not expressly formed as burial societies (i.e., the so-called *collegia funeraticia*), which do not seem to have existed as a separate category before the reign of Hadrian.[89] A second-century B.C.E. cultic association of the Magna Mater, for example, paid for the burial expenses of poorer members of the community through funds from the common chest (IG II² 1327; cf. IG II² 1275, 1277). As J. Albert Harrill comments on this particular group, "The possession of a burial fund does not necessarily imply that this association of *orgeōnes* was a cult of the dead, but seems instead to denote financial charity to persons within its own membership who otherwise would not have been able to belong.... With the burial funds, this group of *orgeōnes* could

---

founders of a second-century B.C.E. θίασος in Knidos, see IKnidos 1:23; the donations range from 300 to 5 drachmae.

[88] Foucart, *Les associations religieuses*, 42–47. For an example of monies from a common fund used to pay rent, see IG II² 2499 and the discussion in William Scott Ferguson, "The Attic Orgeones," *HTR* 37 (1944): 80. For evidence of corporate ownership of property by associations in Hellenistic Rhodes, see P. M. Fraser, *Rhodian Funerary Monuments* (Oxford: Clarendon, 1977), 58–70 (cf. SEG 3:764). Bonz's claim ("Differing Approaches to Religious Benefaction," 149) that "these common funds were used primarily to honor wealthy patrons on whom the various *thiasoi* appear to have been substantively, if not exclusively, financially dependent" fails to account for the use of these funds to pay for the more mundane activities of associations.

[89] See Ausbüttel, *Untersuchungen zu den Vereinen im Westen des Römischen Reiches*, 22–29. For fragmentary evidence of burial practices among a first-century C.E. Jewish σύνοδος, see CPJ 138.

have been assisting a specific segment of its membership, which probably included not only kinless resident aliens, but also a number of others too poor to bear the cost of their own funerals. The necrological fund bonded socially diverse members together."[90] Monies from the common fund were not only used to pay for burial in a common grave owned by the community; these finances also occasionally provided for an engraved epitaph publicly honoring the deceased (SEG 42:625; IG X/2 288; IG X/2 289; IG X/2 503).[91]

Finally, members of Greco-Roman voluntary associations also occasionally pooled financial resources together to fund special projects.[92] For instance, an inscription from a first-century C.E. association of fishermen and fishmongers in Ephesus records the donations made by about one hundred members of the group for the construction of a new customs house (NewDocs 5:5 = IEph Ia 20).[93] The contributions, which, according to standard practice, are listed in order of value from greatest to least, range from the funds for the construction of four large columns – a sizeable expense – to fifty denarii, to five denarii at the end of the list. The descending value of these donations appears to indicate the diverse economic status of the members of the group; while the wealthier members of the group subsidized the bulk of the construction costs, those with lesser means nevertheless also proudly recorded their donations. Similarly, one Publius Hostilius Philadelphus, an *aedile* in Philippi sometime in the second century C.E., set up two Latin inscriptions to commemorate the members of an association of Silvanus worshippers who had donated to the construction and decoration of a temple for the god (CIL III 633/2, 3).[94] These various gifts included a statue of Silvanus, 400 roof tiles for the temple, two small statues of Hercules and Mercury, 250 denarii worth of concrete, a painting of Olympus worth 15 denarii, and assorted monetary contributions from at least seven named individuals.[95]

---

[90] Harrill, *Manumission of Slaves*, 140–41.

[91] For a series of burial inscriptions (second century B.C.E.) from a σύνοδος of foreigners in Tanagra (Boeotia), see IG VII 685–689.

[92] Verbrugge, *Paul's Style of Church Leadership*, 150–57 ignores these kinds of special contributions in his study of the financial activities of Greco-Roman associations and clubs. Verbrugge's claim that "there were voluntary associations to which people belonged, but the manner in which funds were collected was by a set of legal rules and regulations, not by appeals for voluntary contributions of money" (208) fails to account for the gathering of funds for special projects.

[93] Due to the deterioration of the stele, only 89 names are clearly recognizable. See also IEph 5.1503 for an inscription of a woman associated with the Ephesian fishermen, Cominia Junia, who dedicated a statue of Isis. For another association of fishermen, see L. Robert, "Documents D'Asie Mineure," *BCH* 102 (1978): 532–35; SEG 28:561–62.

[94] A text, German translation, and commentary are provided in Peter Pilhofer, *Philippi, Band II: Katalog der Inschriften von Philippi* (WUNT 119; Tübingen: Mohr Siebeck, 2000), 164.

[95] Associations also set up honorific inscriptions, presumably with monies from the group fund, which listed all the members of the association on the stele. See, e.g., IG X/2 68 (38 names); IG X/2 58 (13 names); IG X/2 288 (11 names); NewDocs 1:5. For another example of

Members of Jewish synagogues also contributed to special collections that were used to support the social and religious activities of Jewish associations. In 55 C.E., for example, eighteen members of "the congregation of the Jews" (ἐφάνη τῇ συναγωγῇ τῶν ἐν Βερνεικίδι Ἰουδαίων) in Berenice (Cyrenaica), including two women, donated to a fund used to pay for "repairs of the synagogue" (CJZC 72). Their names were inscribed on a marble stele along with the amount contributed by each individual, ranging from 5 to 28 drachmae.[96] Another first-century honorific inscription from Akmoneia (Phrygia), well known for its mention of the prominent benefactor Julia Severa, refers to renovations to an *oikos* used by the Jewish community:

> The *oikos*, which was constructed by Julia Severa,[97] was renovated by P. Tyrronios Clados, archisynagogos for life, Lucius son of Lucius, archisynagogos, and Popilios Zoticos, archon, from their own funds and from the community treasury [ἔκ τε τῶν ἰδίων καὶ τῶν συνκαταθεμένων]. They decorated the walls and the ceiling, and they made the security of the gates and all the rest of the decoration. The synagogue honors them with a gold shield on account of their excellent leadership and their kindly feelings and zeal toward the synagogue.[98]

While the congregation publicly honors three of its leaders for using their own financial resources to subsidize these restorations, the renovations were also made possible by funds from the common chest (τὰ συνκαταθεμένα). Of course, as we see in this inscription and in several discussed above, Jewish communities, like their pagan neighbors, frequently drew upon the resources of wealthy donors. However, in her study of religious benefaction in antiquity, Marianne Palmer Bonz has suggested that "far more prominent among Jewish donor inscriptions than among their pagan counterparts is the mention of common funds or community revenues."[99] Unfortunately, much of the available evidence comes from the third century C.E. and beyond, but it does seem that, as part of the strategy of avoiding the lavish honors typically bestowed upon patrons and bene-

---

a subscription for a special project, see IG XII/1, 9 (the repair of a wall following an earthquake).

[96] Ten males identified on the inscription as *archons* and one male identified as a priest (ἱερεύς) are listed at the top of the inscription as having contributed 10 drachmae each. These individuals appear to have served as the governing body of the association; see Donald Binder, *Into the Temple Courts: The Place of the Synagogues in the Second Temple Period* (SBLDS 169; Atlanta: Society of Biblical Literature, 1999), 260–62.

[97] It is now generally recognized that Julia Severa, who is known from a number of inscriptions and who was a member of a prominent Galatian family (see Paul R. Trebilco, *Jewish Communities in Asia Minor* [SNTSMS 69; Cambridge: Cambridge University Press, 1991], 58–60), was not Jewish, nor was she a member of this particular Jewish congregation. Instead, she seems to have paid for the construction of a building that was later taken over and renovated by the Jewish community.

[98] The text may be found in MAMA 6.264; CIJ 2:766; and IJO 2:168.

[99] Marianne Palmer Bonz, "Differing Approaches to Religious Benefaction," 139–54.

factors in Greco-Roman antiquity, Jews tended both to emphasize modest gifts from members of the community and also to highlight gifts provided "from the revenue of the synagogue" (ἐκ τῆς προσόδου τῆς συναγωγῆς), a phrase used in a fourth-century inscription from Aegina commemorating the construction of a mosaic pavement (IJO I: Ach 59; cf. IJO III: Syr 84 [244/5 C.E.]). Although coming from a later period, the fourth-century synagogue in Apamea is a case in point. Its beautiful mosaic floor was financed by the donations of at least 15 members of the community – both men and women – each of whom contributed between 35 and 150 feet of flooring.[100] Slightly closer to our period, a lengthy honorific inscription from third-century Aphrodisias, famous for its use of the term θεοσεβής, provides the names of more than 120 individuals who had donated to the πατέλλα – presumably a kind of soup kitchen[101] – and who had helped to construct a building associated with the synagogue and used for charitable distributions. Interestingly, the roster of names not only contains officers, proselytes, and other members of the synagogue, but also (pagan) civic officials and other non-Jews, suggesting a high degree of interaction between Jewish residents of Aphrodisias and their pagan neighbors.[102]

Lastly, both Philo and Josephus testify to the existence of a common fund, as well as shared property, among the Essenes (*Prob.* 84–87; *J.W.* 2.122–144; *Ant.* 18.20–22), although the devotion to the common life among the Essenes exceeds that of almost all other Greco-Roman voluntary associations.[103] The sectarian writings from the Essenes generally confirm the picture painted by Philo and Josephus, for the Qumran community maintained a common fund that was used to provide economic assistance to the needy in the community:

> And this is the rule of the Many, to provide for all their needs: the salary of two days each month at least. They shall place it in the hand of the Inspector and of the judges. From it they shall give to the <[in]jured> and with it they shall support the needy and poor, and to the elder who [is ben]t, and to the af[flic]ted, and to the prisoner of a foreign people, and to the girl who has [n]o re[dee]mer, [and] to the <youth> [w]ho has no-one looking after him; everything is the task of the association and [the house of the

---

[100] The donor inscriptions can be found in IJO III: Syr 53–69, 71.

[101] On the translation of this difficult word, see L. Michael White, *The Social Origins of Christian Architecture*, vol. 2: *Texts and Monuments of the Christian Domus Ecclesiae in Its Environment* (HTS 42; Valley Forge, Pa.: Trinity, 1997), 304 n. 41.

[102] L. Michael White, *The Social Origins of Christian Architecture*, vol. 1: *Building God's House in the Roman World: Architectural Adaptation among Pagans, Jews, and Christians* (HTS 42; Valley Forge, Pa.: Trinity, 1996), 88–90.

[103] While Philo (*Contempl.*) does not indicate that the Therapeutae who lived outside of Alexandria shared common property – perhaps because of his desire to portray this community as purely devoted to the study of philosophy and therefore immune to the temptations of wealth and possessions (see §§13.16–20) – one might suppose that some form of collective financial activity was employed to pay for the weekly community feasts that Philo describes in great detail (§§66–89).

association shall] not [be deprived of] its [means]. (CD XIV, 12–16; cf. 4Q266 10 I, 5–10; see also 1QS VI, 13b–23)[104]

Whether reflected in the payment of membership dues or in the gathering of monetary collections for special projects, collective economic activity was an important part of the communal life of Greco-Roman voluntary associations. The construction and renovation of sacred precincts, the enjoyment of banquets and cultic rites, and the burial of deceased members were all events likely to be financed by monies from an association's common fund. More than merely serving as a resource for the religious and social affairs of the community, however, the common fund also played an important symbolic role in establishing the group's identity. Within the group, contributions to the common fund marked some (wealthier) members as patrons and thus helped to establish a hierarchy of status. Yet Harrill has suggested that "one could envisage an association based on equal contributions, so that the hierarchy based on contribution amount would be diminished."[105] Indeed, this seems to have been a strategy adopted by some Jewish synagogues, whose members preferred to speak of donations from the common fund. Giving to the association's common chest also demonstrated one's loyalty to the group. As John Barclay has recently remarked, "The close tie between giving (or receiving) money and membership of the association meant that all such financial transactions served to solidify the social identity of the group, and clarify the boundaries between insiders and outsiders."[106]

---

[104] Translation from Florentino García Martínez and Eibert J. C. Tigchelaar, eds., *The Dead Sea Scrolls Study Edition* (2 vols.; Leiden: Brill/Grand Rapids: Eerdmans, 1997); see also Catherine M. Murphy, *Wealth in the Dead Sea Scrolls and in the Qumran Community* (STDJ 40; Leiden: Brill, 2002), 83–87, 155–61. The theory that the authors of the documents found at Qumran were Essenes represents the current consensus position, but it has not gone without challenge. See Murphy, *Wealth in the Dead Sea Scrolls*, 401–6; for a discussion of the issues involved and a challenge to the consensus position, see Lena Cansdale, *Qumran and the Essenes: A Re-evaluation of the Evidence* (TSAJ 60; Tübingen: Mohr Siebeck, 1997).

[105] Harrill, *Manumission of Slaves*, 144.

[106] John Barclay, "Money and Meetings: Group Formation among Diaspora Jews and Early Christians," in *Vereine, Synagogen und Gemeinden im kaiserzeitlichen Kleinasien* (ed. Andreas Gutsfeld and Dietrich-Alex Koch; STAC 25; Tübingen: Mohr Siebeck, 2006), 116. There is also evidence for the existence of common funds within second-century churches. Lucian refers to Christians from the cities of Asia sending delegations to visit the imprisoned Peregrinus "at their common expense" (ἀπὸ τοῦ κοινοῦ; *Peregr.* 1.13). In 197 C.E., Tertullian defends the monetary collections taken up within Christian communities with a derogatory comparison to pagan associations: "Even if there is a chest of a sort, it is not made up of money paid in entrance-fees, as if religion were a matter of contract. Every man once a month brings some modest coin – or whenever he wishes, and only if he does wish, and if he can; for nobody is compelled; it is a voluntary offering. You might call them the trust funds of piety (*Haec quasi deposita pietatis sunt*). For they are not spent upon banquets nor drinking-parties nor thankless eating houses; but to feed the poor and to bury them (*sed egenis alendis humandisque*), for boys and girls who lack property and parents, and then for slaves grown old and shipwrecked mariners; and any who may be in mines, islands or

There is no evidence that the members of Paul's churches paid monthly or weekly membership dues, or that community funds were used to subsidize the burial expenses of deceased believers.[107] In fact, Paul's instructions regarding the organization of the contribution for Jerusalem in 1 Cor 16:1–4 seem to imply that the congregations of his mission in Galatia and Corinth did not regularly administer funds. On the other hand, some forms of collective economic activity among the Pauline churches do bear certain similarities to the use of financial resources among pagan and Jewish voluntary associations. First, associations typically used monies from their common chest to finance community meals and religious activities. While Paul's letters do not explicitly disclose the identity of those who paid for the celebration of the Lord's supper in Corinth (κυριακὸς δεῖπνον), Suzanne Watts Henderson has recently argued that 1 Cor 11:17–34 reveals Paul's hope that the Christians of the Corinthian οἶκος (cf. 1 Cor 11:22, 34) will gather together for a community meal, patterned on the self-giving love of Christ, in which the poor are fed from the resources of the wealthy (cf. Gal 6:6; Rom 12:8–10).[108] Second, with respect to the collection for the saints in Jerusalem, the gathering of a one-time communal contribution among the Pauline churches is not dissimilar to the pooling together of material resources for special projects among pagan and Jewish voluntary associations. To the extent that these subscriptions were frequently used to finance the religious activities of these associations, Paul's collection for Jerusalem offers an interesting parallel, since, as I will argue in the next chapter, Paul metaphorically frames the "offering of the Gentiles" (Rom 15:16) as a religious offering.[109] Moreover, we have seen that funds from the common chest of the Qumran community were used to "support the needy and the poor" (CD XIV, 14), a pecuniary purpose that will be explored in the following section.

---

prisons, provided that it is for the sake of God's school, become the pensioners of their confession" (*Apol.* 39.5–6 [Glover, LCL]).

[107] Meeks (*First Urban Christians*, 78) suggests that although "we have no evidence about the funeral practices of Pauline Christians – a silence that in itself would be grounds for doubting a direct identification of the Christian groups with *collegia tenuiorum* – [we] can hardly doubt, in the face of the sort of sentiment expressed in, say 1 Thess. 4:13–5:11 or the enigmatic reference to 'baptism for the dead' in 1 Cor. 15:29, that these groups made appropriate provision for the burial of deceased Christians."

[108] Suzanne Watts Henderson, "'If Anyone Hungers ...': An Integrated Reading of 1 Cor 11.17–34," *NTS* 48 (2002): 195–208; cf. Gerd Theissen, *The Social Setting of Pauline Christianity: Essays on Corinth* (ed. and trans. John Schütz; Philadelphia: Fortress, 1982), 145–74; Schmeller, *Hierarchie und Egalität*, 66–73.

[109] Indeed, among some pagan associations meat, oil, wine, and other material goods, which were used to provide for the association's cultic sacrifices during community banquets, were collected from members *instead of* fees and membership dues. See LSCG 55; SIG³ 985; Kloppenborg, "Edwin Hatch," 236–37.

3.5 Care for the Poor within Associations

At least since publication of Hendrik Bolkestein's *Wohltätigkeit und Armenpflege im vorchristlichen Altertum* in 1939, there has been a tendency to posit a sharp contrast between pagan benefaction and Christian charity.[110] The beneficence of the notables in the pagan world, it is assumed, was largely, if not exclusively, civic, and, moreover, unconcerned with the needs of the poor. That is, patrons and benefactors in Greek and Roman cities directed their assistance toward fellow citizens of the *polis*, none of whom were without means. The category of "the poor," as such, was not, for the most part, an object of pagan benefaction. "There was," as Peter Brown notes, "little room in such a model for the true urban 'poor,' many of whom would, in fact, have been impoverished immigrants, noncitizens, living on the margins of the community."[111] Bolkestein argued that, on the other hand, genuine concern for the destitute by the wealthy and powerful was a Near Eastern ideal introduced into the Mediterranean world by Jews and Christians. The declaration of the Roman emperor Julian, intended to spur charitable giving among the pagan priesthood in the fourth century, is often interpreted as an accurate description of the situation that obtained throughout Greco-Roman antiquity:

> In every city establish frequent hostels in order that strangers may benefit from our benevolence. I do not mean for our own people only, but for others also who are in need of money.... I order that one-fifth of this be used for the poor who serve the priests, and the remainder distributed by us to strangers and beggars. For it is disgraceful that, when no Jew ever has to beg, and the impious Galileans [i.e., the Christians] support not only their own poor but ours as well, all men see that our people lack aid from us [i.e., from the pagan priesthood]. (Julian, *Letter 22* [Wilson, LCL]; cf. Julian, *Misopogon* 363 A-B)

There can be little doubt that "charity," understood as philanthropic giving to the poor and destitute, was not in the main a public virtue in pagan society.[112] With respect to voluntary associations, for example, in spite of the vast number of inscriptions testifying to the receipt of gifts by these groups from wealthy benefactors on any number of occasions – such as the celebration of a banquet, the consecration of a tomb, the funding of sacrifices, the repair of an edifice – there is very little to suggest that the poor were ever singled out as an object of

---

[110] Hendrik Bolkestein, *Wohltätigkeit und Armenpflege im vorchristlichen Altertum: Ein Beitrag zum Problem "Moral und Gesellschaft"* (Utrecht: Oosthoek, 1939). For a more recent attempt to highlight this distinction, see Rodney Stark, *The Rise of Christianity: A Sociologist Reconsiders History* (Princeton: Princeton University Press, 1996), 73–94.

[111] Peter Brown, *Poverty and Leadership in the Later Roman Empire: The Menahem Stern Jerusalem Lectures* (Hanover and London: University Press of New England, 2002), 5.

[112] Hands, *Charities and Social Aid*, 62–88; Moses Finley, *The Ancient Economy* (2d ed.; Berkeley: University of California Press, 1985), 35–40.

charity.¹¹³ Yet careful consideration of the available evidence suggests that the sharp contrast between pagan euergetism and Christian charity is perhaps overstated.¹¹⁴ Even Bolkestein conceded that, by the beginning of the first century C.E., changes in the social, political, and religious environment of the Greco-Roman world – changes caused in part by increased immigration from the East – had introduced "Oriental" notions of charity into the world of the Roman Empire.¹¹⁵

It is true that Jewish and Christian sources often express more respect for the abject poor than do many pagan texts (cf. Isa 58:3–7; 1QH VI, 2–6; 4Q171; Matt 19:21 with Artemidorus, *Onir.*, 3.53;), occasionally even depicting the poor as a category of people under the special protection of God (LXX Ps 71:1–4, 12–14; 139:13; Luke 6:20).¹¹⁶ It is incorrect to suppose, however, that euergetism in the Greco-Roman world benefited only privileged citizens, for there are a number of examples of financial allocations by wealthy benefactors and cities to those explicitly identified as "poor." To cite but one instance of care for the poor among Greek cities, the first-century geographer Strabo describes the system of state-sponsored charity on the island of Rhodes:

> The Rhodians are concerned for the people in general, although their rule is not democratic; still, they wish to take care of their multitude of poor people [τὸ τῶν πενήτων πλῆθος]. Accordingly, the people are supplied with provisions and the needy are supported by the well-to-do; and there are certain liturgies that supply provisions, so that at the same time the poor man receives his sustenance and the city does not run

---

¹¹³ Waltzing, *Étude historique*, 1:300–21. There are, however, different ways to interpret this silence. One might suggest that "the poor" are not identified in the epigraphical record as recipients of these gifts because it was, in fact, "the poor" who authorized the erection of the very inscriptions that memorialized these donations, and "the poor" were loathe to identify themselves as such. As John Kloppenborg ("Collegia and *Thiasoi*," 20) points out in a different context, "For obvious reasons, no collegium identified itself as a *collegium tenuiorum*; that designation derives from the jurist Marcianus."

¹¹⁴ For cautions against ignoring the place of charity and altruism in the pagan world, see Martin R. P. McGuire, "Epigraphical Evidence for Social Charity in the Roman West," *AJPh* 67 (1946): 129–50; L. W. Countryman, "Welfare in the Churches of Asia Minor under the Early Roman Empire," in *Society of Biblical Literature 1979 Seminar Papers* (ed. Paul J. Actemeier; Missoula, Mont.: Scholars Press, 1979), 131–46; Steven C. Muir, "'Caring for All the Weak': Polytheist and Christian Charity in Sardis and Smyrna," in *Religious Rivalries and the Struggle for Success in Sardis and Smyrna* (ed. Richard S. Ascough; SSEJC 14; Waterloo, Ontario: Wilfrid Laurier University Press, 2005), 123–40; and Anneliese Parkin, "'You Do Him No Service': An Exploration of Pagan Almsgiving," in *Poverty in the Roman World* (ed. Margaret Atkins and Robin Osborne; Cambridge: Cambridge University Press, 2006), 60–82.

¹¹⁵ Bolkestein, *Wohltätigkeit und Armenpflege*, 438–84.

¹¹⁶ See Gildas Hamel, *Poverty and Charity in Roman Palestine, First Three Centuries C.E.* (University of California Publications: Near Eastern Studies 23; Berkeley and Los Angeles: University of California Press, 1990), 164–211; Leslie J. Hoppe, *There Shall Be No Poor Among You: Poverty in the Bible* (Nashville: Abingdon, 2004).

short of useful men, and in particular for the manning of the fleets. (Strabo, *Geogr.* 14.2.5 [Jones, LCL])[117]

Nor was pagan euergetism strictly civic. Voluntary associations, in fact, often received banquets and financial distributions from affluent donors who were not members of the group themselves. When Aba of Histria, a wealthy benefactor who had served as a civic priest, celebrated her tenure by hosting a number of festivals for the city, she doled out both money and wine not only to a variety of civic and religious groups, but also to a number of professional associations.[118] As Onno van Nijf points out, "Participation in public commensality appears to have been determined not by citizenship alone, but also by membership of a variety of status groups, which determined the ways in which individuals took part."[119] Although the partaking of voluntary associations in public commensality cannot simply be equated with charity, doubtless the elite citizens who, like Aba, hosted festivals and distributed goods alleviated some of the material needs of those with lesser means, even as these public distributions also served to solidify the hierarchical structure of society.

Even the pursuit of honor (φιλοτιμία) could occasionally be accompanied by what is advertised as genuine concern for the poor. Thus, when the city of Gytheion (in southern Laconia) erected an honorific decree for the physician Damidas in 86 B.C.E., the inscription proclaims that, during Damidas's two-year tenure as resident doctor, "he did what was just for those who had need, lacking nothing in zeal and love of honor, so that there might be equality for all, both rich and poor, slave and free" (ἐποίησε τοῖς χρείαν ἔχουσιν, σπουδᾶς καὶ φιλο[τιμίας οὐ]θὲν ἐλλείπων εἰς τὸ πᾶσιν ἴσος εἶναι κα[ὶ πένησι καὶ] πλουσίοις καὶ δούλοις καὶ ἐλευθέροις, IG V/1 1145, *lines* 17–21; cf. IG XII/1

---

[117] For Aristotle's discussion of a similar though more democratic, arrangement in Tarentum, cf. *Pol.* 6.5. In the Roman West, the situation may have been somewhat different. Even the distribution of *alimenta* by Nerva and Trajan was not intended to address the needs of the abject poor; see Woolf, "Food, Poverty and Patronage." In his study of gift-giving in the Roman world, Koenraad Verboven concludes, "The qualification 'poor' (*pauper*) was a very subjective and vague term that was used very loosely by Roman nobles to indicate almost anyone not belonging to at least the *prima classis*.... Everything indicates, therefore, that the poorest in Roman society rarely – if ever – enjoyed the benefits of patronage, because they rarely – if ever – had anything to offer in return" (*The Economy of Friends: Economic Aspects of Amicitia and Patronage in the Late Republic* [Collection Latomus 269; Brussels: Latomus, 2002], 112–13).

[118] The text and a translation may be found in Van Nijf, *Civic World of Professional Associations*, 149, 251–52 (cf. IHistria 57). Van Nijf also catalogues numerous instances of Greek associations benefiting from public commensality; see e.g., IHistria 61; IPriene 111; IG V/1, 208; IG V/1, 209; IG VII, 2712; Waltzing 3:179. Cf. NewDocs 7:10 for another example of a first-century honorific inscription that praises a civic benefactor, Kleanax, for the wide range of people who enjoyed his distributions, including citizens, foreigners, and non-citizens from the countryside.

[119] Van Nijf, *Civic World of Professional Associations*, 187.

1032).¹²⁰ Damidas had clearly gone beyond the obligations of his contract with the city Gytheion, even working free of charge during a period of fiscal trouble for the *polis* (*lines* 45–47). That this inscription praises Damidas's concern for equality between rich and poor, slave and free, is an indication that "civic" euergetism could occasionally extend beyond the bounds of citizens of the *polis*, and that poverty and lack of social status were not necessarily barriers to medical care (and other forms of assistance?) in certain contexts. Whether this identification of the πένητες as a group worthy of Damidas's assistance is the exception that proves the rule is beyond the scope of the present work, but at the very least it should caution us against assuming too quickly that care for the poor was never a concern of the pagan elite.

The more limited purpose of this section is to investigate care for the poor among Greco-Roman voluntary associations. Of course, defining "the poor" is a tricky matter in its own right. For the purposes of the present study, the category of "the poor" will be understood as "those living at or near subsistence level, whose prime concern it is to obtain the minimum food, shelter and clothing necessary to sustain life, whose lives are dominated by the struggle for physical survival."¹²¹ Of course, we must reckon with the fact that poverty, thus defined, is not a static category. While opportunities for significant economic advancement and entrepreneurial enterprise were available in the Greco-Roman world, they were not common.¹²² More likely was the possibility that one might be thrust suddenly into poverty by crop failure, banditry, war, or some other fiscal crisis. For many ancients, there was a very thin line between living above, at, or below subsistence level.¹²³ Despite the difficulty of defining "the poor," it is necessary to inquire if among Greco-Roman voluntary associations there are forms of caritative activity comparable to the Pauline collection for Jerusalem. While the evidence is hardly overwhelming, there are indications that associations did occasionally provide financial support for the poor among their members.

Perhaps the most important literary testimony to the practice of care for the poor among pagan associations in the Greek world is found in an exchange between Pliny (ca. 61–ca. 112 C.E.), *legatus Augusti* in the province of Bithynia-Pontus from ca. 110 C.E. until his death, and the emperor Trajan (ca. 53–117 C.E.).¹²⁴ Writing on behalf of the citizens of Amisus – a city on the coast of the

---

[120] See H. F. J. Horstmanshoff, "The Ancient Physician: Craftsman or Scientist," *JHMAS* 45 (1990): 176–97; cf. SEG 48:2139 for other literature that deals with IG V/1 1145.

[121] Garnsey and Woolf, "Patronage of the Rural Poor," 153. See now also the helpful collection of essays in Margaret Atkins and Robin Osborne, eds., *Poverty in the Roman World* (Cambridge: Cambridge University Press, 2006).

[122] See Finley, *The Ancient Economy*, 123–49.

[123] Peter Oakes, "Constructing Poverty Scales for Graeco-Roman Society: A Response to Steven Friesen's 'Poverty in Pauline Studies'," *JSNT* 26 (2004): 367–71.

[124] On this exchange, see A. N. Sherwin-White, *The Letters of Pliny: A Historical and Social Commentary* (Oxford: Oxford University Press, 1966), 686–89.

Black Sea that had been granted *libertas* by Julius Caesar and then, after a brief period of control by a local dynast, Augustus – Pliny passes along to Trajan a request for the emperor to consider the right of the Amisians to form ἐρανισταί:

> Amisenorum civitas libera et foederata beneficio indulgentiae tuae legibus suis utitur. In hac datum mihi libellum ad ἐράνους pertinentem his litteris subieci, ut tu, domine, dispiceres quid et quatenus aut permittendum aut prohibendum putares.
>
> The free and confederate city of Amisus enjoys, with your permission, the privilege of administering its own laws. I am sending with this letter a petition handed to me there which deals with the subject of benefit societies [ἐράνους], so that you, Sir, may decide whether and to what extent these clubs are to be permitted or forbidden. (Pliny, *Ep.* 10.92 [Radice, LCL])

The petition of the Amisians appears to have been provoked by an edict of Pliny, issued on the instructions of the emperor, banning clubs in the province of Bithynia-Pontus (Pliny, *Ep.* 10.33–34, 96.7), a prohibition that, incidentally, figures in Pliny's well-known prosecution of Christians (96.7).[125] In that latter context, Pliny writes of "my edict, issued on your instructions, which banned all political societies" (*edictum meum, quo secundum mandata tua hetaerias esse vetueram, Ep.* 10.96.7). The citizens of Amisus, having certain freedoms because of the *libertas* granted to their *polis*, inquire of their privilege, in light of this ban, to form associations. Trajan's response is instructive not only because of its legal significance but also because it sheds light on the practices of these ἐρανισταί in Asia Minor, at least as Trajan understood them. The emperor writes to Pliny:

> Amisenos, quorum libellum epistulae tuae iunxeras, si legibus istorum, quibus beneficio foederis utuntur, concessum est eranum habere, possumus quo minus habeant non impedire, eo facilius si tali collatione non ad turbas et ad inlicitos coetus, sed ad sustinendam tenuiorum inopiam utuntur. In ceteris civitatibus, quae nostro iure obstrictae sunt, res huius modi prohibenda est.
>
> If the citizens of Amisus, whose petition you send with your letter, are allowed by their own laws, granted them by formal treaty, to form a benefit society [*eranum*], there is no reason why we should interfere: especially if the contributions are not used for riotous

---

[125] With reference to meals shared by Christians after worship, Pliny writes to Trajan, "But they had in fact given up this practice since my edict (*post edictum meum*), issued on your instructions, which banned all political societies" (*Ep.* 10.96.7 [Radice, LCL]). This edict banning associations probably does not refer to an imperial policy enacted throughout the empire, as some have suggested; instead, the law prohibiting *collegia* was a regional response to the unstable political situation in Bithynia-Pontus (so Harland, *Associations, Synagogues, and Congregations*, 170–73; Ilias N. Arnaoutglou, "Roman Law and *Collegia* in Asia Minor," *Revue International des droits de l'Antiquité* 49 [2002]: 27–44; idem, "*Collegia* in the Province of Egypt in the First Century AD," *AncSoc* 35 [2005]: 197–216; *pace* Wendy Cotter, "The Collegia and Roman Law: State Restrictions on Voluntary Associations, 64 BCE–200 CE," in *Voluntary Associations in the Graeco-Roman World* [London and New York: Routledge, 1996], 84).

and unlawful assemblies, but to relieve cases of hardship among the poor [*sed ad sustinendam tenuiorum inopiam utuntur*]. In all other cities which are subject to our own law these institutions must be forbidden. (Pliny, *Ep.* 10.93 [Radice, LCL])

Trajan grants the Amisians the right to establish associations on account of the free status of their city, although he cautions Pliny that the clubs must not engage in disorderly and illicit conduct. Lacking other evidence, we can never be certain that these *erani*, or benefit societies, actually engaged in acts of charity on behalf of the poor. Yet this practice is suggested by the fact that Trajan stipulates that the "collections" (*collatione*) taken up by these clubs be used "to relieve cases of hardship among the poor" (*ad sustinendam tenuiorum inopiam utuntur*).[126] Trajan understands these ἐρανισταί to be the Greek equivalent of Roman *collegia tenuiorum*, associations of poor people (*tenuiores*, "the poorer") who met to celebrate religious duties, to provide a respectable burial for deceased members, and, according to Trajan, to gather funds intended to "relieve cases of hardship among the poor."[127] The existence of this type of association is attested as early as the latter half of the reign of Augustus (63 B.C.E – 14 C.E.), at which time a *senatus consultum* granted the right of persons of lesser means to form *collegia* and to make monthly contributions to a community fund that would be used to provide for religious activities and the burial of deceased members.[128] Of course, the meaning of the term "poor" in this context is difficult to pin down, for the ut-

---

[126] On the history and meaning of the word ἔρανος, see Bolkestein, *Wohltätigkeit und Armenpflege*, 240–41, 432–33. These associations appear originally to have been groups that offered their members interest-free loans, but by Trajan's time they had become "Organisationen ad sustinendam tenuiorum inopiam" (241).

[127] Cotter, "The Collegia and Roman Law," 86–87; cf. Marcus Prell, *Sozialökonomische Untersuchunen zur Armut im antiken Rom: Von Gracchen bis Kaiser Diokletian* (BWSG 77; Stuttgart: Franz Steiner, 1997), 258–60. An older scholarly view, advanced by Mommsen and Waltzing, maintained that the *collegia tenuiorum* represented a unique, legally recognized type of association devoted solely to the burial of its members (*collegia funeraticia*). More recently, Ausbüttel and Kloppenborg, among others, have challenged this position, suggesting that *collegia funeraticia* were not officially recognized until the time of Hadrian and, moreover, funerary activities were only one of many important aspects of associations in antiquity, including conviviality and religious practices. Even after Hadrian, however, few associations were formed simply as *collegia funeraticia*, and even those that were combined burial practices with other religious, professional, and social functions. See Kloppenborg, "Collegia and *Thiasoi*," 20–23; Ausbüttel, *Untersuchungen zu den Vereinen im Westen des Römischen Reiches*, 26–29.

[128] This *senatus consultum* is known from the reference to it in the charter inscription of the *cultures Dianae et Antinoi* in Lanuvium. This association was founded in 136 C.E., but its constitution refers to an earlier senatorial decree: "Chapter from a senatorial decree of the Roman people: It is allowed to persons of lesser means to meet and assemble a *collegium*. People wishing to contribute on a monthly basis an amount of money for sacral purposes, they can meet for this purpose as a *collegium*, and not under the guise of an existing *collegium*, unless they gather once a month in order to contribute to a fund, at the expenses of which they are going to bury the deceased" (CIL XIV 2112; translation from Arnaoutoglou, "*Collegia* in the Province of Egypt," 200). For another reference to this earlier senatorial decree, see *Dig.* XLVII 22.4.1.

terly destitute may have been prevented from joining some associations by the relatively high cost of membership fees and banquets.[129] Since the authors of the petition passed from Pliny to the emperor appear to have been citizens of Amisus, with the term *tenuiores* Trajan may, in fact, be referring to members of what Peter Brown has called "the middling classes."[130] On the other hand, with his use of the unusual phrase "to relieve cases of hardship among the poor," Trajan seems to have in mind something more substantial than merely an occasional banquet and the provision of a proper burial at death. The "hardship" (*inopia*) envisioned by Trajan appears to be a form of economic distress. While these ἐρανισταί in the Greek East do not necessarily provide evidence for charitable giving from the wealthy to the poor, they do imply that pagan associations did occasionally adopt economic practices, including taking up collections, intended to provide financial assistance for those in material need.[131]

Other associations included in their community charters rules for providing assistance to destitute members. The regulations of a second-century B.C.E. Demotic religious association in Egypt, for example, stipulate that, should one member of the group come across a poor colleague at the wharf or on the ferry, and fail to render assistance, he will be fined 25 *deben*, unless he affirms in an

---

[129] Verboven, "Associative Order," 12–13. The charter of the *cultures Dianae et Antinoi* in Lanuvium, for example, stipulates that "whoever wishes to become a member of this society shall give as a personal entrance fee 100 sesterces and an *amphora* of good wine, also he shall pay a monthly subscription of 5 *asses*" (CIL XIV 2112). Although recently manumitted slaves were required to pay only one *amphora* of good wine, the abject poor would have been unable to afford these costs of membership.

[130] Brown, *Poverty and Leadership*, 12–16, 79–80. There are, admittedly, numerous problems associated with using the language of "class" to describe the situation in Greco-Roman antiquity, especially if one assumes that "*as a group* they played a significant role in the primary modes of production of the economy as a whole; that they provided an important source for the 'capital' needed to drive the economic system" (Dale B. Martin, "Review Essay: Justin J. Meggitt, *Paul, Poverty and Survival*," *JSNT* 84 [2001]: 53; cf. Meeks, *First Urban Christians*, 51–53). With this term, however, Brown simply refers to the large mass of the population that fell somewhere between the wealthy elite and the destitute. Cf. also Steven J. Friesen, "Poverty in Pauline Studies: Beyond the So-called New Consensus," *JSNT* 26 (2004): 323–61.

[131] *Pace* Meggitt, who claims, "In fact the trade *collegia* rarely took any corporate action to defend their members' economic interests; nor did they have a system for providing assistance from joint funds to members facing financial difficulty. Indeed, nor were they as all-pervasive as is often assumed. The funeral clubs, *collegium funeraticium* or *collegium tenuiorum*, although substantially more popular, particularly amongst those at the bottom of Graeco-Roman society, did not offer anything more to their members than the occasional meal and the eventual fulfillment of the purpose of their creation, a decent burial" (*Paul, Poverty and Survival*, 171–72). Among some Roman *collegia* in the West, *sportulae* were distributed to members of the group from the common fund, although individuals of higher status received more money (cf. CIL VI 10234 = Waltzing, 3:1083; Prell, *Sozialökonomische Untersuchungen*, 259–60).

oath before the god that it was impossible for him to give.¹³² Similarly, members of this association were required to subsidize the burial costs of indigent comrades and to provide "mourner's bread" at the funeral of a deceased associate.¹³³ Perhaps a touch of disdain for the practice of collecting subscriptions for community meals for those without means is found in the retort of Diogenes the Cynic, who, when asked by the leader of an association (ἐρανάρχης) to contribute to the *eranos* of the club, responded with a punning allusion to the Iliad, "Borrow (ἐράνιζ) from the rest; but keep your hands from Hector" (Diogenes Laertius, *Lives* 6.63).¹³⁴

Of course, members of Jewish synagogues throughout the Mediterranean world, whose communal practices were shaped by biblical traditions concerning justice and care for the poor, considered the demonstration of *zedekah* to be an important religious activity.¹³⁵ Charitable institutions such as the *kupah* (קופה), through which weekly material support was donated to the poor, and the *tamhui* (תמחוי), which provided daily meals for the hungry and for strangers, were important aspects of everyday life in ancient synagogues (*m. Demai* 3:1; *m. Pe'ah* 8:7; *t. Pe'ah* 4:9; cf. Acts 6:1–7).¹³⁶ As Ze'ev Safrai remarks, "The Jewish community had a great degree of social awareness and responsibility, and the sages further encouraged this. It is no coincidence that the two general terms of *zedakah* and *mizvah* (lit. commandment) came to be technical phrases for the giving of monies, usually for social welfare purposes, and this certainly indicates the importance of this activity."¹³⁷ We have seen epigraphical evidence from the third-century synagogue in Aphrodisias that implies community giving for the construction and maintenance of a building likely used for charitable distributions. This corresponds to the claim of Josephus that Jews were admired and imitated

---

¹³² P. Cairo 31179; for a transliterated text and French translation, see Françoise de Cenival, *Les associations religieuses en Égypte: D'après les documents démotiques* (Cairo: Publications de l'institut français d'archéologie orientale du Caire, 1972), 63–67 (cf. P. Cairo 30606).

¹³³ Cenival, *Les associations religieuses*, 187–90.

¹³⁴ Had this chapter considered charity among other social institutions in the Greco-Roman world, such as philosophical schools, we might have noted the pecuniary practices of the Pythagorean communities; see Bolkestein, *Wohltätigkeit und Armenpflege*, 238–39.

¹³⁵ Roman Garrison, *Redemptive Almsgiving in Early Christianity* (JSNTSup 77; Sheffield: Sheffield Academic Press, 1993), 46–59.

¹³⁶ See Lee I. Levine, *The Ancient Synagogue: The First Thousand Years* (New Haven and London: Yale University Press, 2000), 372–74; Hamel, *Poverty and Charity*, 216–19; Ze'ev Safrai, *The Economy of Roman Palestine* (London: Routledge, 1994), 50; Emil Schürer, *The History of the Jewish People in the Age of Jesus Christ* (rev. and ed. G. Vermes, F. Millar, M. Black, and M. Goodman; 3 vols.; Edinburgh: T & T Clark, 1973–1987), 2:437; Ben-Zion Rosenfeld and Joseph Menirav, "The Ancient Synagogue as an Economic Center," *JNES* 58 (1999): 259–76, esp. 267–68. On the question of whether or not these institutions existed in Jerusalem in the first century C.E., see David Seccombe, "Was There Organized Charity in Jerusalem before the Christians?" *JTS* 29 (1978): 140–43.

¹³⁷ Safrai, *Economy of Roman Palestine*, 50.

throughout antiquity for, among other things, "our distribution of possessions" (τὴν τῶν ὄντων ἀνάδοσιν; *Ag. Ap.* 2.283; cf. Tacitus, *Hist.* 5.5.1). Finally, we have already noted the practice of collecting two days' worth of salary from members of the Qumran sect in order to "support the needy and poor" (CD XIV, 14).

Edwin Hatch, in comparing the financial practices of Greco-Roman associations with the early Christian tradition of almsgiving, remarked, "Other associations were charitable: but whereas in them charity was an accident, in the Christian associations it was of the essence. They gave to the religious revival which almost always accompanies a period of social strain the special direction of philanthropy. They brought into the European world that regard for the poor which had been for several centuries the burden of Jewish hymns."[138] Aside from Hatch's overly pessimistic view of the state of the Roman economy during the first century of the common era, his assertion that "charity was an accident" in pagan associations needs to be nuanced. On the one hand, it does appear that, for the most part, there was greater concern for the welfare of the poor among Jewish and Christian communities than one typically finds among pagan associations. Paul's explicitly expressed desire to see "equality" (ἰσότης, 2 Cor 8:13–14) between the churches of his mission and the poor among the saints in Jerusalem finds no parallel among the inscriptions left by pagan associations, although we have seen a similar formulation in the honorific decree for Damidas the physician erected by civic officials in Gytheion (IG V/1 1145). Most pagan voluntary associations were composed of those of middling status and wealth – "those rich enough to have left us their epitaphs recording their names and sometimes their ages and professions, but whose achievements were too insignificant to be remembered"[139] – and these individuals did not typically concern themselves with charity. At the same time, given that the collection for Jerusalem seems to have been a one-time caritative donation, we should not overstate the extent to which the charity was "of the essence" in the Pauline churches.

Moreover, the practice of individuals of lesser means forming associations and using their combined financial resources to provide assistance for the needy among their number is attested among the Greek ἐρανισταί, the Jewish sectarian group at Qumran, and Jewish synagogues throughout the Mediterranean world, and these forms of collective assistance seem to offer an interesting analogy to the collection for the saints among the Pauline churches. In addition to these analogous forms of giving, one can also point to the relief fund from Antioch to Jerusalem (Acts 11:27–30; Gal 2:10), a fundraising effort that served as a direct genealogical antecedent for the Pauline collection for the saints.[140] Therefore, to label the contribution for the impoverished believers in Jerusalem taken up

---

[138] Hatch, *Organization of the Early Christian Churches*, 36.
[139] Verboven, *Economy of Friends*, 113.
[140] See the discussion in chapter two, pp. 33–39.

3.5 Care for the Poor within Associations

among the churches of Paul's mission "a unique phenomenon in world history, both religious and social,"[141] as some scholars have done, is a conclusion that not only ignores much of the extant evidence, it is also one that fails to exercise the historical imagination.

How, we might ask, did the nameless and numberless poor in antiquity survive on a daily basis, despite the ever-present threat of food shortage and the less frequent but more devastating danger of famine? This question leaves us, as Garnsey and Woolf succinctly pose the problem, with two paradoxes: (1) "The poor are ubiquitous but are more or less invisible"; (2) "the poor survived (though doubtless for a shorter time span than their social superiors), but we are not told how."[142] In his study of the survival strategies available to subsistence farmers in Greco-Roman antiquity, Peter Garnsey highlights a number of options that peasants might have adopted in order to mitigate disaster during times of food shortage and/or famine. Among these strategies for survival, Garnsey discusses two types of social and economic relationships: *exchange relationships* (i.e., horizontal "relationships with members of [the peasant's] own or neighboring communities") and *patronage relationships* (i.e., vertical "relationships with men of superior wealth and influence").[143] Voluntary associations, it seems, provided access to either one or both of these kinds of economic relationships.[144] Some associations were more dependent upon the beneficence of wealthy patrons, from whom they received not only resources to fund religious and convivial activities, but also material distributions that helped members of these *collegia* to sustain life in times of crisis. If the members of these associations did not expressly identify themselves as "the poor" who benefited from the munificence of the wealthy, perhaps this was because the inscriptions that record these gifts were set up by, or with the approval of, the very individuals who received this assistance, and who did not wish to call themselves as οἱ πτωχοί or οἱ πένητες. Here we may run up against the veil of epigraphical rhetoric.

Other associations, like the ἐρανισταί in Asia Minor and Jewish synagogues throughout the Diaspora, may have been more likely to eschew patronal relationships, instead taking up collections from their members and combining financial

---

[141] Petros Vassiliadis, "Equality and Justice in Classical Antiquity and in Paul: The Social Implications of the Pauline Collection," *SVTQ* 36 (1992): 56.

[142] Garnsey and Woolf, "Patronage of the Rural Poor," 153.

[143] Peter Garnsey, *Famine and Food Supply in the Graeco-Roman World: Responses to Risk and Crisis* (Cambridge: Cambridge University Press, 1988), 55–63. These are Garnsey's terms. In terms of the categories elucidated earlier in this chapter, we might prefer to speak of relationships of familial/balanced reciprocity and relationships of general reciprocity.

[144] Cf. the conclusions of Schmeller (*Hierarchie und Egalität*, 50–51): "Die soziale Struktur von Vereinen ist durch eine Verbindung hierarchischer und egalitärer Element gekennzeichnet.... Die Gewichtung dieser hierarchischen und egalitären Elemente ist von der sozialen Stellung des jeweiligen Vereins abhängig: Je höher ein Verein in der Hierarchie der sozialen Umwelt steht, desto dominanter sind in ihm die hierarchischen Züge."

resources in order "to relieve cases of hardship among the poor." As Garnsey points out, "mutual support between ordinary citizens linked by kinship, proximity of residence or friendship, and exemplified in the interest-free loan, was a defence against poverty, hardship and the personal patronage of the wealthy that was irreconcilable with democratic ideology."[145] To the extent that Greco-Roman associations – pagan, Jewish, and Christian – provided alternative forms of social organization to the structures of both kinship and civic identity, even as they drew from and overlapped with these institutions, one might suppose that these associations also provided protection for the poor against both financial hardship and exploitation by potential patrons. Unfortunately, the evidence is elusive. The voices of the poorest members of Greco-Roman society are lost to us, for, when they did form associations, they could not afford to engrave community regulations and honors on permanent stone. It is interesting that the main evidence for "collections for the poor" among Greek ἐρανισταί comes, not from the associations themselves, but from the literary exchange of two elite politicians, Pliny and Trajan. Paul's endeavor to convince his congregations to provide material relief for the poor among the saints in Jerusalem, however, combined with his efforts to eliminate any hint that the Gentile Christians might justifiably conceive of themselves as patrons of their brothers and sisters in Jerusalem, suggests that "the offering of the Gentiles" finds its closest analogy among those associations that avoided patronal relationships and instead provided for the welfare of the poorer members of their community with charitable distributions from the entire group.

3.6 Translocal Economic Links among Associations

It is often claimed that a major difference between Greco-Roman voluntary associations and the earliest Christian communities is that the voluntary associations were localized whereas the Christian assemblies enjoyed numerous connections with churches in other cities.[146] One of the most important pieces of evidence for translocal links among the Pauline churches, of course, consists of Paul's fundraising efforts on behalf of the saints in Jerusalem, a labor that in-

---

[145] Garnsey, *Famine and Food Supply*, 80.
[146] This claim can be found in Meeks, *First Urban Christians*, 80; Robert Wilken, "Collegia, Philosophical Schools, and Theology," in *The Catacombs and the Coliseum: The Roman Empire as the Setting of Primitive Christianity* (ed. Stephen Benko and John J. O'Rourke; Valley Forge, Pa.: Jusdon, 1971), 269–91, esp. 279; idem, *The Christians as the Romans Saw Them* (New Haven: Yale University Press, 1984), 35; McCready, "*Ekklēsia* and Voluntary Associations," 63–64; and Barton and Horsley, "Hellenistic Cult Group," 28.

volved communities in the regions of Galatia, Achaia, and Macedonia.[147] A recent article by Richard S. Ascough, however, evaluates the primary evidence from voluntary associations and contends that this distinction between pagan associations and Christian churches is not tenable.[148] Associations of foreigners or traders frequently maintained ties with groups in their home cities or in other cities (IG II² 1317; SEG 2:10).[149] Cultic associations devoted to the Egyptian gods Isis and Sarapis throughout the Mediterranean world were often organized and staffed by Egyptian priests (IPriene 195), and members of these associations could expect to be welcomed by different branches of the group when moving from city to city, as is the case for Lucius when he travels from Africa to Rome (Apuleius, *Metam.* 11.26: *fani quidem advena, religionis autem indigena*). Additionally, the guild of Dionysiac artists, an ancient and popular religious association, advertised itself as a "world-wide" (τῆς οἰκουμένης) fellowship with local communities throughout the empire (cf. IEph 22; IG II² 1350).[150] Ascough therefore concludes, "A number of inscriptions point to the maintenance of contact with the place of origin of the association and/or its members as well as contact between associations in various locales. Thus, there seems to be some translocal connections among some voluntary associations."[151] Here we shall consider evidence for translocal economic connections among voluntary associations in different localities in antiquity. While the evidence is slim, there are indications of financial interdependence and examples of mutual assistance among some associations with regional and/or international ties.

Not surprisingly, the pagan clubs most likely to have shared translocal economic connections are the trade associations of merchants (ἔμποροι) and shippers (ναύκληροι) that were scattered among the port cities of the Mediterranean region (cf. IG XVI 1052).[152] To the extent that these associations of foreign traders established financial links with one another, it is likely that these bonds also sometimes involved the mediation of civic bodies in the locales from which these groups originated. This is illustrated in the fascinating inscription of two engraved letters that record the negotiations between city officials in Tyre, in southern Phoenicia, and two associations of Tyrian merchants in Rome and

---

[147] See also Michael B. Thompson, "The Holy Internet: Communication between Churches in the First Christian Generation," in *The Gospels for All Christians: Rethinking the Gospel Audiences* (ed. Richard Bauckham; Grand Rapids: Eerdmans, 1998), 49–70.

[148] Ascough, "Translocal Relationships"; see also idem, *Paul's Macedonian Associations*, 91–108; cf. Larry W. Hurtado, *At the Origins of Christian Worship: The Context and Character of Earliest Christian Devotion* (Grand Rapids: Eerdmans, 2000), 15–17.

[149] George La Piana, "Foreign Groups in Rome during the First Centuries of the Empire," *HTR* 20 (1927): 183–403.

[150] Ascough, *Paul's Macedonian Associations*, 98–100, 107.

[151] Ascough, "Translocal Relationships," 234.

[152] Tod and Hornblower, "Clubs, Greek," 352. See also Poland, *Geschichte des griechischen Vereinswesens*, 107–16.

Puteoli, the latter of which was a valuable port city some 140 miles south of Rome. The text of this correspondence follows:

> Letter written to the city of the Tyrians, sacred, inviolable, autonomous metropolis of Phonecia and of other cities and foremost on the sea.
>
> To the council, the citizens, and those of our sovereign fatherland, the Tyrians who dwell at Puteoli send greetings. To the gods and to the fortune of our Emperor!
>
> If there are any other *stationes* in Puteoli, ours is superior in both beauty and size, as you well know. In times past the Tyrians who dwell in Puteoli have provided for its maintenance, for they were many and wealthy. But now we are only a small group, and considering the expenses that we must bear for the sacrifices and the cultic worship of the gods of our fatherland who reside in temples here, we do not have the means to pay the rent of the *statio*, which is one-hundred thousand *denarii* per year. Even more so, there has fallen on us the burden of the bull-sacrifice in Puteoli. Therefore, we implore you provide for the maintenance of the *statio*, which cannot continue unless you take it upon yourselves to pay the yearly rent of one-hundred thousand *denarii*. As for the expenses and the costs for the repairs of the *statio* for the sacred days of the lord Emperor, we agree to assume them ourselves, so that we do not burden the city. We also remind you that we do not receive any revenue [πρόσοδος] from the ship-merchants and traders here, as is the case in royal Rome. Therefore, we urge and implore you by Fortune to give this matter careful consideration.
>
> Letter written at Puteoli, the sixth day before the calends of August, in the consulship of Gallus and Flaccus Cornelianus.
>
> In the session of the council of December twenty-first of the year three-hundred [Tyrian era; corresponding to December 8, 174 C.E.), under the presidency of Callicrates, son of Pausanius, the president.
>
> The letter of the Tyrians who have a *statio* was read, having been delivered by Laches, one of them. [Here follows a paraphrase of the letter: "In this letter they requested us to give assistance to them in the amount of one-hundred thousand *denarii* for sacrifices and the cultic worship of the gods of our fatherland who reside in temples there..."] After this letter was read, Philocles, son of Diodorus, spoke: The Tyrians who have the *statio* in Rome used to contribute to those in Puteoli the sum of one-hundred thousand *denarii* from the income of their receipts. Those in Puteoli have now asked that this old arrangement be observed, or if those in Rome are not willing to provide them with this amount, those in Puteoli will accept the general administration of the two *stationes* on the same terms. The motion is approved. Philocles has spoken well. Those in Puteoli are in the right. Since this has always been the custom, it must be maintained. This is in the interest of our city. We decreed that the tradition be continued.[153]

It seems that the association of Tyrian merchants in Puteoli had run into economic troubles, and was therefore unable to afford both its required religious sacrifices and the rent of the station in which the group conducted its business. Initially, the Roman association of Tyrians, which had experienced an economic boom after enhancements to the harbor at Ostia under Claudius (41–54 C.E.),

---

[153] CIG 5853; translation modified from La Piana, "Foreign Groups," 257–58. On this group, see also White, *The Social Origins of Christian Architecture*, 1:32.

had provided financial assistance to those in Puteoli. This subsidy had apparently lapsed with the passing of time, however. Facing fiscal crisis, the members of the association in Puteoli wrote a letter to the officials of their home city, asking for financial support. In response, the civic officials in Tyre stipulate that, following the established custom, the association of Tyrian merchants in Rome should pay for the expenses of the group in Puteoli, which amounts to no less than one hundred thousand *denarii* per year. As George La Piana comments on this arrangement, "From this document it is clear that the stationes of the Tyrians both in Puteoli and in Rome were the representative institutions there of the colonies as units, since through them the cults of the national gods and of the emperors were provided for; that they were officially recognized by the senate of Tyre as institutions necessary for the welfare of the citizens both at home and abroad; and finally that between the two stationes there was a connection not only of commercial, but of social, moral, and religious interests, involving mutual obligations."[154] Perhaps it is too generous to label this an act of charity on behalf of the Roman Tyrians, but this correspondence does suggest that pagan voluntary associations occasionally offered financial assistance to, and shared in religious obligations with, similar groups in different localities.[155]

Comparable examples of sharing in mutual obligations are found in the inter-civic economic connections among Jewish groups in antiquity. The Essene community at Qumran appears to have kept ties with other towns in Judea (Philo, *Prob.* 85; Josephus, *J.W.* 2.124).[156] According to Josephus, among the Essenes who inhabited different cities, there was an expectation that hospitality would be shown to visitors from other segments of the sect, to the extent that in

---

[154] La Piana, "Foreign Groups," 258.

[155] Demonstrations of financial assistance among voluntary associations may have paralleled practices of the state, for there are numerous instances of the rendering of economic aid from one city to another during times of crisis. When Hellenistic Rhodes suffered a severe earthquake in 227/6 B.C.E., for example, the city received gifts from a number of cities, rulers, and dynasts (Polybius, *Hist.* 5.88–90). Similarly, Aelius Aristides (117–after 181 C.E.) reports that, when a great earthquake devastated Asia Minor, the city of Smyrna provided other towns in the region with donations of food and money (*Or.* 19.12). For examples of inter-civic donations during periods of food scarcity, see Garnsey, *Famine and Food Supply*, 70–74. As early as the third century B.C.E., branches of the guild of Dionysiac artists in different cities occasionally shared mutual obligations with one another, including sending delegations of performers to cities that had fallen on hard times (CIG 3069; see Sir Arthur Pickard-Cambridge, *The Dramatic Festials of Athens* [2d ed.; Oxford: Clarendon, 1988], 279–305, 315–17).

[156] Ascough's claim ("Translocal Relationships," 235) that the discovery of copies of the Damascus Document at Qumran (4QD^{a-g}; 5Q12; and 6Q15) indicates that the Qumran community also shared ties with Egypt is inaccurate. The unearthing of the Damascus Document in the *geniza* of a synagogue in Cairo cannot be used as evidence for connections between Qumran and an unknown Egyptian community in the Second Temple period. For a helpful overview of the history of the Qumran community, see James C. Vanderkam, "Identity and History of the Community," in *The Dead Sea Scrolls After Fifty Years* (ed. Peter W. Flint and James C. Vanderkam; Leiden, Boston, and Köln: Brill, 1999), 2:487–533.

each town there was a specially appointed officer (κηδεμών) assigned to take care of guests from the sect:

> On the arrival of any of the sect from elsewhere, all the resources of the community are put at their disposal, just as if they were their own; and they enter the houses of men whom they have never seen before as though they were their most intimate friends. Consequently, they carry nothing whatever with them on their journeys, except arms as a protection against brigands. In every city there is one of the order expressly appointed to attend to strangers, who provides them with raiment and other necessaries.... There is no buying or selling among themselves, but each gives what he has to any in need and receives from him in exchange something useful to himself; they are, moreover, freely permitted to take anything from any of their brothers without making any return. (*J.W.* 2.124–127 [Thackeray, LCL]; cf. Philo, *Prob.* 85–86; 2 John 10–11; 3 John 3–8)

Similarly from Palestine, the so-called Theodotus inscription (CIJ 1404) commemorates the construction of a συναγωγή with a guest-room (ξενών) designed to serve "as a lodging place for those in need from foreign places" (εἰς κατάλυμα τοῖς [χ]ρήζουσιν ἀπὸ τῆς ξέ[ν]ης). This room was doubtless used to house and to provide hospitality to religious pilgrims traveling to Jerusalem from the Diaspora.[157]

Members of Jewish synagogues in the Diaspora, moreover, contributed monies to Jerusalem in the form of the temple tax. While this is not strictly an example of giving from one association to another, translocal economic connections among synagogues in the Mediterranean Diaspora were forged through the gathering of funds at regional collection centers before they were brought to Jersualem (cf. *Ant.* 14.110–13; 18.311–312). These connections were especially important in light of the opposition that Jews often faced from pagan neighbors upset with the transportation of such large sums of money away from their local communities.[158] As Barclay notes, "The gathering of such money at regional collection points (Josephus, Ant 14.110–13; Cicero, Pro Flacco 28.66–69) must have helped tie Diaspora communities together across geographical boundaries, while its common delivery to Jerusalem annually reinforced the international links of Diaspora Jews with one another, and with the Jerusalem temple."[159]

The practice of conveying material support from an association in one city to a related group in another region, therefore, appears to have been an uncommon but not unknown activity among pagan voluntary associations in antiquity.

---

[157] On the disputed date of this inscription, see now John S. Kloppenborg Verbin, "Dating Theodotos (CIJ II 1404)," *JJS* 51 (2000): 243–77. Cf. Tosefta, *Sukkah* 4.6 and Philo, *Legat.* 134 for references to a synagogue in Alexandria at which foreigners could also obtain assistance.

[158] Cf. Ciccero, *Flac.* 28.66–69; Josephus, *Ant.* 16.163–170; Philo, *Legat.* 156–157; 311–313; see John M. G. Barclay, *Jews in the Mediterranean Diaspora: From Alexander to Trajan (323 BCE–117 CE)* (Hellenistic Culture and Society 33; Berkeley: University of California Press, 1996), 266–70, 417–18.

[159] Barclay, "Money and Meetings," 119.

Where these translocal economic relationships did exist, it seems, not surprisingly, that ethnic connections and religious duties played a key role in solidifying ties between distant communities. When the association of Tyrian merchants in Puteoli was unable to pay both its rent and its required religious sacrifices, its members appealed to the civic authorities in their hometown as *Tyrians*, and their countrymen who owned a *statio* in Rome were enlisted by officials in Tyre to provide assistance. Among Diaspora Jews, who shared a common ethnic and religious identity, translocal economic relationships were forged through their attachment to Jerusalem.

That Paul spent so much time and energy raising funds from the churches of his mission for the saints in Jerusalem does stand out when compared to the pecuniary practices of pagan associations. Ascough, in fact, suggests that the difficulties Paul faced in soliciting contributions for the collection from the believers in Corinth may have been due, in part, to the inability of the Corinthians to understand their obligations to a community so far removed from their own: "What confuses the Corinthians [about the collection] is not the fact that they have to donate, but that the monies are going to Jerusalem rather than the common fund of the local congregation."[160] We might add that perhaps it was not only the distance of the Jerusalem church that posed a problem for the reluctant givers in Corinth, but also the ethnicity of the recipients. We know that Diaspora Jews consistently faced derision and hostility from pagans for the Jewish practice of sending funds each year to the temple in Jerusalem. From the perspective of their non-Jewish neighbors, the exportation of substantial quantities of gold was a serious drain on the local economy: "For cities struggling to meet their tax obligations and unable to repair their own temples, it must have been galling to discover that such sums were regularly donated to a foreign temple."[161] In defending the governor L. Valerius Flaccus against the charge of confiscating well over one hundred and twenty pounds of gold destined for Jerusalem from Jewish communities in four cities in Asia Minor, Cicero clearly aims to exploit anti-Jewish sentiment among his jurors:

> When every year it was customary to send gold to Jerusalem on the order of the Jews from Italy and from all our provinces, Flaccus forbade by an edict its exportation from Asia. Who is there, gentlemen, who could not honestly praise this action? The senate often earlier and also in my consulship most urgently forbade the export of gold. But to resist this barbaric superstition [*barbara superstitio*] was an act of firmness. (*Flac.* 28.67 [Lord, LCL]; cf. Josephus, *J.W.* 6.335–336)[162]

---

[160] Ascough, *Paul's Macedonian Associations*, 104.
[161] Barclay, *Jews in the Mediterranean Diaspora*, 267.
[162] On this episode, see Anthony J. Marshall, "Flaccus and the Jews of Asia (Cicero *Pro Flacco* 28.67–69)," *Phoenix* 29 (1975): 139–54. In his *Antiquities of the Jews*, Josephus offers a catena of no less than six decrees and letters from Roman officials that all allow, among other things, Jews the liberty to transport sacred monies to the temple in Jerusalem (*Ant.* 16.160–174; cf.

Whether or not the Pauline collection was patterned on the Jewish temple tax, the notion of consigning money to the Jewish-Christian community in Jerusalem, in light of the widespread pagan resentment of Jewish offerings to a distant temple, might have given some members of Paul's churches pause when they were asked to fund a monetary contribution for the saints in this foreign city.

Finally, the one demonstrable predecessor for the offering raised among the Gentile churches of Paul's mission is the relief fund dispatched from Antioch to Jerusalem in Acts 11:27–30. This earlier collection of funds, organized in anticipation of a worldwide famine predicted by the prophet Agabus and delivered by Barnabas and Saul (i.e., Paul) to the elders in Jerusalem, should also be considered in evaluating the evidence for translocal economic connections among ancient associations.[163] This διακονία, as the narrator makes clear, is the result, not of the patronage of a few wealthy members of the community, but of contributions from each (ἕκαστος αὐτῶν, 11:29) of the disciples.

3.7 Conclusion

This chapter has focused on the monetary practices of Greco-Roman voluntary associations in the attempt to discern forms of giving analogous to the Pauline collection for Jerusalem, rather than genealogical antecedents to that contribution. The comparative task has been given precedence over the competing quests for uniqueness and sameness.[164] Paul's collection for Jerusalem was neither a unique event in world history nor was it merely a repetition of some earlier model. We have seen examples of collective economic activity among pagan and Jewish associations that, in both their similarities and differences, shed light on Paul's efforts to organize a collection for the saints in Jerusalem. Members of pagan associations, Jewish synagogues, and the Pauline churches were all bound together through their communal economic practices. Within each of these groups, relationships were formed and symbolized through the distribution of benefits, the observance of sacred rites, the celebration of community meals, the

---

Philo, *Legat.* 311–313). That Josephus is compelled to provide such a thorough catalogue of this provision is an indication of the severity of pagan opposition to this Jewish practice. Cf. Sze-kar Wan, "Collection for the Saints as Anticolonial Act: Implications of Paul's Ethnic Reconstruction," in *Paul and Politics: Ekklesia, Israel, Imperium, Interpretation; Essays in Honor of Krister Stendahl* (ed. Richard H. Horsley; Harrisburg, Pa.: Trinity, 2000), 201–3.

[163] Ascough does not mention evidence from the book of Acts in his discussions of translocal connections within early Christianity. The point here is not the historical accuracy of Acts, although I have argued in chapter two that here Acts does provide reliable information about Paul's involvement in the administration of a contribution from Antioch. Instead, it is enough to maintain that the author of Acts described an episode of translocal financial assistance among the early Christian communities.

[164] Smith, *Drudgery Divine*, 36–53.

3.7 Conclusion

collection of funds, and the provision of mutual assistance. Collective economic activity, therefore, was part and parcel of the daily life of ancient associations.

Recently, Vincent Gabrielsen, in a study of the associations of Hellenistic Rhodes, has posed the following question, aimed at moving beyond the concern of many classicists to interpret associations in antiquity in light of medieval guilds: "the current discourse about the relation of [the multiple functions performed by a corporate body] to economic activity needs to be redirected, by abandoning its traditional (and narrow) concern with whether or not ancient *koina/collegia* acted like the mediaeval guilds – i.e., as regulatory or protective agencies in their respective trades – in favor of an inquiry into how, and in which areas, the habit of pooling and articulating human action through *koinoniai* interacted with a given social environment and its political regime."[165] This is a worthwhile question, and it is hoped that this chapter has shed some light on the social context of the Pauline collection for Jerusalem and, more generally, on the relationship between Paul's churches and Greco-Roman voluntary associations. To the extent that members of pagan and Jewish voluntary associations shared financial resources in order to fund religious and social activities, cared for the poor within their communities, and established or solidified financial links with similar groups in other localities, the monetary practices of Greco-Roman associations shed light on Paul's efforts to raise a relief fund for Jerusalem.

Yet we might also extend Gabrielsen's question by asking, with respect to Paul's efforts to organize a contribution for the poor among the saints in Jerusalem, not only how "the habit of pooling and articulating human action through *koinoniai* interacted with a given social environment and its political regime," but also how this activity interacted with a given set of theological convictions. We have already seen evidence to suggest that certain Jewish communities and authors in antiquity practiced or advocated restraint in the awarding of prolific honors to benefactors and patrons, in part because of the theological conviction that all benefactions originate from God. In what sense is Paul's rhetoric of the Jerusalem collection shaped by or reflective of his own theological convictions? This question is the burden of the following chapter, which shall provide a detailed examination of the theological presentation of the collection for Jerusalem in 1 Cor 16:1–4; 2 Cor 8:1–9:15; and Rom 15:14–32.

---

[165] Gabrielsen, "Rhodian Associations," 219. For the standard assessment of the relationship between ancient *collegia* and medieval trade guilds, see Finley, *Ancient Economy*, 137–38.

Chapter 4

The Collection as an Act of Worship: Paul's Cultic Rhetoric

4.1 Introduction

Having examined the Pauline collection for Jerusalem in its chronological and socio-cultural contexts, it is now time to undertake a detailed exegetical study of those passages in which Paul explicitly discusses the collection for the saints, namely, 1 Cor 16:1–4; 2 Cor 8:1–9:15; and Rom 15:14–32. With the aim of exploring Paul's presentation of the theological significance of the Jerusalem collection (i.e., Paul's *theologizing* about the collection[1]), this chapter will focus on two related questions. First, as we saw in the second chapter of the present work, Paul's efforts to organize a relief fund for Jerusalem met with considerable resistance in Corinth (and perhaps in Galatia as well). Given this opposition, what rhetorical strategies does Paul employ in order to persuade his readers in Corinth to adopt a reoriented theological conception of the collection for the saints, and so contribute to the fund? Second, Paul's rhetoric of the collection – indeed, his discussion of economic matters in general (cf. Phil 2:17; 4:10–20) – is marked by a high concentration of religious or cultic language.[2] What role, therefore, do Paul's cultic metaphors play in the attempt to determine the theological significance of the Jerusalem collection for Paul's mission as apostle to the Gentiles?

After a brief discussion of the ways in which recent theoretical study of metaphor might inform the interpretation of the cultic language that Paul uses with reference to the Jerusalem collection, I shall investigate each of the passages

---

[1] On the concept of Paul's "theologizing," see Paul W. Meyer, "Pauline Theology: A Proposal for a Pause in Its Pursuit," in *Pauline Theology*, vol. 4: *Looking Back, Pressing On* (ed. E. Elizabeth Johnson and David M. Hay; SBLSymS 4; Atlanta: Scholars Press, 1997), 140–60, esp. 150.

[2] With the term "cultic language," I refer loosely to language taken from the realm of Jewish or pagan ritual religious practice, particularly the activity of sacrifice and the role of the priesthood. For an exploration of the function of cultic language in another New Testament document, see Christian A. Eberhart, "Characteristics of Sacrificial Metaphors in Hebrews," in *Hebrews: Contemporary Methods, New Insights* (ed. Gabriella Gelardini; Biblical Interpretation Series 75; Leiden and Boston: Brill, 2005), 37–64; and Ekkehard W. Stegemann and Wolfgang Stegemann, "Does the Cultic Language in Hebrews Represent Sacrificial Metaphors? Reflections on Some Basic Problems," in *Hebrews: Contemporary Methods, New Insights* (ed. Gabriella Gelardini; Biblical Interpretation Series 75; Leiden and Boston: Brill, 2005), 13–23.

in which Paul mentions the relief fund, focusing my exegesis particularly on the two questions identified above. The aim of this chapter is to demonstrate that Paul presents the collection for Jerusalem to the (largely) Gentile congregations of his mission in Achaia and to the (mixed Jewish-Gentile) Christian community in Rome as a religious offering.[3] Although one intention of this gift was, undoubtedly, the material relief of impoverished believers in Jerusalem, the collection in Paul's letters is portrayed primarily, and especially through the use of several cultic metaphors, as an act of corporate worship that will result in thanksgiving and praise, not to human benefactors, as the dominant ideology of euergetism in the Greco-Roman world would have claimed, but rather to God, the one through whom all human benefaction is ultimately possible. Paul metaphorically frames his readers' responsive participation in the collection as an act of cultic worship, and in so doing he underscores the point that benefaction within the community of believers results in praise to God. This rhetorical strategy represents a challenge to the ideologies of patronage and benefaction that, as we saw in the previous chapter, so decisively shaped conventions of gift-giving in the Greco-Roman world – including the pecuniary practices of ancient voluntary associations – for it not only minimizes the competition for honor among the members of Paul's churches, it also suggests that even the very human action of raising money for those in material need originates in ἡ χάρις τοῦ θεοῦ and will eventuate in χάρις τῷ θεῷ (2 Cor 9:14–15). Paul uses the metaphor "collection is an act of worship," along with the metaphor "collection is an act of harvest," to invite his readers to conceptualize gift-giving within the community of believers in terms of an alternative economy characterized by generosity and aimed at worship.

4.2 Methodological Considerations

In anticipation of the exegesis of Paul's cultic metaphors that will follow, it is necessary first to provide a very brief sketch of some of the theoretical concepts that underlie the discussion of metaphor in the present chapter. Recent study of metaphor – by both literary theorists and biblical scholars – has emphasized that, far from being limited to instances of linguistic decoration, metaphor lies at the

---

[3] On the problem of the audience for Romans, see Karl Donfried, ed., *The Romans Debate: Revised and Expanded Edition* (Peabody, Mass.: Hendrickson, 1991). Recently, A. Andrew Das (*Solving the Romans Debate* [Minneapolis: Fortress, 2007]) has contended that Paul wrote to "Roman congregations composed exclusively of gentiles" (1), but his argument fails to account for evidence in Romans that suggests the presence of at least some Jewish believers in the audience of Romans (cf. Rom 16:3, 7, 11; 1:7: "to *all* God's beloved in Rome"; see David J. Downs, review of *Solving the Romans Debate* by A. Andrew Das, *Review of Biblical Literature* [2007] http://www.bookreviews.org/pdf/5772_6197.pdf).

root, not just of human language, but also of human thought and experience.[4] At least since the publication of I. A. Richards' seminal monograph *The Philosophy of Rhetoric* in 1936, metaphor has increasingly been viewed as "central to the task of accounting for our perspectives on the world: how we think about things, make sense of reality, and set the problems we later try to solve."[5] As George Lakoff and Mark Johnson argue in their now-classic book *Metaphors We Live By*, because metaphors can provide a frame through which we view the world, the introduction of a metaphor into a particular rhetorical context is potentially also an invitation to reframe one's view of reality.[6] A central argument of the present chapter will be that, among a number of rhetorical strategies that Paul employs in his discussions of the collection for the poor among the saints in Jerusalem,

---

[4] A very helpful introduction to some recent developments in the study of metaphor is provided in Zoltán Kövecses, *Metaphor: A Practical Introduction* (Oxford: Oxford University Press, 2002). See also the brief history of the debate in Wendell V. Harris, "Metaphor," in *Dictionary of Concepts in Literary Criticism and Theory* (New York: Greenwood, 1992), 222–31. Another useful outline of various theories of metaphor can be found in Janet Martin Soskice, *Metaphor and Religious Language* (Oxford: Clarendon, 1985), 24–53.

A number of recent works in biblical studies have engaged contemporary metaphor theory. See, e.g., Peter W. Macky, *The Centrality of Metaphors to Biblical Thought: A Method for Interpreting the Bible* (SBEC 19; Lewiston: Edwin Mellen, 1990); Steven J. Kraftchick, "Death in Us, Life in You: The Apostolic Medium," in *Pauline Theology*, vol. 2: *1 and 2 Corinthians* (SBLSymS 22; ed. David M. Hay; Minneapolis: Fortress, 1993), 156–81; Beverly Roberts Gaventa, "Our Mother St. Paul: Toward the Recovery of a Neglected Theme," *PSB* 17 (1996): 29–44; Gregory W. Dawes, *The Body in Question: Metaphor and Meaning in the Interpretation of Ephesians 5:21–33* (Biblical Interpretation Series 30; Leiden: Brill, 1998); Trevor J. Burke, *Family Matters: A Socio-Historical Study of Kinship Metaphors in 1 Thessalonians* (JSNTSup 247; London and New York: T & T Clark, 2003); Sarah J. Dille, *Mixing Metaphors: God as Mother and Father in Deutero-Isaiah* (JSOTSup 398; Gender, Culture, Theory 13; London and New York: T & T Clark, 2004); Mary Shields, *Circumscribing the Prostitute: The Rhetorics of Intertextuality, Metaphor, and Gender in Jeremiah 3.1–4.4* (JSOTSup 387; London and New York: T & T Clark, 2004); Cilliers Breytenbach, "Civic Concord and Cosmic Harmony: Sources of Metaphoric Mapping in *1 Clement* 20:3," in *Early Christianity and Classical Culture: Comparative Studies in Honor of Abraham J. Malherbe* (NovTSup 110; Atlanta: Society of Biblical Literature, 2005), 259–73; Stegemann and Stegemann, "Does the Cultic Language in Hebrews Represent Sacrificial Metaphors?" 13–23; P. Van Hecke, ed., *Metaphor in the Hebrew Bible* (BETL 187; Leuven: Peeters, 2006); and Nijay K. Gupta, "Principles for Interpreting Metaphors in Paul: *Prosagōgēn* (Rom 5.2) as a Case Study" (paper presented at the annual meeting of the Society of Biblical Literature, San Diego, Calif., 18 November 2007). David J. Williams's book *Paul's Metaphors: Their Context and Character* (Peabody, Mass.: Hendrickson, 1999) represents a detailed thematic catalogue of Paul's metaphors in their cultural context, but the focus is more historical and exegetical.

[5] Donald Schön, "Generative Metaphor," in *Metaphor and Thought* (2d ed.; ed. Andrew Ortony; Cambridge: Cambridge University Press, 1993), 137; see I. A. Richards, *The Philosophy of Rhetoric: The Mary Flexner Lectures on the Humanities; Bryn Mawr College, 1936* (New York and Oxford: Oxford University Press, 1936).

[6] George Lakoff and Mark Johnson, *Metaphors We Live By* (Chicago and London: University of Chicago Press, 1980).

several distinct yet related cultic metaphors are used in order to invite readers to adopt an appropriate theological framework for the offering.

Lakoff and Johnson define metaphor, quite simply, as "understanding and experiencing one kind of thing in terms of another."[7] Central to their theory of metaphor is their conviction that metaphor is far more than "a device of the poetic imagination and the rhetorical flourish – a matter of extraordinary rather than ordinary language."[8] Instead, Lakoff and Johnson maintain that metaphor is pervasive in human thought and action: "Our ordinary conceptual system, in terms of which we both think and act, is fundamentally metaphorical in nature.... Our concepts structure what we perceive, how we get around in the world, and how we relate to other people. Our conceptual system thus plays a central role in defining everyday realties."[9]

To illustrate how metaphor functions as part of our conceptual system, Lakoff and Johnson point to the metaphor ARGUMENT IS WAR, a structural metaphor that can be observed in any number of everyday expressions:

> Your claims are *indefensible*.
> He *attacked every weak point* in my argument.
> His criticisms were *right on target*.
> I *demolished* his argument.
> I've never *won* an argument with him.
> You disagree? Okay, *shoot!*
> If you use that *strategy*, he'll *wipe you out*.
> He *shot down* all of my arguments.[10]

Their point is that the metaphor ARGUMENT IS WAR structures how we think about and experience the activity of arguing. This metaphor does not exist merely at the linguistic level, but it structures our language, our thought, and our experience of the concept of argument. Indeed, Lakoff and Johnson claim that "[m]etaphors as linguistic expressions are possible precisely because there are metaphors in a person's conceptual system."[11] It is possible to envision a culture in which argument is not viewed in terms of this particular structural metaphor. For example, Lakoff and Johnson suggest that we might "imagine a culture where an argument is viewed as a dance, the participants are seen as performers,

---

[7] Ibid., 5.

[8] Ibid., 3.

[9] Ibid. Lakoff and Johnson's notion of "conceptual metaphors" is similar to Max Black's claim that "every metaphor is the tip of a submerged model"; see Max Black, *Models and Metaphors: Studies in Language and Philosophy* (Ithaca, N.Y.: Cornell University Press, 1979); and idem, "More about Metaphor," in *Metaphor and Thought* (ed. Andrew Ortony; 2d ed.; Cambridge: Cambridge University Press, 1993), 19–41.

[10] Lakoff and Johnson, *Metaphors We Live By*, 4.

[11] Ibid., 6. This point is debatable, and one weakness of Lakoff and Johnson's work may be their assumption that there are no "dead" metaphors. See Soskice, *Metaphors and Religious Language*, 81; Dawes, *The Body in Question*, 37, 66–68.

and the goal is to perform in a balanced and aesthetically pleasing way."[12] In contemporary American culture, however, the structural metaphor ARGUMENT IS WAR takes precedence over the metaphor ARGUMENT IS DANCE.

The thesis of this chapter is that a close reading of the language used to describe the Jerusalem collection in Paul's letters reveals a particular conceptual metaphor that structures Paul's own understanding and presentation of the activity of collecting money within the believing community.[13] In short, Paul works with the conceptual metaphor that collecting money for the poor in Jerusalem is an act of cultic worship; or, to frame the statement in a pithier form: COLLECTION IS WORSHIP.

Of course, as Lakoff and Johnson demonstrate, specific concepts like "argument" can be structured with different, sometimes logically inconsistent, metaphors. Although the metaphor ARGUMENT IS DANCE is not particularly common in American culture, a number of other structural metaphors are regularly used to speak of the concept "argument," including ARGUMENT IS A JOURNEY ("*So far*, we haven't *covered much ground*"), ARGUMENT IS A BUILDING ("If you don't *support* your argument with *solid* facts, the whole thing will *collapse*") and ARGUMENT IS A CONTAINER ("Your argument *won't hold water*").[14] According to Lakoff and Johnson, "[e]ach metaphor focuses on one aspect of the concept ARGUMENT: in this, each serves a single purpose. Moreover, each metaphor allows us to understand one aspect of the concept in terms of a more clearly delineated concept, e.g., JOURNEY or CONTAINER. The reason we need two metaphors is because there is no one metaphor that will do the job – there is no one metaphor that will allow us to get a handle simultaneously on both the direction of the argument and the content of the argument. These two purposes cannot both be served at once by a single metaphor."[15]

---

[12] Lakoff and Johnson, *Metaphors We Live By*, 5.

[13] Methodologically, I begin with metaphors at the textual level (i.e., "metaphors as linguistic expressions") and from them work back to the larger conceptual metaphor structured by these particular linguistic expressions. This, as I understand it, is also the approach of Lakoff and Johnson, and this method differs significantly from that of Steven J. Kraftchick in his article "Death in Us, Life in You." Kraftchick begins with what he calls the "generative metaphor" of the "death and resurrection of Jesus" in 2 Corinthians, and moves from there to a study of the "rhetorical metaphors" that occur at the level of the text. The question of whether Kraftchick's notion of a "generative metaphor" is, in fact, actually a "metaphor" is rightly raised by Beverly Roberts Gaventa, "Apostle and Church in 2 Corinthians: A Response to David M. Hay and Steven J. Kraftchick," in *Pauline Theology*, vol. 2: *1 and 2 Corinthians* (SBLSymS 22; ed. David M. Hay; Minneapolis: Fortress, 1993), 182–99, esp. 189. Similarly, Stephan Joubert's (*Paul as Benefactor: Reciprocity, Strategy and Theological Reflection in Paul's Collection* [WUNT 2:124; Tübingen: Mohr Siebeck, 2000], 172) discussion of "the metaphorical application of family language by Paul in 2 Corinthians 8–9" suffers from the fact that, while Paul does address his readers as ἀδελφοί in 8:1, the apostle nowhere employs patriarchal language in 2 Corinthians 8–9.

[14] Lakoff and Johnson, *Metaphors We Live By*, 97–105.

[15] Ibid., 95.

4.2 Methodological Considerations

Recognizing that many concepts are organized by different structural metaphors, Lakoff and Johnson draw an important distinction between inconsistent and coherent metaphors. Metaphors are consistent if "one clearly delineated concept" can account for both of them. For example, in Isa 45:10 the metaphor of God as father ("Woe to anyone who says to a father, 'What are you begetting?'") is consistent with the metaphor of God as mother ("or to a woman, 'With what are you in labor?'") because both metaphors can be described by the single concept GOD IS PARENT.[16] Yet "complete consistency across metaphors is rare."[17] Therefore, Lakoff and Johnson propose that logically inconsistent metaphors can nevertheless be coherent. Metaphorical coherence is determined by what Lakoff and Johnson call "shared entailments,"[18] by which term they mean an overlap of purpose:

> A metaphorical structuring of a concept, say the JOURNEY metaphor for arguments, allows us to get a handle on one aspect of the concept. Thus a metaphor works when it satisfies a purpose, namely, understanding an aspect of the concept. When two metaphors successfully satisfy two purposes, then overlaps in the purposes will correspond to overlaps in the metaphors. Such overlaps, we claim, can be characterized in terms of shared metaphorical entailments and the cross-metaphorical correspondences established by them.[19]

Thus, both the metaphors ARUMENT IS A JOURNEY and ARUMENT IS A CONTAINER, though logically inconsistent, are nevertheless "coherent" because they share certain metaphorical entailments.[20] Seemingly mixed metaphors, therefore, which may be logically inconsistent, can still function coherently based on shared entailments. Moreover, since diverse metaphors structure the same concepts, metaphors are also able to "highlight certain features [of a concept] while suppressing others."[21] Lakoff and Johnson point to the structural metaphor LOVE IS A COLLABORATIVE WORK OF ART. This metaphor entails such convictions as "love is work," "love requires cooperation," and "love involves creativity." Thus the metaphor highlights certain aspects of love (e.g., activity) while at the same time downplaying or masking others (e.g., the emotional aspects of love).[22]

---

[16] See Dille, *Mixing Metaphors*, 102–27.

[17] Lakoff and Johnson, *Metaphors We Live By*, 96.

[18] Ibid., 93; see also Kövecses, *Metaphor*, 93–105.

[19] Lakoff and Johnson, *Metaphors We Live By*, 97.

[20] In this case, the ARGUMENT IS A JOURNEY metaphor assumes that "as more of a surface is created, the argument covers more ground" and the ARGUMENT IS A CONTAINER that "as more of a surface is created, the argument gets more content." Thus, one entailment is "as we make an argument, more of a surface is created" (*Metaphors We Live By*, 94).

[21] Lakoff and Johnson, *Metaphors We Live By*, 141.

[22] For further discussion of metaphorical highlighting and hiding, see Kövecses, *Metaphor*, 79–83.

The notion that some concepts can be structured by several different, perhaps even inconsistent, metaphors is an issue that will present itself in the study of Paul's rhetoric for the collection. Along with the conceptual metaphor COLLECTION IS WORSHIP, which comes to expression in a number of places in the Pauline epistles (1 Cor 16:1–2; 2 Cor 8:6, 11–12; 9:12; Rom 15:16, 27–28), Paul also uses at least one additional conceptual metaphor to describe the Jerusalem collection, namely, COLLECTION IS HARVEST (2 Cor 9:6–10; Rom 15:28). Since Paul has occasionally been accused of an inability to express himself clearly with metaphorical language, careful attention to Lakoff and Johnson's notion of "metaphorical coherence" may shed light on Paul's seemingly mixed metaphors.[23] Furthermore, as we shall see, Paul's cultic metaphors for the Jerusalem collection highlight certain aspects of that activity (e.g., worship) while at the same time hiding others (e.g., competition).

Finally, the work of Lakoff and Johnson is suggestive of how metaphors can be used to shape human experience and behavior. Metaphors not only reflect but also help to create social realities, as research on the use of metaphor in the realm of public policy has shown.[24] According to Lakoff and Johnson, "New metaphors, like conventional metaphors, can have the power to define reality. They do this through a coherent network of entailments that highlight some features of reality and hide others. The acceptance of the metaphor, which forces us to focus *only* on those aspects of our experience that it highlights, leads us to view the entailments of the metaphor as being *true*."[25] As we shall see, the metaphors that Paul uses to describe the Jerusalem collection invite his readers to perceive this fundraising project in a new way, the goal of which epistemological reorientation is to encourage both support for the project and, most importantly, the worship of God.

---

[23] Beverly Gaventa notes that C. H. Dodd (*The Epistle of Paul to the Romans* [New York: Ray Long and Richard R. Smith, 1932], 103), commenting on the analogy to marriage in Rom 7:1–6, writes, "[Paul lacks] the gift for sustained illustration of ideas through concrete images (though he is capable of a brief illuminatory metaphor. It is probably a defect of imagination" (cited in Gaventa, "Our Mother St. Paul," 33 n. 10). Several articles by Gaventa on maternal imagery in Paul's letters have shed light on Paul's (effective) use of mixed metaphors; see Beverly Roberts Gaventa, "Apostles as Babes and Nurses in 1 Thessalonians 2:7," in *Faith and History: Essays in Honor of Paul W. Meyer* (ed. John T. Carroll, Charles H. Cosgrove, and E. Elizabeth Johnson; Atlanta: Scholars Press, 1990), 193–207; "Mother's Milk and Ministry in 1 Corinthians 3," in *Theology and Ethics in Paul and His Interpreters: Essays in Honor of Victor Paul Furnish* (ed. Eugene H. Lovering Jr. and Jerry L. Sumney; Nashville: Abingdon, 1996), 101–13; "The Maternity of Paul: An Exegetical Study of Galatians 4:19," in *The Conversation Continues: Studies in Paul and John in Honor of J. Louis Martyn* (ed. Robert T. Fortna and Beverly R. Gaventa; Nashville: Abingdon, 1990), 189–201.

[24] Schön, "Generative Metaphor," 137–63; George Lakoff, *Moral Politics* (Chicago: University of Chicago Press, 1996).

[25] Lakoff and Johnson, *Metaphors We Live By*, 156.

4.3 First Corinthians 16:1–4: The Collection of Money as an Element of Worship in the Pauline Churches

We begin our exegesis with 1 Cor 16:1–4, the earliest extant comments about the offering for Jerusalem gathered among the Pauline churches. Paul's brief treatment of the organizational mechanics of collection in this passage, introduced with the formulaic clause περὶ δέ (cf. 1 Cor 7:1, 25; 8:1; 12:1; 16:12), is intended to answer a question posed by the Corinthians about the relief fund for the saints.[26] Paul responds to their query by providing instructions regarding the gathering of the fund: "Now concerning the collection for the saints: just as I directed the churches in Galatia, you yourselves should also do likewise. Every Sunday, each of you individually should set aside and gather in accordance with how you fare, so that there need not be collections when I come. And when I arrive, I will send those whom you approve with letters to take your benefaction[27] to Jerusalem. If it seems right for me to go also, they will go together with me" (1 Cor 16:1–4). As has often been observed, the authoritative tenor of Paul's directives in this passage suggests little of the conflict that would ultimately plague his fundraising efforts in Corinth, troubles reflected plainly in 2 Cor 8:1–9:15. Here Paul appears confident in the willingness and ability of the Corinthians to obey the instructions set forth in 1 Cor 16:1–4.[28]

The first point to make in this context is the close connection between the procedure for collecting monies for Jerusalem, on the one hand, and the worship life of the nascent Christian communities in Corinth and Galatia, on the other.

---

[26] Dieter Georgi (*Remembering the Poor: The History of Paul's Collection for Jerusalem* [Nashville: Abingdon, 1992], 51–52) makes the intriguing observation that 1 Cor 16:1–4 is linked to the material concerning the resurrection of the dead in the preceding chapter by means of the "historic indebtedness on the part of later Jesus-believing congregations to the first witnesses" (cf. 1 Cor 15:3–8).

[27] It is extremely difficult to find a consistent English translation for the term χάρις when it appears as a designation for the Jerusalem collection in 1 Cor 16:3; 2 Cor 8:4, 6, 7, and 19. In light of the frequency with which the word appears in benefaction contexts in the ancient sources (see James R. Harrison, *Paul's Language of Grace in Its Graeco-Roman Context* [WUNT 2:172; Tübingen: Mohr Siebeck, 2003], 26–209), I have attempted to render the word "benefit/benefaction," even when Paul speaks of the χάρις τοῦ θεοῦ (2 Cor 8:1) or of the χάρις τοῦ κυρίου ἡμῶν Ἰησοῦ Χριστοῦ (2 Cor 8:9). This does not solve the problem of how to translate the phrase χάρις τῷ θεῷ in 2 Cor 8:16 and 9:15, however.

[28] So also Joubert, *Paul as Benefactor*, 162–64. Pace Verbrugge (Verlyn D. Verbrugge, *Paul's Style of Church Leadership Illustrated by His Instructions to the Corinthians on the Collection* [San Francisco: Mellen Research University Press, 1992], 58–67), who argues that 1 Cor 16:1–2 represents an example of the epistolary form called the "commanding letter" and who claims that Paul adopts this literary form in order to combat a reluctance among the Corinthians to contribute to the fund. Not only does Verbrugge fail to provide sufficient evidence to confirm the existence of the genre of "commanding letter" in the ancient world, even if such a literary form did exist, Verbrugge's strategy of isolating 1 Cor 16:1–2 from its present literary context and claiming that these two verses represent the genre of "commanding letter" is dubious.

Paul's letter to the Corinthians provides a wealth of information about the worship practices of the believing community at Corinth (cf. 1 Cor 10:14–22; 11:2–34; 14:1–40), and the apostle's comments in 1 Cor 16:1–4 indicate that the collection of funds for the poor among the saints in Jerusalem was to be an important element of the weekly meeting of Christians in Corinth (and presumably in Galatia as well). A focal point in the debate about the historical origins of the Christian practice of meeting regularly on Sunday (cf. Acts 20:7; Rev 1:10) instead of on the Jewish Sabbath has been the question whether 1 Cor 16:2 testifies to an offering taken up during a weekly Christian assembly or to an offering gathered privately each week by individuals at home. Recently, S. R. Llewelyn has argued for the former option, pointing to a number of grammatical parallels which suggest that the prepositional phrase παρ' ἑαυτῷ, when it follows the distributive adjective ἕκαστος in 1 Cor 16:2, should be translated "individually" instead of "at home" (cf. Aristotle, *Hist. an.* 511b; Dio Cassius, *Hist.* 63.28.5; Herodian, *Ab excessu divi Marci* 4.3.8).[29] Indeed, the construction παρ' ἑαυτῷ in 1 Cor 16:2 seems more naturally to qualify the preceding subject ἕκαστος ὑμῶν than the following verbal clause τιθέτω θησαυρίζων: Paul instructs each member of the church in Corinth individually to donate to the common fund on the first day of the week (cf. the practice in Acts 11:29, where the distributive pronoun ἕκαστος is also found). Moreover, as Llewelyn points out, it is difficult to explain why Paul names Sunday (κατὰ μίαν σαββάτου) as the day for the occasion of this contribution, if a Christian gathering is not in mind.[30]

We have already noted that Greco-Roman voluntary associations frequently collected funds from members during regular, usually monthly, group meetings

---

[29] S. R. Llewelyn, "The Use of Sunday for Meetings," *NovT* 43 (2001): 205–23, esp. 209–10. For a counter to Llewelyn's perspective, see Norman H. Young, "'The Use of Sunday for Meetings of Believers in the New Testament': A Response," *NovT* 45 (2003): 111–22. The preposition παρά followed by a dative form of the reflexive pronoun ἑαυτοῦ does not occur often in the epigraphical record, but to the list of literary texts cited by Llewelyn should be added IG XI/4 1040, a proxeny decree of the League for the Thebans for two benefactors, Hypatodoros and Kaphisodoros (ca. 287 B.C.E.). The inscription stipulates that "each of the cities individually should engrave the decree and make dedications in their temples, which is their custom" (ἀναγράψαι δὲ καὶ τὰς πόλεις ἑκάστας παρ' ἑαυταῖς τὸ ψήφισμα καὶ ἀναθεῖναι εἰς τὰ ἱερὰ οὗ ἔθος ἐστὶν αὐταῖς). Cf. also SEG 43:26, an honorific inscription from Acharnai for the ταμίας of a deme (315/14 B.C.E.), which notes that Acharneusis "paid the remaining money for each member for financial administration" ([τὸ π]ερι[ὸν] ἀργύριον παρ' ἑαυτῶι ἐκ τῆς διοικήσεως κατ[αβέ]βληκεν). Also noteworthy is the construction ἕκαστος εἰς τοὺς καθήκοντας παρ' ἑαυτῷ συνέλεξαν in LXX Exod 16:18 (cf. Philo, *Her.* 191), especially since Paul cites an earlier portion of that same scriptural verse with reference to the collection in 2 Cor 8:15.

[30] Llewelyn ("The Use of Sunday Meetings," 209) also notes that suggestions that this directive "reflects sound budgetary planning [suffer] from anachronistic considerations in a period when income was not determined by weekly pay periods." So also Anthony C. Thiselton, *The First Epistle to the Corinthians: A Commentary on the Greek Text* (NIGTC; Grand Rapids: Eerdmans, 2000), 1323.

for religious and social purposes (cf. IG II² 1368). The practice of donating monies to a common chest during weekly gatherings, even for a special project like the collection for the saints, therefore, would not have been unfamiliar to the believers in Corinth. In 1 Cor 16:1–4, Paul seems to envision a situation in which contributions to the Jerusalem offering were collected during Sunday worship meetings in Corinth and Galatia. Paul's assertion that this procedure would ensure "that there need not be collections" on the occasion of his impending visit to Corinth might be interpreted as an indication that the monies would already have been gathered into a central ecclesiastical fund, such as those maintained among clubs and guilds, upon Paul's arrival in Corinth.[31] Had members of the Corinthian church simply been storing up funds privately at home, there would have been little reason for Paul to send delegates like Titus and two unnamed brothers to the church in Corinth to oversee the completion of this task (2 Cor 8:6, 16–24), unless Paul intended for these representatives to make door-to-door visitations in order to supervise the gathering of the fund. Instead, this oversight involves the corporate activity of the Corinthian church, and Paul's instruction that the collection of funds take place during Sunday meetings implies that the offering for the saints was gathered in the context of Christian worship.[32]

Given this connection with the worship practices of the Pauline house churches in Corinth, Paul's terminology for the collection is noteworthy. In this setting, Paul initially refers to the collection as ἡ λογεία ἡ εἰς τοὺς ἁγίους (1 Cor 16:1). Although Georgi claims that λογεία "in this context means a collection of funds, nothing else," there is reason to believe that the term should be included among the cluster of cultic metaphors that Paul uses to describe the collection for Jerusalem.[33] The word λογεία, which does not occur in the literary record before 1 Cor 16:1–4, is employed in epigraphical and papyrological sources to denote collections of various sorts, including money gathered for public subscriptions (SEG 45:1070 = LSCG 48; IFayum 152; SE 221:3), collections of corn (IKret III 4:9; IMagnMai 105), and harvests of other types of plants (*PHamb* 184, 186). Yet as Deissmann observed almost a century ago, the term is used "chiefly of religious collections for a god, a temple, etc."[34]

---

[31] See pp. 143–54.

[32] See also Ralph P. Martin, *Worship in the Early Church* (Grand Rapids: Eerdmans, 1987), 77–80.

[33] Georgi, *Remembering the Poor*, 53. In the context of this quotation, Georgi is actually arguing against the hypothesis that the λογεία was a tax levied upon the Pauline communities by the Jerusalem church. In a footnote, Georgi writes, "Λογεία also denotes the cult-connected collections" (188 n. 14). Jerome Murphy-O'Connor (*The Theology of the Second Letter to the Corinthians* [Cambridge: Cambridge University Press, 1991], 76) calls λογεία "a commercial term," although he does note cite evidence for the use of this word in commercial contexts.

[34] Adolf Deissmann, *Light from the Ancient East: The New Testament Illustrated by Recently Discovered Texts of the Graeco-Roman World* (trans. Lionel R. M. Strachan; New York: George H. Doran,

Deissmann cites an ostracon from Thebes (63 C.E.) that records the donation of four drachmae and one obol for "the collection of Isis" (τὴν λογίαν "Ισιδος).[35] Similarly, a first-century C.E. inscription from Smyrna (ISmyrna 753 = Syll³ 996) speaks of a religious association founded by one Apollonios Sparos, who financed "a vessel which is gilded and clothed for the collection and procession of the gods" (τὴν λογήαν καὶ πομπὴν τῶν θεῶν). It seems that this vessel was used to gather monetary contributions for the gods from onlookers during a cultic procession. Even compulsory subscriptions were often related to the religious activity of temples, as is seen in the attempt of local priests in 95 B.C.E. to assemble monetary collections from each individual in the village of Magdola (Egypt) for the maintenance and restoration of the temple of Heron (IFayum 152: ἐν ταῖς γινομέναις παρ' ἕκαστον ἐν τῆι κώμηι λογείαις ἐπιχιρ[ε]ῖν τοὺς ἐκ τού[τ]ου ἱερεῖς πράσσειν παρὰ τὸ καθῆκον τὸ ὅμοιον).[36] Moreover, the term λογεία is occasionally found in relation to the cultic practices of pagan voluntary associations: a fragmentary inscription from Physkos (ca. 66 C.E.) refers to collections for the sacrifices and offerings of a *koinon* (IRhodB 501 = LSCG 143),[37] and the sacred law of the cult of Sarapis, Isis, and Apis at Priene (ca. 200 B.C.E.) may mention the collection of funds (λογεῖαι) by the priest of the association, although this reference to the word λογεία unfortunately depends upon an editor's restoration (IPriene 195 = LSAM 36).[38]

In applying the term λογεία to the monetary contribution organized among the Corinthian and Galatian churches, therefore, Paul appears to draw upon language typically associated with cultic and sacral collections for temples and gods in order metaphorically to frame the Jerusalem fund as a religious offering. The two uses of λογεία in 1 Cor 16:1–4 do not, of course, provide sufficient evidence on their own to establish this as one of Paul's rhetorical and theological strate-

---

1927), 105. BDAG also points out that the term λογεία denotes "esp. a collection for sacred purposes" (597).

[35] Deissmann, *Light from the Ancient East*, 105. For the use of this term in sacral contexts, see also Ulrich Wilcken, ed., *Griechische Ostraka aus Aegypten und Nubien: Ein Beitrag zur antiken Wirtschaftsgeschichte* (2 vols.; Amsterdam: Adolf M. Hakkert, 1970), 1:253–56 (cf. no. 360; 402; 412–418; 420); Kittel, "Λογεία," *TDNT* 4:282; Georg Petzl, ed., *Die Inschriften von Smyrna* (2 vols.; IGSK 23–24; Bonn: Habelt, 1987), 255. The spelling of the word λογεία is far from consistent. Here, as in many of the papyri, the word is spelled λογία; in *PHamb* 184, it appears as ἡ λογέα; and in *PHamb* 186, ἡ λογεία.

[36] On this text, see also the commentary of André Bernand, ed., *La Prose sur Pierre dans l'Égypte hellénistique et romaine* (2 vols.; Paris: Éditions du centre national de la recherché scientifique, 1992), no. 32 (1:80–83; 2:79–83).

[37] The editor of the text, Wolfgang Blümel (*Die Inschriften der rhodischen Peraia* [2 vols.; IGSK 41–42; Bonn: Habelt, 1992], 120), cites Hiller von Gärtringen, who calls this "eine zu einem sakralen Zweck vorgenommene Kollekte."

[38] IG XII/5 156 uses the cognate verb λογεύω to refer to a collection "for the restoration of the fountain, the altar, and the inner-room" of a temple in Paros (third century B.C.E.; cf. Amyzon 38).

gies, since λογεία can just as well refer to more mundane collections. Combined with the cultic language found in discussions of the Jerusalem collection elsewhere in Paul's letters, however, the usage of the word λογεία in 1 Cor 16:1–4 should be interpreted as the first among a cluster of cultic metaphors that depict the collection as a religious offering consecrated to God. More to the point, the fact that Paul instructs his readers in Corinth to gather these λογεῖαι during Sunday meetings of the believing community indicates that, for Paul, "the offering of money is an integral part of Christian worship": "Money which had been honestly gained in the toil of the week is to be brought to the assembly of the Church and thus made part of the Sunday worship."[39]

4.4 Second Corinthians 8–9: The Collection as a Religious Offering

After the success of his so-called "letter of tears" (2 Cor 2:4), which helped to repair the relationship between the Corinthian church and its apostle that had been broken in the aftermath of the controversy surrounding Paul's second visit to Corinth, Paul wrote an epistle now preserved as 2 Corinthians 1–9.[40] Paul does not broach the subject of the Jerusalem collection in this missive until he has already covered other important topics, including the reasons for his postponed visit to Corinth (1:8–2:13), a "major digression" on the nature of apostolic ministry (2:14–7:4),[41] and a report of his encouragement at the Corinthians' grief and repentance over their formerly fractured bond with their apostle (7:5–16). Paul's heartfelt expression of his joy and confidence in his restored relationship with the Corinthians in 2 Cor 7:5–16 paves the way for the next substantial section of the letter. Written with the aim of persuading the Corinthians to resume their now-stalled participation in the contribution for Jerusalem, 2 Corinthians 8–9 provides us with Paul's most extensive discussion of the collection for the saints. In these two chapters, Paul employs a number of rhetorical strategies and metaphors in order to encourage the believers in Achaia to support the offering for Jerusalem.

4.4.1 8:1–6: The Example of the Macedonians

Paul opens his appeal in 2 Cor 8:1–6 by immediately drawing the attention of his readers to the outstanding demonstration of χάρις among believers in the region of Macedonia. Already in 1 Cor 16:3, Paul had referred to the collection as ἡ χάρις ὑμῶν ("your benefaction"). Here, by contrast, χάρις is first described as a

---

[39] Martin, *Worship in the Early Church*, 79–80.
[40] See pp. 42–49.
[41] Murray J. Harris, *The Second Epistle to the Corinthians* (NIGTC; Grand Rapids: Eerdmans: 2005), 522. Many commentators consider 6:14–7:1 to be a non-Pauline interpolation; see p. 75 n. 53.

benefit given by God to the Christian communities in Macedonia (τὴν χάριν τοῦ θεοῦ τὴν δεδομένην ἐν ταῖς ἐκκλησίαις τῆς Μακεδονίας).[42] Paul will go on to highlight the exceptional generosity shown by the Macedonians through their support of the collection in vv. 2–6: in spite of their own affliction and deep poverty, they gave beyond their means and voluntarily,[43] petitioning Paul and his associates "for the benefit of partnership[44] in the ministry for the saints" (v. 4). Yet with Paul's use of the term χάρις to denote the gracious activity of God in v. 1, the initial emphasis is on the fact that "the collection itself – on the face of it a human endeavor – has its origin and energy in God's grace."[45]

It has often been observed that Paul's description of the generosity of the Macedonians in 2 Cor 8:1–6 establishes an implicit rivalry between them and the recalcitrant Corinthians. Stephan Joubert, for example, has termed this section an "agonistic exemplum."[46] Similarly, drawing on agonistic imagery and terminology from honorific inscriptions, James Harrison has argued that here "Paul employs traditional inscriptional rivalry and imitation motifs to encourage the Corinthians not to become benefactors of himself but rather of others through the Jerusalem collection." At the same time, Harrison contends that "there remain several significant departures from inscriptional convention that highlight what is central for Paul: χάρις and ἀγάπη."[47]

The rivalry motif was frequently employed in benefaction contexts. The public nature of honorific inscriptions was itself an implicit invitation for rival patrons to compete with one another for the public recognition typically offered in

---

[42] As pointed out by Beverly Roberts Gaventa ("The Economy of Grace: Reflections on 2 Corinthians 8 and 9," in *Grace upon Grace: Essays in Honor of Thomas A. Langford* [ed. Robert K. Johnston, L. Gregory Jones, and Jonathan R. Wilson; Nashville: Abingdon, 1999], 61 n. 12), "Technically, it is possible to translate the churches of Macedonia as an instrumental dative, so that God's grace was given by the churches of Macedonia, but it is difficult to imagine anything in Paul's letters that would support such a translation."

[43] The word αὐθαίρετος, which Paul uses in 2 Cor 8:3 to indicate that the Macedonians "gave of their own volition" (cf. 2 Cor 8:17), and the related adverb αὐθαιρέτως are often used in inscriptions to refer to the voluntary assumption of religious duties and liturgies: Meletemata 11 K2; IPontEux 2:39, 54; IG XII.5 660, 668; IG XII *Supplementum* 238; IMagnMai 163; IEph 944, 950, 957, 959, 961, 963; ISardBR VII.1 41; SEG 8:641.

[44] The construction τὴν χάριν καὶ τὴν κοινωνίαν is an example of hendiadys, "the combining of two different nouns by a conjunction in order to express one complex thought: here, in order to avoid a piling-up of genitives" (Victor P. Furnish, *II Corinthians: Translated with Introduction, Notes, and Commentary* [AB 32A; Garden City: Doubleday, 1984], 401; cf. Kieran J. O'Mahony, *Pauline Persuasion: A Sounding in 2 Corinthians 8–9* (JSNTSup 199; Sheffield: Sheffield Academic Press, 2000), 114; see also BDF 442).

[45] Gaventa, "Economy of Grace," 55.

[46] Joubert, *Paul as Benefactor*, 173–76; cf. Richard R. Melick, "The Collection for the Saints: 2 Corinthians 8–9," *Criswell Theological Review* 4 (1989): 107–8; Frederick W. Danker, *Benefactor: Epigraphic Study of a Graeco-Roman and New Testament Semantic Field* (St. Louis: Clayton, 1982), 437–38.

[47] Harrison, *Paul's Language of Grace*, 315. The *exemplum* (or παράδειγμα) was also a technique of ancient rhetoric; see O'Mahony, *Pauline Persuasion*, 123–24.

response to gifts. More explicitly, the decrees of cities and voluntary associations frequently invite competition among potential benefactors by encouraging patrons to rival one another in terms of their support of the institution. For example, the phrase ὅπως ἂν οὖν ἐφάμιλλον ᾖ plus an infinitive like εὐεργετεῖν or φιλοτιμεῖσθαι and an accusative object such as τὸν δῆμον or τὸ κοινὸν ("so that there might be a competition to benefit the *dēmos*/association") is standard language in Athenian inscriptions.[48] Moreover, the rhetoric of zeal (ζῆλος) is often used in inscriptions to encourage potential benefactors to imitate the enthusiastic giving of their predecessors. An honorific decree of the association of Tyrian merchants and sailors on the island of Delos (153/2 B.C.E.) that details the honors awarded to the patron of the guild (ironically named Patron) provides the following inducement for future benefactors from the membership of the association:

> So that, therefore, for the remaining time [Patron] may also render himself (to be one who does not need to be) summoned (in regard to beneficence) and that the guild may manifestly take thought of the men who are benevolently disposed to itself and that it may return worthy favors to the benefactors and that more of the other (members) from the guild may be zealous imitators on account of the (guild's) thankfulness for this (generosity of Patron) and that those whose love of honor may outdo (each other) to achieve something for the guild. (IDelos 1519)[49]

Yet while Paul does encourage the Corinthians to consider the example of the churches of Macedonia, the nature of the rivalry in 2 Cor 8:1–6 is quite different from that found in Greco-Roman inscriptions. As Harrison points out, conspicuously absent in Paul's letters is the terminology used in inscriptions to promote competition among potential patrons (ἐφάμιλλος; ἀμιλλᾶσθαι; παραμιλλᾶσθαι). Instead, Paul is ultimately interested in the excellence of the Corinthians' love (ἀγάπη), although the genuineness of this love is tested against the "zeal" (σπουδή) of the Macedonians (v. 8).[50] Additionally, Paul does not intimate that a rivalry between the Corinthians and Macedonians will result in the receipt of thanksgiving and honor for the benefactors in this context. The award of thanksgiving (εὐχαριστία) and the pursuit of public honor were crucial motivating factors for benefactors according to the ideology of euergetism, as the language of the inscriptions makes clear. The standard rivalry clause in Attic inscriptions cited above (ὅπως ἂν οὖν ἐφάμιλλον ᾖ), for example, is typically

---

[48] Cf. IG II² 330, 663, 667, 670, 691, 700, 712, 721, 786, 798, 801, 808, 859, 884, 931, 984, 1045, 1227, 1281, 1292, 1293, 1297, 1301, 1319, 1327. For instances of the same construction in non-Attic inscriptions, see IG XII/5 653, 818; IG XII/8 666.

[49] Translation from Harrison, *Paul's Language of Grace*, 318.

[50] Harrison's claim that "Paul avoided ζηλωτής in imitation contexts [because of] its association with Jewish zeal for the Law from the Maccabean era onwards" (*Paul's Language of Grace*, 319) fails to account for the use of the term ζῆλος in 2 Cor 9:2, where Paul informs the Corinthians that "your zeal has provoked most of [the Macedonians]."

followed by a promise that donors will "know that each [benefactor] will receive thanks in proportion to his benefaction."[51] Yet here and elsewhere Paul seems almost consciously to avoid any suggestion that the Corinthians will receive this kind of public honor and recognition from their beneficiaries in Jerusalem in response to Corinthian support of the collection.[52] That Paul does not indicate that the Corinthians will receive thanksgiving from the recipients of their gift may be viewed as a deliberate strategy on the apostle's part to avoid any competition between the Macedonians and the Corinthians for praise of their munificence. In fact, Paul's insistence that the enthusiastic participation in the collection effort among the Macedonians in the face of their own extreme poverty is first and foremost a testimony to the χάρις given them by God stands in marked contrast to the honorific inscriptions of Greco-Roman voluntary associations, and therefore minimizes any competition for honor among these "rival" benefactors in Macedonia and Achaia.

4.4.2 8:7–12: Plea for Generous Giving

Having described the grace-infused example of the Macedonians, Paul turns in vv. 7–12 "to an intense urging of the Corinthians in an exhortation that weaves a narrow path between repeated commands and outright cajoling."[53] The appeal begins in v. 7 with an affirmation of the Corinthians' excellence "in faith, in speech, in knowledge, in all zeal, and in the love derived from us and present in you" (cf. 1 Cor 1:5) – an affirmation that, given Paul's previous difficulties with the church in Corinth, might be regarded as an expression of hope, if not a softening-up. Paul then invites the Corinthians to "abound also in this χάρις" (8:7), by which term, as in v. 6, he means the collection for the saints.[54] After immediately qualifying this request in v. 8 by indicating that he envisions this offering as a voluntary expression of love rather than the fulfillment of a command (οὐ κατ' ἐπιταγὴν λέγω),[55] Paul offers the Corinthians another *exemplum* in the χάρις of

---

[51] Cf., e.g., IG II² 663, 670.

[52] O'Mahony's (*Pauline Persuasion*, 149) conclusion that Paul's use of the terminology of benefaction "means that Paul is offering the Corinthians an opportunity to attain prestige, for their contributions to the welfare of the saints in Jerusalem" is fundamentally mistaken. Nowhere in 2 Corinthians 8–9 does Paul offer the accretion of "prestige" as an incentive for contributing to the relief fund.

[53] Harris, *Second Epistle*, 572.

[54] There is some debate about whether the ἵνα clause in v. 7b should be regarded as carrying the force of an imperative (so Furnish, *II Corinthians*, 403; Harris, *Second Epistle*, 574) or as an expression of a wish (so Verbrugge, *Paul's Style of Church Leadership*, 251; M. E. Thrall, *A Critical and Exegetical Commentary on the Second Epistle to the Corinthians* (2 vols.; ICC; London: T & T Clark, 1994, 2000), 529). Given Paul's explicit assertion in the following sentence that he is not issuing a command, the latter of these options is to be preferred.

[55] As Hans Dieter Betz (*2 Corinthians 8 and 9: A Commentary on Two Administrative Letters of the Apostle Paul* [Hermeneia; Philadelphia: Fortress, 1985], 59) points out, the formula κατ' ἐπιταγὴν frequently appears in "connection with votive offerings in Greek religious texts" (see, e.g., IG II²

Jesus Christ: "that on your account he became poor, although he was rich, in order that by his poverty you might become rich" (v. 9). The christological example – with its allusion to the Corinthians' knowledge (γινώσκετε γὰρ) of the narrative of Jesus' incarnation, life, death, and resurrection – demonstrates the close connection between christology and ethics with respect to the Jerusalem collection. Although the Corinthians are not called merely to duplicate Christ's self-giving impoverishment (cf. v. 13), their anticipated support of the collection for the saints is implicitly presented as an *imitatio Christi*.

Again with caution, seemingly aware of the necessity to tread lightly when broaching this matter, Paul offers his own carefully weighed opinion with regard to the Corinthians' resumption of their support for the relief fund: "for this is in your interest, you who had previously made a start last year, not only to act but also to prove willing. Now, then, also complete the action, so that its completion may correspond with your willingness – completion in accordance with your means. For if the eagerness is present, that is acceptable according to what one has, not according to what one does not have" (vv. 10–12). In v. 11, Paul uses two forms of the verb ἐπιτελέω to encourage the completion of the offering, an imperative (τὸ ποιῆσαι ἐπιτελέσατε) and an articular infinitive (τὸ ἐπιτελέσαι), the former of which is the only formal imperative in all of chapters 8 and 9. Paul had already used the same verb in v. 6, when he spoke of his hope that Titus might "complete this benefaction among you as well" (ἐπιτελέσῃ εἰς ὑμᾶς καὶ τὴν χάριν ταύτην).

Although the verb ἐπιτελέω might mean nothing more than "carry out" or "accomplish," its frequent usage in religious contexts to denote the performance of cultic rites or religious duties suggests that this word, too, should be included among the cluster of cultic metaphors with which Paul describes the activity associated with the Jerusalem collection. A recent article by Richard Ascough has explored a number of occurrences of ἐπιτελέω in Greek inscriptions, focusing on its usage to describe the performance of sacred rites (SIG³ 985 = LSAM 20; SIG³ 695, 820; IG II² 1368; LSAM 53; IG V/1 1390; cf. Philo, *Ebr.* 129) – including sacrifices (θυσία; cf. Josephus, *Ant.* 1.58) and mysteries (μυστήρια) – the fulfillment of oaths (SIG³ 694, 1007; IG V/1 1390), and benefaction in religious contexts (IG II² 1271; IDelos 1519, 1520; SIG³ 695). Ascough demonstrates that, while the meaning of a given word can never be determined apart from its literary context, the frequency with which the term ἐπιτελέω is used in the epigraphical record to speak of the fulfillment of religious obligations implies that, for Paul, "the collection is to be carried out in the same manner, with the same attitude, as one would carry out a religious duty within the cults and associations of the cities of the Greco-Roman world." Therefore, Ascough concludes, "When Paul used this word within the argument of 2 Cor 8.1–15 he could rely on the

---

4038, 4519, 4773, 5172; SEG 45:770; SEG 47:196b; IG V.1 245; IDelos 2346, 2413). Here, however, Paul explicitly avows that he is *not* speaking in terms of a command.

shared cultural experiences of his audience, which would include having seen ἐπιτελέω used in the context of religious duty. Thus Paul's choice of ἐπιτελέω is not without significance. By using it within the argument of 2 Cor 8.1–15 Paul is appealing to the Corinthians' sense of religious duty."[56]

Ascough's interpretation of the religious background of the verb ἐπιτελέω in 2 Corinthians 8 is consistent with other uses of the word in Paul's letters. Outside of 2 Cor 8:6, 11, the verb ἐπιτελέω is found only four other times in the Pauline corpus. First, at the conclusion of the ethical exhortation in 2 Cor 6:14–7:4, with its reflection on the metaphor of the body as a living temple (6:16; cf. 1 Cor 3:10–17),[57] ἐπιτελέω occurs in combination with cultic language in 2 Cor 7:1: "Therefore, beloved, since we have these promises, let us cleanse ourselves (καθαρίσωμεν ἑαυτοὺς) from every defilement of body and spirit, and let us complete our consecration (ἐπιτελοῦντες ἁγιωσύνην) in reverence to God" (cf. Heb 9:6). However one judges the relationship of this section to the rest of the epistle, the directive in 2 Cor 7:1 is closely related to the temple metaphor in 6:16, for "bringing such holiness to completion is an appropriate task for those who are 'the temple of the Living God'."[58] The verb is also used along with several cultic metaphors in Rom 15:28, another passage in which Paul discusses the collection for the saints (see below). The word ἐπιτελέω does not always appear to have a cultic nuance in Paul's letters, however. It is used with the more mundane meaning of "complete" or "finish" in Gal 3:3 and Phil 1:6.

In his study, Ascough emphasizes the obligatory nature of this religious offering.[59] This interpretation of Paul's use of ἐπιτελέω in its present literary context is not fully convincing, however. In Rom 15:27, where Paul speaks of believers in Macedonia and Achaia as "debtors" (ὀφειλέται) of their brothers and sisters in Jerusalem, the collection is perhaps presented as a religious duty.

---

[56] Richard S. Ascough, "The Completion of a Religious Duty: The Background of 2 Cor 8.1–15," *NTS* 42 (1996): 599.

[57] See John R. Lanci, *A New Temple for Corinth: Rhetorical and Archaeological Approaches to Pauline Imagery* (StBL 1; New York: Peter Lang, 1997); D. R. De Lacey, "οἵτινές ἐστε ὑμεῖς: The Function of a Metaphor in St Paul," in *Templum Amicitiae: Essays on the Second Temple Period Presented to Ernst Bammel* (ed. William Horbury; JSNTSup 48; Sheffield: JSOT Press, 1991), 391–409; Christfried Böttrich, "'Ihr seid der Tempel Gottes': Tempelmetaphorik und Gemeinde bei Paulus," in *Gemeinde ohne Tempel: Zur Substituierung und Transformation des Jerusalemer Tempels und seines Kult im Alten Testament, antiken Judentum und frühen Christentum* (ed. Beate Ego, Armin Lange, and Peter Pilhofer; WUNT 118; Tübingen: Mohr Siebeck, 1999), 411–25; Jean-Nöel Aletti, "Le statut de l'Église dans les lettres pauliniennes: Réflexions sur quelques paradoxes," *Bib* 83 (2002): 153–74.

[58] Frank J. Matera, *II Corinthians: A Commentary* (The New Testament Library; Louisville: Westminster John Knox, 2003), 168.

[59] Ascough calls the collection "an obligation which [Paul] had assumed at the Jerusalem council (Gal 2.10) in exchange for Gentile Christians' release from the requirements of the Mosaic Law," and he suggests that Paul "is appealing to the Corinthians' sense of religious duty in order to have them complete their collection" ("Completion of a Religious Duty," 598–99).

Yet Paul's consistent emphasis on the voluntary character of the contribution in his appeal to the Corinthians (cf. 2 Cor 8:3, 8, 10; 9:7) indicates that the cultic and religious associations with the word may figure more prominently in Paul's appeal in 2 Cor 8:1–24 than any emphasis on duty or obligation. To be sure, Paul does believe that the Corinthians have an ethical responsibility to render financial assistance to the impoverished believers in Jerusalem. Yet his carefully constructed rhetoric highlights the fact that the collection for the saints is an offering to which the Corinthians are encouraged to contribute voluntarily. Paul's thrice-repeated use of the verb ἐπιτελέω, therefore, may function more as a subtle invitation to view the completion of this χάρις metaphorically as an act of cultic worship, from which realm the term ἐπιτελέω comes.

4.4.3 8:13–15: The Aim of Equality

In the first twelve verses of his appeal to the Corinthians, Paul has said nothing of the actual needs of those for whom this χάρις is designated, namely, the "poor among the saints in Jerusalem" (Rom 15:26). He focuses instead on the example of the Macedonians (vv. 1–6), the example of Christ (v. 9), and the necessity for the Corinthians to complete the task of supporting the collection (vv. 7–8, 10–12). In vv. 13–15, however, Paul provides a rationale for the collection by describing the relationship that will obtain between the Corinthians and the recipients of this gift – whom Paul calls "others" (ἄλλοι, v. 13) – as a result of Corinthian support for the fund. According to Paul, one purpose of this χάρις is the establishment of "equality" (ἰσότης). This principle of equality is first stated negatively in v. 13: Paul does not desire that the recipients of the offering should have "relief" (ἄνεσις) while the Corinthian contributors suffer "affliction" (θλῖψις). Instead, Paul envisions a reciprocal relationship in which the present abundance of the Corinthians will help to alleviate the material needs of the saints in Jerusalem (and in which the situation may in the future be reversed), "so that there may be equality" (v. 14).[60]

With his emphasis on equality in this section, Paul may be drawing on conventions associated with the concept of friendship in the Greco-Roman world.[61] At the same time, Paul supports this goal of equality by citing the biblical precedent of Exod 16:18 at the conclusion of his argument: "As it is written, 'The one who had much did not have too much, and the one who had little did not have too little'" (2 Cor 8:15).[62] This scriptural quotation, with its allusion to the story

---

[60] As Justin Meggitt (*Paul, Poverty and Survival* [Studies of the New Testament and Its World; Edinburgh: T & T Clark, 1998], 159–61) has argued, Paul may envision a time in the future when economic troubles for the Corinthians will require financial assistance from believers in Jerusalem.

[61] See Johan C. Thom, "'Harmonious Equality': The *Topos* of Friendship in Neopythagorean Writings," in *Greco-Roman Perspectives on Friendship* (SBLRBS 34; ed. John T. Fitzgerald; Atlanta: Scholars Press, 1997), 77–103; Luke Timothy Johnson, "Making Connections: The Material Expression of Friendship in the New Testament," *Int* 58 (2004): 158–71, esp. 165–67.

[62] On the differences between LXX Exod 16:18 and Paul's citation, see Harris, *Second Epistle*,

of God's provision of manna to the Israelites wandering in the wilderness, does more than merely provide a pithy summation of, and warrant for, the principle of Christian equality. Richard Hays has argued that attention to the larger narrative context of Exod 16:18 shows that "Paul sees in this manna story an economic parable whose moral is that God provides for those who rely on him for their daily bread, taking no thought for the morrow."[63] Given Paul's consistent emphasis on divine χάρις throughout this chapter (v. 1, 9, 16), as well as the stress placed on God's abundant and gracious provision elsewhere in 2 Corinthians 1–9 (1:3–11, 18–22; 2:14–17; 3:4–6; 4:1–15; 5:1–5, 14–21; 6:6; 7:6–7; 9:8–15), Hays's interpretation is of a piece with the larger literary context of v. 15. As Young and Ford propose, Paul declares to his readers that "the extraordinary grace of God" (2 Cor 9:14) allows believers to participate in an "economy of abundance" that transforms all human relationships and economic bonds within the Christian community:

> This is an economy in which freedom is precious, and Paul is trying to encourage a free response in the Corinthians. Therefore, his appeal is both a celebration of God's grace and an invitation to the Corinthians to recognize afresh what they are part of and to draw the practical consequences. Vis-à-vis Hellenistic reciprocity, what seems to have happened is that the inexhaustible generosity of God places everyone in the position of his clients and therefore owing him thanks; but among the clients themselves there is no basis for anything other than equality or uncalculating generosity, and so all patron-client relationships are relativized.[64]

4.4.4 8:16–24: Commendation of Delegates

After Paul's appeal for contributions to the collection for the saints in 2 Cor 8:1–15 there appears a section in which the apostle announces how he intends to co-ordinate the realization of the Corinthians' promised support (vv. 16–24). Paul states that he plans to send a three-person delegation to Corinth, consisting of Titus and two unnamed brothers, a party charged with the responsibility of both helping the Corinthians to fulfill their religious commitment to the saints in Jerusalem and, at the same time, ensuring the propriety of the fund. Second Corinthians 8:16–24, therefore, functions as a letter of recommendation for these emissaries.

593; and Christopher D. Stanley, *Paul and the Language of Scripture: Citation Technique in the Pauline Epistles and Contemporary Literature* (SNTSMS 74; Cambridge: Cambridge University Press, 1992), 231–33. Philo also associates this episode in Exod 16:11–36 with the principle of ἰσότης in *Her.* 191, which has led to speculations that Paul and Philo drew upon a common Hellenistic-Jewish tradition that associated Exod 16:18 with ἰσότης (so Georgi, *Remembering the Poor*, 84–91).

[63] Richard B. Hays, *Echoes of Scripture in the Letters of Paul* (New Haven and London: Yale University Press, 1989), 90.

[64] Frances Young and David F. Ford, *Meaning and Truth in 2 Corinthians* (Grand Rapids: Eerdmans, 1988), 179.

Titus's reliability and his close relationship with the Corinthian church have already been affirmed by what is said of him in 2 Cor 7:6–16 and 8:6. It was Titus who reported to Paul the grief and consolation with which the Corinthians received Paul's "letter of tears" (2 Cor 7:6–8; cf. 2:3–4), and it was Titus who, along with this earlier epistle, appears to have played a key role in the Corinthians' repentance (7:15). In 2 Cor 8:16, however, Titus's zeal for the Corinthians is directly attributed to the activity of God, the one who placed the same zeal (τὴν αὐτὴν σπουδὴν) for the Corinthians into the heart of Titus as that possessed by Paul, and the one to whom thanksgiving is due (χάρις δὲ τῷ θεῷ) for Titus's enthusiastic willingness to participate in the organization of the fund.

Along with Titus, Paul indicates that he is sending to Corinth two "messengers of the churches" (ἀπόστολοι ἐκκλησιῶν, v. 23) – one known for his "praise in the gospel" and appointed by the churches "in association with this benefaction administered by us for the glory of the Lord and for our zeal" (vv. 18–19), the other reported to have been "tested often and in many ways since he is zealous, but who is now all the more zealous because of his great confidence in you" (v. 22). Given the likelihood that Paul had earlier faced severe criticism from some members of the Corinthian community on account of his financial policies – with accusations focused specifically on the apostle's handling of the collection fund – his decision to dispatch this delegation is entirely understandable. As Paul himself concedes in vv. 20–21, these emissaries are charged with the responsibility of ensuring the financial integrity of this benefaction: "We are taking this preparation[65] lest anyone blame us concerning this lavish gift that is being administered by us. For we pay attention to what is honorable, not only 'in the sight of the Lord' but also 'in the sight of human beings.'"[66] As Harris points out, Paul's validation of these representatives is at once personal (τὴν αὐτὴν σπουδὴν ὑπὲρ ὑμῶν ἐν τῇ καρδίᾳ Τίτου, v. 16; κοινωνὸς ἐμὸς, v. 23; ἀδελφοὶ ἡμῶν, v. 23), ecclesiological (διὰ πασῶν τῶν ἐκκλησιῶν, v. 18; χειροτονηθεὶς ὑπὸ τῶν ἐκκλησιῶν, v. 19; ἀπόστολοι ἐκκλησιῶν, v. 23), and christological (πρὸς τὴν αὐτοῦ τοῦ κυρίου δόξαν, v. 19; ἐνώπιον κυρίου, v. 21; δόξα Χριστοῦ, v. 23).[67] Moreover, although the importance of this mission is highlighted by Paul's attempt to accredit these emissaries, his description of the two unnamed brothers as the δόξα Χριστοῦ (v. 23) "relativizes their importance in relation to the glory which is due to Christ."[68]

---

[65] Reading στελλόμενοι with Thrall (*2 Corinthians*, 550–51) as "taking preparation" (*pace* BDAG).

[66] Clearly this is an adaptation of Prov 3:4 (LXX). For an example of donations recorded publicly "before the association" (ἐνώπιον κοινοῦ) in a pagan club in Thessalonica (11 C.E.), see Jean Bousquet, "Affranchissements de Larissa (Thessalie) note complémentaire," *BCH* 95 (1971): 561–66.

[67] Harris, *Second Epistle*, 595–96.

[68] O'Mahony, *Pauline Persuasion*, 130.

4.4.5 9:1–5: Boasting and Appeal

In 2 Cor 9:1–5, Paul again employs the rivalry motif, although this time he reports, in a reversal of his strategy in 8:1–6, that it is the "eagerness" (προθυμία) of the *Corinthians* on behalf of "the ministry for the saints" that has stirred up most of the *Macedonians*. Yet despite his boast of their preparation "since last year" (v. 2), Paul is still aware of the possibility that the Corinthians will not have made sufficient progress in raising funds for the offering by the time of the apostle's imminent visit to Corinth, taking with him representatives from the Macedonian churches (v. 4). Concerned that he and his envoy might arrive to find the Achaians unprepared, Paul indicates that he has already dispatched "the brothers," by which designation he means Titus and the other delegates mentioned in 2 Cor 8:16–24, so that his boasting to the Macedonians will not be in vain and so that the honor of both Paul and the Corinthians will be preserved (vv. 3–4).[69] In this section, Paul also refers to the collection as a "ministry" (διακονία, v. 1; cf. 9:12) and a "blessing" (εὐλογία, v. 5), the latter term perhaps playing on his earlier use of the word λογεία as a designation for the offering in 1 Cor 16:1.[70]

4.4.6 9:6–10: Generosity That Comes from God

In 2 Cor 9:6–10, Paul clarifies his point with a metaphor drawn from the realm of agricultural practice, one that highlights the generative activity of God in the act of human beneficence. The opening statement in v. 6, which indicates that one reaps whatever one sows, is a chiastic maxim that appears to draw on the Jewish sapiential tradition (Job 4:8; Prov. 11:26; Sir 7:3; *3 Bar.* 15.2; cf. Gal 6:7–9), although no precise parallel can be found in the extant literature. The notion that giving to the relief fund is like sowing seed plays on Paul's designation of the collection as an εὐλογία in v. 5, with the adverbial prepositional phrase ἐπ' εὐλογίαις used to indicate that "the one who sows blessedly will also reap

---

[69] If 2 Cor 9:1–15 represents a separate letter, sent to Corinth – or perhaps as a circular letter to the region of Achaia, including its capital city, Corinth – shortly after 2 Corinthians 1–8, perhaps Paul dispatched this epistle shortly after 2 Corinthians 1–8 because the extent of the Macedonian enthusiasm for the collection encouraged Paul to travel to Corinth sooner than he had originally anticipated (so Thrall, *2 Corinthians*, 43).

[70] So Hans Windisch, *Der zweite Korintherbrief* (KEK 6; Göttingen: Vandenhoeck und Ruprecht, 1924), 276. It is possible that Paul's use of the word διακονία as a designation for the collection in 9:1 (cf. Rom 15:31; and διακονέω in 2 Cor 8:19, 20; and Rom 15:25) also carries cultic connotations. In Josephus, the verbal form διακονέω occasionally indicates priestly service rendered to God (*Ant.* 3.155; 7.365; 10.72). On Diakonos as a cultic functionary, see IEph 3416–18; CCCA I 289; Philip A. Harland, *Associations, Synagogues, and Congregations: Claiming a Place in Ancient Mediterranean Society* (Minneapolis: Fortress, 2003), 299 n. 4; Richard S. Ascough, *Paul's Macedonian Associations: The Social Context of Philippians and 1 Thessalonians* (WUNT 2:161; Tübingen: Mohr Siebeck, 2003), 82–83; cf. John N. Collins, *Diakonia: Re-interpreting the Ancient Sources* (New York and Oxford: Oxford University Press, 1990), 163–64.

blessedly" (v. 6). Paul does not, however, advocate a self-interested giving, for the "blessed" return of this agrarian investment is not merely credited to the sower, but also to the recipients of the harvest, who experience the benefits of this "blessed gift" (v. 5).[71] As Harris observes, "[As] the general principle of v. 6b is applied to the Corinthian situation in vv. 8–14, the harvest to be reaped from lavish and joyful sowing is declared to be God's material and spiritual prospering to make further liberal giving possible (vv. 8–11), the relief of need (v. 12a), and prayers of thanksgiving and intercession on the part of the beneficiaries of the sowing (vv. 12b–14)."[72]

Paul's emphasis on God's enabling grace continues in vv. 7–10. Repeating the refrain that donations to the collection fund are not compulsory (cf. 8:3, 8), Paul stresses the importance of viewing one's support of the collection as a voluntary and joyful offering, with the amount of one's donation determined "in the heart, not reluctantly or under compulsion, for God loves a cheerful giver" (v. 7). Moreover, as in 8:1, where the beneficence of the Macedonians was credited to the χάρις given by God, behind this human act of charity lies the power of God to provide for the Corinthians "every benefit (πᾶσαν χάριν) in abundance," so that they might abound in good deeds (v. 8). It is God, therefore, who will stand behind and empower the Corinthians' support of the needy in Jerusalem, as the explicit citation of LXX Psalm 111:9 in v. 9 confirms.[73]

---

[71] So Bart B. Bruehler, "Proverbs, Persuasion and People: A Three-Dimensional Investigation of 2 Cor 9.6–15," NTS 48 (2002): 213–14.

[72] Harris, Second Epistle, 633–34.

[73] There is some debate concerning the identity of the implied subject of the scriptural citation in 2 Cor 9:9. Is the subject God (Betz, 2 Corinthians 8 and 9, 111–12; Furnish, II Corinthians, 448–49; Murphy-O'Connor, Second Letter, 92), the righteous individual who shares his possessions with the poor (Thrall, 2 Corinthians, 580–83; Harris, Second Epistle, 640; Joubert, Paul as Benefactor, 196), or even Christ (A. T. Hanson, Studies in Paul's Technique and Theology [Grand Rapids: Eerdmans, 1974], 179–80)? Although in its original setting LXX Psalm 111:9 clearly speaks of the righteousness of the pious individual who gives to the poor, Paul's citation of this text in 2 Cor 9:9 seems to suggest that God is the subject of the verbs ἐσκόρπισεν and ἔδωκεν, for God is the subject of vv. 8 and 10. The reference to "his righteousness" in this verse would, therefore, be to the divine, covenant faithfulness of God and not, as some have suggested, to the demonstration of human righteousness through the practice of almsgiving (pace Klaus Berger, "Almosen für Israel," NTS 23 [1977]: 200; Byung-Mo Kim, Die paulinische Kollekte [TANZ 38; Tübingen: Francke, 2002], 78–80). Perhaps Georgi's (Remembering the Poor, 99) position best accounts for the ambiguity in the quotation: "Paul and his readers both knew that in the passage quoted from the psalm the subject is the pious person – and Paul does not change that. Yet, in the light of the peculiar bond between Psalms 111 and 112, the deliberate vagueness of the way the quotation is incorporated into the Pauline context necessarily leads one to realize that God is the true origin of human compassion and that his righteousness is the true source of our righteousness." More recently, Christopher D. Stanley (Arguing with Scripture: The Rhetoric of Quotations in the Letters of Paul [New York and London: T & T Clark, 2004], 105–9) has argued that readers with different levels of familiarity with the biblical text would have interpreted this scriptural citation in different ways. Members of what Stanley calls the "informed audience" might have recognized that the

Paul returns to the agrarian metaphor in v. 10,[74] where he summarizes his argument in this section, declaring to the Corinthians that "he who supplies the seed to the sower and bread for food will supply and multiply your seed and will increase the harvest of your righteousness." Paul again draws upon the language of scripture to frame his appeal, this time alluding to LXX Isa 55:10, which, in a passage that compares the effectiveness of God's word to the inevitable power of natural forces to produce crops, asserts that the earth "gives seed to the sower and bread for food" (δῷ σπέρμα τῷ σπείροντι καὶ ἄρτον εἰς βρῶσιν). Since in this allusion Paul has transformed the subject of this clause from γῆ in LXX 55:10 to θεός (i.e., ὁ ἐπιχορηγῶν σπόρον) in 2 Cor 9:10, we might be open to the possibility that he adopts a similar hermeneutical strategy in v. 9, altering the subject from the pious individual in the LXX Psalm 111 to God. The God of abundance, according to Paul, will not only provide for the material resources of the Corinthians, he will "also increase (καὶ αὐξήσει) the material and spiritual benefits that would accrue to them and to the poor in Jerusalem as a result of their generous benevolence."[75] As in 1 Cor 3:6–9, another passage in which Paul makes use of an agrarian metaphor, the fundamental assumption behind this imagery is that God is the one who authenticates and sustains human effort: God is responsible for multiplying both the seed for sowing and the increase of the harvest.

4.4.7 9:11–15: Generosity That Glorifies God

The conclusion of Paul's appeal for the Corinthians to contribute to the collection for the saints is found in vv. 11–15. It is noteworthy that v. 11 represents the first occurrence of the word εὐχαριστία in 2 Corinthians 8–9, and Paul's usage of this term here and in v. 12 is indicative of his distinctly theological conception of the Jerusalem collection. As we saw in the preceding chapter, the accumulation of honor, praise, and thanksgiving – what some anthropologists refer to as "symbolic capital" – was a crucial motivating factor in the dissemination of gifts and benefits in the Greco-Roman world. According to the ideologies of patronage and euergetism in antiquity, the receipt of a gift was properly acknowledged with a public demonstration of thanksgiving. This reciprocation may have come in the form of a verbal expression of gratitude, an honorary inscription, or even the material return of a gift of equal or greater value. Seneca's treatise *De beneficiis* stands out as an illustrative commentary on this system of "general reciprocity." According to Seneca, "not to return gratitude for benefits

---

psalm praises the righteous person who freely gives to the poor, whereas members of the "competent" and "minimal" audiences, who possessed less knowledge of the original literary context of this verse, would have understood God as the subject of the citation.

[74] The scriptural citation in 2 Cor 9:9 may also be a continuation of the agricultural metaphor. The verb σκορπίζω ("scatter") is used to describe the spreading of fertilizer over a field in PLond 131:421.

[75] Harris, *Second Epistle*, 644.

is a disgrace and the whole world counts it as such" (*Ben.* 3.1.1). The remains of thousands of inscriptions, many of which preserve the records of ancient clubs and guilds, also testify to the necessity of reciprocating benefits with proper acknowledgements of thanksgiving, as is seen in the frequency with which εὐχαριστία appears in honorific decrees.[76] We have seen already that a standard clause in honorific inscriptions designed to promote a rivalry among potential benefactors explicitly proclaimed that "each [donor] will receive thanks (εὐχαριστία) in proportion to their benefaction."

What is striking about 2 Cor 9:11–12 is not so much Paul's use of the term εὐχαριστία in a context in which he is exhorting his readers to contribute to a gift for the needy in Jerusalem, but rather his affirmation of God as the sole object of thanksgiving. Given the importance of donors in Greco-Roman antiquity being recognized with public thanksgiving and praise for their benefactions, one would perhaps expect Paul to remind the Corinthians that their support of the offering for Jerusalem will result in "thanksgiving to you." Yet Paul does not echo anything like the inscriptional refrain that the Corinthians "will receive thanks in proportion to their benefaction." Instead, Paul twice intimates that εὐχαριστία in this context is properly ascribed only to the God whose abundant grace makes this offering possible.[77] In v. 11, Paul affirms that the "generosity" of the Corinthians – itself the result of God's enrichment – "will produce thanksgiving *to God* through us." Presumably the thanksgiving of which Paul speaks here will be offered by the recipients of this offering in Jerusalem, although the thanksgiving will be directed to the "one who supplies the seed" (v. 10) and not to the Corinthian benefactors. Paul essentially repeats this refrain in v. 12, declaring that "this ministry of service not only supplies the needs of the saints but also abounds with many thanksgivings *to God*." Should the Corinthians prove faithful in this task, their obedience to the confession of the gospel and their "partnership-forming contribution" will ultimately bring glory to the God whose abundant χάρις enables their own χάρις (v. 13). Indeed, what Paul says of the thanksgiving rendered to God because of the collection echoes what he has already said about the nature of his apostolic ministry in 2 Cor 4:15: "For everything is for your sake, so that grace [χάρις], as it widens its scope through more and more people, may increase thanksgiving, to the glory of God."[78] This rhetorical strategy subtly subverts the dominant ideology of pagan benefaction by highlighting the honor, praise, and thanksgiving due God, the one from

---

[76] On the usage of εὐχαριστία in benefaction contexts, see G.W. Peterman, *Paul's Gift from Philippi* (SNTSMS 92; Cambridge: Cambridge University Press, 1997), 51–89; Harrison, *Paul's Language of Grace*, 269–73.

[77] Similarly, in both 2 Cor 8:16 and 9:15, Paul uses the related word χάρις in the expression χάρις τῷ θεῷ. These declarations also indicate that God is the one who truly deserves thanks (i.e., χάρις) for the offering of the Corinthians.

[78] On the thematic connection between 2 Cor 4:15 and 2 Cor 8–9, see Kraftchick, "Death in Us, Life in You," 177–79.

whom all benefactions ultimately originate, thus also minimizing any competition for honor, praise, and thanksgiving among the Corinthians. As Bart Bruehler nicely summarizes Paul's strategy, "The return of gratitude and public honour to the human benefactor is replaced by thanks and worship being offered to God because of the grace-enabled gift."[79]

Moreover, the notion that the Corinthians' participation in the collection effort will result in the worship of God permeates 2 Cor 9:11–16. This motif of worship is found not only in the two instances of εὐχαριστία ascribed to God (vv. 11, 12), in the reference to "glorifying God" (δοξάζοντες τὸν θεόν) in v. 13, or in the "liturgical-sounding expression of gratitude to God for his indescribable gift"[80] with which the passage concludes (v. 15), but also in Paul's terminology for the relief fund in v. 12. In that verse, Paul refers to the collection as ἡ διακονία τῆς λειτουργίας ταύτης ("this ministry of service"). We have seen already that in 2 Cor 8:1–15 Paul metaphorically frames the collection as a religious offering, and the designation ἡ διακονία τῆς λειτουργίας ταύτης in 2 Cor 9:12 is consistent with this earlier use of cultic metaphor.

In classical Greek usage, the word λειτουργία denoted an act of service, particularly with reference to public duties performed by wealthy citizens, such as the financing of regular festivals or the payment of special taxes designed to fund the military during times of war. Eventually, however, this concept of service was applied more specifically to religious or cultic activities, which is how the λειτουργ- word family is frequently used in papyri and inscriptions from the Hellenistic and Imperial periods.[81] In the LXX, λειτουρέω and λειτουργία are essentially technical terms associated with priestly and levitical service offered to God in the tabernacle or temple (e.g., Num 16:9; Deut 18:5). Therefore, most scholars posit that the phrase ἡ διακονία τῆς λειτουργίας in 2 Cor 9:12 should be read with cultic connotations.[82] With this designation for the Jerusalem

---

[79] Bruehler, "Proverbs, Persuasion, and People," 223.

[80] Thrall, *2 Corinthians*, 594; see also David W. Pao, *Thanksgiving: An Investigation of a Pauline Theme* (NSBT 13; Downers Grove, Ill.: InterVarsity Press, 2002), 84–85.

[81] Cf., e.g., IG V/1 1390; IMagnMai 98; IG II² 1028, 1039. Several inscriptions record λειτουργία as the object of the verb ἐπιτελέω in cultic contexts. See, e.g., IKerameikos 3.5 (1st BCE: φιλοτίμως ἐπιτελοῦσι τὰς λειτουργίας); IMiletMcCabe 415 (2nd CE). For a thorough discussion of the history of the word λειτουργία, see Sibel Ayse Tuzlak, "Service and Performance: *Leitourgia* and the Study of Early Christian Worship" (Ph.D. diss., Syracuse University, 2001), 1–49; cf. C. Spicq, "λειτουργέω, λειτουργία, λειτουργικός, λειτουργός," *TLNT* 2:378–84; Verbrugge, *Paul's Style of Church Leadership*, 147–50.

[82] So Thrall, *2 Corinthians*, 586–87; Furnish, *II Corinthians*, 451; Harris, *Second Epistle*, 648–49. Philipp D. Bachmann (*Der zweite Brief des Paulus an die Korinther* [KNT 8; Leipzig: A Diechert, 1909], 330) writes, "Das Kollektenwerk ... hießt jetzt ἡ διακονία τῆς λειτουργίας ταύτης und wird damit eine Beziehung sakral-kultischer Art hineingehoben: in diesem Dienst vollzieht sich ein gottesdienstliches Handeln höchster Art." Paul also clearly uses the word λειτουργία in a cultic sense in Phil 2:17, where he speaks of himself being "poured out as a libation over the sacrifice and the offering of your [i.e., the Philippians'] faith" (σπένδομαι ἐπὶ τῇ θυσίᾳ καὶ

collection, then, Paul invites his readers in Corinth to view their participation in the collection as an act of priestly service offered to God.[83] When framed as a religious offering, God is the one who receives thanksgiving for this caritative act (vv. 12, 15). As caretakers of this priestly liturgy, the Corinthians participate in an act of service that results in the worship and praise of God.

4.4.8 Conclusion

Paul employs a number of rhetorical strategies in 2 Cor 8:1–9:15 in his cautious attempt to persuade the Corinthians to resume their support of the collection for the saints. Throughout these two chapters, Paul is at pains to emphasize the initiative and activity of God in this fundraising effort.[84] Although the Macedonians and the Corinthians are both called to support this endeavor, the success of the collection is not finally dependent on human activity, but rather upon the God whose abundant χάρις will enable this gift. As one part of his strategy of highlighting the fact that this undertaking has its "origin and energy in God's grace," Paul metaphorically frames the activity of contributing to the collection as a religious offering that will result in the worship of God.[85] First, in 2 Cor 8:6, 11, Paul uses the verb ἐπιτελέω, with its resonance of the completion of sacral offerings and duties in the Greco-Roman world, in order to urge the completion of the offering. Second, in 2 Cor 9:12, Paul speaks of the collection as a "ministry of service," using the phrase ἡ διακονία τῆς λειτουργίας. In viewing the collection as a λειτουργία, the Corinthians are invited to understand their contribution as a priestly service offered to God. As such, the praise and thanksgiving for their support of this benefaction is rightly directed toward the God who stands behind their offering. In order to sustain my claim that the cultic language in 2 Cor 8:1–9:15 represents two linguistic expressions of a larger conceptual metaphor that structures Paul's thought regarding the collection, however, it will be

---

λειτουργίᾳ τῆς πίστεως ὑμῶν; see below). According to Heinrich A. W. Meyer (*Kritisch exegetisches Handbuch über den zweiten Brief an die Korinther* [Göttingen: Vandenhoeck und Ruprecht's, 1870], 245–46), the collection is to be regarded as "ein (den Empfängern zu Gute kommendes) priesterliches *Opferdarbringen*." Pace Sze-kar Wan, "Collection for the Saints as Anticolonial Act: Implications of Paul's Ethnic Reconstruction," in *Paul and Politics: Ekklesia, Israel, Imperium, Interpretation; Essays in Honor of Krister Stendahl* (ed. Richard H. Horsley; Harrisburg, Pa.: Trinity, 2000), 208–9, 212.

[83] Georgi (*Remembering the Poor*, 103) translates v. 12, "Indeed, the enactment of this priestly service not only covers the needs of the saints, it also leads to abundance through the great number of (ensuing) thanksgiving prayers to God."

[84] See Gaventa, "Economy of Grace," 58–60; Wan ("Collection for the Saints," 214) argues a similar point: "While suggesting to the Corinthians that they contribute generously, Paul reiterates the assertion that all generosity and all wealth ultimately come from God, and that the final aim and goal of the collection is likewise the glorification and thanksgiving to God. Accordingly, the Corinthians are no more than middlemen who must be faithful stewards of what has been entrusted to them."

[85] Gaventa, "Economy of Grace," 55.

necessary also to examine Rom 15:14–32, where we find a similar use of cultic language with reference to the Jerusalem collection.

In addition to the cultic metaphors applied to the collection in 2 Corinthians 8–9, Paul also employs agrarian imagery in 2 Cor 9:6–11 by depicting support of the fund as sowing seed and the fulfillment of the fund as a harvest of righteousness. If the cultic metaphors indicate that one conceptual metaphor for the collection is COLLECTION IS WORSHIP, the agricultural metaphor suggests that a second conceptual metaphor for the fund is COLLECTION IS HARVEST. As we shall see, this metaphor, too, reappears with reference to the Jerusalem collection in Romans 15.

4.5 Romans 15:14–32: "The Offering of the Gentiles"[86]

4.5.1 Introduction

Paul's emphasis on the collection as an act of cultic worship offered to God is even stronger in his comments about the offering in Rom 15:14–32, a passage written in anticipation of the apostle's delivery of the fund to Jerusalem.[87] Indeed, Paul's use of cultic metaphors in order to frame the Jerusalem collection as a religious offering presented in the worship of God in Rom 15 builds on the theme of worship as it is developed throughout the epistle to the Romans. When, at the beginning of the letter, Paul speaks of humanity's captivity to sin, he diagnoses as the root problem a fundamental failure properly to acknowledge and worship God: "For although they knew God, they did not praise him as God or give thanks to him [οὐχ ὡς θεὸν ἐδόξασαν ἢ ηὐχαρίστησαν], but they became futile in their thoughts and their senseless minds were darkened" (1:21). As a result of this spiritual bankruptcy, Paul declares, God handed humanity over to the powers of sin and death.[88] In Rom 12:1, at a key transition point in the argument of the epistle, Paul presents a vision of the Christian life as one of rational worship offered to God. Moreover, if Rom 1:21–23 highlights at the beginning of the epistle the cosmic implications of humanity's failure to offer rightly ordered worship to God, Rom 14:1–15:13 deals near the letter's end with

---

[86] Much of the material in this section is drawn from my article "'The Offering of the Gentiles' in Romans 15.16," *JSNT* 29 (2006): 173–86.

[87] Ben Witherington III (*Conflict and Community in Corinth: A Socio-Rhetorical Commentary on 1 and 2 Corinthians* [Grand Rapids: Eerdmans, 1995], 425) writes, "In Rom. 15:23–32 Paul seems to see the collection as an act of worship offered up to God, a religious 'liturgy' that prompts thanksgiving."

[88] See Beverly Roberts Gaventa, "God Handed Them Over: Reading Romans 1:18–32 Apocalyptically," *ABR* 53 (2005): 42–53; idem, "Interpreting the Death of Jesus Apocalyptically: Reconsidering Romans 8:32," in *Jesus and Paul Reconsidered: Fresh Pathways Into an Old Debate* (ed. Todd D. Still; Grand Rapids and Cambridge: Eerdmans, 2007), 125–45 .

practical problems for the Roman church's worship life caused by disputes about law observance. Francis Watson has suggested that the long section on the weak and the strong in Rom 14:1–15:13 represents an attempt to mediate between two groups in Rome whose differing perspectives on the law likely left them unable to share in common worship.[89] Paul's exhortation for these factions to "welcome one another, therefore, just as Christ has welcomed you" (15:7) stems from his hope that "together with one voice you might glorify the God and Father of our Lord Jesus Christ" (15:6). The entire section is appropriately punctuated in 15:7–13 with a catena of scriptural testimonies that bear witness to Paul's vision of the Gentiles joining with God's people Israel in a chorus of praise and worship (vv. 9b–12).[90]

Following this hopeful expression of a unified community praising and worshipping God together, Paul provides a précis of his apostolic ministry (15:14–21) and announces to his audience in Rome his dual desire for their future support of his Spanish mission as well as for their prayers for his safety and the successful delivery of the collection for the saints during his journey to Jerusalem (15:22–32). Although it is only in Rom 15:25–32 that Paul directly discusses the relief fund for Jerusalem, I shall argue that there is also a reference to the collection earlier in this section, in Rom 15:16. My claim is that the phrase ἡ προσφορὰ τῶν ἐθνῶν in Rom 15:16 should be read as a subjective genitive that refers to the monetary offering raised among the Gentile churches of Paul's mission. This reading holds great significance for the understanding of the collection in Rom 15, particularly for the claim that Paul presents the Jerusalem collection as a religious offering that results in the worship of God.

4.5.2 "The Offering of the Gentiles"

In Rom 15:15–16, Paul explains to his readers that he has written rather boldly to them on some points "because of the grace given [to him] by God to be a minister of Christ Jesus to the Gentiles, so that the offering of the Gentiles [ἡ προσφορὰ τῶν ἐθνῶν] may be acceptable, sanctified by the Holy Spirit." The phrase ἡ προσφορὰ τῶν ἐθνῶν is taken by almost all interpreters – both ancient and modern – as a genitive of apposition, indicating that the offering of which

---

[89] Francis Watson, "The Two Roman Congregations: Romans 14:1–15:3," in *The Romans Debate: Revised and Expanded Edition* (ed. Karl P. Donfried; Peabody, Mass.: Hendrickson, 1991), 203–15. For a helpful overview of the differing interpretations of this passage, see Mark Reasoner, *The Strong and the Weak: Romans 14.1–15.13 in Context* (SNTSMS 103; Cambridge: Cambridge University Press, 1999), 1–23; see also John M. G. Barclay, "Do We Undermine the Law? A Study of Romans 14.1–15.6," in *Paul and the Mosaic Law: The Third Durham Tübingen Research Symposium on Earliest Christianity and Judaism* (ed. J. D. G. Dunn; WUNT 89; Tübingen: J. C. B. Mohr, 1996), 287–308.

[90] See J. Ross Wagner, "The Christ, Servant of the Jew and Gentile: A Fresh Approach to Romans 15:8–9," *JBL* 116 (1997): 473–85.

Paul speaks consists of his Gentile converts themselves.[91] According to this reading, the phrase "the offering of the Gentiles," in its context, "denotes the evangelized Gentiles who are consecrated and offered to God as an acceptable sacrifice through Paul's evangelization of them."[92] While there is not space here to recite the history of interpretation of this verse, it seems that such an appositional reading received decisive support in the work of Johannes Munck, who proposed in his book *Paul and the Salvation of Mankind* that Paul's understanding of the mission to the Gentiles was profoundly shaped by the apostle's appropriation of Old Testament traditions regarding an eschatological pilgrimage of the nations to Zion.[93] Among scholars who prefer an appositional genitive in

---

[91] Among the many modern interpreters who take τῶν ἐθνῶν as epexegetical or appositional are included: Charles Hodge, *Commentary on the Epistle to the Romans* (2d ed.; Edinburgh: Andrew Elliot, 1875), 436–37; F. Godet, *Commentaire sur L'Épitre aux Romains* (2d ed.; Paris: Grassart, 1890), 560–61; W. Sanday and A. C. Headlam, *The Epistle to the Romans* (ICC; 5th ed.; Edinburgh: T & T Clark, 1902), 403; John Murray, *The Epistle to the Romans: The English Text with Introduction, Exposition, and Notes* (2 vols.; NICNT; Grand Rapids: Eerdmans, 1965), 210–11; C. E. B. Cranfield, *A Critical and Exegetical Commentary on the Epistle to the Romans*, vol. 2: *Commentary on Romans IX–XVI and Essays* (ICC; Edinburgh: T & T Clark, 1979), 756; Ernst Käsemann, *Commentary on Romans* (trans. G. W. Bromiley; Grand Rapids: Eerdmans, 1980), 393; Rudolf Pesch, *Römerbrief* (NEchtB 6; Würzburg: Echter, 1983), 104; James D. G. Dunn, *Romans* (2 vols.; WBC 38; Dallas: Word, 1988), 2:860; John Ziesler, *Paul's Letter to the Romans* (TPINTC; Philadelphia: Trinity, 1989), 342; C. K. Barrett, *The Epistle to the Romans* (BNTC; 2d ed.; London: A & C Black, 1991), 252; Douglas J. Moo, *The Epistle to the Romans* (NICNT; Grand Rapids: Eerdmans, 1996), 890; Brendan Byrne, *Romans* (SP 6; Collegeville: Minn.: Liturgical, 1996), 438; Thomas R. Schreiner, *Romans* (BECNT; Grand Rapids: Baker, 1998), 767; Terence L. Donaldson, *Paul and the Gentiles: Remapping the Apostle's Convictional World* (Minneapolis: Fortress, 1997), 256; and Klaus Haacker, *Der Brief des Paulus an die Römer* (THKNT 6; Leipzig: Evangelische Verlagsanstalt, 1999). Joseph Fitzmyer (*Romans: A New Translation with Introduction and Commentary* [AB 33; Garden City: Doubleday, 1993], 712) and Eduard Lohse (*Der Brief an die Römer* [KEK 15; Göttingen: Vandenhoeck and Ruprecht, 2003], 395) both classify the phrase as an objective genitive, but there is no real difference in meaning (cf. also R. St. John Parry, ed., *The Epistle of Paul the Apostle to the Romans* [CGTSC; Cambridge: Cambridge University Press, 1921], 189). Though he does not provide a grammatical classification, Karl Barth (*The Epistle to the Romans* [trans. Edwyn C. Hoskyns; Oxford: Oxford University Press, 1933], 530) understands the phrase as an offering up of the Gentiles themselves, as does Adolph Schlatter (*Gottes Gerechtigkeit: Ein Kommentar zum Römerbrief* (Stuttgart: Calwer, 1836), 386.

[92] Fitzmyer, *Romans*, 712.

[93] See Johannes Munck, *Paul and the Salvation of Mankind* (Atlanta: John Knox, 1959), esp. chapter 10. Munck himself seems to have built upon the work of Joachim Jeremias, whose delivery of the Franz Delitzsch lectures in 1953 argued for the importance of the so-called eschatological pilgrimage tradition for the mission of Jesus; see Joachim Jeremias, "The Gentile World in the Thought of Jesus," *SNTA* 3 (1952): 18–28; idem, *Jesus' Promise to the Nations: The Franz Delitzsch Lectures for 1953* (trans. S. H. Hooke; London: SCM, 1958). Cf. Terence L. Donaldson, "Proselytes or 'Righteous Gentiles'? The Status of Gentiles in Eschatological Pilgrimage Patters of Thought," *JSP* 7 (1990): 3–27.

A brief look at the history of interpretation of Rom 15:16 suggests that most pre-modern interpreters also take "the offering of the Gentiles" as a reference to Paul's symbolic offering to

Rom 15:16, the "offering of the Gentiles" is frequently interpreted as an intended fulfillment of the eschatological narrative of Isa 66:20, a passage that speaks of a remnant of Jews from the Diaspora taken by Gentiles to Jerusalem "from all the nations as a gift to the Lord" (LXX Isa 66:20; ἄξουσιν τοὺς ἀδελφοὺς ὑμῶν ἐκ πάντων τῶν ἐθνῶν δῶρον κυρίῳ).[94] Paul is sometimes thought to have reversed this scenario rather dramatically: within his own ministry it is the Gentiles, instead of the Jews, who are being gathered as an offering to God. Hence Roger Aus has proposed:

> Paul read this Isaiah text [i.e., Isa 66:20–21] to mean that Christian missionaries, primarily he himself with his helpers, were, in a complete reversal of the normal Jewish thought regarding the end time, to gather representatives from all the *Gentile* nations and to bring them, the Gentiles, and not the diaspora Jews, to Jerusalem as an 'offering' or 'gift' to the Lord Jesus, the Messiah. This would be the "offering of the Gentiles" of which Paul speaks in Rom. xv 16.[95]

There is, however, another way to read the phrase ἡ προσφορὰ τῶν ἐθνῶν in Rom 15:16, namely, as a subjective genitive ("the offering given by the Gentiles").[96] If the genitive is taken subjectively, one apparent referent for an offering

---

God of his Gentile converts, though without allusion to eschatological pilgrimage passages. So Justin Martyr (*ANF* 1:257); Origen (*Comm. Rom.*, 5:214–16); Augustine (*Augustine on Romans*, 49); Pelagius (*Pelagius's Commentary on Romans*, 147–48); Calvin (*Commentaries on the Epistle of Paul to the Romans* [trans. John Owen; Grand Rapids: Eerdmans, 1948], 527); Luther (*Lectures on Romans: Glosses and Scholia*, vol. 25 of *Luther's Works*, [ed. Hilton C. Oswald; Saint Louis: Concordia, 1972], 516–17); and John Locke (*A Paraphrase and Notes on the Epistles of St. Paul to the Galatians, 1 and 2 Corinthians, Romans, Ephesians*, vol. 2 [ed. Arthur W. Wainwright; Oxford: Clarendon, 1987], 598–99). The eschatological reading of this phrase, with its emphasis on the allusion to Isaiah, does not seem to have arisen until after Munck.

[94] Those who find in Rom 15:16 an allusion to Isa 66:20 include Murray, *Romans*, 210–11; Roger D. Aus, "Paul's Travel Plans to Spain and the 'Full Number of the Gentiles of Rom. XI 25," *NovT* 21 (1979): 232–62; Dunn, *Romans*, 860; Schreiner, *Romans*, 767; Fitzmyer, *Romans*, 712; Moo, *Epistle to the Romans*, 890; Byrne, *Romans*, 438; Rainer Riesner, *Paul's Early Period: Chronology, Mission Strategy, Theology* (trans. Doug Stott; Grand Rapids: Eerdmans, 1998), 245–53; Burkhard Beckheuer, *Paulus und Jerusalem: Kollekte und Mission im theologischen Denken des Heidenapostels* (Europäische Hochschulschriften 23; Frankfurt am Main: Peter Lang, 1997), 221–23; Richard J. Dillon, "The 'Priesthood' of St Paul, Romans 15:15–16," *Worship* 74 (2000): 156–68. Ziesler (*Romans*, 342) does not explicitly mention Isaiah 66, but he does refer to "the coming of the Gentiles into the (Christian) people of God as the fulfillment of the hope that in the last days they would stream to Zion." LXX Isaiah 66 itself is no easy passage to interpret; for a helpful summary of the difficult issues, see David A. Baer, *When We All Go Home: Translation and Theology in LXX Isaiah 56–66* (JSOTSup 318; Sheffield: Sheffield Academic Press, 2001).

[95] Aus, "Paul's Travel Plans," 241.

[96] Both A. M. Denis ("La Fonction apostolique et la liturgie nouvelle en Esprit: Étude thématique des métaphores pauliniennes du culte nouveau," *RSPT* 42 [1958]: 401–36) and D. W. B. Robinson ("The Priesthood of Paul in the Gospel of Hope," in *Reconciliation and Hope: New Testament Essays on Atonement and Eschatology Presented to L.L. Morris on His Sixtieth Birthday* [ed. Robert Banks; Grand Rapids: Eerdmans, 1974], 231–45) argue for a subjective genitive in Rom

made by the Gentiles would then be the collection for Jerusalem, which is Paul's explicit subject in 15:25–32. While the noun προσφορά often refers to religious offerings in Jewish and Christian literature (e.g., LXX Ps 39:7; Sir 14:11; Acts 21:26; Heb 10:18), it can equally designate more mundane gifts and benefactions (Sophocles, *Oed. col.* 581, 1270; Theophrastus, *Char.* 30.19; Josephus, *A.J.* 19.8.2), including victuals (Hippocrates, *Aph.* 2.33). There is, therefore, no compelling linguistic reason that with the designation ἡ προσφορά τῶν ἐθνῶν Paul cannot be referring to a monetary contribution from his Gentile churches (cf. 15:27), especially if the noun προσφορά is taken metaphorically. Moreover, within the same section, the noun ἔθνος occurs in a comparable genitival construction, ὑπακοὴν ἐθνῶν (15:18), and in this latter case the phrase is best understood as a subjective genitive: Paul does not dare to speak of anything except that which Christ has worked through him for *the obedience that proceeds from the Gentiles*, which is made known in both word and deed, by the power of signs and wonders, by the power of the Spirit of God (Rom 15:18–19a).[97]

15:16. Denis, noting that most commentators in his day read the phrase as an objective genitive, declares: "Cependant l'emploi avec un génitif subjectif, offrande de celui qui offre, existe aussi et de façon bien naturelle" (405). He takes the phrase as a reference to the cultic worship of the Gentiles, relating it back to Rom 12:1 (cf. Walter Schmithals, *Der Römerbrief: Ein Kommentar* [Gütersloher: Gütersloher Verlagshous, 1988], 528–29). Robinson, on the other hand, sees the "offering" as "what the Gentiles offer to Christ, namely their own glorifying of God (15:9), or their obedience (15:18)" (231). Hans Asmussen (*Der Römerbrief* [Stuttgart: Evangelisches Verlagswerk, 1952], 292–93) earlier made a case for a subjective genitive. Joseph Ponthot ("L'expression cultuelle du ministère paulinien selon Rm 15,16," in *L'Apôtre Paul: Personnalité, Style et Conception du Ministère* [ed. A. Vanhoye; BETL 73; Leuven: Leuven University Press, 1986], 254–62) hedges between the two options: "En fait, ce deuxième sens [i.e., an appositional genitive] n'est pas exclusif du premier [i.e., a subjective genitive], car les nations ne peuvent être offertes qu'en consentant elles-mêmes à cette offrande" (259).

The only modern interpreter known to me who even suggests the possibility that ἡ προσφορά τῶν ἐθνῶν can be read as a subjective genitive that refers to the monetary collection for Jerusalem is Sze-kar Wan ("Collection for the Saints," 191–215, esp. 204–10). However, Wan thinks that this allusive phrase can be taken both objectively and subjectively, and that therefore the expression "contains a double reference: While it speaks of the Gentiles as Paul's offering, it also alludes to the Gentiles' contribution, namely the collection, as an offering" (206). While my perspective is fundamentally indebted to a number of Wan's insightful observations, the argument in this section is that τῶν ἐθνῶν is primarily a reference to the monetary contribution of the Gentiles.

[97] Note also the parallel in the authorizing and authenticating role ascribed to the Holy Spirit in both 15:16 and 15:19. Relating the phrase ὑπακοὴν ἐθνῶν back to εἰς ὑπακοὴν πίστεως ἐν πᾶσιν τοῖς ἔθνεσιν in Rom 1:5, Käsemann (*Commentary on Romans*, 393–94), Barrett (*Epistle to the Romans*, 253), and Moo (*Epistle to the Romans*, 892) find in Rom 15:18 a reference to the acceptance of the gospel of Christ among the Gentiles. However, while not ignoring this parallel, Don Garlington (*Faith, Obedience, and Perseverance: Aspects of Paul's Letter to the Romans* [WUNT 79; Tübingen: J.C.B. Mohr, 1994], 24–30) develops a strong contextual case for viewing ὑπακοὴν ἐθνῶν in 15:18 as a reference to both an obedience that "springs from faith" and an "obedience that consists in faith," especially in light of the parenetic section from 14:1–15:13.

Taking τῶν ἐθνῶν as a subjective genitive would then indicate that Isaiah 66 does not figure in the background of Rom 15:16, despite the speculations of a number of scholars.[98] An allusion to Isa 66:20 in this verse is already tentative, not least because those who interpret Rom 15:16 in light of this Isaianic narrative must posit a complete reversal of the prophetic tradition. As Terence Donaldson, who reads τῶν ἐθνῶν epexegetically and yet objects to the Old Testament allusion, opines, "It is quite a jump to think that Paul grounded his ministry as a Jewish apostle bringing Gentiles as an offering, on a text which speaks of Gentiles bringing Jews."[99] Although close verbal parallels between LXX Isa 49:1–6 and Gal 1:15 suggest that Paul probably understood his divine calling as apostle to the Gentiles in terms of this earlier Isaianic servant passage,[100] there is no such overlap in the vocabulary of Isa 66:18–24 and Rom 15:16.[101] In fact, nowhere else in his letters does Paul appear to cite or allude to the eschatological scenario in Isaiah 66, or any of the other so-called eschatological pilgrimage texts.[102] Ultimately, without the notion of Paul presenting the Gentiles themselves as an offering to God in Rom 15:16, the potential allusion to Isaiah 66 disappears altogether.

An example from Paul's correspondence with the Philippians may shed some light on the difficult genitival construction in Rom 15:16. In an attempt to refute the claim made by Denis that the phrase ἡ προσφορὰ τῶν ἐθνῶν in Rom 15:16 is a subjective genitive that refers to an offering of obedience and cultic worship made by the Gentiles, Fitzmyer rightly draws attention to a similar locution in Phil 2:17: ἐπὶ τῇ θυσίᾳ καὶ λειτουργίᾳ τῆς πίστεως ὑμῶν ("the sacrifice and

---

[98] The most extensive arguments for an allusion to Isa 66 in Rom 15:16 are found in Aus, "Paul's Travel Plans," 232–62, and Riesner, *Paul's Early Period*, 245–53. For a more critical view, see James M. Scott, *Paul and the Nations: The Old Testament and Jewish Background of Paul's Mission to the Nations with Special Reference to the Destination of Galatians* (WUNT 84; Tübingen: J.C.B. Mohr, 1995), 136–47. Scott points out that the geographical scope of the mission in Isa 66 does not exactly correspond to the direction of Paul's mission, according to Rom 15:14–21, from Jerusalem to Illyricum to Spain. Although the "table of nations" tradition may have informed Paul's theological geography, it is not necessary to appeal specifically to Isa 66 as the source of this information, since, as Scott demonstrates, the "table of nations" tradition is fairly widespread in both the Old Testament and in later Jewish sources.

[99] Donaldson, *Paul and the Gentiles*, 363 n. 38.

[100] Ibid., 253–54.

[101] The word for gift in Isa 66:20 is δῶρον, which does not occur in the authentic Pauline epistles (but cf. Eph 2:8 and δωρεάν in Rom 3:24; 2 Cor 11:7; and Gal 2:21). For an interesting and more easily demonstrable usage of LXX Isa 66:20 in early Jewish literature, see *Ps. Sol.* 17.31.

[102] E.g., Isa 2:2–4; 11:10–12; 25:6–10; 56:6–8; 60:1–14; Mic 4:1–4; Jer 3:17; Zech 14:16–21. So Donaldson, *Paul and the Gentiles*, 363 n. 38; J. Ross Wagner, *Heralds of the Good News: Isaiah and Paul 'in Concert' in the Letter to the Romans* (NovTSup 101; Leiden: Brill, 2002), 215 n. 287. For a different view from a disputed (and, in the present writer's view, pseudonymous) epistle, 2 Thessalonians, see Stephen G. Brown, "The Intertextuality of Isaiah 66.17 and 2 Thessalonians 2.7: A Solution for the 'Restrainer' Problem," in *Paul and the Scriptures of Israel* (JSNTSup 83; SSEJC 1; ed. Craig A. Evans and James A. Sanders; Sheffield: Sheffield Academic Press, 1993), 254–77.

the offering of your [i.e., the Philippians'] faith"). Fitzmyer and other commentators also take this phrase as an epexegetical genitive, so that the πίστις represents the sacrificial service of the Philippians.[103] Although there is not an exact verbal correspondence between these two texts (the words are θυσιά and λειτουργία in Phil 2:17 and προσφορά in Rom 15:16), there is both a grammatical parallel and also an overlapping of cultic language. However, Phil 2:17 would actually seem to support the argument that ἡ προσφορὰ τῶν ἐθνῶν in Rom 15:16 should be taken as a reference to the collection for the saints, since it is also possible to read the construction ἐπὶ τῇ θυσίᾳ καὶ λειτουργίᾳ τῆς πίστεως ὑμῶν in Phil 2:17 as a subjective genitive, or a genitive of origin, referring to an offering that proceeds from or is made possible by the faith of the Philippians, namely, the gift dispatched to Paul from the church in Philippi (4:10–20).[104] Confirmation for this reading of a subjective genitive in Phil 2:17 is found in 4:18, where Paul calls the gift sent to him by the Philippians through their representative Epaphroditus "a fragrant offering, a sacrifice acceptable [θυσίαν δεκτήν] and pleasing to God." The "offering and sacrifice of your faith" in 2:17 signifies the same gift from the Philippians that Paul discusses in 4:10–20. Here, too, as in Paul's comments about the collection for the saints, a monetary contribution is metaphorically framed as a cultic offering. Epaphroditus is already described in 2:25 as a minister (λειτουργός; cf. Rom 15:16) to Paul's needs, a role certainly related to his delivery of the Philippians' gift (4:10–20). The application of the term λειτουργός to both the gift-bearing delegate Epaphroditus in Phil 2:15 and to Paul in Rom 15:16 strengthens the claim that Paul's priestly service on behalf of the gospel of God in Romans is related to his delivery of the collection to Jerusalem. Dieter Georgi, noting the similarities in language that obtain between Paul's acknowledgment of the Philippians' gift in Phil 4:10–20 and discussions of the collection elsewhere in the Pauline epistles, has suggested that "the theological argumentation on which Paul elaborates in Philippians 4:10–20 [is] an exegetical model for the further interpretation of all Pauline literature pertaining to the collection."[105] Whatever the relationship between the Philippians' gift to Paul and Paul's own efforts to raise funds for Jerusalem, the point here is sufficiently made if the phrase "the offering and sacrifice of your faith" in Phil 2:17 is also understood as a subjective genitive.[106]

---

[103] E.g., Peter T. O'Brien, *The Epistle to the Philippians* (NIGTC; Grand Rapids: Eerdmans, 1991), 310.

[104] So Gerald F. Hawthorne, *Philippians* (rev. and enl. by Ralph P. Martin; WBC 43; Nashville: Thomas Nelson, 2000), 148; cf. Gordon D. Fee, *Paul's Letter to the Philippians* (NICNT; Grand Rapids: Eerdmans, 1995), 255. Interestingly, outside of Philippians the word λειτουργία is found in the Pauline corpus only in 2 Cor 9:12, where it describes the collection for the saints.

[105] Georgi, *Remembering the Poor*, 66.

[106] Since the letter to the Philippians was likely written after Paul's delivery of the relief fund to Jerusalem, the gift in 4:10–20 is not related to the collection for the saints, although the church in Philippi doubtless contributed to that earlier offering as well (2 Cor 8:1–6; 9:1–5; Rom 15:25–

4.5 Romans 15:14–32: "The Offering of the Gentiles"

Of course, even if a subjective genitive is granted in Rom 15:16, it might be claimed that the offering made by the Gentiles does not refer to the collection at all, but rather represents an extension of the metaphor in Rom 12:1, where Paul instructs his audience "to present your bodies as a living sacrifice, holy and acceptable to God, which is your spiritual worship."[107] I would not want to rule out the possibility that the phrase ἡ προσφορὰ τῶν ἐθνῶν refers also to the obedience of the Gentiles in a wider sense, with the collection standing as one concrete manifestation of that obedience (cf. vv. 18–19). The noun προσφορά can indicate either (1) the act of bringing an offering or (2) the offering which is brought as a voluntary expression,[108] and there is no easy way to decide between these two options in Rom 15:16. Paul does go on to speak of "what Christ has accomplished through me for the obedience of the Gentiles, by word and deed, by the power of signs and wonders, by the power of the Spirit of God, so that from Jerusalem and around even to Illyricum I have fully proclaimed the good news of Christ" (vv. 18–19), and this missionary activity includes but is not limited to the collection for the saints. At the same time, the passive form of Rom 15:16 seems to move in a slightly different direction from the active presentation of bodies as an act of spiritual worship in Rom 12:1: the "offering of the Gentiles" in Rom 15:16 has been entirely entrusted to the priestly service of Paul, and through him it becomes acceptable.[109] This is similar to the way in which Paul, with reference to the collection, speaks of "his ministry" (ἡ διακονία μου ἡ εἰς Ἰερουσαλήμ) being acceptable to the saints in Jerusalem in 15:31.

As is so often the case, however, the issue cannot be decided by grammar alone, so we must turn to verbal and conceptual links between Rom 15:16 and 15:25–32 to test further the claim that the phrase ἡ προσφορὰ τῶν ἐθνῶν refers to Paul's collection for the saints in Jerusalem.[110] First, two explicit verbal links establish a connection between these passages. The word εὐπρόσδεκτος, which is used in 15:16 to describe the acceptable offering of the Gentiles, occurs only

---

26). For an engaging study of Phil 4:10–20 in the context of Greco-Roman practices of giving and receiving gifts, see Peterman, *Paul's Gift from Philippi.*

[107] So Denis, "Fonction apostolique," 405–7; cf. Dunn, *Romans*, 2:860.

[108] BDAG, 887.

[109] Dillon ("The 'Priesthood' of St. Paul," 165) writes, "The consistent focus on Paul as the one and only acting subject in 15:14–21 forbids the intrusion of 'the Gentiles' as actors in the offering." While the Gentiles have, of course, been active participants in the fundraising project, it is Paul's own *delivery* of the contribution that is at issue in Rom 15:16. Note how frequently Paul's statements about the delivery of the collection are dominated by first-person verbs and pronouns: 1 Cor 16:3–4; Rom 15:30–31.

[110] Although Donaldson takes ἡ προσφορὰ τῶν ἐθνῶν as an epexegetical genitive, he does highlight some of the overlapping language between 15:16 and 15:25–33: "While the 'offering of the Gentiles' of Rom 15:16 cannot be simply equated with the collection from the Gentile congregations, there are nevertheless several indications ... that the one is at least a sign and preliminary manifestation of the other" (*Paul and the Gentiles*, 257). See also Wan, "Collection for the Saints," 205–6.

three other times in the Pauline corpus, and one of those instances is with explicit reference to the collection in 15:31: "that my ministry to Jerusalem may be acceptable [εὐπρόσδεκτος] to the saints." Interestingly, in 2 Cor 8:12 the word εὐπρόσδεκτος is also used of the collection.[111] A similar verbal link between Paul's discussion of his Gentile mission in 15:14–21 and his statements about the collection in 15:25–32 is forged by the use of the cognate words λειτουργός in 15:16 and λειτουργέω in 15:27: Paul, the *servant* to the Gentiles, is organizing an offering from the Gentiles because they recognize their obligation *to serve sacrificially* the poor among the saints in Jerusalem.[112]

Second, scholars have often noted that there is a high concentration of cultic terminology employed in Rom 15:16: λειτουργός, ἱερουργέω, προσφορά, εὐπρόσδεκτος, and ἁγιάζω all resonate with overtones of the temple cultus.[113] The language is metaphorical, and the power of this metaphor rests almost as much in the aggregation of symbolic language as it does in the incongruity created when the terminology of cultic worship is applied to Paul's mission to the Gentiles – a mission that ostensibly had as one of its primary goals the elimination of boundaries between the sacred and the secular.[114] Stanley Stowers has, in fact, pointed out that one of the truly distinguishing features of the early Christian movement was its apparent disregard for many of the most important aspects of the ancient religions: "In Pauline Christianity, there are no temples on the land, no ties to or concern for the land, no animal or other types of sacrifice, and no agricultural festivals or festivals for other types of productivity.... All that is missing here constituted the heart of ancient religion."[115]

---

[111] The only other time this word is used in Paul's extant writings comes in a gloss on a quotation of Isa 49:8 in 2 Cor 6:2, where the word δεκτός is found in the scriptural text.

[112] On λειτουργέω in 15:27, Moo (*Epistle to the Romans*, 905 n. 51) writes, "The choice of this verb (cf. also Acts 13:2; Heb. 10:11) may suggest that Paul views the collection as an act of worship, since it is often used in the LXX with reference to the cult. But the verb is also used in secular Greek of the work of civil servants. It is possible, though not clear, that the priestly associations of the cognate word λειτουργός from 15:16 are still present here." The word λειτουργός is found also in Rom 13:6, where the ruling authorities are described as God's λειτουργοί.

[113] So Dunn, *Romans*, 2:859–81; Moo, *Epistle to the Romans*, 889–91; Schreiner, *Romans*, 766–68; Dillon, "The 'Priesthood' of St Paul," 162; Ponthot, "Expression cultuelle," 254–62.

[114] Dunn, *Romans*, 2:867. On the notion that the abolishment of religious distinctions between the holy and the profane stands at the heart of Paul's apocalyptic gospel, see J. Louis Martyn, *Theological Issues in the Letters of Paul* (Nashville: Abingdon, 1997), esp. 47–69, 77–84.

[115] Stanley K. Stowers, "Does Pauline Christianity Resemble a Hellenistic Philosophy?" in *Paul Beyond the Judaism/Hellenism Divide* (ed. Troels Engberg-Pedersen; Louisville: Westminster John Knox, 2001), 81–102; see also idem, "Greeks Who Sacrifice and Those Who Do Not: Toward an Anthropology of Greek Religion," in *The Social World of the First Christians: Essays in Honor of Wayne A. Meeks* (ed. L. Michael White and O. Larry Yarbrough; Minneapolis: Fortress, 1995), 293-33; and Wayne A. Meeks, *The First Urban Christians: The Social World of the Apostle Paul* (New Haven and London: Yale University Press, 1983), 140–42.

It is somewhat odd, then, to find such strong cultic imagery in Rom 15:16. With the ear pricked by the cultic metaphors applied to Paul's mission to the Gentiles in Rom 15:16, it is significant that one finds a recurrence of cultic language, using some of the very same terminology, in Paul's discussion of the collection in Rom 15:25–32. While the verb λειτουργέω, which is used in Rom 15:27 to describe the action of the Gentile Christians toward the saints in Jerusalem, does not always have a cultic nuance, it should be read with cultic overtones in 15:27 because of its proximity to the priestly language of 15:16, and also because of the cognate cultic designation for the collection in 2 Cor 9:12 (ἡ διακονία τῆς λειτουργίας).[116] The Gentiles minister as priests to their Jewish-Christian benefactors in Jerusalem. This is supported in the next sentence by Paul's assertion that "having completed [ἐπιτελέσας] this, and having sealed [σφραγισάμενος] to them [i.e., the Jerusalem Christians] this fruit [τὸν καρπὸν τοῦτον]," he plans to travel through Rome to Spain (15:28). We have seen already in 2 Cor 8:6, 11 that Paul's use of the term ἐπιτελέω appears to draw on the contemporary usage of this word to denote the observation of religious rites and sacrifices. In many of the inscriptions in which the verb is used, ἐπιτελέω designates the performance, sometimes by priests, of cultic rites, sacrifices, and mysteries.[117] It might additionally be noted that, while many commentators take σφραγίζω in this context as a reference to the agricultural practice of sealing sacks of grain for delivery,[118] this verb perhaps also has cultic overtones, since in the Greek world the priest responsible for the official sealing of the temple sacrifices was called the ἱερομοσχοσφραγιστής.[119]

Therefore, it seems possible on grammatical, linguistic, and contextual grounds to take the phrase "offering of the Gentiles" in Rom 15:16 as a subjective genitive and thus as a reference to the collection for the saints in Jerusalem. But would Paul's readers have picked up on an allusion to the relief fund in the phrase ἡ προσφορὰ τῶν ἐθνῶν? On the one hand, it could be objected that this expression is a rather opaque reference compared to the more direct discussion found in Rom 15:25–32. On the other, we might consider the possibility that the Christians in Rome would have had some knowledge of the collection before

---

[116] So Dunn, *Romans*, 2:876; contra Strathmann, "λειτουργέω κτλ.," *TDNT* 4:227; Schreiner, *Romans*, 777 (given the concentration of cultic language in Phil 2:17–30, Schreiner's appeal to Phil 2:30 does not help his case).

[117] Ascough, "Completion of a Religious Duty," 590–94. Of note in light of Paul's language in Rom 15:27–28 is a first-century inscription from Ephesus that reads: μυστήρια καὶ θυσίαι ... ἐπιτελοῦνται; οἱ ὀφείλοντες τὰ μυστήρια ἐπιτελεῖν (*Syll.*³ 820, *lines* 3–4, 14; cited in "Completion," 591).

[118] BDAG, 980.

[119] See Gottfried Fitzer, "σφραγίς κτλ.," *TDNT* 7:943 for a discussion of seals in ancient cultic practice. For example, Fitzer cites Plutarch's descrption of Egyptian priests called "sealers" (οἱ σφραγισταὶ) in *De Iside et Osiride* (§31): τὸν δὲ μέλλοντα θύεσθαι βοῦν οἱ σφραγισταὶ λεγόμενοι τῶν ἱερέων κατεσημαίνοντο.

reading the letter that Paul had written to them.[120] Assuming that Rom 16 was originally addressed to the church in Rome, Paul would certainly have had some personal contacts among the Christian community in Rome familiar with his efforts to raise support for the Jerusalem church, particularly since that fundraising endeavor extended over a period of several years.[121] Moreover, we might also imagine Phoebe from Cenchrea to have been an ideal source of additional information on the history of Paul's efforts to raise a collection for Jerusalem in Corinth (Rom 16:1–2). The fact that Paul opens and closes the section on the collection in Rom 15:25–32 with a form of the idiom ἡ διακονία τοῖς ἁγίος, a veritable "'*terminus technicus*' for the collection" (15:25, 31; cf. 1 Cor 16:15; 2 Cor 8:4; 9:1), may also indicate familiarity with the project among his readers in Rome.[122] Paul's summary report of the history of the fundraising effort in Rom 15:26–27 would then be understood as both an expansion of a tradition with which the Roman Christians were already familiar and as further information intended to explain the delay of Paul's visit to Rome.

4.5.3 Metaphorical Mapping

Thus, if the phrase ἡ προσφορὰ τῶν ἐθνῶν in Rom 15:16 is read as a subjective genitive and taken as an allusion to the Jerusalem collection, we have two references to the collection in Rom 15, both of which are couched in metaphorical language taken from the realm of cultic worship. In the first instance, the cultic metaphors are clustered around Paul's own priestly ministry to the Gentiles, through which, and with the help of the Holy Spirit, the collection (i.e., "the offering of the Gentiles") might be deemed acceptable. In the second, with the verb λειτουργέω in Rom 15:27 used to describe the service of the Gentile churches, the cultic metaphor is extended to include the willing participants in the collection from Paul's communities in Macedonia and Achaia as they fulfill their obligation to the saints in Jerusalem. In this way, Paul's own priestly ministry as caretaker of the relief fund (15:16, 28) is "mapped" onto the Gentiles' priestly participation in the collection.[123] The controlling image, or the structural

---

[120] Cf. the thesis of A. J. M. Wedderburn ("The Purpose and Occasion of Romans Again," in *The Romans Debate: Revised and Expanded Edition* [ed. Karl P. Donfried; Peabody, Mass.: Hendrickson, 1999], 195–202) that one of the reasons for Paul's letter to the Romans was to ensure prayer support for his collection among competing groups of Gentile Christians who maintained different positions toward Judaism.

[121] See pp. 58–60.

[122] Joubert, *Paul as Benefactor*, 128. On the role of letter carriers in the Pauline mission, see Margaret M. Mitchell, "New Testament Envoys in the Context of Greco-Roman Diplomatic and Epistolary Conventions: The Example of Timothy and Titus," *JBL* 111 (1992): 641–62.

[123] The notion that metaphors, by virtue of their ability to introduce disjunction and incongruity, are able to "map one conceptual structure onto another, permitting the digitalization of information in previously analog form" is developed in Kraftchick, "Death in Us, Life in You," 156–81.

metaphor, used to describe the service of the apostle and of his Gentile churches in meeting the needs of the saints in Jerusalem is painted with the brushstrokes of cultic metaphor. In mapping his own cultic ministry onto the activity of the Gentiles, Paul frames their responsive participation in the collection as an act of cultic worship, and in doing so he underscores the point that the fulfillment of mutual obligations within the Christian community results in praise to God.

4.6 Conclusion

This investigation of Paul's discussions of and appeals to the collection in 1 Cor 16:1–4; 2 Cor 8:1–9:15; and Rom 15:14–32 has shown that Paul employs a number of cultic metaphors to speak of "the offering of the Gentiles" (Rom 15:16). This clustering of cultic language suggests that Paul's understanding of the collection is governed by a particular structural metaphor, which I have identified as COLLECTION IS WORSHIP. This metaphorical concept structures the way Paul thinks about, experiences, and presents the activity of collecting money for the poor among the saints in Jerusalem. That is, in metaphorically depicting the activity of collecting money for Jerusalem in terms of cultic practice, Paul frames participation in the relief fund primarily as an act of worship. Several implications follow from this conclusion.

First, this use of cultic metaphor should not be narrowly defined solely in terms of Paul's "Jewish background" or interpreted simply in terms of the Jewish temple cultus in Jerusalem.[124] Not only are the dichotomous categories of "Jewish" and "Greek" increasingly recognized as problematic among interpreters of Paul, but, as Lakoff and Johnson point out, metaphors are grounded in cultural experience,[125] and the worship practices of pagans in localities throughout the Greco-Roman world – and therefore the religious experiences of the pagan converts in Paul's churches before their conversion to Christianity – were no less cultic than those of pious Jews in Jerusalem. Temples, priests, sacrifices – these were ubiquitous features of religion in antiquity.[126] "To worship through offering

---

[124] This is a mistake made by Wan. Wan ("Collection for the Saints," 203–10) uses Paul's cultic language in Romans 15 to interpret the collection in light of "Jewish universalism" and to highlight parallels with the Jewish temple tax. He writes, "while Paul insists that the collection for the saints is entirely voluntary in nature, and while he affirms the universal ecumenicity between Jews and Gentiles in the worldwide community, he also makes it quite clear to his readers that it is a Jewish institution (the temple?) into which Gentiles have been incorporated" (209). This statement is based on Wan's assumption that Paul's cultic language is essentially "Jewish," however. D. W. B. Robinson ("The Priesthood of Paul," 231) correctly observes, "This image is probably drawn from cultic religion in general, rather than from the levitical system in particular."

[125] Lakoff and Johnson, *Metaphors We Live By*, 61–68.

[126] See, e.g., the collection of essays in Richard Buxton, ed., *Greek Religion* (Oxford: Oxford

sacrificial animals, libations, and incense on special altars in areas consecrated and purified by dedicated priests was standard religious behaviour for almost everyone in the ancient world."[127] That the members of the Pauline congregations did not participate in this kind of cultic religion is not only one of the distinctive marks of nascent Christianity; it is also precisely what makes Paul's use of cultic language with reference to the Jerusalem collection metaphorical.[128]

Second, it is the nature of structural metaphors both to highlight certain features of a concept or experience and, at the same time, to hide or downplay others. The structural metaphor COLLECTION IS WORSHIP, of course, highlights the properly religious and/or theological dimensions of this fundraising project. No mundane benefaction, the Jerusalem collection is represented as an offering consecrated to God. Additionally, in depicting the fund as act of worship, a liturgy offered in the praise of God, Paul's cultic metaphors have the effect of downplaying certain aspects of the Greco-Roman benefaction system inimical to Paul's theological conception of the collection for the saints. To view the activity of supporting the collection as a cultic act, for example, downplays the inherently competitive and potentially oppressive nature of benefaction in the Greco-Roman world. Paul's attempt to frame the collection as an act of corporate worship offered in service to God functions to subvert the values of patronage and euergetism by depicting an alternate mode of benefaction, one that brings glory, praise, and thanksgiving to God rather than to human benefactors.[129] In fact, we have already observed this strategy while looking at benefaction among Jewish synagogues in antiquity in the previous chapter. Given the difficulties that Paul consistently experienced in negotiating issues of patronage and power in his re-

---

University Press, 2000); cf. H. S. Versnel, ed., *Faith, Hope, and Worship: Aspects of Religious Mentality in the Ancient World* (Studies in Greek and Roman Religion 2; Leiden: Brill, 1981).

[127] Martin Goodman, "The Temple in First Century CE Judaism," in *Temple and Worship in Biblical Israel: Proceedings of the Oxford Old Testament Seminar* (ed. John Day; LHBOTS 422; London: T & T Clark, 2005), 459.

[128] In comparing the cultic language employed in the inscription of a Hellenistic voluntary association with that found in Paul's letters, S. C. Barton and G. H. R. Horsley ("A Hellenistic Cult Group and the New Testament Churches," *JAC* 24 [1981]: 30), write, "As in Dionysius' cult, [the Christian's god] was the focus of the individual group's activities – of its prayers, hymns, prophecies, teaching, communal meals and acts of mutual aid. Unlike it, however, he was not present in each gathering in the form of a concrete image nor were altars dedicated to him, since it was held that he indwelt every believer (e.g. 1 Thess. 3.8; Rom. 8.1/11). This belief gave the Christian group a remarkably non-cultic character: its members' worship of the deity and their service of one another were understood as inextricably linked, a fact which explains the apparent desacralisation of cultic terminology in early Christian writing about the church and the markedly fraternal character of early Christian worship. As an example of the former we may cite Paul's reference to the financial aid sent by his churches as ὀσμὴν εὐωδίας, θυσίαν δεκτήν, εὐάρεστον τῷ θεῷ" (Barton and Horsley, "Hellenistic Cult," 30).

[129] So also Wan ("Collection for the Saints," 210–15), who labels 2 Cor 8–9 "an antipatronal appeal."

lationship with the Corinthian church, this rhetorical strategy is entirely understandable.[130] Nowhere in his comments about the collection in the Corinthian correspondence does Paul suggest that the contributors to the relief fund will attain prestige for their support of the offering, nor does Paul claim that the recipients of this gift will reciprocate with thanksgiving to their benefactors. Instead, the successful delivery of the offering of the Gentiles will result in thanksgiving to God.

Finally, the structural metaphor COLLECTION IS WORSHIP coexists and overlaps with at least one other clustering of metaphorical expressions for the collection. In 2 Cor 9:6–10, Paul compares the activity of contributing to the collection to that of sowing and reaping, and he declares that God "will supply and multiply your seed and will increase the harvest of your righteousness" (v. 10). This agricultural metaphor is picked up again in Rom 15:28, when Paul designates the collection a καρπός to be "sealed" (σφραγισάμενος) to the Jewish-Christian community in Jerusalem. These linguistic expressions, therefore, suggest that Paul also works with the conceptual metaphor COLLECTION IS HARVEST. Despite any apparent inconsistency between these two structural metaphors, they share several entailments that allow us to understand them as coherent metaphors. For example, in the ancient world cultic sacrifices and offerings frequently represented some form of food, such as a consecrated animal, a libation, or grain.[131] To offer a cultic sacrifice, therefore, was, more often than not, to offer to the god(s) a source of physical nourishment.[132] Similarly, sowing and harvesting seed is, of course, an activity that produces food for nourishment. There may even be a hint of this overlap between worship and harvest in Paul's declaration that "having sealed to them [i.e., Jerusalem] this fruit," he plans to travel through Rome to Spain (Rom 15:28), for the sealing of offerings was "a guarantee of inviolability in the cultic sphere."[133] Additionally, because God is central to the experience of human worship and to the success of agricultural effort (cf. 1 Cor 3: 6–9), both worship and farming are conceived of as human actions that require divine empowerment. Perhaps the strongest note of coherence between the structural metaphors COLLECTION IS WORSHIP and COLLECTION IS HARVEST, then, is their singular focus on the power of God to authenticate human activity.

This matter cuts to the very heart of Paul's apocalyptic gospel. With respect to the issue of soteriology, I would agree with J. Louis Martyn's insistence on the

---

[130] See John K. Chow, *Patronage and Power: A Study of Social Networks in Corinth* (JSNTSup 75; Sheffield: Sheffield Academic Press, 1992). Chow's book concentrates almost exclusively on 1 Corinthians, but these issues remained pressing concerns in the exchanges that followed this text.

[131] See Gary A. Anderson, "Sacrifice and Sacrificial Offerings (OT)," *ABD* 5:870–86.

[132] See Peter Garnsey, *Food and Society in Classical Antiquity* (Cambridge: Cambridge University Press, 1999), 128–38. This does not, of course, include votive offerings, on which see F. T. van Straten, "Gifts for the Gods," in *Faith, Hope, and Worship: Aspects of Religious Mentality in the Ancient World* (ed. H. S. Versnel; Studies in Greek and Roman Religion 2; Leiden: Brill, 1981), 65–151.

[133] Fitzer, *TDNT*, 7:943.

invasive primacy of God's act of rectification in Paul's theology. "God has set things right without laying down a prior condition of any sort," writes Martyn. "God's rectifying act, that is to say, is no more God's response to human faith in Christ than it is God's response to human observance of the Law. God's rectification is not God's response at all. It is the *first* move; it is God's initiative, carried out by him in Christ's faithful death."[134]

Paul's appeals to and discussions of the Jerusalem collection, which are addressed to those whose lives have already been transformed by the rectifying power of God, do not dwell on the logic of salvation. Yet in framing participation in the collection for the saints as an act of corporate worship and as a bountiful harvest produced by God, Paul implies that even this activity of human beneficence is one that depends on the χάρις of God. As Beverly Gaventa succinctly puts the matter, "God's economy is not one in which the sum needed for salvation comes from a contribution from God (however large) and another contribution from humanity (however small). Everything in this economy comes from a single source, that of God's grace."[135] For Paul, there is no distinction between the economy of salvation and the economy of the collection, for both are dependent upon the activity of the God whose gracious power stands behind every human action. If God's χάρις is the first move in salvation, it is also the first move in the collection.

---

[134] Martyn, *Theological Issues*, 151.
[135] Gaventa, "Economy of Grace," 59.

Chapter 5

Conclusion

This monograph has investigated the Pauline collection for Jerusalem in its chronological, cultural, and cultic contexts, with the goal of understanding the significance of this relief fund for Paul's mission and theology. Chapter one attempted to situate this project in the history of scholarship on the Jerusalem collection. I considered and evaluated four major, though not necessarily mutually exclusive, interpretations of the relief fund for the poor among the saints: the collection as an eschatological event, the collection as an obligation, the collection as an ecumenical offering, and the collection as material relief. I concluded that, of these four interpretations, the latter two represent the most faithful explanations of the reasons that Paul himself gives for his efforts to organize this contribution for the Jerusalem church. There is no indication in Paul's letters that the apostle conceptualized the collection as a fulfillment of the eschatological pilgrimage to Zion by Gentiles depicted in some Old Testament and early Jewish texts. Moreover, there is little reason to believe that Paul viewed his attempt to organize a relief fund for the poor among the saints as the fulfillment of an obligation laid upon him by the leadership of the Jerusalem church.

Yet it does appear that "the offering of the Gentiles" (Rom 15:16) served an important ecumenical purpose. This gift, according to Paul, symbolized the unity of Jews and Gentiles under the one gospel of Jesus Christ, and the offering may also have served as an olive branch offered by Paul to the leadership of the Jerusalem church, with whom the apostle had, by all accounts, experienced a rocky relationship since at least as early as the conflict at Antioch reported in Gal 2:11–14. Paul uses the term κοινωνία several times with reference to the collection in order to indicate that the fund is a "partnership-forming contribution" (2 Cor 8:4, 23; 9:3, 13; Rom 15:26) that demonstrates materially the spiritual unity shared by Jews and Gentiles. At the same time, the collection also functioned to strengthen connections between the separate Gentile churches of the Pauline mission in the regions of Galatia, Macedonia, and Achaia. Moreover, interpreters clearly are correct to stress the social and caritative aspects of the offering. A primary purpose of the Pauline collection was to provide financial assistance to a destitute segment of the Jerusalem church.

Chapter two endeavored to provide a chronological sketch of Paul's fundraising efforts on behalf of the Jewish-Christian community in Jerusalem using the methodological principle that evidence from the authentic epistles is to be given priority over information from Acts. I argued that Paul was involved in the administration of at least two relief funds for the Jerusalem church. The earlier effort came during Paul's association with the church in Antioch, and the arrangement and delivery of this gift is reported in Gal 2:10 and Acts 11:27–30. Many years after Paul's split with Antioch, however, the apostle conceived of organizing a collection for the saints in Jerusalem from the largely Gentile churches of his own mission, a project first reported in 1 Cor 16:1–4. The chronology of Paul's efforts to coordinate this fund can be pieced together from what he says about the offering in the Corinthian correspondence and in Romans.

The last word about the collection for the saints from the pen of the apostle Paul is found in Rom 15:14–32, a passage written on the eve of his impending journey to Jerusalem to deliver the monies to the believing community there. The theory that the Pauline collection represents a different fundraising project from the one agreed to in Gal 2:10 helps to explain Paul's trepidation over the possibility of the Jerusalem church's rejection of his efforts in Rom 15:30–31. The book of Acts narrates Paul's voyage to Jerusalem but, interestingly, never mentions the collection for the saints. Most scholars have assumed that Acts refers to the Pauline collection, either in 11:27–30 or 24:17. Against this consensus, I argued that the narrative of Acts, when read on its own terms and without the imposition of information from the Pauline epistles, neither mentions nor alludes to the collection for Jerusalem organized among the churches of Paul's mission. In its narrative context, the reference to "alms" in Acts 24:17, far from being an allusion to the collection, identifies Paul before his accusers as a faithful Jew whose individual piety is demonstrated by almsgiving and worship. Information from the book of Acts, therefore, cannot be used to write the final chapter of the historical reconstruction of the Pauline collection for Jerusalem. This conclusion should, at the very least, caution scholars against too easily reading information from the Pauline epistles *into* the narrative of Acts.

Chapter three explored the socio-cultural context of the collection for the saints by considering the phenomenon of benefaction within ancient pagan and Jewish voluntary associations. Chapter one had already identified a number of proposed analogies to and backgrounds of the Pauline collection, including the eschatological offering of the Gentiles, the Jewish temple tax, the Jewish tradition of redemptive almsgiving, the general exchange of benefits and obligations in the Mediterranean world, and the Greek tradition of ἐπίδοσις. Chapter two had also suggested at least one direct antecedent for the Pauline collection, namely, the contribution administered for Jerusalem by Paul and Barnabas as delegates of Antioch. Building on recent scholarship that has suggested pagan and Jewish voluntary associations as a helpful comparative model for understanding the organization and activity of the Pauline churches, in chapter three I examined benefaction, monetary collections, and the sharing of resources within ancient associations. I argued that, rather than focusing on the quest for genealogical antecedents to the Pauline collection for Jerusalem, the task of comparing the relief fund from the Pauline churches with gift-giving practices among pagan and Jewish associations is a worthwhile endeavor in its own right. The communal economic practices of pagan associations, Jewish synagogues, and the Pauline churches served to knit together tightly the various members of these respective groups. Within each of these groups, relationships were formed and symbolized through the distribution of benefits, the observance of sacred rites, the celebration of community meals, the collection of funds, and the provision of mutual assistance. This chapter also identified benefaction and patronage as the two dominant models that shaped the gift-giving practices of ancient voluntary associations. These two related forms of what has been called "general reciprocity" were inherently asymmetrical in that recipients of gifts from wealthy donors, unable to respond in kind, were encouraged to reciprocate with public honors and thanksgiving. This system of pagan benefaction provides an appropriate sociocultural context for Paul's efforts to organize a relief fund for the Jerusalem church, and it helps to explain the rhetoric that Paul uses to frame the offering as an act of cultic worship.

Chapter four provided an exegetical examination of the passages in which Paul specifically discusses the collection for the saints, namely, 1 Cor 16:1–4; 2 Cor 8:1–9:15; and Rom 15:14–32. I began with a brief discussion of the ways in which recent theoretical work on metaphor might inform the interpretation of the cultic metaphors that Paul employs with reference to the Jerusalem collection. A number of linguists and biblical scholars have lately claimed that metaphors represent far more than instances of linguistic or rhetorical flourish; instead, metaphors can provide a framework for understanding one's world. Drawing particularly on the notion of "conceptual metaphors" developed by George Lakoff and Mark Johnson, I argued that the particular linguistic expressions in Paul's rhetoric that depict the collection in cultic terms (1 Cor 16:1–2; 2 Cor 8:6, 11–12; 9:12; Rom 15:16, 27–28) reflect a larger conceptual metaphor, which I identified as COLLECTION IS WORSHIP. Another conceptual metaphor, COLLECTION IS HARVEST, is reflected in those passages in which Paul speaks of the activity of collecting money in agrarian terms (2 Cor 9:6–10; Rom 15:28). My thesis was that the conceptual metaphors COLLECTION IS WORSHIP and COLLECTION IS HARVEST serve to subvert conventions of gift-giving in Paul's and his audience's cultural context. In metaphorically framing the activity of collecting money for the poor among the saints as an act of cultic worship, Paul underscores the point that the fulfillment of mutual obligations within the Christian community results in praise, not to human benefactors, as the dominant ideology of pagan euergetism would have suggested, but to God, the one from whom all benefactions come. In metaphorically framing the activity of collecting money for the poor among the saints as an act of harvest, Paul also emphasizes that it is God who is ultimately responsible for this bountiful produce. Even the very human action of raising money for those in material need originates in ἡ χάρις τοῦ θεοῦ and will eventuate in χάρις τῷ θεῷ (2 Cor 9:14–15). This matter cuts to the very heart of Paul's apocalyptic gospel, for it suggests that, just as God is the active, invasive agent in the event of human rectification, God is also the source of and power behind every act of human beneficence.

From here more work remains to be done. Additional research into the role of metaphor in Pauline theology is one endeavor that would bear much fruit.[1] This project has concentrated on the cultic metaphors Paul uses to describe the economic activity of collecting money for the poor among the saints in Jerusalem. Far from being incidental examples of rhetorical flourish, these metaphors reveal something of fundamental importance about the nature of Paul's theology: behind the human action of collecting money stands the God whose χάρις empowers and authenticates this activity. What other conceptual metaphors does Paul employ to describe the gospel and its effects on those whose lives are invaded by it, and how are these conceptual metaphors related to one another? To cite but one example of how the work done here might be expanded to include other areas of Pauline scholarship, Paul also employs cultic language to refer to the gift sent to him in prison by the Philippian church through their delegate Epaphroditus (Phil 2:17; 4:10–20), a fact I have mentioned only briefly. Paul's discussion of this contribution in Phil 4:10–20, often noted for its concentration of commercial terminology (δόσις καὶ λῆμψις in v. 15; ἐπιζητῶ τὸ δόμα, ἀλλὰ ἐπιζητῶ τὸν καρπὸν τὸν πλεονάζοντα εἰς λόγον ὑμῶν in v. 17), also describes the gift as "a fragrant offering, an acceptable sacrifice, pleasing to God" (ὀσμὴν εὐωδίας, θυσίαν δεκτήν, εὐάρεστον τῷ θεῷ, v. 18). A Pauline theology of finances attentive to the role of metaphor in Paul's thought – a project obviously beyond the scope of this book – would need to account for this cultic metaphor in Philippians and its overlap with the cultic metaphors applied to the Jerusalem collection in the Corinthian correspondence and in Romans.

This work has focused on one crucially important economic endeavor that siphoned off a substantial portion of Paul's time and energy over the course of a number of years. Yet while the collection for Jerusalem was a vital undertaking for Paul, we should not overstate the impact that the offering had in its own day. It is quite possible that the leadership of the Jerusalem church rejected Paul's efforts on their behalf, although our historical knowledge of the Pauline collection ends with the apostle's comments about the project in Romans 15. Even if the gift was accepted, the donation of a relatively small sum of money gathered among the Gentile churches of Paul's mission for poor believers in Jerusalem hardly stands out as a remarkable event in the history of philanthropic giving. So far as we can tell, no inscription was erected in Jerusalem or Corinth or Thes-

---

[1] For some suggestions along these lines, see Steven J. Kraftchick, "Death in Us, Life in You: The Apostolic Medium," in *Pauline Theology*, vol. 2: *1 and 2 Corinthians* (SBLSymS 22; ed. David M. Hay; Minneapolis: Fortress, 1993), 179–81.

salonica or Philippi to commemorate this achievement, and no doubt Paul would have objected to such a memorial, had one been proposed, on the grounds that thanksgiving and honor for this offering were properly rendered only to the God whose abundant χάρις empowered this human act of beneficence. This, at least, is the implication of Paul's rhetorical strategy in his explicit comments about the offering.

Yet Paul's letters were eventually collected and canonized, and even before receiving that official designation they began to shape the gift–giving practices of the emerging Christian church. Reflection on Paul's letters, in particular his appeals to the collection, played a central role in the development of what Peter Brown has called "a revolution in the social imagination" that reached its climax in the fourth and fifth centuries of the Common Era, when being "a 'lover of the poor' became a public virtue."[2] Classical euergetism, in which wealthy donors contributed to cities and voluntary associations, was eventually replaced by charitable giving to the poor and destitute of society. In short, "Late antiquity witnessed the transition from one model of society, in which the poor were largely invisible, to another, in which they came to play a vivid imaginative role."[3] Certainly Paul's voice was joined by other voices in the canon to effect this social transformation. Paul's vision, then, for an "economy of grace," shaped by a countercultural understanding of God as the ultimate source and actor of human beneficence, was crucial for the articulation of a new social model that emphasized care for the poor as a meaningful public virtue. Perhaps Paul's vision also has the potential to help contemporary communities of faith to articulate and embody models of giving and care for the poor that bring glory and thanksgiving to the God who still stands behind human beneficence.

---

[2] Peter Brown, *Poverty and Leadership in the Later Roman Empire: The Menahem Stern Jerusalem Lectures* (Hanover and London: University Press of New England, 2002), 1. For an interesting monograph that touches on this question in spite of its focus on the christological interpretation of 2 Cor 8:9, see Pius Angstenberger, *Der reich und der arme Christus: Die Rezeptionsgeschichte von 2 Kor 8,9 zwischen dem zweiten und dem sechsten Jahrhundert* (Hereditas 12; Bonn: Borengässer, 1997).

[3] Brown, *Poverty and Leadership*, 74. See also Richard Finn, *Almsgiving in the Later Roman Empire: Christian Promotion and Practice, 313–450* (Oxford Classical Monographs; Oxford: Oxford University Press, 2006), esp. 221–57.

Bibliography

Primary Sources

Aland, Barbara, Kurt Aland, Johannes Karavidopoulos, Carlo M. Martini, and Bruce M. Metzger, eds. *Novum Testamentum Graece. Nestle-Aland²⁷*. Stuttgart: Deutsche Bibelgesellschaft, 1993.
The Apostolic Fathers. Edited and translated by Bart D. Ehrman. 2 vols. Loeb Classical Library. Cambridge: Harvard University Press, 2003.
Apuleius. *Metamorphoses*. Translated by J. Arthur Hanson. 2 vols. Loeb Classical Library. Cambridge: Harvard University Press, 1989.
Charlesworth, James H., ed. *The Old Testament Pseudepigrapha*. 2 vols. New York: Doubleday, 1983–1985.
Dio Chrysostom. Translated by J. W. Cohoon and H. Lamar Crosby. 5 vols. Loeb Classical Library. Cambridge: Harvard University Press, 1932–1951.
Elliger, K. and W. Rudolph, eds. *Biblia Hebraica Stuttgartensia*. Stuttgart: Deutsche Bibelgesellschaft, 1977.
Holmes, Michael W., ed. *The Apostolic Fathers: Greek Texts and English Translations*. Grand Rapids: Baker, 1999.
Josephus. Translated by H. St. J. Thackeray et al. 10 vols. Loeb Classical Library. Cambridge: Harvard University Press, 1926–1965.
Julian. *The Works of the Emperor Julian*. Translated by Wilmer Cave Wright. 3 vols. Loeb Classical Library. New York: Macmillan and G. P. Putnam's Sons, 1913–1923.
Lucian. Translated by A. M. Harmon et al. 8 vols. Loeb Classical Library. Cambridge: Harvard University Press, 1913–1967.
Martínez, Florentino García and Eibert J. C. Tigchelaar, eds. *The Dead Sea Scrolls Study Edition*. 2 vols. Leiden: Brill/Grand Rapids: Eerdmans, 1997.
Philo. Translated by F. H. Colson and G. H. Whitaker. 10 vols. Loeb Classical Library. Cambridge: Harvard University Press, 1929–1953.
Pliny. *Letters and Panegyricus*. Translated by Betty Radice. 2 vols. Loeb Classical Library. Cambridge: Harvard University Press, 1969.
Rahlfs, Alfred, ed. *Septuaginta: Id est Vetus Testamentum Graece iuxta LXX interpretes*. Stuttgart: Deutsche Bibelgesellschaft, 1979. Seneca. *Moral Essays*. Translated by John W. Basore. 3 vols. Loeb Classical Library. Cambridge: Harvard University Press, 1935. Strabo. *The Geography of Strabo*. Translated by Horace Leonard Jones. 8 vols. Loeb Classical Library. Cambridge: Harvard University Press, 1917–1932.
Tertullian. *Apology*. Translated by T. R. Glover. Loeb Classical Library. Cambridge: Harvard University Press, 1931.
Watson, Alan, ed. *The Digest of Justinian*. 2 vols. Philadelphia: University of Pennsylvania Press, 1998.
White, Robert J., ed. *The Interpretation of Dreams (Oneirocritica) by Artemidorus*. 2d ed. Torrance, Calif.: Original, 1990.

Epigraphical and Palaeographical Sources

Bean, George Ewart, and Terence Bruce Mitford, eds. *Journeys in Rough Cilicia, 1962–1963*. Österreichische Akademie der Wissenschaften, Philosophisch-historische Klasse, Denkschriften 85. Vienna: Böhlau, 1965.

—. *Journeys in Rough Cilicia, 1964–1968*. Österreichische Akademie der Wissenschaften, Philosophisch-historische Klasse, Denkschriften 102. Vienna: Böhlau, 1970.

Bernand, André, ed. *La prose sur Pierre dans l'Égypte hellénistique et romaine*. 2 vols. Paris: Éditions du centre national de la recherché scientifique, 1992.

Bernand, Étienne, ed. *Recueil des inscriptions Grecques du Fayoum*. 3 vols. Cairo: Institut Français d'Archéologie Orientale du Caire, 1975–1981.

Blümel, Wolfgang, ed. *Die Inschriften von Knidos*. 2 vols. Inschriften griechischer Städte aus Kleinasien 41–42. Bonn: Habelt, 1992.

—. *Die Inschriften der rhodischen Peraia*. Inschriften griechischer Städte aus Kleinasien 38. Bonn: Habelt, 1991.

Boeckh, Augustine. *Corpus Inscriptionum Graecarum*. 4 vols. Berlin: Reimer, 1828–1877.

Cenival, Françoise de. *Les associations religieuses en Égypte: D'après les documents démotiques*. Cairo: Publications de l'institut français d'archéologie orientale du Caire, 1972.

Cross, Frank Moore. "The Hebrew Inscriptions from Sardis." *Harvard Theological Review* 95 (2002): 3–19.

Fränkel, Max. *Die Inschriften von Pergamon*. Altertümer von Pergamon 8:1–2. Berlin: Spemann, 1890–1895.

Gaetringen, F. Hiller von. *Die Inschriften von Priene*. Königliche Museen zu Berlin. Berlin: Reimer, 1906.

Horsley, G. H. R., and John A. L. Lee. "A Preliminary Checklist of Abbreviations of Greek Epigraphic Volumes." *Epigraphica* 56 (1994): 129–69.

Kent, J. H. *Inscriptions 1926–1950: Corinth viii. Part Three*. Princeton: The American School of Classical Studies at Athens, 1966.

Kenyon, F. G., et al., eds. *Greek Papyri in the British Museum*. 7 vols. London: British Museum, 1893–1917.

Kroll, John H. "The Greek Inscriptions of the Sardis Synagogue." *Harvard Theological Review* 94 (2001): 5–127.

Lüderitz, Gert, and Joyce M. Reynolds, eds. *Corpus jüdischer Zeugnisse aus der Cyrenaika*. Wiesbaden: Reichert, 1983.

Meyer, P.M, B. Snell, and A. Dietrich, eds. *Griechische Papyrusurkunden der Hamburger Staats und Universitätsbibliothek*. 3 vols. Leipzig: 1911–1955.

Noy, David, and William Horbury, eds. *Jewish Inscriptions of Graeco-Roman Egypt, with an Index of Jewish Inscriptions of Egypt and Cyrenaica*. Cambridge: Cambridge University Press, 1992.

Noy, David, Alexander Panayotov, Hanswulf Bloedhorn, and Walter Ameling, eds. *Inscriptiones Judaicae Orientis*. 3 vols. Texts and Studies in Ancient Judaism 99, 101, 102. Tübingen: Mohr Siebeck, 2004.

Petzl, Georg, ed. *Die Inschriften von Smyrna*. 2 vols. Inschriften Griechische Städte aus Kleinasien 23–24. Bonn: Habelt, 1987.

Rehm, Albert. *Didyma. Zweiter Teil: Die Inschriften*. Edited by Richard Harder. Deutsches Archäologisches Institut. Berlin: Mann, 1958.

Rhodes, P. J., and Robin Osborne, eds. *Greek Historical Inscriptions: 404–323 B.C.* Oxford: Oxford University Press, 2004.

Pierre, Roussel, and Marcel Launey, eds. *Inscriptions de Délos*. Vol. 5. Paris: Libraire Ancienne Honoré Champion, 1937.

Şahin, M. Çetin. *Die Inschriften von Stratonikeia.* Teil I: *Panamara.* Inschriften Griechischer Städte aus Kleinasien 21. Bonn: Habelt, 1981.
Sokolowski, Franciszek, ed. *Lois sacrées des cités grecques.* Travaux et mémoires des members étrangers de l'école et de divers savants 18. Paris: E. de Boccard, 1969.
—. *Lois sacrées de l'Asie Mineure.* Travaux et mémoires des anciens members étrangers de l'école et de divers savants 9. Paris: E. de Boccard, 1955.
Tcherikover, Victor A., and Alexander Fuks. *Corpus Papyrorum Judaicarum.* 3 vols. Cambridge, Mass.: Harvard University Press, 1957–1964.
Wilcken, Ulrich, ed. *Griechische Ostraka aus Aegypten und Nubien: Ein Beitrag zur antiken Wirtschaftsgeschichte.* 2 vols. Amsterdam: Adolf M. Hakkert, 1970.

Secondary Sources

Achtemeier, Paul J. *The Quest for Unity in the New Testament Church: A Study in Paul and Acts.* Philadelphia: Fortress, 1987.
Aejmelaeus, Lars. "The Question of Salary in the Conflict Between Paul and the 'Super Apostle' in Corinth." Pages 343–76 in *Fair Play: Diversity and Conflicts in Early Christianity. Essays in Honour of Heikki Räisänen.* Edited by Ismo Dunderberg, Christopher Tuckett, and Kari Syreeni. Supplements to Novum Testamentum 103. Leiden: Brill, 2002.
Aletti, Jean-Noël. "Le statut de l'Église dans les lettres pauliniennes: Réflexions sur quelques paradoxes." *Biblica* 83 (2002): 153–74.
Alexander, Loveday. "*IPSE DIXIT*: Citation of Authority in Paul and in the Jewish and Hellenistic Schools." Pages 103–27 in *Paul Beyond the Judaism/Hellenism Divide.* Edited by Troels Engberg-Pedersen. Louisville: Westminster John Knox, 2001.
—. "Paul and the Hellenistic Schools: The Evidence of Galen." Pages 60–83 in *Paul in His Hellenistic Context.* Edited by Troels Engberg-Pedersen. Minneapolis: Fortress, 1995.
Amstutz, Joseph. *HAPLOTĒS: Eine begriffsgeschichtliche Studie zum jüdisch-christlichen Griechisch.* Theophaneia 19. Bonn: Hanstein, 1968.
Andreau, Jean. *Banking and Business in the Roman World.* Key Themes in Ancient History. Translated by Janet Lloyd. Cambridge: Cambridge University Press, 1999.
Angstenberger, Pius. *Der reiche und der arme Christus: Die Rezeptionsgeschichte von 2 Kor 8,9 zwischen dem zweiten und dem sechsten Jahrhundert.* Studien zur Alten Kirchengeschichte 12. Bonn: Borengässer, 1997.
Arnaoutglou, Ilias N. "*Collegia* in the Province of Egypt in the First Century CE," *Ancient Society* 35 (2005): 197–216.
—. "Roman Law and *Collegia* in Asia Minor." *Revue International des droits de l'Antiquité* 49 (2002): 27–44.
Ascough, Richard S. "The Completion of a Religious Duty: The Background of 2 Cor 8.1–15." *New Testament Studies* 42 (1996): 584–99.
—. "Greco-Roman Philosophic, Religious, and Voluntary Associations." Pages 3–24 in *Community Formation in the Early Church and the Church Today.* Edited by Richard N. Longenecker. Peabody, Mass.: Hendrickson, 2002.
—. *Paul's Macedonian Associations: The Social Context of Philippians and 1 Thessalonians.* Wissenschaftliche Untersuchungen zum Neuen Testament 2:161. Tübingen: Mohr Siebeck, 2003.
—. "The Thessalonian Christian Community as a Professional Voluntary Association." *Journal of Biblical Literature* 119 (2000): 311–28.
—. "Translocal Relationships among Voluntary Associations and Early Christianity." *Journal of Early Christian Studies* 5 (1997): 223–41.

———. *What Are They Saying About the Formation of the Pauline Churches?* New York and Mahwah, N.J.: Paulist, 1998.

Ascough, Richard S., ed. *Religious Rivalries and the Struggle for Success in Sardis and Smyrna*. Studies in Christianity and Judaism/Études sur le christianisme et le judaïsme 14. Waterloo, Ontario: Wilfrid Laurier University Press, 2005.

Asmussen, Hans. *Der Römerbrief*. Stuttgart: Evangelisches Verlagswerk, 1952.

Atkins, Margaret and Robin Osborne, eds. *Poverty in the Roman World*. Cambridge: Cambridge University Press, 2006.

Aus, Roger D. "Paul's Travel Plans to Spain and the 'Full Number of the Gentiles' of Rom. XI 25." *Novum Testamentum* 21 (1979): 232–62.

Ausbüttel, Frank M. *Untersuchungen zu den Vereinen im Westen des römischen Reiches*. Frankfurter Althistorische Studien 11. Kallmünz: Michael Lassleben, 1982.

Bachmann, D. Philipp. *Der zweite Brief des Paulus an die Korinther*. Kommentar zum Neuen Testament 8. Leipzig: A Diechert, 1909.

Baer, David A. *When We All Go Home: Translation and Theology in LXX Isaiah 56–66*. Journal for the Study of the Old Testament Supplement Series 318. The Hebrew Bible and Its Versions 1. Sheffield: Sheffield Academic Press, 2001.

Baker, Murray. "Paul and the Salvation of Israel: Paul's Ministry, the Motif of Jealousy, and Israel's Yes." *Catholic Biblical Quarterly* 67 (2005): 469–84.

Barclay, John M. G. "'Do We Undermine the Law?': A Study of Romans 14.1–15.6." Pages 287–308 in *Paul and the Mosaic Law: The Third Durham Tübingen Research Symposium on Earliest Christianity and Judaism*. Edited by J. D. G. Dunn. Wissenschaftliche Untersuchungen zum Neuen Testament 89. Tübingen: J. C. B. Mohr, 1996.

———. *Jews in the Mediterranean Diaspora: From Alexander to Trajan (323 BCE – 117 CE)*. Hellenistic Culture and Society 33. Berkeley: University of California Press, 1996.

———. "Money and Meetings: Group Formation among Diaspora Jews and Early Christians." Pages 113–27 in *Vereine, Synagoge und Gemeinden im kaiserzeitlichen Kleinasien*. Edited by Andreas Gutsfeld and Dietrich-Alex Koch. Studien und Texte zu Antike und Christentum 25. Tübingen: Mohr Siebeck, 2006.

———. "Poverty in Pauline Studies: A Response to Steven Friesen." *Journal for the Study of the New Testament* 26 (2004): 363–66.

Barrett, C. K. *A Critical and Exegetical Commentary on the Acts of the Apostles*. 2 vols. International Critical Commentaries. Edinburgh: T & T Clark, 1994–1998.

———. *The Epistle to the Romans*. Black's New Testament Commentaries. 2d ed. London: A & C Black, 1991.

———. *The Second Epistle to the Corinthians*. Harper's New Testament Commentaries. New York: Harper & Row, 1973.

Barry, Thomas F. "Metaphor." Pages 754–55 in *Encyclopedia of Literary Critics and Criticism*. Edited by Chris Murray. 2 vols. London and Chicago: Fitzroy Dearborn, 1999.

Barth, Karl. *The Epistle to the Romans*. Translated by Edwyn C. Hoskyns. Oxford: Oxford University Press, 1933.

Barton, S. C., and G. H. R. Horsley. "A Hellenistic Cult Group and the New Testament Churches." *Jahrbuch für Antike und Christentum* 24 (1981): 7–41.

Bartsch, Hans Werner. "'...Wenn ich ihnen diese Frucht versiegelt habe' (Röm 15.28): Ein Beitrag zum Verständnis der paulinischen Mission." *Zeitschrift für die neutestamentliche Wissenschaft und die Kunde der älteren Kirche* 63 (1972): 95–107.

Bassler, Jouette M. *God and Mammon: Asking for Money in the New Testament*. Nashville: Abingdon, 1991.

Bauckham, Richard, ed. *The Gospels for All Christians: Rethinking the Gospel Audiences*. Grand Rapids: Eerdmans, 1998.

Baumgarten, Albert. "Graeco-Roman Voluntary Associations and Ancient Jewish Sects." Pages 93–111 in *Jews in a Graeco-Roman World*. Edited by Martin Goodman. Oxford: Clarendon, 1998.
Becker, Eve-Marie. *Letter Hermeneutics in 2 Corinthians: Studies in Literarkritik and Communication Theory*. Translated by Helen S. Heron. Journal for the Study of the New Testament Supplement Series 279. London and New York: T & T Clark, 2004.
Becker, Jürgen. *Paul: Apostle to the Gentiles*. Translated by O. C. Dean Jr. Louisville: Westminster John Knox, 1993. Translation of *Paulus: Der Apostel der Völker*. Tübingen: Mohr Siebeck, 1989.
Beckheuer, Burkhard. *Paulus und Jerusalem: Kollekte und Mission im theologischen Denken des Heidenapostels*. Europäische Hochschulschriften 23. Frankfurt am Main: Peter Lang, 1997.
Berger, Klaus. "Almosen für Israel." *New Testament Studies* 23 (1977): 180–204.
Betz, Hans Dieter. *2 Corinthians 8 and 9: A Commentary on Two Administrative Letters of the Apostle Paul*. Hermeneia. Philadelphia: Fortress, 1985.
—. *Galatians: A Commentary on Paul's Letter to the Churches in Galatia*. Hermeneia. Philadelphia: Fortress, 1979.
Binder, Donald D. *Into the Temple Courts: The Place of the Synagogues in the Second Temple Period*. Society of Biblical Literature Dissertation Series 169. Atlanta: Society of Biblical Literature, 1999.
Black, Max. *Models and Metaphors: Studies in Language and Philosophy*. Ithaca, N.Y.: Cornell University Press, 1979.
—. "More about Metaphor." Pages 19–41 in *Metaphor and Thought*. Edited by Andrew Ortony. 2d ed. Cambridge: Cambridge University Press, 1993.
Blomberg, Craig L. *Neither Poverty nor Riches: A Biblical Theology of Possessions*. New Studies in Biblical Theology 7. Downers Grove, Ill.: InterVarsity Press, 1999.
Boer, W. Den. *Private Morality in Greece and Rome: Some Historical Aspects*. Mnemosyne: Bibliotheca Classica Batava. Leiden: Brill, 1979.
Bolkestein, Hendrik. *Wohltätigkeit und Armenpflege im vorchristlichen Altertum: Ein Beitrag zum Problem 'Moral und Gesellschaft.'* Utrecht: Oosthoek, 1939.
Bonz, Marianne Palmer. "Differing Approaches to Religious Benefaction: The Late Third-Century Acquisition of the Sardis Synagogue." *Harvard Theological Review* 86 (1993): 139–54.
Böttrich, Christfried."'Ihr seid der Tempel Gottes': Tempelmetaphorik und Gemeinde bei Paulus." Pages 411–25 in *Gemeinde ohne Tempel: Zur Substituierung und Transformation des Jerusalemer Tempels und seines Kult im Alten Testament, antiken Judentum und frühen Christentum*. Edited by Beate Ego, Armin Lange, and Peter Pilhofer. Wissenschaftliche Untersuchungen zum Neuen Testament 118. Tübingen: Mohr Siebeck, 1999.
Bourdieu, Pierre. "Ökonomisches Kapital, kulturelles Kapital, soziales Kapital." Pages 183–98 in *Soziale Ungleichheiten*. Edited by Reinhard Kreckel. Göttingen: Otto Schartz, 1983.
Bowen, Clayton Raymond. "Paul's Collection and the Book of Acts." *Journal of Biblical Literature* 42 (1923): 49–58.
Brändle, Rudolf. "Geld und Gnade (zu II Kor 8, 9)." *Theologische Zeitschrift* 41 (1985): 264–71.
Bremer, Jan-Maarten. "The Reciprocity of Giving and Thanksgiving in Greek Worship." Pages 127–37 in *Reciprocity in Ancient Greece*. Edited by Christopher Gill, Norman Postlethwait, and Richard Seaford. Oxford: Oxford University Press, 1998.
Breytenbach, Cilliers. "Civic Concord and Cosmic Harmony: Sources of Metaphoric Mapping in *1 Clement* 20:3." Pages 259–73 in *Early Christianity and Classical Culture: Comparative Studies in Honor of Abraham J. Malherbe*. Edited by John T. Fitzgerald, Thomas H. Olbricht, and L. Michael White. Supplements to Novum Testamentum 110. Atlanta: Society of Biblical Literature, 2005.
—. *Paulus und Barnabas in der Provinz Galatien: Studien zu Apostelgeschichte 13f.; 16.6; 18.23 und den Adressaten des Galaterbriefes*. Arbeiten zur Geschichte des antiken Judentums und des Urchristentums 38. Leiden: Brill, 1996.

Brown, Peter. *Poverty and Leadership in the Later Roman Empire. The Menahem Stern Jerusalem Lectures.* Hanover and London: University Press of New England, 2002.

Brown, Stephen G. "The Intertextuality of Isaiah 66.17 and 2 Thessalonians 2.7: A Solution for the 'Restrainer' Problem." Pages 254–77 in *Paul and the Scriptures of Israel.* Edited by Craig A. Evans and James A. Sanders. Journal for the Study of the New Testament Supplement Series 83. Studies in Early Judaism and Christianity 1. Sheffield: Sheffield Academic Press, 1993.

Bruce, F. F. *The Acts of the Apostles: The Greek Text with Introduction and Commentary.* 3d ed. Grand Rapids: Eerdmans, 1990.

———. *The Epistle to the Galatians: A Commentary on the Greek Text.* The New International Greek Testament Commentary. Grand Rapids: Eerdmans, 1982.

Bruehler, Bart B. "Proverbs, Persuasion and People: A Three Dimensional Investigation of 2 Cor 9.6–15." *New Testament Studies* 48 (2002): 209–24.

Buck, Charles H. "The Collection for the Saints." *Harvard Theological Review* 43 (1950): 1–30.

Bultmann, Rudolf. *The Second Letter to the Corinthians.* Translated by Roy A. Harrisville. Minneapolis: Augsburg, 1985. Translation of *Der zweite Brief an die Korinther.* Edited by Erich Dinkler. Göttingen: Vandenhoeck & Ruprecht, 1976.

———. "Zur Frage nach den Quellen der Apostelgeschichte." Pages 68–80 in *New Testament Essays: Studies in Memory of Walter Manson, 1893–1958.* Edited by J. B. Higgins. Manchester: Manchester University Press, 1959.

Burke, Trevor J. *Family Matters: A Socio-Historical Study of Kinship Metaphors in 1 Thessalonians.* Journal for the Study of the New Testament Supplement Series 247. London and New York: T & T Clark, 2003.

Byrne, Brendan. *Romans.* Sacra Pagina 6. Collegeville, Minn.: Liturgical, 1996.

Byrskog, Samuel. "History or Story in Acts—A Middle Way? The 'We' Passages, Historical Intertexture, and Oral History." Pages 257–83 in *Contextualizing Acts: Lukan Narrative and Greco-Roman Discourse.* Edited by Todd Penner and Caroline Vander Stichele. Society of Biblical Literature Symposium Series 20. Atlanta: Society of Biblical Literature, 2003.

Campbell, Douglas A. "An Anchor for Pauline Chronology: Paul's Flight from 'The Ethnarch of King Aretas' (2 Corinthians 11:32–33)." *Journal of Biblical Literature* 121 (2002): 279–302.

———. "Possible Inscriptional Attestation to Sergius Paul[l]us (Acts 13:6–12), and the Implications for Pauline Chronology." *Journal of Theological Studies* 56 (2005): 1–29.

———. *The Quest for Paul's Gospel: A Suggested Strategy.* London and New York: T & T Clark, 2005.

Campbell, William Sanger. *The "We" Passages in the Acts of the Apostles: The Narrator as Narrative Character.* Studies in Biblical Literature 14. Atlanta: Society of Biblical Literature, 2007.

Cansdale, Lena. *Qumran and the Essenes: A Re-evaluation of the Evidence.* Texte und Studien zum antiken Judentum 60. Tübingen: Mohr Siebeck, 1997.

Catchpole, D. R. "Paul, James and the Apostolic Decree." *New Testament Studies* 23 (1977): 428–44.

Chacko, James. "Collection in the Early Church." *Evangelical Review of Theology* 24 (2000): 177–83.

Cherian, Jacob. "Toward a Commonwealth of Grace: A Plutocritical Reading of Grace and Equality in Second Corinthians 8:1–15." Ph.D. diss., Princeton Theological Seminary, 2007.

Chow, John K. *Patronage and Power: A Study of Social Networks in Corinth.* Journal for the Study of the New Testament Supplement Series 75. Sheffield: Sheffield Academic Press, 1992.

Clemente, Guido. "Il patronato nei collegia dell'impero Romano." *Studi classici e orientali* 21 (1972): 142–229

Collins, Raymond F. *First Corinthians.* Sacra Pagina 7. Collegeville, Minn.: Liturgical, 1999.

Combes, I. A. H. *The Metaphor of Slavery in the Writings of the Early Church: From the New Testament to the Beginning of the Fifth Century.* Journal for the Study of the New Testament Supplement Series 156. Sheffield: Sheffield Academic Press, 1998.

Conzelmann, Hans. *1 Corinthians.* Hermeneia. Translated by James W. Leitch. Edited by George W. MacRae. Philadelphia: Fortress, 1975.

———. *Acts of the Apostles*. Translated by James Limburg, A. Thomas Kraabel, and Donald H. Juel. Hermeneia. Philadelphia: Fortress, 1987.
Cosgrove, Charles H. "The Divine ΔΕΙ in Luke-Acts." *Novum Testamentum* 26 (1984): 168–90.
Countryman, L. William. *The Rich Christian in the Church of the Early Empire: Contradictions and Accommodations*. New York and Toronto: Edwin Mellen, 1980.
———. "Welfare in the Churches of Asia Minor under the Early Roman Empire." Pages 131–46 in *Society of Biblical Literature 1979 Seminar Papers*. Edited by Paul J. Actemeier. Missoula, Mont.: Scholars Press, 1979.
Corley, Bruce, ed. *Colloquy on New Testament Studies: A Time for Reappraisal and Fresh Approaches*. Macon, Ga.: Mercer University Press, 1983.
Cranfield, C. E. B. *A Critical and Exegetical Commentary on the Epistle to the Romans*. 2 vols. International Critical Commentaries. Edinburgh: T & T Clark, 1975–1979.
Croix, G. E. M. De Ste. "Suffragium: From Vote to Patronage." *British Journal of Sociology* 5 (1954): 33–48.
Crook, Zeba A. *Reconceptualising Conversion: Patronage, Loyalty, and Conversion in the Religions of the Ancient Mediterranean*. Beihefte zur Zeitschrift für die neutestamentliche Wissenschaft und die Kunde der älteren Kirche 130. Berlin and New York: Walter de Gruyter, 2004.
———. "Reflections on Culture and Social-Scientific Models." *Journal of Biblical Literature* 124 (2005): 515–20.
Cullmann, Oscar. "The Early Church and the Ecumenical Problem." *Anglican Theological Review* 40 (1958): 181–89, 294–301.
Cumont, Franz. *Les religions orientales dans le paganisme romain*. Paris: Leroux, 1929.
Dahl, Nils A. "Paul and Possessions." Pages 22–39 in *Studies in Paul: A Theology for Early Christian Missions*. Philadelphia: Fortress, 1977.
Danker, Frederick W. *Benefactor: Epigraphic Study of a Graeco-Roman and New Testament Semantic Field*. St. Louis: Clayton, 1982.
———. "On Stones and Benefactors." *Currents in Theology and Mission* 8 (1981): 351–56.
———. "Paul's Debt to the *De Corona* of Demosthenes: A Study of Rhetorical Techniques in Second Corinthians." Pages 262–80 in *Persuasive Artistry: Studies in New Testament Rhetoric in Honor of George A. Kennedy*. Edited by Duane F. Watson. Journal for the Study of the New Testament Supplement Series 50. Sheffield: Sheffield Academic Press, 1991.
Das, A. Andrew. *Solving the Romans Debate*. Minneapolis: Fortress, 2007.
Davids, Peter H. "The Test of Wealth." Pages 355–84 in *The Missions of James, Peter, and Paul: Tensions in Early Christianity*. Edited by Bruce Chilton and Craig Evans. Supplements to Novum Testamentum 115. Leiden: Brill, 2005.
Dawes, Gregory W. *The Body in Question: Metaphor and Meaning in the Interpretation of Ephesians 5:21–33*. Biblical Interpretation Series 30. Leiden: Brill, 1998.
De Boer, Martinus C. "The Composition of 1 Corinthians." *New Testament Studies* 40 (1994): 229–45.
De Lacey, D. R. "οἵτινές ἐστε ὑμεῖς: The Function of a Metaphor in St Paul." Pages 391–409 in *Templum Amicitiae: Essays on the Second Temple Period Presented to Ernst Bammel*. Edited by William Horbury. Journal for the Study of the New Testament Supplement Series 48. Sheffield: JSOT Press, 1991.
De Vos, Craig Steven. *Church and Community Conflicts: The Relationships of the Thessalonian, Corinthian, and Philippian Churches with Their Wider Civic Communities*. Society of Biblical Literature Dissertation Series 168. Atlanta: Scholars Press, 1999.
Deissmann, Adolf. *Light from the Ancient East: The New Testament Illustrated by Recently Discovered Texts of the Graeco-Roman World*. Translated by Lionel R. M. Strachan. New York: George H. Doran, 1927.
Denis, Albert-Marie. "La Fonction apostolique et la liturgie nouvelle en Esprit: Étude thématique

des métaphores pauliniennes du culte nouveau." *Revue des sciences philosphiques et théologiques* 42 (1958): 401–36.
deSilva, David A. *Honor, Patronage, Kinship and Purity: Unlocking New Testament Culture*. Downers Grove, Ill.: InterVarsity Press, 2000.
Dibelius, Martin. *Studies in the Acts of the Apostles*. Translated by Mary Ling. Edited by Heinrich Greeven. London: SCM, 1956. Translation of *Aufsätze zur Apostelgeschichte*. Edited by Heinrich Greeven. Göttingen: Vandenhoeck & Ruprecht, 1951.
Dignas, Beate. *Economy of the Sacred in Hellenistic and Roman Asia Minor*. Oxford Classical Monographs. Oxford: Oxford University Press, 2002.
Dille, Sarah J. *Mixing Metaphors: God as Mother and Father in Deutero-Isaiah*. Journal for the Study of the Old Testament Supplement Series 398. Gender, Culture, Theory 13. London and New York: T & T Clark, 2004.
Dillon, Richard J. "The 'Priesthood' of St. Paul, Romans 15:15–16." *Worship* 74 (2000): 156–68.
Donaldson, Terence L. *Paul and the Gentiles: Remapping the Apostle's Convictional World*. Minneapolis: Fortress, 1997.
———. "'Proselytes or 'Righteous Gentiles'? The Status of Gentiles in Eschatological Pilgrimage Patterns of Thought." *Journal for the Study of the Pseudepigrapha* 7 (1990): 3–27.
Donaldson, Terence L., ed. *Religious Rivalries and the Struggle for Success in Caesarea Maritima*. Studies in Christianity and Judaism/Études sur le christianisme et le judaïsme 8. Waterloo, Ontario: Wilfrid Laurier University Press, 2000.
Donfried, Karl P. *Paul, Thessalonica, and Early Christianity*. Grand Rapids: Eerdmans, 2002.
———. *The Romans Debate: Revised and Expanded Edition*. Peabody, Mass.: Hendrickson, 1991.
Downs, David J. "Chronology of the NT." Pages 633–36 in *The New Interpreter's Dictionary of the Bible*. Vol. 1. Edited by Katharine Doob Sakenfeld. Nashville: Abingdon, 2006.
———. "'Early Catholicism' and Apocalypticism in the Pastoral Epistles." *Catholic Biblical Quarterly* 67 (2005): 641–61.
———. "'The Offering of the Gentiles' in Rom 15.16." *Journal for the Study of the New Testament* 29 (2006): 173–86.
———. "Paul's Collection and the Book of Acts Revisited." *New Testament Studies* 52 (2006): 50–70.
Dunn, James D. G. *The Acts of the Apostles*. Narrative Bible Commentaries. Harrisburg, Pa.: Trinity, 1996.
———. *Romans*. 2 vols. Word Biblical Commentary 38. Dallas: Word, 1988.
Dupont, Jacques. "La mission de Paul 'à Jérusalem' (Actes xii, 25)." *Novum Testamentum* 1 (1956): 275–303.
———. *The Sources of Acts: The Present Position*. New York: Herder and Herder, 1964.
Eastman, Brad. *The Significance of Grace in the Letters of Paul*. Studies in Biblical Literature 11. New York: Peter Lang, 1999.
Ebel, Eva. *Die Attraktivität früher christlicher Gemeinden: Die Gemeinde von Korinth im Spiegel griechisch-römischer Vereine*. Wissenschaftliche Untersuchungen zum Neuen Testament 2:178. Tübingen: Mohr Siebeck, 2004.
Eckert, Jost. "Die Kollekte des Paulus für Jerusalem." Pages 65–80 in *Kontinuität und Einheit: Für Franz Mussner*. Edited by Paul-Gerhard Müller and Werner Stenger. Freiburg: Herder, 1981.
Eilers, Claude. *Roman Patrons of Greek Cities*. Oxford Classical Monographs. Oxford: Oxford University Press, 2002.
Eisenstadt, S. N., and Louis Roniger. "Patron-Client Relations as a Model of Structuring Social Exchange." *Comparative Studies in Society and History* 22 (1980): 42–77.
Elliott, John H. "Patronage and Clientage." Pages 144–56 in *The Social Sciences and New Testament Interpretation*. Edited by Richard Rohrbaugh. Peabody, Mass.: Hendrickson, 1996.
———. "Patronage and Clientism in Early Christian Society." *Forum* 3 (1987): 39–48.

Fee, Gordon D. "CARIS in 2 Corinthians 1:15: Apostolic Parousia and Paul-Corinth Chronology." *New Testament Studies* 24 (1977): 533–38.
———. *Paul's Letter to the Philippians*. New International Commentary on the New Testament. Grand Rapids: Eerdmans, 1995.
Fellows, Richard G. "Was Titus Timothy?" *Journal for the Study of the New Testament* 81 (2001): 33–58.
Ferguson, William Scott. "The Attic Orgeones." *Harvard Theological Review* 37 (1944): 61–140.
Finlan, Stephen. *The Background and Content of Paul's Cultic Atonement Metaphors*. Academia Biblica 19. Atlanta: Society of Biblical Literature, 2004.
Finley, Moses. *The Ancient Economy*. Sather Classical Lectures 43. 2d ed. Berkeley: University of California Press, 1985.
Finn, Richard. *Almsgiving in the Later Roman Empire: Christian Promotion and Practice, 313–450*. Oxford Classical Monographs. Oxford: Oxford University Press, 2006.
Fitzmyer, Joseph. *The Acts of the Apostles: A New Translation with Introduction and Commentary*. Anchor Bible 31. New York: Doubleday, 1998.
———. *Romans: A New Translation with Introduction and Commentary*. Anchor Bible 33. Garden City: Doubleday, 1993.
Foucart, P. *Des associations religieuses chez les Grecs: thiases, éranes, orgéons*. Paris: Klincksieck, 1873.
Fowl, Stephen E. "Know Your Context: Giving and Receiving Money in Philippians." *Interpretation* 56 (2002): 45–58.
Fransen, Paul S. "Mission, Money and Right Administration: Reflections on II Corinthians 8 and 9." *Trinity Seminary Review* 22 (2000): 7–18.
Fraser, P. M. *Rhodian Funerary Monuments*. Oxford: Clarendon, 1977.
Friesen, Steven J. "Poverty in Pauline Studies: Beyond the So-called New Consensus." *Journal for the Study of the New Testament* 26 (2004): 323–61.
Furnish, Victor P. *II Corinthians*. Anchor Bible 32A. Garden City: Doubleday, 1984.
Gabrielsen, Vincent. "The Rhodian Associations and Economic Activity." Pages 215–44 in *Hellenistic Economies*. Edited by Zofia H. Archibald, John Davies, Vincent Gabrielsen, and G. J. Oliver. London and New York: Routledge, 2001.
———. "The Rhodian Associations Honouring Dionysodoros from Alexandria." *Classica et Mediaevalia* 45 (1994): 137–60.
Gamble, Harry, Jr. *The Textual History of the Letter to the Romans: A Study in Textual and Literary Criticism*. Studies and Documents 42. Grand Rapids: Eerdmans, 1977.
Gardner, Gregg. "Jewish Leadership and Hellenistic Civic Benefaction in the Second Century B.C.E." *Journal of Biblical Literature* 126 (2007): 327–43.
Garlington, Don. *Faith, Obedience, and Perseverance: Aspects of Paul's Letter to the Romans*. Wissenschaftliche Untersuchungen zum Neuen Testament 79. Tübingen: J. C. B. Mohr, 1994.
Garnsey, Peter. *Famine and Food Supply in the Graeco-Roman World: Responses to Risk and Crisis*. Cambridge: Cambridge University Press, 1988.
———. *Food and Society in Classical Antiquity*. Cambridge: Cambridge University Press, 1999.
Garrison, Roman. *Redemptive Almsgiving in Early Christianity*. Journal for the Study of the New Testament Supplement Series 77. Sheffield: JSOT Press, 1993.
Gaston, Lloyd. "Paul and Jerusalem." Pages 61–72 in *From Jesus to Paul: Studies in Honour of Francis Wright Beare*. Edited by Peter Richardson and John C. Hurd. Waterloo: Wilfried Laurier University Press, 1984.
Gauthier, Philippe. *Les cités grecques et leur bienfaiteurs (IVe-Ier avant J.-C.): Contribution à l'histoire des institutions*. Suppléments du bulletin de correspondance hellénique 12. Athènes: École Française D'Athènes, 1985.
Gaventa, Beverly Roberts. *The Acts of the Apostles*. Abingdon New Testament Commentaries. Nashville: Abingdon, 2003.

—."Apostle and Church in 2 Corinthians: A Response to David M. Hay and Steven J. Kraftchick." Pages 182–199 *Pauline Theology*. Vol. 2: *1 and 2 Corinthians*. Society of Biblical Literature Symposium Series 22. Edited by David M. Hay. Minneapolis: Fortress, 1993.

—. "Apostles as Babes and Nurses in 1 Thessalonians 2:7." Pages 193–207 in *Faith and History: Essays in Honor of Paul W. Meyer*. Edited by John T. Carroll, Charles H. Cosgrove, and E. Elizabeth Johnson. Atlanta: Scholars Press, 1990.

—. "The Economy of Grace: Reflections on 2 Corinthians 8 and 9." Pages in 51–62 in *Grace Upon Grace: Essays in Honor of Thomas A. Langford*. Edited by Robert K. Johnston, L. Gregory Jones, and Jonathan R. Wilson. Nashville: Abingdon, 1999.

—. "Galatians 1 and 2: Autobiography as Paradigm." *Novum Testamentum* 28 (1986): 309–26.

—. "God Handed Them Over: Reading Romans 1:18–32 Apocalyptically." *Australian Biblical Review* 53 (2005): 42–53.

—. "Interpreting the Death of Jesus Apocalyptically: Reconsidering Romans 8:32." Pages 125–45 in *Jesus and Paul Reconsidered: Fresh Pathways Into an Old Debate*. Edited by Todd D. Still. Grand Rapids and Cambridge: Eerdmans, 2007.

—. "The Maternity of Paul: An Exegetical Study of Galatians 4:19." Pages 189–201 in *The Conversation Continues: Studies in Paul and John in Honor of J. Louis Martyn*. Edited by Robert T. Fortna and Beverly R. Gaventa. Nashville: Abingdon, 1990.

—. "Mother's Milk and Ministry in 1 Corinthians 3." Pages 101–13 in *Theology and Ethics in Paul and His Interpreters: Essays in Honor of Victor Paul Furnish*. Edited by Eugene H. Lovering Jr. and Jerry L. Sumney. Nashville: Abingdon, 1996.

—. "Our Mother St. Paul: Toward the Recovery of a Neglected Theme." *Princeton Seminary Bulletin* 17 (1996): 29–44.

Gelardini, Gabriella, ed. *Hebrews: Contemporary Methods—New Insights*. Biblical Interpretation Series 75. Leiden and Boston: Brill, 2005.

Georgi, Dieter. *The Opponents of Paul in Second Corinthians*. Philadelphia: Fortress, 1986. Translation of *Die Gegner des Paulus im 2. Korintherbrief: Studien zur religiösen Propaganda in der Spätantike*. Theologische Forschung 38. Neukirchen-Vluyn: Neukirchener, 1964.

—. *Remembering the Poor: The History of Paul's Collection for Jerusalem*. Nashville: Abingdon, 1992. Translation of *Geschichte der Kollekte des Paulus für Jerusalem*. Hamburg: Herbert Reich, 1965.

Godet, F. *Commentaire sur L'Épitre aux Romains*. 2d ed. Paris: Grassart, 1890.

Goguel, Maurice. "La collecte en faveur des Saints." *Revue d'histoire et de philosophie religieuses* 5 (1925): 301–18.

Golag, Paton J. *A Critical and Exegetical Commentary on the Acts of the Apostles*. Edinburgh: T & T Clark, 1870.

Goodman, Martin. "The Temple in First Century CE Judaism." Pages 459–68 in *Temple and Worship in Biblical Israel: Proceedings of the Oxford Old Testament Seminar*. Edited by John Day. Library of Hebrew Bible/Old Testament Studies 422. London: T & T Clark, 2005.

Grant, Robert. *Early Christianity and Society: Seven Studies*. San Francisco: Harper & Row, 1977.

Günther, Matthias. *Die Frühgeschichte des Christentums in Ephesus*. Arbeiten zur Religion und Geschichte des Urchristentums 1. Frankfurt: Lang, 1995.

Gupta, Nijay K. "Principles for Interpreting Metaphors in Paul: *Prosagōgēn* (Rom 5.2) as a Case Study." Paper presented at the annual meeting of the Society of Biblical Literature, San Diego, Calif., November 18, 2007.

Haacker, Klaus. *Der Brief des Paulus an die Römer*. Theologischer Handkommentar zum Neuen Testament 6. Leipzig: Evangelische Verlagsanstalt, 1999.

Hainz, Josef. "Gemeinschaft (κοινωνία) zwischen Paulus und Jerusalem (Gal 2,9f.): Zum paulinischen Verständnis von der Einheit der Kirche." Pages 30–42 in *Kontinuität und Einheit: Für Franz Mussner*. Edited by Paul-Gerhard Müller and Werner Stenger. Freiburg: Herder, 1981.

—. *Koinonia: "Kirche" als Gemeinschaft bei Paulus*. Biblische Untersuchungen 16. Regensburg: Pustet, 1982.
Hall, David R. "St. Paul and Famine Relief: A Study in Galatians 2:10." *Expository Times* 82 (1971): 309–11.
—. *The Unity of the Corinthian Correspondence*. Journal for the Study of the New Testament Supplement Series 251. London: T & T Clark, 2003.
Hamel, Gildas. *Poverty and Charity in Roman Palestine, First Three Centuries C.E*. University of California Publications: Near Eastern Studies 23. Berkeley and Los Angeles: University of California Press, 1990.
Hands, A. R. *Charities and Social Aid in Greece and Rome*. Aspects of Greek and Roman Life. Ithaca, N.Y.: Cornell University Press, 1968.
Hanson, A. T. *Studies in Paul's Technique and Theology*. Grand Rapids: Eerdmans, 1974.
Harland, Philip A. Associations, Synagogues, and Congregations: Claiming a Place in Ancient Mediterranean Society. Minneapolis: Fortress, 2003.
—. "Connections with Elites in the World of the Early Christians." Pages 385–408 in *Handbook of Early Christianity: Social Science Approaches*. Edited by Anthony J. Blasi, Jean Duhaime, and Paul-André Turcotte. Walnut Creek, Calif.: Altamira, 2002.
—. "The Economy of First-Century Palestine: State of the Scholarly Discussion." Pages 511–27 in *Handbook of Early Christianity: Social Science Approaches*. Edited by Anthony J. Blasi, Jean Duhaime, and Paul-André Turcotte. Walnut Creek, Calif.: Altamira, 2002.
—. "Familial Dimensions of Group Identity: 'Brothers' ('Αδελφοί) in Associations of the Greek East." *Journal of Biblical Literature* 124 (2005): 491–513.
—. "Familial Dimensions of Group Identity (II): 'Mothers' and 'Fathers' in Associations and Synagogues of the Greek World," *Journal for the Study of Judaism in the Persian, Hellenistic, and Roman Periods* 38 (2007): 57–79
—. "Spheres of Contention, Claims of Pre-eminence: Rivalries among Associations in Sardis and Smyrna." Pages 53–63 in *Religious Rivalries and the Struggle for Success in Sardis and Smyrna*. Edited by Richard S. Ascough. Studies in Early Christianity and Judaism/Études sur les christianisme et le judaïsme 14.Waterloo, Ontario: Wilfrid Laurier University Press, 2005.
Harrill, J. Albert. *The Manumission of Slaves in Early Christianity*. Hermeneutische Untersuchungen zur Theologie 32. Tübingen: J. C. B. Mohr, 1995.
—. "Servile Functionaries or Priestly Leaders? Roman Domestic Religion, Narrative Intertextuality, and Pliny's Reference to Slave Christian *Ministrae* (Ep. 10,96,8)." *Zeitschrift für die neutestamentliche Wissenschaft und die Kunde der älteren Kirche* 97 (2006): 111–30.
Harris, Murray J. *The Second Epistle to the Corinthians*. The New International Greek Testament Commentary. Grand Rapids: Eerdmans/Milton Keynes: Paternoster, 2005.
Harris, Wendell V. *Dictionary of Concepts in Literary Criticism and Theory*. New York: Greenwood, 1992.
Harrison, James R. *Paul's Language of Grace in its Graeco-Roman Context*. Wissenschaftliche Untersuchungen zum Neuen Testament 2:172. Tübingen: Mohr Siebeck, 2003.
—. "Paul's House Churches and the Cultic Associations." *The Reformed Theological Review* 58 (1999): 31–47.
Hatch, Edwin. *The Organization of the Early Christian Churches: Eight Lectures Delivered Before the University of Oxford, in the Year 1880*. Bampton Lectures. London: Rivingtons, 1881.
Hawthorne, Gerald F. *Philippians*. Revised and enlarged by Ralph P. Martin. Word Biblical Commentary 43. Nashville: Thomas Nelson, 2000.
Hays, Richard B. *Echoes of Scripture in the Letters of Paul*. New Haven and London: Yale University Press, 1989.
Hecke, P. van, ed. *Metaphor in the Hebrew Bible*. Bibliotheca Ephemeridum Theologicarum Lovaniensium 187. Leuven: Peeters, 2006.

Henderson, Suzanne Watts. "'If Anyone Hungers …': An Integrated Reading of 1 Cor 11.17–34." *New Testament Studies* 48 (2002): 195–208.

Hendrix, Holland. "Benefactor/Patron Networks in the Urban Environment: Evidence from Thessalonica." *Semeia* 56 (1991): 39–59.

Hock, Ronald F. *The Social Context of Paul's Ministry: Tentmaking and Apostleship*. Philadelphia: Fortress, 1980.

Hodge, Charles. *Commentary on the Epistle to the Romans*. 2d ed. Edinburgh: Andrew Elliot, 1875.

Holl, Karl. "Der Kirchenbegriff des Paulus in seinem Verhältnis zu dem der Urgemeinde." Pages 920–47 in *Sitzungsbericht der Berliner Akademie* (1921). Repr. in pages 44–67 of *Gesammelte Aufsätze zur Kirchengeschichte, II*. Tübingen: J. C. B. Mohr, 1928.

Holloway, Paul A. *Consolation in Philippians: Philosophical Sources and Rhetorical Strategy*. Society for New Testament Studies Monograph Series 112. Cambridge: Cambridge University Press, 2001.

Holmberg, Bengt. *Paul and Power: The Structure of Authority in the Primitive Church as Reflected in the Pauline Epistles*. Philadelphia: Fortress, 1978.

Hoppe, Leslie J. *There Shall Be No Poor Among You: Poverty in the Bible*. Nashville: Abington, 2004.

Horn, Friedrich Wilhelm. "Die Kollektenthematik in der Apostelgeschichte." Pages 135–56 in *Die Apostelgeschichte und die hellenistische Geschichtsschreibung: Festschrift für Eckhard Plümacher zu seinem 65. Geburtstag*. Edited by Cilliers Breytenbach and Jens Schröter. Ancient Judaism and Early Christianity 57. Leiden and Boston: Brill, 2004.

Horstmanshoff, H. F. J. "The Ancient Physician: Craftsman or Scientist?" *Journal of the History of Medicine and Allied Sciences* 45 (1990): 176–97.

Horrell, David. "Paul's Collection: Resources for a Materialist Theology." *Epworth Review* 22 (1995): 74–83.

———. "'The Lord Commanded … But I Have Not Used': Exegetical and Hermeneutical Reflections on 1 Cor 9:14–15." *New Testament Studies* 43 (1997): 587–603.

Horsley, G. H. R. "A Fishing Cartel in First-Century Ephesos." Pages 95–114 in *New Documents Illustrating Early Christianity*. Vol. 5: *Linguistic Essays*. Macquarie: Macquarie University, 1989.

Hurtado, Larry W. "The Jerusalem Collection and the Book of Galatians." *Journal for the Study of the New Testament* 5 (1979): 46–62.

Jeremias, Joachim. "The Gentile World in the Thought of Jesus." *Studiorum Novi Testamenti Societas Auxilia* 3 (1952): 18–28.

———. *Jesus' Promise to the Nations*. Translated by S. H. Hooker. London: SCM, 1958.

Jewett, Robert. *A Chronology of Paul's Life*. Philadelphia: Fortress, 1979.

———. "Ecumenical Theology for the Sake of Mission: Romans 1:1–17 + 15:14–16:24." Pages 89–108 in *Pauline Theology*. Vol. 3: *Romans*. Edited by David M. Hay and E. Elizabeth Johnson. Society of Biblical Literature Symposium Series 23. Atlanta: Society of Biblical Literature, 2002.

———. "Paul, Shame, and Honor." Pages 551–74 in *Paul in the Greco-Roman World: A Handbook*. Edited by J. Paul Sampley. Harrisburg, Pa.: Trinity, 2003.

Johnson, Luke Timothy. *The Literary Function of Possessions in Luke-Acts*. Society of Biblical Literature Dissertation Series 39. Missoula, Mont.: Scholars Press, 1977.

———. "Making Connections: The Material Expression of Friendship in the New Testament." *Interpretation* 58 (2004): 158–71.

Jones, C. P. *The Roman World of Dio Chrysostom*. Loeb Classical Monographs. Cambridge: Harvard University Press, 1978.

Jones, Nicholas F. *The Associations of Classical Athens: The Response to Democracy*. New York and Oxford: Oxford University Press, 1999.

Joubert, Stephan. "ΧΑΡΙΣ in Paul: An Investigation into the Apostle's 'Performative' Application of the Language of *Grace* within the Framework of His Theological Reflection on the Event/Process of Salvation." Pages 187–211 in *Salvation in the New Testament: Perspectives on the Soteriology*. Edited by Jan G. van der Watt. Leiden and Boston: Brill, 2005.

—. "Coming to Terms with a Neglected Aspect of Ancient Mediterranean Reciprocity: Seneca's Views on Benefit-Exchange in *De beneficiis* as the Framework for a Model of Social Exchange." Pages 47–63 in *Social Scientific Models for Interpreting the Bible: Essays by the Context Group in Honor of Bruce J. Malina*. Edited by John J. Pilch. Biblical Interpretation Series 53. Leiden: Brill, 2001.

—. "One Form of Social Exchange or Two: Euergetism, Patronage and Testament Studies." *Biblical Theology Bulletin* 31 (2001): 17–25.

—. *Paul as Benefactor: Reciprocity, Strategy, and Theological Reflection in Paul's Collection*. Wissenschaftliche Untersuchungen zum Neuen Testament 2:124. Tübingen: Mohr Siebeck, 2000.

Judge, E. A. "Did the Churches Compete with Cult Groups?" Pages 501–24 in *Early Christianity and Classical Culture: Comparative Studies in Honor of Abraham J. Malherbe*. Edited by John T. Fitzgerald, Thomas H. Olbricht, and L. Michael White. Supplements to Novum Testamentum 110. Leiden and Boston: Brill, 2003.

Käsemann, Ernst. *Commentary on Romans*. Translated by Geoffrey W. Bromiley. Grand Rapids: Eerdmans, 1980.

Keck, Leander. "Christology, Soteriology, and the Praise of God (Romans 15:7–13)." Pages 85–97 in *The Conversation Continues: Studies in Paul and John in Honor of J. Louis Martyn*. Edited by Robert T. Fortna and Beverly R. Gaventa. Nashville: Abingdon, 1990.

—. "The Poor among the Saints in Jewish Christianity and Qumran." *Zeitschrift für die neutestamentliche Wissenschaft und die Kunde der älteren Kirche* 57 (1966): 54–78.

—. "The Poor among the Saints in the New Testament." *Zeitschrift für die neutestamentliche Wissenschaft und die Kunde der älteren Kirche* 56 (1965): 100–29.

Kiley, Mark. *Colossians as Pseudepigraphy*. The Biblical Seminar 4. Sheffield: JSOT Press, 1986.

Kim, Byung-Mo. *Die paulinische Kollekte*. Texte und Arbeiten zum neutestamentlichen Zeitalter 38. Tübingen and Basel: Francke, 2002.

Kittel, G., and G. Friedrich, eds. *Theological Dictionary of the New Testament*. Translated by G. W. Bromiley. 10 vols. Grand Rapids: Eerdmans, 1964–1976.

Klinghardt, Matthias. "The Manual of Discipline in Light of Statutes of Hellenistic Associations." Pages 251–70 in *Methods of Investigation of the Dead Sea Scrolls and the Khirbet Qumran Site: Present Realities and Future Prospects*. Edited by Michael O. Wise, Norman Golb, John J. Collins, and Dennis G. Pardee. Annals of the New York Academy of Sciences 722. New York: The New York Academy of Sciences, 1994.

Kloppenborg, John S. "Edwin Hatch, Churches and *Collegia*." Pages 212–38 in *Origins and Method: Towards a New Understanding of Judaism and Christianity. Essays in Honour of John C. Hurd*. Edited by Bradley H. McLean. Journal for the Study of the New Testament Supplement Series 86. Sheffield: JSOT Press, 1993.

Kloppenborg, John S., and Stephen G. Wilson, eds. *Voluntary Associations in the Graeco-Roman World*. London: Routledge, 1996.

Knox, John. *Chapters in a Life of Paul*. Rev. ed. Macon, Ga.: Mercer University Press, 1987.

—. "'Fourteen Years Later': A Note on the Pauline Chronology." *Journal of Religion* 16 (1936): 341–49.

—. "On the Pauline Chronology: Buck-Taylor-Hurd Revisited." Pages 258–74 in *The Conversation Continues: Studies in Paul and John in Honor of J. Louis Martyn*. Edited by R. T. Fortna and B. R. Gaventa. Nashville: Abingdon, 1990.

—. "The Pauline Chronology." *Journal of Biblical Literature* 58 (1939): 15–29.

—. "Romans 15:14–33 and Paul's Conception of His Apostolic Mission." *Journal of Biblical Literature* 83 (1964): 1–11.

Koch, Dietrich-Alex. "Kollektenbericht, 'Wir'-Bericht und Itinerar: Neue [?] Überlegungen zu einem alten Problem." *New Testament Studies* 45 (1999): 367–90.

Koch, Dietrich-Alex, and Andreas Gutsfeld, eds. *Vereine, Synagogen und Gemeinden im kaiserzeitlichen Kleinasien*. Studien und Texte zu Antike und Christentum 25. Tübingen: Mohr Siebeck, 2006.

Konstan, David. "Patrons and Friends." *Classical Philology* 90 (1995): 328–42.
Kövecses, Zoltán. *Metaphor: A Practical Introduction.* Oxford: Oxford University Press, 2002.
Kraemer, Ross S. "Jewish Tuna and Christian Fish: Identifying Religious Affiliation in Epigraphic Sources." *Harvard Theological Review* 84 (1991): 141–62.
—."On the Meaning of the Term 'Jew' in Greco-Roman Inscriptions." *Harvard Theological Review* 82 (1989): 35–53.
Kraftchick, Steven J. "Death in Us, Life in You: The Apostolic Medium." Pages 156–81 in *Pauline Theology*. Vol. 2: *1 and 2 Corinthians*. Society of Biblical Literature Symposium Series 22. Edited by David M. Hay. Minneapolis: Fortress, 1993.
Krüger, M. A. "*Tina Karpon*, 'Some Fruit,' in Rom. 1:13." *Westminster Theological Journal* 49 (1987): 167–73.
La Piana, George. "Foreign Groups in Rome during the First Centuries of the Empire." *Harvard Theological Review* 20 (1927): 183–403.
Lakoff, George, and Mark Johnson. *Metaphors We Live By*. Chicago and London: The University of Chicago Press, 1980.
Lanci, John R. *A New Temple for Corinth: Rhetorical and Archaeological Approaches to Pauline Imagery*. Studies in Biblical Literature 1. New York: Peter Lang, 1997.
Lambrecht, Jan. "Paul's Boasting About the Corinthians: A Study of 2 Cor. 8:24–9:5." *Novum Testamentum* 40 (1998): 352–68.
—. *Second Corinthians*. Sacra Pagina 8. Collegeville, Minn.: Liturgical, 1999.
Lampe, Peter. *From Paul to Valentinus: Christians at Rome in the First Two Centuries*. Translated by Michael Steinhauser. Minneapolis: Fortress, 2003. Translation of *Die stadtrömischen Christen in den ersten beiden Jahrhunderten: Untersuchungen zur Sozialgeschichte*. Wissenschaftliche Untersuchungen zum Neuen Testament 2:18. Tübingen: J. C. B. Mohr, 1989.
—. "Paul, Patrons, and Clients." Pages 488–523 in *Paul in the Greco-Roman World: A Handbook*. Edited by J. Paul Sampley. Harrisburg, Pa.: Trinity, 2003.
Levine, Lee I. *The Ancient Synagogue: The First Thousand Years*. New Haven and London: Yale University Press, 2000.
Liebenam, Willy. *Zur Geschichte und Organisation des römischen Vereinswesens: Drei Untersuchungen*. Leipzig: Teubner, 1890.
Llewelyn, S. R. "The Use of Sunday for Meetings of Believers in the New Testament." *Novum Testamentum* 43 (2001): 205–23.
Lohse, Eduard. *Der Brief an die Römer*. Kritisch-exegetischer Kommentar über das Neue Testament 15. Göttingen: Vandenhoeck and Ruprecht, 2003.
Longenecker, Bruce W. "Good News to the Poor: Jesus, Paul, and Jerusalem." Pages 37–65 in *Jesus and Paul Reconnected: Fresh Pathways into an Old Debate*. Edited by Todd D. Still. Grand Rapids and Cambridge: Eerdmans, 2007.
—. "Lukan Aversion to Humps and Hollows: The Case of Acts 11.27–12.25." *New Testament Studies* 50 (2004): 185–204.
Longenecker, Richard N. *Galatians*. Word Biblical Commentary 41. Dallas: Word, 1990.
Lüdemann, Gerd. *Early Christianity according to the Traditions in Acts: A Commentary*. Minneapolis: Fortress, 1989. Translated by John Bowden. Translation of *Das frühe Christentum nach den Traditionen der Apostelgeschichte: Ein Kommentar*. Göttingen: Vandenhoeck & Ruprecht, 1987.
—. *Paul: Apostle to the Gentiles: Studies in Chronology*. Translated by F. Stanley Jones. Philadelphia: Fortress, 1984.
—. *Primitive Christianity: A Survey of Recent Studies and Some New Proposals*. Translated by John Bowden. London: T & T Clark, 2003.
Macky, Peter W. *The Centrality of Metaphors to Biblical Thought: A Method for Interpreting the Bible*. Studies in the Bible and Early Christianity 19. Lewiston, N.Y.: Edwin Mellen Press, 1990.

MacMullen, Ramsay. "The Epigrpahic Habit in the Roman Empire." *The American Journal of Philology* 103 (1982): 233–46.

———. "The Frequency of Inscriptions in Roman Lydia." *Zeitschrift für Papyrologie und Epigraphik* 65 (1986): 237–38.

Magness, Jodi. "The Date of the Sardis Synagogue in Light of the Numismatic Evidence." *American Journal of Archaeology* 109 (2005): 443–47.

Malherbe, Abraham J. "The Corinthian Contribution." *Restoration Quarterly* 3 (1959): 221–33.

———. *The Letters to the Thessalonians: A New Translation with Introduction and Commentary*. Anchor Bible 32B. New York: Doubleday, 2000.

Malina, Bruce J. *The New Testament World: Insights from Cultural Anthropology*. 3d ed. Louisville: Westminster John Knox, 2001.

Marshall, Anthony. "Flaccus and the Jews of Asia (Cicero *Pro Flacco* 28.67–69." *Phoenix* 29 (1975): 139–54.

Marhsall, I. Howard. *The Acts of the Apostles: An Introduction and Commentary*. Grand Rapids: Eerdmans, 1980.

Marshall, Peter. *Enmity in Corinth: Social Conventions in Paul's Relations with the Corinthians*. Wissenschaftliche Untersuchungen zum Neuen Testament 23. Tübingen: J. C. B. Mohr, 1987.

Martin, Dale B. "Review Essay: Justin J. Meggitt, *Paul, Poverty and Survival*." *Journal for the Study of the New Testament* 24 (2001): 51–64.

Martin, Ralph P. *2 Corinthians*. Word Biblical Commentary 40. Waco, Tex.: Word, 1986.

———. *Worship in the Early Church*. Grand Rapids: Eerdmans, 1987.

Martyn, J. Louis. *Galatians: A New Translation with Introduction and Commentary*. Anchor Bible 33A. New York: Doubleday, 1997.

———. *Theological Issues in the Letters of Paul*. Nashville: Abingdon, 1997.

Matera, Frank J. *II Corinthians: A Commentary*. The New Testament Library. Louisville: Westminster John Knox, 2003.

McGuire, Martin R. P. "Epigraphical Evidence for Social Charity in the Roman West." *The American Journal of Philology* 67 (1946): 129–50.

McKay, K. L. "Observations on the Epistolary Aorist in 2 Corinthians." *Novum Testamentum* 37 (1995): 154–58.

McKnight, Scot. "Collection for the Saints." Pages 143–47 in *Dictionary of Paul and His Letters*. Edited by Gerald F. Hawthorne, Ralph P. Martin, and Daniel G. Reid. Downers Grove, Ill.: InterVarsity Press, 1993.

McLean, Bradley H. "The Agrippinilla Inscription: Religious Associations and Early Church Formation." Pages 239–70 in *Origins and Method: Towards a New Understanding of Judaism and Christianity. Essays in Honour of John C. Hurd*. Edited by Bradley H. McLean. Journal for the Study of the New Testament Supplement Series 86. Sheffield: JSOT Press, 1993.

———. *An Introduction to Greek Epigraphy of the Hellenistic and Roman Periods from Alexander the Great down to the Reign of Constantine (323 B.C. – A.D. 337)*. Ann Arbor: University of Michigan Press, 2002.

Meeks, Wayne. *The First Urban Christians: The Social World of the Apostle Paul*. 2d ed. New Haven: Yale University Press, 2003.

Meggitt, Justin J. *Paul, Poverty and Survival*. Studies of the New Testament and Its World. Edinburgh: T & T Clark, 1998.

———. "Response to Martin and Theissen." *Journal for the Study of the New Testament* 24 (2001): 85–94.

Meiggs, Russell. *Roman Ostia*. 2d ed. Oxford: Clarendon, 1973.

Melick, Richard R. "The Collection for the Saints: 2 Corinthians 8–9." *Criswell Theological Review* 4 (1989): 97–117.

Metzger, Bruce M. *A Textual Commentary on the Greek New Testament*. 2d ed. New York: United Bible Societies, 1994.

Meyer, Heinrich August Wilhelm. *Kritisch exegetisches Handbuch über den zweiten Brief an die Korinther.* Göttingen: Vandenhoeck und Ruprecht's, 1870.

Meyer, Paul W. "Pauline Theology: A Proposal for a Pause in Its Pursuit." Pages 140–60 in *Pauline Theology.* Vol. 4: *Looking Back, Pressing On.* Edited by E. Elizabeth Johnson and David M. Hay. Society of Biblical Literature Symposium Series 4. Atlanta: Scholars Press, 1997.

Migeotte, Léopold. *Les souscriptions publiques dans les cités grecques.* Québec and Geneva: Droz, 1992.

Minear, Paul S. "The Jerusalem Fund and Pauline Chronology." *Anglican Theological Review* 25 (1943): 389–96.

Mitchell, Margaret M. "Concerning ΠΕΡΙ ΔΕ in 1 Corinthians." *Novum Testamentum* 31 (1989): 229–56.

—. "New Testament Envoys in the Context of Greco-Roman Diplomatic and Epistolary Conventions: The Example of Timothy and Titus." *Journal of Biblical Literature* 111 (1992): 641–62.

—. *Paul and the Rhetoric of Reconciliation: An Exegetical Investigation of the Language and Composition of 1 Corinthians.* Louisville: Westminster/John Knox, 1993.

—. "Paul's Letters to Corinth: The Interpretive Intertwining of Literary and Historical Reconstruction." Pages 306–38 in *Urban Religion in Roman Corinth: Interdisciplinary Approaches.* Edited by Daniel N. Schowalter and Steven J. Friesen. Harvard Theological Studies 53. Cambridge, Mass.: Harvard University Press, 2005.

Mommsen, Theodore. *De collegiis et sodaliciis romanorum.* Kiliae: Libraria Schwersiana, 1843.

Moo, Douglas J. *The Epistle to the Romans.* The New International Commentary on the New Testament. Grand Rapids: Eerdmans, 1996.

Morgado, Joe. "Paul in Jerusalem: A Comparison of His Visits in Acts and Galatians." *Journal of the Evangelical Theological Society* 37 (1994): 55–68.

Mott, Stephen C. "The Power of Giving and Receiving: Reciprocity in Hellenistic Benevolence." Pages 60–72 in *Current Issues in Biblical and Patristic Interpretation: Studies in Honor of Merrill C. Tenney Presented by His Former Students.* Edited by Gerald F. Hawthorne. Grand Rapids: Eerdmans, 1975.

Moule, C. F. D. *An Idiom Book of New Testament Greek.* 2d ed. Cambridge: Cambridge University Press, 1959.

Munck, Johannes. *The Acts of the Apostles: Introduction, Translation, and Notes.* Anchor Bible 31. Garden City, N.Y.: Doubleday, 1967.

—. *Paul and the Salvation of Mankind.* Atlanta: John Knox, 1959.

Murphy, Catherine M. *Wealth in the Dead Sea Scrolls and in the Qumran Community.* Studies on the Texts of the Desert of Judah 40. Leiden: Brill, 2002.

Murphy-O'Connor, Jerome. *Paul: A Critical Life.* Oxford: Clarendon, 1996.

—. *The Theology of the Second Letter to the Corinthians.* New Testament Theology. Cambridge: Cambridge University Press, 1991.

Murray, John. *The Epistle to the Romans: The English Text with Introduction, Exposition, and Notes.* 2 vols. New International Commentary on the New Testament. Grand Rapids: Eerdmans, 1965.

Nanos, Mark D. *The Mystery of Romans: The Jewish Context of Paul's Letter.* Minneapolis: Fortress, 1996.

Nickle, Keith F. *The Collection: A Study in Paul's Strategy.* Studies in Biblical Theology 48. Naperville, Ill.: Allenson, 1966.

Oakes, Peter. "Constructing Poverty Scales for Graeco-Roman Society: A Response to Steven Friesen's 'Poverty in Pauline Studies.'" *Journal for the Study of the New Testament* 26 (2004): 367–71.

O'Brien, Peter T. *The Epistle to the Philippians.* New International Greek Testament Commentary. Grand Rapids: Eerdmans, 1991.

Öhler, Markus. "Die Jerusalemer Urgemeinde im Spiegel des antiken Vereinswesens." *New Testament Studies* 51 (2005): 393–415.

O'Mahony, Kieran J. *Pauline Persuasion: A Sounding in 2 Corinthians 8–9*. Journal for the Study of the New Testament Supplement Series 199. Sheffield: Sheffield Academic Press, 2000.
Oppenheimer, Aharon. "Benevolent Societies in Jerusalem at the End of the Second Temple Period." Pages 149–65 in *Intertestamental Essays in Honour of Jozef Tadeusz Milik*. Qumranica Mogilanensia 6. Edited by Zdzislaw J. Kapera. Kraków: Enigma, 1992.
Orchard, R. K. "The Significance of Ecumenical Travel." *Journal of Ecumenical Studies* 15 (1978): 477–502.
O'Rourke, John J. "The Participle in Rom 15,25." *Catholic Biblical Quarterly* 29 (1967): 116–18.
Ortony, Andrew, ed. *Metaphor and Thought*. 2d ed. Cambridge: Cambridge University Press, 1993.
Pao, David W. *Thanksgiving: An Investigation of a Pauline Theme*. New Studies in Biblical Theology 13. Downers Grove, Ill.: InterVarsity Press, 2002.
Pearson, Birger A. "Philanthropy in the Greco-Roman World and in Early Christianity." Pages 186–213 in *The Emergence of the Christian Religion: Essays on Early Christianity*. Harrisburg, Pa.: Trinity, 1997.
Pesch, Rudolf. *Die Apostelgeschichte*. Evangelisch-katholischer Kommentar zum Neuen Testament 5:2. Zürich: Neukirchener, 1986.
———. *Römerbrief*. Neue Echter Bibel 6. Würzburg: Echter, 1983.
Peterman, G. W. *Paul's Gift from Philippi: Conventions of Gift Exchange and Christian Giving*. Society for New Testament Studies Monograph Series 92. Cambridge: Cambridge University Press, 1997.
———. "Romans 15:26: Make a Contribution or Establish Fellowship." *New Testament Studies* 40 (1994): 457–63.
———. "Romans 15.26 Eleven Years Later: Make a Contribution or Establish Fellowship." Paper presented at the annual meeting of the Society of Biblical Literature. Philadelphia, Pa., November 19, 2005.
Pickard-Cambridge, Sir Arthur. *The Dramatic Festivals of Athens*. 2d ed. Revised by John Gould and D. M. Lewis. Oxford: Clarendon, 1988.
Pilhofer, Peter. *Philippi*. Band I: *Die erste christliche Gemeinde Europas*. Wissenschaftliche Untersuchungen zum Neuen Testament 87. Tübingen: Mohr Siebeck, 1995.
———. *Philippi*. Band II: *Katalog der Inschriften von Philippi*. Wissenschaftliche Untersuchungen zum Neuen Testament 119. Tübingen: Mohr Siebeck, 2000.
Poland, Franz. *Geschichte des griechischen Vereinswesens*. Leipzig: Teubner, 1909.
Polhill, John B. *Acts*. New American Commentary. Nashville: Broadman, 1992.
Ponthot, Joseph. "L'expression cultuelle de ministère paulinien selon Rm 15,16." 254–62 in *L'Apôtre Paul: Personnalité, style et conception du ministère*. Edited by A. Vanhoye. Bibliotheca Ephemeridum Theologicarum Lovaniensium 73. Leuven: Leuven University Press, 1986.
Porter, Stanley E. *Paul in Acts*. Library of Pauline Studies. Peabody, Mass.: Hendrickson, 2001.
Praeder, Susan Marie. "The Problem of First Person Narration in Acts." *Novum Testamentum* 29 (1987): 193–218.
Prell, Marcus. *Sozialökonomische Untersuchungen zur Armut im antiken Rom: Von den Gracchen bis Kaiser Diokletian*. Beiträge zur Wirtschafts und Sozialgeschichte 77. Stuttgart: Franz Steiner, 1997.
Quass, Friedemann. "Bemerkungen zur 'Honoratiorenherrschaft' in den griechischen Städten der hellenistischen Zeit." *Gymnasium* 99 (1992): 422–34.
Rajak, Tessa. "Benefactors in the Greco-Jewish Diaspora." Pages 305–19 in *Geschichte-Tradition-Reflexion: Fetschrift für Martin Hengel zum 70. Geburtstag*. Vol. 1. Edited by Hubert Cancik, Hermann Lichtenberger, and Peter Schäfer. Tübingen: J. C. B. Mohr, 1996.
Rapske, Brian. *The Book of Acts and Paul in Roman Custody*. Vol. 3 of *The Book of Acts in Its First Century Setting*. Edited by Bruce W. Winter. Grand Rapids: Eerdmans, 1994.
Reasoner, Mark. *The Strong and the Weak: Romans 14.1–15.13 in Context*. Society for New Testament Studies Monograph Series 103. Cambridge: Cambridge University Press, 1999.

Reicke, Bo. *Re-Examining Paul's Letters: The History of the Pauline Correspondence.* Edited by David Moessner and Ingalisa Reicke. Harrisburg, Pa.: Trinity Press International, 2001.

Renan, Ernest. *The Apostles.* New York: Carleton, 1870.

Richards, I. A. *The Philosophy of Rhetoric: The Mary Flexner Lectures on the Humanities.* Bryn Mawr College, 1936. New York and Oxford: Oxford University Press, 1936.

Richardson, Peter. "Building 'A *Synodos* ... And a Place of Their Own'." Pages 187–205 in *Building Jewish in the Roman East.* Supplements to the Journal for the Study of Judaism 92. Waco, Tex.: Baylor University Press, 2004.

Riesner, Rainer. *Paul's Early Period: Chronology, Mission Strategy, Theology.* Translated by Doug Stott. Grand Rapids: Eerdmans, 1998.

Roberts, C. H., T. C. Skeat, and A. D. Nock. "The Guild of Zeus Hypsistos." *Harvard Theological Review* 29 (1936): 39–88.

Robinson, D. W. B. "The Priesthood of Paul in the Gospel of Hope." Pages 231–45 in *Reconciliation and Hope: New Testament Essays on Atonement and Eschatology presented to L.L. Morris on his 60th Birthday.* Edited by Robert Banks. Grand Rapids: Eerdmans, 1974.

Rogers, Guy M. "Demosthenes of Oenoanda and Models of Euergetism." *Journal of Roman Studies* 81 (1991): 91–100.

Rosenfeld, Ben-Zion, and Joseph Menirav. "The Ancient Synagogue as an Economic Center." *Journal of Near Eastern Studies* 58 (1999): 259–76.

Safrai, Ze'ev. *The Economy of Roman Palestine.* London: Routledge, 1994.

Sahlins, Marshall D. "On the Sociology of Primitive Exchange." Pages 139–236 in *The Relevance of Models for Social Anthropology.* Edited by M. Banton. New York: Praeger, 1965.

Saller, Richard P. *Personal Patronage under the Early Empire.* Cambridge: Cambridge University Press, 1982.

Sanday, W. and A. C. Headlam. *The Epistle to the Romans.* International Critical Commentary. 5th ed. Edinburgh: T & T Clark, 1902.

Sanders, E. P. *Jesus and Judaism.* Minneapolis: Fortress, 1985.

—. *Paul, the Law, and the Jewish People.* Minneapolis: Fortress, 1983.

Sanders, Jack T. "Paul's 'Autobiographical' Statements in Galatians 1–2." *Journal of Biblical Literature* 85 (1966): 335–43.

Schäfer, Ruth. *Paulus bis zum Apostelkonzil: Ein Beitrag zur Einleitung in den Galaterbrief, zur Geschichte der Jesusbewegung und zur Pauluschronologie.* Wissenschaftliche Untersuchungen zum Neuen Testament 2:179. Tübingen: Mohr Siebeck, 2004.

Schlatter, Adolph. *Gottes Gerechtigkeit: Ein Kommentar zum Römerbrief.* Stuttgart: Calwer, 1836.

Schmeller, Thomas. *Hierarchie und Egalität: Eine sozialgeschichtliche Untersuchung paulinischer Gemeinden und griechisch-römischer Vereine.* Stuttgarter Bibelstudien 162. Stuttgart: Katholisches Bibelwerk, 1995.

Schmithals, Walter. "Die Kollekten des Paulus für Jerusalem." Pages 78–106 in *Paulus, die Evangelien und das Urchristentum. Beiträge von und zu Walter Schmithals zu seinem 80. Geburtstag.* Edited by Cilliers Breytenbach. Arbeiten zur Geschichte des antiken Judentums und des Urchristentums 54. Leiden and Boston: Brill, 2004.

—. *Der Römerbrief: Ein Kommentar.* Gütersloher: Gütersloher, 1988.

Schnabel, Eckhard. "Die ersten Christen in Ephesus: Neuerscheinungen zur frühchristlichen Missionsgeschichte." *Novum Testamentum* 41 (1999): 349–82.

Schneider, Gerhard. *Die Apostelgeschichte.* Teil II: *Kommentar zu Kap. 9,1–28,31.* Herders theologischer Kommentar zum Neuen Testament 5:2. Freiburg: Herder, 1982.

Schön, Donald. "Generative Metaphor." Pages 137–63 in *Metaphor and Thought.* Edited by Andrew Ortony. 2d ed. Cambridge: Cambridge University Press, 1993.

Schowalter, Daniel N., and Steven J. Friesen, eds. *Urban Religion in Roman Corinth: Interdisciplinary Approaches.* Harvard Theological Studies 53. Cambridge: Harvard University Press, 2005.

Schreiner, Thomas R. *Romans*. Baker Exegetical Commentary on the New Testament. Grand Rapids: Baker Books, 1998.
Schürer, Emil. *The History of the Jewish People in the Age of Jesus Christ*. Revised and edited by G. Vermes, F. Millar, M. Black, and M. Goodman. 3 vols. Edinburgh: T & T Clark, 1973–1987.
Scott, James M. *Paul and the Nations: The Old Testament and Jewish Background of Paul's Mission to the Nations with Special Reference to the Destination of Galatians*. Wissenschaftliche Untersuchungen zum Neuen Testament 84. Tübingen: J. C. B. Mohr, 1995.
Seccombe, David. "Was There Organized Charity in Jerusalem before the Christians?." *Journal of Theological Studies* 29 (1978): 140–43.
Silva, Moisés. *Interpreting Galatians: Explorations in Exegetical Method*. 2d ed. Grand Rapids: Baker Academic, 2001.
Shields, Mary. *Circumscribing the Prostitute: The Rhetorics of Intertextuality, Metaphor, and Gender in Jeremiah 3.1–4.4*. Journal for the Study of the Old Testament Supplement Series 387. London and New York: T & T Clark, 2004.
Sherwin-White, A. N. *The Letters of Pliny: A Historical and Social Commentary*. Oxford: Oxford University Press, 1966.
Slingerland, Dixon. "Acts 18:1–8, the Gallio Inscription, and Absolute Pauline Chronology." *Journal of Biblical Literature* 110 (1991): 439–49.
———. "Acts 18:1–17 and Luedemann's Pauline Chronology." *Journal of Biblical Literature* 109 (1990): 686–90.
Smiga, George. "Romans 12:1–12 and 15:30–32 and the Occasion of the Letter to the Romans." *Catholic Biblical Quarterly* 53 (1991): 257–73.
Smith, Jonathan Z. *Drudgery Divine: On the Comparison of Early Christianities and the Religions of Late Antiquity*. Jordan Lectures in Comparative Religion 14. Chicago: University of Chicago Press, 1990.
———. *Relating Religion: Essays in the Study of Religion*. Chicago and London: University of Chicago Press, 2004.
———. *To Take Place: Toward Theory in Ritual*. Chicago: University of Chicago Press, 1987.
Soskice, Janet Martin. *Metaphor and Religious Language*. Oxford: Clarendon, 1985.
Spencer, F. Scott. *Acts*. Readings: A New Biblical Commentary. Sheffield: Sheffield Academic Press, 1997.
Stanley, Christopher D. *Arguing with Scripture: The Rhetoric of Quotations in the Letters of Paul*. New York and London: T & T Clark, 2004.
———. *Paul and the Language of Scripture: Citation Technique in the Pauline Epistles and Contemporary Literature*. Society for New Testament Studies Monograph Series 74. Cambridge: Cambridge University Press, 1992.
Stark, Rodney. *The Rise of Christianity: A Sociologist Reconsiders History*. Princeton: Princeton University Press, 1996.
Stegemann, Ekkehard W., and Wolfgang Stegemann. *The Jesus Movement: A Social History of Its First Century*. Translated by O. C. Dean Jr. Minneapolis: Fortress, 1999. Translation of *Urchristliche Sozialgeschichte: Die Anfänge im Judentum und die Christusgemeinden in der mediterranen Welt*. Stuttgart: Kohlhammer, 1995.
Stowers, Stanley K. "A Cult from Philadelphia: Oikos Religion or Cultic Association?" Pages 287–301 in *The Early Church in Its Context: Essays in Honor of Everett Ferguson*. Edited by Abraham J. Malherbe, Frederick W. Norris, and James W. Thompson. Supplements to Novum Testamentum 90. Leiden and Boston: Brill, 1998.
———. "Does Pauline Christianity Resemble a Hellenistic Philosophy?" Pages 81–102 in *Paul Beyond the Judaism/Hellenism Divide*. Edited by Troels Engberg Pedersen. Louisville: Westminster John Knox, 2001.
———. "Greeks Who Sacrifice and Those Who Do Not: Toward an Anthropology of Greek

Religion." Pages 293–33 in *The Social World of the First Christians: Essays in Honor of Wayne A. Meeks.* Edited by L. Michael White and O. Larry Yarbrough. Minneapolis: Fortress, 1995.

—. "*Peri Men Gar* and the Integrity of 2 Cor. 8 and 9." *Novum Testamentum* 32 (1990): 340–48.

Strelan, Rick. *Paul, Artemis, and the Jews in Ephesus.* Beihefte zur Zeitschrift für die neutestamentliche Wissenschaft 80. Berlin: Walter de Gruyter, 1996.

Suhl, Alfred. "Der Beginn der Selbständigen Mission des Paulus: Ein Beitrag zur Geschichte des Urchristentums." *New Testament Studies* 38 (1992): 430–47.

Sumney, Jerry L. *Identifying Paul's Opponents: The Question of Method in 2 Corinthians.* Journal for the Study of the New Testament Supplement Series 40. Sheffield: JSOT Press, 1990.

Tatum, Gregory. *New Chapters in the Life of Paul: The Relative Chronology of His Career.* The Catholic Biblical Quarterly Monograph Series 41. Washington, D.C.: The Catholic Biblical Association of America, 2006.

Talbert, C. H. "Money Management in Early Mediterranean Christianity: 2 Corinthians 8–9." *Review and Expositor* 86 (1989): 359–70.

Tannehill, Robert C. *The Narrative Unity of Luke-Acts: A Literary Interpretation.* 2 vols. Minneapolis: Fortress, 1986–1990.

Taylor, Justin. *Les Actes Des Deux Apôtres. VI. Commentaire Historique (Act. 18,23–28,31).* Paris: Librairie Lecoffre, 1996.

Taylor, N. H. "The Composition and Chronology of Second Corinthians." *Journal for the Study of the New Testament* 44 (1991): 67–87.

—. "The Jerusalem Decrees (Acts 15.20, 29 and 21.25) and the Incident at Antioch (Gal 2.11–14)." *New Testament Studies* 46 (2001): 372–80.

—. *Paul, Antioch and Jerusalem: A Study in Relationships and Authority in Earliest Christianity.* Journal for the Study of the New Testament Supplement Series 66. Sheffield: Sheffield Academic Press, 1992.

Tellbe, Mikael. "The Temple Tax as a Pre-70 CE Identity Marker." Pages 19–44 in *The Formation of the Early Church.* Edited by Jostein Ådna. Wissenschaftliche Untersuchungen zum Neuen Testament 1:183. Tübingen: Mohr Siebeck, 2005.

Theissen, Gerd. "Social Conflicts in the Corinthian Community: Further Remarks on J. J. Meggitt, *Paul, Poverty and Survival.*" *Journal for the Study of the New Testament* 25 (2003): 371–91.

—. *The Social Setting of Pauline Christianity: Essays on Corinth.* Edited and translated by John Schütz. Philadelphia: Fortress, 1982.

—. "The Social Structure of Pauline Communities: Some Critical Remarks on J. J. Meggitt, *Paul, Poverty and Survival.*" *Journal for the Study of the New Testament* 24 (2001): 65–84.

Thiselton, Anthony C. *The First Epistle to the Corinthians: A Commentary on the Greek Text.* The New International Greek Testament Commentary. Grand Rapids: Eerdmans, 2000.

Thom, Johan C. "'Harmonious Equality': The *Topos* of Friendship in Neopythagorean Writings." Pages 77–103 in *Greco-Roman Perspectives on Friendship.* Edited by John T. Fitzgerald. Society of Biblical Literature Resources for Biblical Study 34. Atlanta: Scholars Press, 1997.

Thompson, Michael B. "The Holy Internet: Communication between Churches in the First Christian Generation." Pages 49–70 in *The Gospels for All Christians: Rethinking the Gospel Audiences.* Edited by Richard Bauckahm. Grand Rapids: Eerdmans, 1998.

Thrall, M. E. *A Critical and Exegetical Commentary on the Second Epistle to the Corinthians.* 2 vols. International Critical Commentary. London: T & T Clark, 1994–2000.

—. "The Offender and the Offence: A Problem of Detection in 2 Corinthians." Pages 65–78 in *Scripture: Meaning and Method. Essays Presented to Anthony Tyrrell Hanson for His Seventieth Birthday.* Edited by Barry P. Thompson. Hull: Hull University Press, 1987.

Trebilco, Paul. *The Early Christians in Ephesus from Paul to Ignatius.* Wissenschaftliche Untersuchungen zum Neuen Testament 1:166. Tübingen: Mohr Siebeck, 2004.

—. *Jewish Communities in Asia Minor.* Society for New Testament Studies Monograph Series 69. Cambridge: Cambridge University Press, 1991.
Tuzlak, Sibel Ayse. "Service and Performance: *Leitourgia* and the Study of Early Christian Worship." Ph.D. diss., Syracuse University, 2001.
Van Nijf, Onno M. *The Civic World of Professional Associations in the Roman East.* Dutch Monographs on Ancient History and Archaeology 17. Amsterdam: J. C. Gieben, 1997.
Van Straten, F. T. "Gifts for the Gods." Pages 65–151 in *Faith, Hope, and Worship: Aspects of Religious Mentality in the Ancient World.* Edited by H. S. Versnel. Studies in Greek and Roman Religion 2. Leiden: Brill, 1981.
Vanderkam, James C. "'Identity and History of the Community." Pages 487–533 in *The Dead Sea Scrolls After Fifty Years: A Comprehensive Assessment.* Vol. 2. Edited by Peter W. Flint and James C. Vanderkam. Leiden, Boston, and Köln: Brill, 1999.
Vassiliadis, Petros. *ΧΑΡΙΣ–ΚΟΙΝΩΝΙΑ–ΔΙΑΚΟΝΙΑ: Ο κοινωνικός χαρακτήρας του παύλειου προγράμματος της λογείας* (Εισαγωγή και ερμηνευτικό υπόμνημα στο Β Κορ 8–9) (Bibliotheca Biblica 2; Thessaloniki: Pournaras, 1985).
—. "The Collection Revisited." *Deltion Biblikon Meleton* 11 (1992): 42–48.
—. "Equality and Justice in Classical Antiquity and in Paul: The Social Implications of the Pauline Collection." *St. Vladimir's Theological Quarterly* 36 (1992): 51–59.
Verbin, John S. Kloppenborg. "Dating Theodotos (CIJ II 1404)." *Journal of Jewish Studies* 51 (2000): 243–77.
Verboven, Koenraad. "The Associative Order: Status and Ethos among Roman Businessmen in Late Republic and Early Empire." *Athenaeum* 95 (2007): 861–93.
—. *The Economy of Friends: Economic Aspects of Amicitia and Patronage in the Late Republic.* Collection Latomus 269. Brussels: Latomus, 2002.
Verbrugge, Verlyn D. *Paul's Style of Church Leadership Illustrated by His Instructions to the Corinthians on the Collection.* San Francisco: Mellen Research University Press, 1992.
Veyne, Paul. *Bread and Circuses: Historical Sociology and Political Pluralism.* Translated by Brian Pearce. London: Penguin, 1992. Translation of *Le Pain et le cique.* Paris: Seuil, 1976.
Vouga, François. *An die Galater.* Handbuch zum Neuen Testament 10. Tübingen: Mohr Siebeck, 1998.
Wagner, J. Ross. "The Christ, Servant of Jew and Gentile: A Fresh Approach to Romans 15:8–9." *Journal of Biblical Literature* 116 (1997): 473–85.
—. *Heralds of the Good News: Isaiah and Paul "In Concert" in the Letter to the Romans.* Supplements to Novum Testamentum 101. Leiden: Brill, 2002.
Walaskay, Paul W. *Acts.* Westminster Bible Companion. Louisville: Westminster John Knox, 1998.
Walker, William O. "Galatians 2:7b–8 as a Non-Pauline Interpolation." *Catholic Biblical Quarterly* 65 (2003): 568–87.
—. "Why Paul Went to Jerusalem: The Interpretation of Galatians 2:1–5." *Catholic Biblical Quarterly* 54 (1992): 503–10.
Wallace-Hadrill, Andrew, ed. *Patronage in Ancient Society.* London and New York: Routledge, 1989.
Waltzing, J. P. *Étude historique sur les corporations professionnelles chez les Romains depuis les origines jusqu' à chute de l'Empire d'Occident.* 4 vols. Louvain: Peeters, 1895–1900.
Wan, Sze-kar. "Collection for the Saints as Anticolonical Act: Implications of Paul's Ethnic Reconstruction." Pages 191–215 in *Paul and Politics: Ekklesia, Israel, Imperium, Interpretation. Essays in Honor of Krister Stendahl.* Edited by Richard H. Horsley. Harrisburg, Pa.: Trinity, 2000.
Watson, Francis. "The Two Roman Congregations: Romans 14:1–15:3." Pages 203–15 in *The Romans Debate: Revised and Expanded Edition.* Edited by Karl P. Donfried. Peabody, Mass.: Hendrickson, 1991.

Weber, Valentin. *Die antiochenische Kollekte, die übersehene Hauptorientierung für die Paulusforschung: Grundlegende Radikalkur zur Geschichte des Urchristentums.* Würzburg: Echterhaus, 1917.
Wedderburn, Alexander J. M. *A History of the First Christians.* London: T & T Clark, 2004.
—. "Paul's Collection: Chronology and History." *New Testament Studies* 48 (2002): 95–110.
—. *The Reasons for Romans.* Studies of the New Testament and Its World. Edinburgh: T & T Clark, 1988.
—. "The 'We'-Passages in Acts: On the Horns of a Dilemma." *Zeitschrift für die neutestamentliche Wissenschaft und die Kunde der älteren Kirche* 93 (2002): 78–98.
Weinfeld, Moshe. *The Organizational Pattern and the Penal Code of the Qumran Sect: A Comparison with Guilds and Religious Associations of the Hellenistic-Roman Period.* Novum Testamentum et Orbis Antiquus 2. Fribourg and Göttingen: Vandenhoeck & Ruprecht, 1986.
Whelan, Caroline F. "*Amica Pauli*: The Role of Phoebe in the Early Church." *Journal for the Study of the New Testament* 49 (1993): 67–85.
White, L. Michael. *The Social Origins of Christian Architecture.* Vol. 1: *Building God's House in the Roman World: Architectural Adaptation among Pagans, Jews, and Christians.* Harvard Theological Studies 42. Valley Forge, Pa.: Trinity, 1996.
—. *The Social Origins of Christian Architecture.* Vol. 2: *Texts and Monuments of the Christian Domus Ecclesiae in Its Environment.* Harvard Theological Studies 42. Valley Forge, Pa.: Trinity, 1997.
Wilken, Robert. *The Christians as the Romans Saw Them.* New Haven: Yale University Press, 1984.
—. "Collegia, Philosophical Schools, and Theology." Pages 269–91 in *The Catacombs and the Coliseum: The Roman Empire as the Setting of Primitive Christianity.* Edited by Stephen Benko and John J. O'Rourke. Valley Forge, Pa.: Jusdon, 1971.
Williams, David J. *Paul's Metaphors: Their Context and Character.* Peabody, Mass.: Hendrickson, 1999.
Windisch, Hans. *Der zweite Korintherbrief.* Kritisch-exegetischer Kommentar über das Neue Testament 6. Göttingen: Vandenhoeck und Ruprecht, 1924.
Winger, Michael. "Act One: Paul Arrives in Galatia." *New Testament Studies* 48 (2002): 548–67.
Winter, Bruce W. "Acts and Food Shortages." Pages 59–78 in *The Book of Acts in Its Graeco-Roman Setting.* Edited by David W. J. Gill and Conrad Gempf. Vol. 2 of *The Book of Acts in Its First Century Setting.* Edited by Bruce W. Winter. Grand Rapids: Eerdmans, 1994.
—. "The Importance of the *Captatio Benevolentiae* in the Speeches of Tertullus and Paul in Acts 24:1–21." *Journal of Theological Studies* 42 (1991): 505–31.
—. *Seek the Welfare of the City: Christians as Benefactors and Citizens.* First Century Christians in the Graeco-Roman World. Grand Rapids: Eerdmans, 1994.
Witherington, Ben, III. *The Acts of the Apostles: A Socio-Rhetorical Commentary.* Grand Rapids: Eerdmans, 1998.
—. *Conflict and Community in Corinth: A Socio-Rhetorical Commentary on 1 and 2 Corinthians.* Grand Rapids: Eerdmans, 1995.
Woolf, Greg. "Food, Poverty and Patronage: The Significance of the Epigraphy of the Roman Alimentary Schemes in Early Imperial Italy." *Papers of the British School at Rome* 58 (1990): 197–228.
Young, Frances, and David F. Ford. *Meaning and Truth in 2 Corinthians.* Grand Rapids: Eerdmans, 1988.
Young, Norman H. "'The Use of Sunday for Meetings of Believers in the New Testament': A Response." *Novum Testamentum* 45 (2003): 111–22.
Ziesler, John. *Paul's Letter to the Romans.* TPI New Testament Commentaries. Philadelphia: Trinity, 1989.

Index of Ancient Sources

1. Hebrew Bible / LXX

Exodus
16:11–36	138
16:18	128, 137–38

Numbers
16:9	144

Deuteronomy
18:5	144

Job
4:8	140

Psalms
22:28	3
39:7	150
72:9–11	3
96:3	3
96:8	3
96:10	3
111	141–42
112	141
119:9	141

Proverbs
11:26	140

Isaiah
2:1–4	8
2:2	3
2:2–4	4, 151
2:3	3
11:10	3, 7
11:10–12	151
14:30–32	19
19:24–25	3
25:6–8	3
25:6–10	151
40:5	3
45:10	125
45:14	3
45:23	3
49:1–6	151
49:8	154
49:23	3
50:1	3
55:5	3
56:6–8	6, 8, 151
55:10	142
56:7	3
58:3–7	101
60:1–14	6, 8, 151
60:3	3
60:5	4
60:5–14	3
62:10	3
66	6, 151
66:18	3
66:18–20	3, 8
66:18–24	151
66:20	149, 151
66:20–21	149
66:19–24	3

Jeremiah
3:17	3, 151
16:9	3

Micah
4:1–2	4
4:1–4	151
7:12	3
7:17	3

Zephaniah
3:9	3
3:9–12	19

Haggai
2:7	3

Zechariah		Sirach	
2:13	3	7:3	140
8:21–23	3	14:11	150
14:16	3		
14:16–21	151		

2. New Testament

Matthew		16:6–10	64
10:1–15	51	16:10–17	32
10:10	51	17	54
19:21	103	18:22	38
		19:21	63
Mark		20	7
6:7–11	51	20:4	4, 6–8, 64, 65
		20:4–21:17	70
Luke		20:5–15	32
9:1–5	51	20:7	128
10:1–16	50	20:16	64–65, 69
10:7	51	20:22–23	65
		20:24	55, 65
Acts		20:25	65
2:42–47	25	20:35	53
3:1–10	67, 68	20:36–38	65
3:2	68	21	8
3:3	68	21:1–18	32
3:10	68	21:1–28:30	61
4:32–37	25	21:4	65
6:1–7	109	21:1–14	65
9:26–27	38	21:14	65
9:36	68	21:15–23:30	38
9:36–43	68	21:17–26	8, 13
10:1–33	68	21:18–36	70
10:2	68	21:23–24	8
10:4	68	21:26	68, 150
10:31	68	22:1–21	67
11:27–30	22, 27, 37–39, 61, 69, 73, 110, 117, 162	23:1–10	67
		23:12–13	67
11:28	37, 74	23:14	67
11:29	37, 61, 74, 128	23:15	67
11:30	38	23:17	67
12:25	37	24	65, 68
13:1–2	64	24:5–6	66
13:4	64	24:11	63, 66–67
15:1–29	28	24:14	66–67
15:1–30	38	24:14–16	66
15:36–19:41	32	24:17	11, 12, 61–64, 66–69, 162
16–18	54–55	24:17–18	67

Index of Ancient Sources

24:17–21	66	15:26	10–11, 15–17, 19–21, 53, 137, 161
24:18	67	15:26–27	11, 54, 156
27:1–28:16	32	15:27	16–17, 23, 25, 136, 150, 154–56

Romans

1–16	53
1:7	121
1:13	35, 59–60
1:16	16
1:21	146
1:21–23	146
3:24	151
6:21–22	59
8:1	157
8:11	157
9–11	4–6, 9
11:13	16
11:25	4, 7
12:1	146, 150, 153
12:4–5	18
12:8–10	101
12:13	17, 23
14:1–15:13	146–47, 150
15	13, 42, 60, 70, 146, 156–57, 164
15:6	147
15:7	147
15:7–9	16
15:7–13	9, 147
15:9–12	17
15:12	7
15:14–21	6, 147, 151, 154
15:14–32	1, 5, 8–9, 13–14, 28, 39, 119, 120, 146–57, 162–63
15:15–16	147
15:16	6, 16, 27, 58, 60, 126, 147–57, 161, 163
15:18	150
15:18–19	150, 153
15:19	150
15:22–32	17
15:23–32	146
15:24	18
15:25	8, 16, 21, 156
15:25f.	13
15:25–26	53, 64
15:25–32	7–9, 14, 25, 42, 58, 60, 69, 71, 147, 150, 153–56
15:25–33	153
15:27–28	126, 163
15:28	59, 126, 136, 156, 159, 163
15:30–31	1, 4, 36, 59, 153, 162
15:31	8–9, 16, 18, 21, 27, 153–54
16	53, 156
16:1	18
16:1–2	53, 156
16:1–27	53
16:3	121
16:3–16	18
16:7	121
16:11	121
16:21–23	18
16:23	53

1 Corinthians

1:5	134
1:11	18, 43, 71
1:14	53
3:6–9	142, 159
5:1–5	46
5:9	40, 71
7:1	40, 43, 71, 127
7:17	41
7:25	40, 43, 127
8:1	40, 43, 127
8:4	40, 43
9:1	51
9:3–12	1
9:3–18	45, 50
9:7	35
9:8–18	1
9:11	35
9:14	41
9:14–15	51
10:14–22	128
11:2–34	128
11:17–34	101
11:22	101
11:34	41, 101
12:1	40, 43, 127
12:27	18
14:1–40	128
14:6	39

14:26	39	2:14–17	138
15:32	56	2:14–7:4	131
15:36–44	35	2:17	1
16:1	1, 8, 16, 21, 40, 43, 129, 140	3:4–6	138
16:1–2	41, 126, 127, 163	3:10–17	136
16:1–4	1, 13–14, 28, 39, 42–44, 71, 101, 119, 120, 127–31, 157, 161, 163	4:1–15	138
		4:15	143
		5:1–5	138
16:1–20	55	5:14–21	138
16:2	11, 128	6:2	154
16:3	16, 21, 45, 64, 127, 131	6:6	138
16:3–4	4, 7, 44, 45, 153	6:14–7:1	43, 49
16:5–7	44	6:14–7:4	136
16:5–9	44	6:16	136
16:7–8	43	7	48
16:8	44	7:1	136
16:9–20	18	7:2–8:24	43
16:10–12	18	7:5	47, 71
16:12	40, 43, 127	7:5–16	46, 71, 131
16:15	47, 156	7:6–7	138
16:19	56	7:6–12	47
		7:6–16	139
2 Corinthians		7:8–12	46
1–8	45	7:12	46
1–9	37, 44, 47–49, 71, 131, 138	7:23–16	18
1:1	47	8–9	13–14, 21, 26, 50, 131–46, 157
1:1–6:13	43		
1:1–9:15	49	8	136
1:1–8:24	49	8:1	45, 127, 132, 138
1:3–11	138	8:1–6	19, 42, 47, 54, 131–34, 137, 140
1:8	56		
1:8–2:13	131	8:1–15	135–36, 138, 144
1:15	44–45	8:1–24	49
1:15–16	44–45, 47	8:1–9:15	1, 13–14, 25, 28, 39, 48, 54, 119–20, 127, 145, 156, 163
1:15–2:11	71		
1:16	45	8:2	42
1:17–22	44	8:2–6	132
1:18–22	138	8:3	11, 132, 137
1:19	43	8:4	8, 15, 16–17, 21, 45, 127, 132, 156, 161
2:1	47		
2:1–4	43, 45, 71	8:6	45, 48, 126–27, 129, 134, 136, 155, 163
2:1–5	43		
2:1–11	46	8:7	45, 127, 134
2:3–4	46, 139	8:7–8	137
2:4	47, 131	8:7–12	134–37
2:5	46	8:8	11, 133–34, 137
2:5–11	46	8:9	127, 135, 137–38
2:10	46	8:10	11, 48, 137
2:12	45	8:10–12	135, 137
2:13	47, 71	8:11	135–36, 155

8:11–12	126, 163	9:15	127, 143–45
8:12	154	10–13	37, 43, 50–53, 71
8:13	16, 135, 137	10:1–13:14	43
8:13–14	21, 110	10:2	52
8:13–15	137–38	10:10	52
8:14	23, 25, 137	11:5	50
8:15	128, 137–38	11:7	50, 151
8:16	7, 127, 138–39, 143	11:7–11	1
8:16–24	4, 7, 18, 129, 138–40	11:7–12	50, 51, 71
8:16–9:4	7	11:8	1
8:17	11, 132	11:15	51
8:18	139	11:32–33	33
8:18–19	7, 139	12:11	50, 51
8:19	45, 48, 127	12:13–18	51, 71
8:20	7, 47	12:14	45, 53
8:20–21	139	12:17–18	51
8:22	7, 139	13:1–2	45, 53
8:23	15, 47, 139, 161	13:1–3	52
9	49		
9:1	8, 16, 21, 140, 156	*Galatians*	
9:1–5	140	1–2	12, 38
9:1–15	43, 49	1:1	12
9:2	45, 48, 133, 140	1:6–11	12
9:2–4	54	1:11	39
9:2–5	19	1:12	12
9:3	7, 15, 48, 161	1:15	151
9:3–4	140	1:15–17	12
9:3–5	18	1:20	38
9:4	45, 49, 140	1:21	35
9:5	11, 49, 140–41	2	35
9:6	35, 141	2:1–10	12, 16, 33–39, 54, 71
9:6–10	126, 140–42, 159, 163	2:2	12, 35, 39
9:6–11	146	2:4	17
9:7	59, 137	2:6	12
9:8	23	2:9	15, 16
9:8–11	141	2:9–10	34
9:8–14	141	2:10	9–10, 12–14, 19, 20, 27, 33–36,
9:8–15	138		38, 55, 62, 69, 73, 74, 110, 162
9:9	141	2:11–12	39
9:10	142–43, 159	2:11–13	35
9:11	142–44	2:11–14	35, 39, 161
9:11–12	143	2:12	17, 35
9:11–15	142–45	2:21	151
9:11–16	144	3:3	136
9:12	16, 140–45, 155, 163	5:22	59
9:12–14	141	6:6	101
9:13	17, 143, 161	6:6–10	34
9:13–14	25	6:7–9	35, 140
9:14	138	6:9	23
9:14–15	29, 121, 164	6:16	5

Ephesians		*1 Thessalonians*	
2:11–4:16	57	2:9–10	55
		2:9–12	1
Philippians		3:1	47
1:1–3:1	55	3:6	18
1:3–5	54	3:8	158
1:6	136		
1:11	59, 60	*1 Timothy*	
1:13	55	1:2–4	56
1:20–21	55		
1:22	59, 60	*2 Timothy*	
2:15	152	1:18	56
2:17	120, 144, 151–52, 164		
2:25	152	*Philemon*	
2:25–30	18	18–19	1
3:2–4:3	55	22	18, 23
4:10–20	1, 13, 54–55, 120, 152, 164	23	18
4:11	23		
4:15	164	*Hebrews*	
4:15–18	55	9:6	136
4:17	59, 164	10:18	150
4:18	152, 164		
4:21–22	18	*2 John*	
4:22	55	10–11	115
Colossians		*3 John*	
4:7–10	18	3–8	115
4:10–17	18		
4:19	18	*Revelation*	
		1:10	128

3. Early Christian Writings

1 Clement			
2:1	53	Origen	
		Commentary on Romans	
Augustine		5:214–16	149
Augustine on Romans			
49	149	Pelagius	
		Pelagius's Commentary on Romans	
Ignatius		147–148	149
Ephesians	149		
		Tertullian	
Justin Martyr		*Apologia*	
ANF		38.1	80
1:257	149	39.5–6	100

4. Other Greco-Roman and Jewish Writings

3 Baruch
15.2   140

Apuleius
Metamorphoses
11.26   113

Aristotle
Ethica eudemia
6.5   103
1245b25–27 77

Historia animalium
511b   128

Politica
1253a30–31 77

Artemidorus
Onirocritica
3.53   103

Cicero
Pro Flacco
28.66–69   116
28.67   117

Dead Sea Scrolls
1QH
VI, 2–6   103

1QM
XIII, 12–14 20

1QpHab
XII, 2–3   20

1QS
VI, 13b–23 99

4Q171
II, 9–10   20
III, 10   20

4Q266
10 I, 5–10 99

CD
XIV, 12–16 99
XIV, 14   101, 109

Demosthenes
3 Philippic
28.1–6   17

Dio Cassius
Historia Romana
63.28.5   128

Dio Chrysostom
Discourses (Rhod.)
31.16   91

Diogenes Laertius
Lives of Eminent Philosophers
6.63   109

Herodian
Ab excessu divi Marci
4.3.8   128

Hesiod
Opera et dies
723   95

Hippocrates
Aphorisms
2.33   150

Josephus
Against Apion
2.122–144   99
2.205   92
2.217   92
2.274   92
2.283   109

Jewish Antiquities
1.58   135
3.155   140
3.320–22   38
7.107   17
7.365   140

10.72	140		*De vita contemplativa*	
11.329–30	8		13.16–20	99
14.110–13	116		13.66–89	99
14.214–16	96			
16.160–74	117		*Legatio ad Gaium*	
16.163–70	116		23	8
18.20–22	99		134	116
19.8.2	150		156–57	116
20.51–53	38		311–13	116–17

Jewish War

Quis rerum divinarum heres sit

2.124	115		191	128, 139
2.124–27	115			
2.408–11	8		*Quod deterius potiori insidari soleat*	
2.409–10	59		33–34	92
6.335–36	117			

Quod omnis probus liber sit

Julian

Letter 22	102		84–87	99
			85	115
			85–86	115

Misopogon

363 A-B	102		*De specialibus legibus*	
			1.76–78	73, 94

Justinian
Digest

Plato
Respublica

3.4.1.1	95–96		371b5–6	17

Lucian
De morte Peregrini

Pliny the Elder
Naturalis historia

1.13	100		5.58	38
11	80		18.1168	38

Mishnah
m. Demai

Pliny the Younger
Epistulae

3:1	109		10.33–34	106
			10.92	105–6
m. Pe'ah			10.93	106
8:7	109		10.96.7	106
			96.7	106

Philo
De cherubim

Plutarch
De Iside et Osiride

117	92		31	155
122–23	92–93			

De decalogo

Polybius
Histories

1.4	92		5.31.1	17
1.6	92		5.88–90	115

De ebrietate

129	135

Psalms of Solomon
17.31   151

Seneca
De beneficiis
1.4.2   85
3.1.1   142–43

Strabo
Geographica
14.2.5   103

Suetonius
Divus Claudius
18–19   38

Tacitus
Historiae
5.5.1   109

Talmud
t. Pe'ah
4:9   109

Theophrastus
Characteres
30.19   150

5. Inscriptions and Papyri

CCCA
I
289   140

CIG
119   81
120   81
3069   115
5859   114

CIJ
II
766   98
1404   116–17

CIL
III
633/2, 3   97
703   89
704   89
707   89
VI
10234   108

XIV
2112   107

CJZC
72   98

CPJ
138   96
139   96

Foucart
43   84

IDelos
1519   84, 133, 135
1520   90, 135
1791   89
2346   135
2413   135

IEph
20   97
22   113
944   132
1503   97
3416–18   140

IFayum
152   129, 130

IG
II²
330   133
633   133
663   134

667	133	68	97
670	133–34	192	89
691	133	220	89
700	133	259	90
721	133	260	90
786	133	288	97
798	133	289	97
801	133	503	97
808	133		
859	133	XI/4	
884	133	1040	128
931	133		
984	133	XII/1	
1028	144	9	97
1039	144	155	83, 90
1045	133	937	89
1227	133	1032	104
1261	81		
1271	135	XII/5	
1275	96	156	130
1277	96	653	133
1293	133	660	132
1297	133	668	132
1301	133		
1307	112	XII/8	
1319	133	666	133
1324	81		
1325	83	XII Supplementum	
1326	83	238	132
1327	83, 96, 133		
1350	113	XVI	
1368	96, 129, 134	1052	113
2499	96		
4038	135	IHistria	
4519	135	57	90, 104
5172	135		
		IJO	
V/1		I	
208	104	Ach 59	99
209	104	Mac 1	93
245	135		
1145	104, 110	II	
1390	135, 144	40	82
		168	98
VII			
685–89	97	III	
2712	104	40	93
		Syr 53–69	99
X/2		Syr 71	99
58	89, 97	Syr 84	99

Index of Ancient Sources

IKerameikos
3.5   144

IKilikiaBM
2:201   75

IKnidos
1:23   89, 96

IKret
III
4:9   129

ILS
II/2
7212   95

IMagnMai
98   144
105   129
163   132

IMakedD
920   90
1104   89

IMiletMcCabe
415   144

IRhodB
501   130

ISardH
4   83

ISmyrna
753   130

LSAM
20   135
20.5–6   84
20.15–16 84
20.53–54 84
36   130
53   135

LSCG
48   129
55   101
143   130

MAMA
6:264   98

NewDocs
1:5   97
5:5   84, 97
7:10   104
8:12   93

OGI
488   84

IPriene
111   104
195   113, 130

P. Cairo
30606   108
31179   108

P. Hamb
184   129–30
186   129–30

PLond
131:421   142
2193   83
2710   83

SEG
2:10   112
3:764   96
8:641   132
8:694   95
24:1233   89
28:561–62 97
32:809–10 93
32:810   93
42:625   97
43:26   128
45:770   135
45:1070   129
46:745   80
47:196b   135
47:954   89
48:2139   104

SIG³
694   135
695   135

820	135		Syll³	
985	84, 101, 135		820:3–4	155
1109	96		820:14	155
			966	130
SIRIS				
123	89			

Index of Modern Authors

Ascough, Richard S., 18, 76–77, 83, 85, 112–13, 115–17, 135–36
Aus, Roger D., 149
Bachmann, Philipp D., 144
Barclay, John M. G., 100, 116, 161
Barrett, C. K., 66
Barton, S. C., 158
Becker, Jürgen, 42, 65
Beckheuer, Burkhard, 6, 73
Berger, Klaus, 11, 28, 73
Black, Max, 123
Bolkestein, Hendrik, 102–3
Bonz, Marianne Palmer, 94, 98
Bourdieu, Peirre, 90
Bowen, Clayton R., 63, 69
Brown, Peter, 102, 108, 165
Buck, Charles H., 37–38
Bultmann, Rudolf, 49
Cranfield, C. E. B., 16, 58
Cullman, Oscar, 15
Das, A. Andrew, 121
Deissmann, Adolf, 129–30
Denis, A. M., 150–51
Donaldson, Terrence
Dunn, James D. G., 16
Fee, Gordon, 44–45
Fitzmyer, Joseph, 62, 148, 151–52
Ford, David F., 138
Friesen, Steven J., 24
Furnish, Victor P., 49, 51–52, 133
Gabrielsen, Vincent, 77, 118–19
Garnsey, Peter, 22–23, 87, 105, 110–11
Gauthier, Philippe, 88
Gaventa, Beverly Roberts, 63–64, 69, 126, 132, 160
Georgi, Dieter, 2–6, 9, 19–20, 28, 34–35, 49, 56, 129, 152
Günther, Matthias, 57
Hainz, Josef, 15–16
Harland, Philip A., 78, 91
Harrill, J. Albert, 96, 100
Harris, Murray J., 53, 134, 139, 141–42
Harrison, James R., 14–15, 28, 45, 73, 132–33

Hatch, Edwin, 80–81, 109–8
Hays, Richard B., 138
Heinrici, Georg, 81
Henderson, Suzanne Watts, 101
Hendrix, Holland, 86–87
Holl, Karl, 9–10, 19, 28
Horrell, David, 9, 21
Horsley, G. H. R., 158
Hurtado, Larry W., 34
Jeremias, Joachim, 3–6
Johnson, Mark, 28, 122–26, 157, 163
Joubert, Stephan, 12–14, 28, 33, 61, 73, 132
Keck, Leander, 5, 10, 20
Kim, Byung-Mo, 28, 70, 73
Kloppenborg, John S., 79, 103
Knox, John, 28, 30, 36, 56–57
Kraftchick, Steven J., 124
La Piana, George, 114–15
Lakoff, George, 28, 122–26, 157, 163
Llewelyn, S. R., 128
Longenecker, Bruce W., 34
Lüdemann, Gerd, 40, 56
MacMullen, Ramsay, 77–78
Martin, Dale B., 26, 108
Martyn, J. Louis, 31, 34, 36–37, 41, 54–55, 160
Meeks, Wayne A., 81–82, 84–85, 101
Meggitt, Justin J., 22–26, 108
Mitchell, Margaret M., 41
Moo, Douglas J., 60, 154
Munck, Johannes, 4–7, 28, 73, 148
Nickle, Keith F., 2–7, 16, 28, 73
Nijf, Onno van, 88, 91–92, 104
Peterman, G. W., 13, 16–17
Ponthot, Joseph, 150
Rajak, Tessa, 93–94
Renan, Ernest, 81
Richards, I. A., 122
Saller, Richard P., 85–86
Smith, Jonathan Z., 75–77
Stegemann, Ekkehard, 89
Stegemann, Wolfgang, 89
Stowers, Stanley, 154

Strelan, Rick, 57–58
Tannehill, Robert C., 63
Theissen, Gerd, 51
Thrall, Margaret, 46, 48
Vassiliadis, Petros, 21–22
Verbrugge, Verlyn, 11, 26, 28, 73–74, 97, 127
Veyne, Paul, 86, 88
Wan, Sze-kar, 16, 28, 73, 145, 150, 157
Watson, Francis, 147
Wedderburn, Alexander J. M., 30, 35, 54–55, 64
Witherington, Ben, III, 146
Woolf, Greg, 22–23, 87, 105, 110–11
Young, Francis, 138

Index of Subjects

Achaia, 1, 16, 31, 42–43, 47–50, 53–54, 56, 58, 62–64, 72–73, 112, 121, 131, 134, 136, 156, 161
Agabus, 37, 39, 61, 65, 73, 118
almsgiving, 11–12, 23, 28, 62–63, 67–69, 73–74, 109, 162
analogies for the collection, 11, 22, 28, 72–79, 110, 112, 118, 162
Antioch, 10–11, 27, 32–39, 59, 61, 70, 72–75, 117, 161–62
Asia, 31, 45, 49, 55–58, 71, 106, 111, 117
Athens, 32, 47, 79, 86, 96,
Augustus, 105, 107
banquets, 87, 90, 95–96, 100, 102, 104, 107
Barnabas, 9–10, 12, 16, 27, 33–35, 37–38, 61–62, 70, 118, 162
benefaction, 12–14, 19, 22, 24–29, 48, 54, 74–76, 85–94, 98, 102–4, 119, 121, 132–35, 139, 143–45, 158–59, 162–63, *see also* benefit exchange; euergetism; reciprocity
benefit exchange, 12–13, 25, 28, 33, 72–73, 86–93, 162, *see also* benefaction; euergetism; reciprocity
burial expenses, 79, 81, 96–97, 100–101, 107–8
Calvin, John, 149
charis, 14, 29, 44–45, 94, 121, 131–32, 134, 137–39, 141, 143, 145, 160, 164–65, *see also* grace
charity, 5, 11, 20, 22–24, 87, 96, 102–4, 106, 109–10, 115, 141, *see also* generosity
circumcision, 5, 11
common chest, 95–96, 98, 100–101, 129
common meals, 80–81, 95–96, 101, 108–9, 118, 163
competition, 19, 29, 78–79, 83, 88, 91, 121, 126, 132–34, 144, 158, *see also* honor
Corinth, 18, 23, 25, 32, 42–55, 57–58, 71, 101, 117, 127–29, 131, 139–40, 164
Corinthian correspondence, 43–44, 46–51, 53, 71
cultic language, 23, 130–31, 136, 145–46, 152, 155, 157–58, 164

delegates, 4–8, 17, 71, 138–40, 162
Delos, 93, 133
Epaphroditus, 152, 164
Ephesus, 32, 44–46, 49, 55–57, 65, 84, 97
Epidosis, 26, 28, 73, 162
eschatology, 3–9, 19–20, 23, 73–74, 148–49, 151, 161–62, *see also* offering of the Gentiles; pilgrimage to Zion
Essenes, 75–76, 99, 115, *see also* Qumran
euergetism, 19, 87–88, 91–92, 103–4, 121, 133, 142, 158, 163, 165, *see also* benefaction; benefit exchange; reciprocity
famine, 37–38, 71, 74, 110–11, 118, *see also* food shortage
Felix, 62–63, 65–68
food shortage, 23–24, 26, 37, 87, 110–11, *see also* famine
friendship, 17, 86, 111, 137
fundraising, 7, 14, 18, 21, 25–26, 28, 35, 41–42, 56, 62, 70–71, 110, 112, 126–27, 145, 156, 158, 161–62
Galatia, 1, 20, 27, 31, 34–35, 40–42, 54, 62, 71–73, 101, 112, 127–29, 161
generosity, 14, 21, 25, 42, 54, 88, 92, 121, 132–37, 140–45
grace, 14, 21, 45, 51, 59, 132, 138, 141, 143–45, 160, 165, *see also charis*
Hadrian, 79, 96
harvest, 60, 121, 126, 141–42, 146, 159–60, 163
Holy Spirit, 37, 58, 63–65, 147, 150, 153, 156
honor, 14, 20, 29, 74, 85, 87–94, 96–99, 104, 112, 119, 132–34, 139–40, 142–44, 163, 165, *see also* competition
imprisonment, 55, 60–61, 65, 99–100, 164
James, 13–14, 34–35, 68, *see also* pillar apostles
Jerusalem authorities, 9, 11–12, 14, 20, 27, 31, 33, 35–37, 59, 61–62, 66, 69–70, 72, 78, 118, 161, 163, *see also* pillar apostles
Jerusalem conference, 16, 33, 35–36, 70
Julian, 102
Julius Caesar, 115–16

koinōnia, 15–18, 161
Letter of tears, 46, 52, 71, 131, 139
Locke, John, 149
Luther, Martin, 149
Macedonia, 1, 16, 31, 42, 44, 47–51, 52–58, 63–64, 71–72, 112, 131–34, 140–41, 161
metaphor, 10, 13, 28, 101, 120–26, 129–31, 135–37, 140, 142, 144–46, 152–59, 163–64
mutualism, 23, 25–26
mystery cults, 75, 80
offering of the Gentiles, 7, 27–28, 42, 58, 60–61, 68, 73, 101, 112, 146–53, 154–57, 59, 161–62, *see also* eschatology; pilgrimage to Zion
patronage, 14, 19, 85–88, 111, 118, 121, 142, 158, 163
Pentecost, 44, 64–65, 69
persecution, 57, 65
Peter, 39, 68, *see also* pillar apostles
Philippi, 32, 54–55, 97, 152, 165
Phoenicia, 113
piety, 20, 63, 67–69, 162
pilgrimage to Zion, 3–9, 66, 73–74, 148, 151, 161, *see also* eschatology; offering of the Gentiles
pillar apostles, 16, 33, *see also* James; Jerusalem leaders; Peter

poverty, 2, 10–12, 19–25, 26, 33–34, 51, 74–76, 78, 96–97, 101–12, 119, 164–65
Qumran, 20, 99, 101, 109–10, 115, *see also* Essenes
reciprocity, 12–15, 33, 72, 86, 88–90, 137–38, 142–43, 149, 163, *see also* benefaction; benefit exchange; euergetism
Rhodes, 83, 90–91, 103, 118
Rome, 25, 42, 53, 55, 58–61, 63–64, 95, 113–14, 116, 121, 147, 155–56, 159
Sabbath, 11, 128
Spain, 58–60, 155, 159
synagogue, 76–77, 80, 82, 84, 93–94, 98–100, 109–11, 116, 118, 158, 163
temple, 8, 38, 66–70, 116, 157
temple tax, 10–11, 22, 28, 72–73, 116–17, 162
Thessalonica, 32, 54, 83, 89
Tiberius Claudius, 37
Timothy, 43
Titus, 7, 33, 35, 47–48, 51, 54, 71, 129, 135, 138–40
Trajan, 80, 105–8, 112
Tyre, 65, 113–14, 116
unity, 5, 15–17, 72, 161
voluntary associations, 19, 26, 28, 73–120, 128, 130, 133–34, 162–63, 165
worship, 3, 5–6, 13, 28–29, 38, 63, 66–69, 74, 120–60, 162–63

www.ingramcontent.com/pod-product-compliance
Lightning Source LLC
Chambersburg PA
CBHW032004220426
43664CB00005B/138